Seventy Years of the International Law Commission

Seventy Years of the International Law Commission

Drawing a Balance for the Future

Edited by

The United Nations

BRILL
NIJHOFF

LEIDEN | BOSTON

Library of Congress Cataloging-in-Publication Data

Title: Seventy years of the International Law Commission : drawing a balance for the future / edited by The United Nations.
Other titles: 70 years of the International Law Commission
Description: Leiden, The Netherlands : Koninklijke Brill NV, [2021] | Summary: "Seventy Years of the International Law Commission: Drawing a Balance for the Future> brings together voices from academia and practice to celebrate and critically evaluate the work of the United Nations International Law Commission (ILC) over the past seventy years. The edited volume draws on the events commemorating the seventieth anniversary of the Commission, which took place in New York and Geneva in May and July 2018. At a time when multilateral law-making has become increasingly challenging, the edited volume appraises the role of one the most important driving forces behind the codification of international law and discusses the ILC's future contribution to the development of international law"– Provided by publisher.
Identifiers: LCCN 2020030046 (print) | LCCN 2020030047 (ebook) | ISBN 9789004434264 (hardback) | ISBN 9789004434271 (ebook)
Subjects: LCSH: United Nations. International Law Commission–History.
Classification: LCC KZ1287.I59 S48 2021 (print) | LCC KZ1287.I59 (ebook) | DDC 341–dc23
LC record available at https://lccn.loc.gov/2020030046
LC ebook record available at https://lccn.loc.gov/2020030047

Typeface for the Latin, Greek, and Cyrillic scripts: "Brill". See and download: brill.com/brill-typeface.

ISBN 978-90-04-43426-4 (hardback)
ISBN 978-90-04-43427-1 (e-book)

This book is printed on acid-free paper and produced in a sustainable manner.

Contents

PART 2
Drawing a Balance for the Future: the Geneva Symposium

SECTION 3
The Commission and Its Impact

SECTION 4
The Working Methods of the Commission

SECTION 5
The Function of the Commission: How Much Identifying Existing Law, How Much Proposing New Law?

SECTION 6
The Changing Landscape of International Law

SECTION 7
The Authority and the Membership of the Commission

PART 3
Celebratory Contributions on the Occasion of the Seventieth Anniversary of the Commission

SECTION 8
Commemorative Speeches Delivered in New York

Foreword

The present publication results from the commemorative events in celebration of the seventieth anniversary session of the International Law Commission.

The preparatory work for these events straddled two sessions of the Commission: the sixty-ninth in 2017 and the seventieth in 2018. The Commission recommended that events be held during its seventieth session, in 2018, at meetings in New York and in Geneva. To this end, it was recommended, first, to convene a solemn half-day meeting of the Commission with high-level dignitaries in New York, followed by an informal half-day meeting with representatives of the Sixth Committee of the General Assembly to exchange views on the work of the Commission, its relationship with the Sixth Committee, and the role of the two bodies in the promotion of the progressive development of international law and its codification. Second, it was recommended that another solemn high-level event be organized in Geneva, which would be followed by a symposium dedicated to the work of the Commission, involving legal advisers of States and international organizations, academics and other distinguished international lawyers, including former members of the Commission. An Advisory Group was established, composed of the Chairs of the Commission at the sixty-ninth and seventieth sessions, as well as Commission members Yacouba Cissé, Shinya Murase and Pavel Šturma, to assist the Secretariat in the organizational arrangements. The two of us, as Chairs of the sixty-ninth and seventieth sessions, were honoured and privileged to make the necessary arrangements. The Secretariat of the Commission, the Codification Division of the Office of Legal Affairs of the United Nations, under the supervision of its Director, Huw Llewellyn, with the assistance of Arnold Pronto, Trevor Chimimba, Christiane Ahlborn, Bart Smit Duijzentkunst, Marianne Sooksatan and Stavroula Alexandropoulou worked tirelessly with us towards the organization of the events both in New York and Geneva, as well as in the editing of the present publication.

The events in New York were held on 21 May 2018, and in Geneva on 5 and 6 July 2018, under the overarching theme of 'Seventy years of the International Law Commission – Drawing a Balance for the Future'. Pursuant to General Assembly resolution 72/116 of 7 December 2017, States were encouraged to make voluntary contributions to the trust fund for the Office of Legal Affairs to support the promotion of international law in order to facilitate the commemoration of the seventieth anniversary of the Commission. Contributions were received in cash and in kind. On behalf of the Commission, we thank Austria, Chile, China, Cyprus, Czech Republic, Finland, Germany, India, Ireland, Japan,

Portugal, Qatar, Republic of Korea, Romania, Singapore, Sri Lanka, Switzerland, Turkey, the United Kingdom of Great Britain and Northern Ireland and Viet Nam, as well as Istanbul Bilgi University and others who wished to remain anonymous, for their generosity of spirit.

The story of the Commission is one of continuity, the past and the present, and of collegiality, its diverse members working together in the service of international law. The Commission forms an essential part of the United Nations architecture that emerged from the ashes of the Second World War. It has progressively developed and codified international law as a foundation for peaceful international relations, gradually building upon the achievements of the past in order to secure the future of the international legal order. As an institution created to assist the General Assembly in pursuing the aims of Article 13, paragraph 1 (a), of the Charter of the United Nations, its work is informed by this founding instrument, which remains as relevant today as at the time of the creation of the United Nations. The determination of the peoples of the United Nations to establish conditions under which justice and respect for the obligations arising from treaties and other sources of international law can be maintained is not a mere platitude; it is the driving force behind the Commission's codification efforts.

Since the Commission held its first session in 1949, the world has witnessed major upheavals and an increasingly complex and challenging set of realities: the continuing scourge of armed conflict, including, increasingly, those of a non-international nature; terrorism and growing extremism; climate change and natural disasters causing horrific loss of life and suffering; and exponential increases in scientific and technological advances, challenging a wide range of branches of the law to adapt to new circumstances.

In the seventy years since its establishment, the Commission has worked diligently towards the progressive development of international law and its codification to contribute to securing a world firmly based on the rule of law in international relations. Through its works, the Commission has sought to provide the common language, a rules-based system, for the conduct of peaceful and harmonious relations among States, guided by the principles and purposes of the Charter of the United Nations. The presence of the visible college of international lawyers and jurists at both events in New York and Geneva was uplifting and fortified our belief in the power and vitality of international law, even in troubled times. This publication constitutes a retrospective and prospective look at the accomplishments and challenges of the Commission.

Eduardo Valencia Ospina *Georg Nolte*

Notes on Contributors

François Alabrune
Director of Legal Affairs of the Ministry of Europe and Foreign Affairs of France

Danae Azaria
Associate Professor in Law, Faculty of Laws, University College London

Davinia Aziz
Senior State Counsel, International Affairs Division, Attorney-General's Chambers, Singapore; Adjunct Assistant Professor, Faculty of Law, National University of Singapore

Laurence Boisson de Chazournes
Professor of International Law, University of Geneva; Associate member, *Institut de Droit international*

Yifeng Chen
Associate Professor, Peking University

Corinne Cicerón Bühler
Director of the Directorate of International Law and Legal Advisor for the Swiss Federal Department of Foreign Affairs

Pedro Comissário Afonso
Former member and Chair of the International Law Commission

Concepción Escobar-Hernández
Professor of International Law, Universidad Nacional de Educación a Distancia (UNED), Spain; Member of the International Law Commission

Janine Felson
Deputy Permanent Representative of Belize to the United Nations in New York

Burhan Gafoor
Permanent Representative of Singapore to the United Nations in New York; Chair of the Sixth Committee of the General Assembly at its seventy-second session

Aleksandar V. Gajić
Professor of Public International Law, Faculty of Law, Belgrade University, Serbia; Chief Legal Advisor of the Ministry of Foreign Affairs of the Republic of Serbia

Kate Gilmore
United Nations Deputy High Commissioner for Human Rights

Claudio Grossman Guiloff
Professor of Law and Dean Emeritus, American University Washington College of Law; Member of the International Law Commission

Hajer Gueldich
Professor, Université de Carthage, Tunis; Member of the African Union Commission on International Law

Elinor Hammarsjköld
Director-General for Political Affairs, Ministry of Foreign Affairs, Sweden

Hussein A. Hassouna
Ambassador; Member of the International Law Commission

Mahmoud D. Hmoud
Ambassador of the Hashemite Kingdom of Jordan to the Republic of Singapore; Member of the International Law Commission

Angel Horna
Legal Adviser, Permanent Mission of Peru to the United Nations in New York

Maurice Kamto
Professor, University of Yaoundé II; Former member, Chair and Special Rapporteur of the International Law Commission

Miroslav Lajčák
Minister of Foreign Affairs of Slovakia; President of the General Assembly of the United Nations at its seventy-second session

Jürg Lauber
Permanent Representative of Switzerland to the United Nations in New York

Keun-Gwan Lee
Professor, School of Law, Seoul National University

Djamchid Momtaz
Professor of International Law, University of Tehran; Former member and Chair of the International Law Commission

Shinya Murase
Professor Emeritus, Sophia University Faculty of Law; Member of the International Law Commission

Sean D. Murphy
Manatt/Ahn Professor of International Law, George Washington University Law School; Member and Special Rapporteur of the International Law Commission; President of the American Society of International Law

Jennifer Newstead
Legal Adviser of the Department of State of the United States of America

Georg Nolte
Professor of International Law at Humboldt University of Berlin; Member and former Chair of the International Law Commission

Ernest Petrič
Member of the International Law Commission

Mónica Pinto
Professor Emerita, University of Buenos Aires; Associate member, *Institut de Droit international*

Alejandro Rodiles
Professor, Instituto Tecnológico Autónomo de México (ITAM)

Nico Schrijver
Professor of Public International Law, Leiden University; President of the *Institut de Droit international* (2017–2019)

Miguel de Serpa Soares
Under-Secretary-General for Legal Affairs and United Nations Legal Counsel

Pavel Šturma
Professor and Head of the Department of International Law, Charles University, Prague; Chair and Special Rapporteur of the International Law Commission

Dire Tladi
Professor of International Law, University of Pretoria; Member of the International Law Commission

Zuzana Trávníčková
Senior Lecturer, Jan Masaryk Centre for International Studies, Faculty of International Relations, University of Economics, Prague

Eduardo Valencia-Ospina
Member, former Special Rapporteur and Chair of the International Law Commission

Abdulqawi A. Yusuf
President of the International Court of Justice

Evgeny Zagaynov
Director of the Legal Department of the Ministry of Foreign Affairs, Russian Federation; Member of the International Law Commission

Ineta Ziemele
President of the Constitutional Court of the Republic of Latvia; Professor of International Law, Riga Graduate School of Law

Introduction

Secretariat of the International Law Commission

The International Law Commission convened its seventieth session in New York from 30 April to 1 June and in Geneva from 2 July to 10 August 2018 under the overarching theme: "Seventy Years of the International Law Commission – Drawing a Balance for the Future".[1] To commemorate the anniversary session, events were organized in New York on 21 May 2018 and in Geneva on 5 and 6 July 2018. At each venue, a solemn celebratory segment was followed by substantive panel discussions: a "conversation" with delegates to the Sixth (Legal) Committee of the General Assembly in New York; and a symposium with legal advisers of foreign ministries and other international law experts in Geneva.

1 Drawing a Balance for the Future

The commemoration of the seventieth anniversary was the fourth in a series of such commemorations for the Commission. The twenty-fifth anniversary was commemorated in 1973 with a solemn event.[2] The fiftieth anniversary was commemorated with a colloquium on the Progressive Development and Codification of International Law in New York in 1997,[3] and a seminar in Geneva in

1 ILC, 'Report of the International Law Commission on the work of its sixty-ninth session' (2017) UN Doc A/72/10, 217 at paras 279–281.

2 The Commission ccommemorated the twenty-fifth anniversary of the opening of the Commission's first session at its twenty-sixth session with a solemn event, ILC, 'Report of the International Law Commission on the work of its twenty-sixth session' [1974] II(1) ILC Ybk, 5–6 at paras 15–17.

3 For an overview of the Commission's achievements, see United Nations, *'Introduction' in Making Better International Law: The International Law Commission at 50, The Proceedings of United Nations Colloquium on the Progressive Development and Codification of International Law* (United Nations 1998). See also United Nations, *International Law as a Language for International Relations* (Kluwer Law International/United Nations 1996), *International Law on the Eve of the Twenty-First Century: Views from the International Law Commission* (United Nations 1997); *The International Law Commission Fifty Years After: An Evaluation, Proceedings of the Seminar to Commemorate the Fiftieth Anniversary of the International Law Commission* (United Nations 2000). See also Shabtai Rosenne, 'The Role of the International Law Commission' (1970) 64 ASILPROC 24–37; Shabtai Rosenne, 'Codification Revisited after 50 Years' (1998) 2 MaxPlanckYrbkUNL 1–22; Christian Tomuschat, 'The International Law

 | DOI:10.1163/9789004434271_002

1998 with the theme 'The International Law Commission fifty years after: An evaluation'. These latter events were convened during the United Nations Decade of International Law (1989–1999), a time of great optimism in world affairs in the immediate aftermath of the end of the Cold War. The 1997 colloquium sought to generate concrete and practical suggestions for enhancing the working capacity of the Commission and for making international law more effective and relevant to decision-making by States. The 1998 seminar included a retrospective assessment of the work of the Commission (1948–1998),[4] and a forward-looking discussion of possible future topics for the Commission and the challenges inherent in the international legislative process. The Commission also published a collection of essays by its members.[5]

When the Commission marked its sixtieth anniversary in Geneva on 19 and 20 May 2008, optimism had begun to wane and the mood had swung toward doubt and concern for the future. As Georg Nolte, Chair of the Commisson at its sixty-ninth session, expresses it "… there was a certain sense of crisis".[6] This sense was articulated in the title of an academic article at the time by a former member of the Commission: "The International Law Commission – An Outdated Institution?".[7] It was also reflected in the theme for the event: "The International Law Commission: Sixty Years … And Now?" The Commission was at a crossroads, having completed many major codification projects. Uncertainties for the future were prevalent. To facilitate dialogue, self-appraisal and critical analysis, the one-and-half days of meetings in 2008 involving legal advisers of United Nations Member States and other international law experts proceeded on the basis of the 'Chatham House rule' – no publication was issued.[8]

The commemoration of the seventieth anniversary took place in 2018 under the overarching theme: "70 years of the International Law Commission – Drawing

Commission – An Outdated Institution?' (2006) 49 GYIL 77–105. See also Mohamed El Baradei, Thomas M. Franck and Robert Trachtenberg, *The International Law Commission: The Need for a New Direction* (United Nations Institute for Training and Research 1981) and Michael R. Anderson et al., *The International Law Commission and the Future of International Law* (BIICL 1998).

4 See United Nations, *Making Better International Law: The International Law Commission at 50* (n 3); ILC 'Report of the International Law Commission on the work of its fiftieth session' [1998] II(2) ILC Ybk 109 at paras 546–550.

5 See United Nations, *International Law on the Eve of the Twenty-first Century* (n 3).

6 See the introductory remarks by George Nolte to Part 2 of this volume.

7 Tomuschat (n 3).

8 But see Georg Nolte (ed), *Peace Through International Law: The Role of the International Law Commission* (Springer Verlag 2009), which is a publication on a colloquium at the occasion of the sixtieth anniversary of the Commission at which members of the Commission participated.

a balance for the future". It is not immediately apparent from this theme whether it signals an upswing in confidence from the doubts and concerns expressed at the time of the sixtieth anniversary, nor what "balance" is to be drawn – what are the competing factors to be balanced, and what is the desired result of balancing them?

When the other language versions of "Drawing a balance for the future" are taken into account, the intention becomes clearer. The French, in particular, "*Dresser le bilan pour l'avenir*" suggests a retrospective stocktaking of the Commission's achievements and challenges, and an assessment of where this stocktaking should lead the Commission for the future. This understanding is reflected in the introductory comments by both Eduardo Valencia Ospina, Chair of the Commission at its seventieth session, and Georg Nolte, Chair of the Commission at its sixty-ninth session. Eduardo Valencia Ospina noted that drawing a balance for the future "... reflects the very human desire for introspection and exploration: learning the lessons of the past in order to create a better future".[9] Georg Nolte stated that it "... signals an ambition" – to commemorate, not simply in a self-congratulatory manner, but "... to use the occasion for reflections to prepare the Commission for challenges which lie ahead".[10]

The commemorative events were thus also an opportunity for the speakers and panelists to articulate what they consider to be the global challenges that form the backdrop for the Commission's work. They emphasised the increasingly complex and challenging set of realities that prevails, including the scourge of war and its adverse impact on humanity and the environment;[11] international terrorism and growing extremism;[12] climate change and natural disasters;[13] and the growing inequality between rich and poor.[14] Among the challenges underlined as most closely connected with the Commission's work were: the current "turbulent" state of international relations, in which the "... painstaking yet constructive process towards the achievement of multilateralism [... since the Second World War] is being threatened by the unilateral actions of some major players on the world stage and the outsized role that

9 See the introductory remarks by Eduardo Valencia-Ospina in Section 9 of this volume.
10 See the introductory remarks by George Nolte to Part 2 of this volume.
11 See e.g. the contribution by Janine Felson in Section 1 and Hajer Gueldich in Section 6 of this volume.
12 See e.g. the keynote address by Nico Schrijver in Section 8 of this volume.
13 See e.g. the contribution by Hajer Gueldich in Section 6 of this volume.
14 See the contribution by Hajer Gueldich in Section 6, and the keynote address by Nico Schrijver in Section 8.

'national interest' is playing in their exercise of sovereignty";[15] the greatly increased number of Member States of the United Nations, with varying interests and cultural perspectives;[16] the plurality of other actors on the international stage, including international organizations, individuals, and corporations;[17] and perhaps most immediately challenging for the Commission, the phenomenon of multilateral "treaty fatigue" on the part of States.[18]

Against the background of this challenging environment, the speakers and panelists at the commemorative events addressed a number of questions designed to help assess the Commission's role and contribution to date, and its potential impact in the future. Summaries of their written contributions to this edited volume are set out in section 4 of this Introduction. Section 2 deals briefly with the establishment of the Commission and its historical context as part of the "codification movement". Section 3 distils and introduces some of the main themes arising in the different contributions. It does not attempt to do so comprehensively, but rather aims to give a flavour of what is to come in the later parts of this publication.

There are aspects of the discussion that follows, particularly in sections 3 and 4, where we, as the Secretariat of both the Commission and the Sixth Committee of the General Assembly, have a particular institutional knowledge or perspective that may help in understanding the issues raised in the various panels.[19] Our views are offered in this spirit.

2 Establishment of the Commission and Brief Historical Context

Although the first session of the Commission was in 1949, the Commission had been established by the United Nations General Assembly two years earlier, in 1947, by its resolution 174 (II).[20] Under its statute, the object of the Commission

15 See the statement by Eduardo Valencia-Ospina in Section 8 of this volume.

16 See the keynote address by Abdulqawi A. Yusuf in Section 9 of this volume.

17 See e.g. the contribution by Ineta Ziemele in Section 5 of this volume.

18 See e.g. the contribution by Laurence Boisson de Chazournes in Section 3 of this volume.

19 On the role of the Secretariat of the International Law Commission, see the contributions by Maurice Kamto and Shinya Murase in Section 4 of this volume.

20 Statute of the ILC, adopted 21 November 1947, UNGA Res 174 (II) (The resolution and the statute were adopted at the 123rd meeting of the General Assembly by 44 votes to none, with 6 abstentions). The UNGA resolved to establish the Commission, 'which shall be constituted and shall exercise its functions in accordance with the provisions of the … statute', annexed to the resolution. The statute has been amended by UNGA Res 485(V) (12 December 1950); UNGA Res 984(X) (3 December 1955); UNGA Res 985(X) (3 December 1955); and UNGA Res 36/39 (18 November 1981).

is the promotion of the progressive development of international law and its codification. Its primary concern is public international law, although it is not precluded from pursuing matters that concern private international law.[21] By that same resolution, the Assembly decided to elect the first members of the Commission the following year. The Commission was thus born on 21 November 1947, its membership was constituted on 3 November 1948, and it was convened for its first session on 12 April 1949.

The idea of codification, which gave rise to the 'codification movement' in international law,[22] has a long pedigree.[23] It had already commenced more than a century before the Commission's establishment. Jeremy Bentham, writing in the late 18th century (1786–1789), coined the terms 'international law' and 'codification', and was the first theorist to assert the value of publishing the law of nations in the form of rules, written as a code.[24] The first private association to advance international law as a 'juridical science of the civilized world' was the *Institut de Droit international*, formed at Ghent in September 1873.[25] The International Law Association was established in October the same year in Brussels, following the convening of the Conference for the reform and codification of international law.[26]

The role of States in the codification movement is fundamental, of course. The Conference of Vienna of September 1814 to June 1815, convened after the fall of Napoleon Bonaparte, is often referred to as the first conscious effort by governments to develop international law.[27] The Powers (Austria, Great Britain, France, Prussia, Russia, Sweden, Spain, and Portugal), signatories of the Treaty of Paris of 1814, adopted Regulations regarding the rank of diplomatic agents on 19 March 1815, a Declaration concerning the abolition of the slave trade on 8 February 1815, and a Regulation regarding free navigation on rivers on 29 March 1815.[28] Subsequently, the development of international

---

21 Article 1 of the ILC statute.

22 Lassa Oppenheim *International Law: A Treatise*, vol I (Longmans 1905) 35.

23 See the contribution by Keun-Gwan Lee Section 6 and also the contribution by Yifeng Chen in Section 5 of this volume.

24 Ernest Nys 'Codification of International Law' (1911) 5 AJIL 871 876–877.

25 See generally Irwin Abrams 'The Emergence of the International Law Societies' (1957) 19 The Review of Politics 361–380. See also Martii Koskenniemi, *The Gentle Civilizer of Nations. The Rise and Fall of International Law 1870–1960* (CUP 2001).

26 ILA, 'History of the International Law Association' in *Report of the Seventieth Conference, held in New Delhi, 2–6 April 2002* (ILA 2002) 76–77.

27 UN Secretariat 'Historical Survey of Development of International Law and its Codification by International Conferences' UN document A/AC.10/5 reproduced in (1947) 41 AJIL Supplement 32.

28 Ibid, at 32 quoting *Martens, Nouveau Receuil V. II* (1818), 432, 434, 449.

law was pursued at over one hundred international conferences between 1864 and 1914, including the two Hague Peace Conferences of 1899 and 1907, resulting in the conclusion of over two hundred and fifty international instruments.[29]

The establishment of the League of Nations after the devastation of the First World War offered an organizational structure to revitalize the codification movement. When the First Assembly of the League of Nations met in 1920, it recommended that the Council of the League request the most authoritative institutions devoted to the study of international law to consider what would be the best methods of cooperative work for the more precise definition and more complete coordination of the rules of international law.[30] This request led to the establishment of the Committee of Experts for the Progressive Codification of International Law, composed of persons possessing the required qualifications and expertise, and also composed as a body representing "the main forms of civilization and the principal legal systems of the world." It was tasked to "draw up a provisional list of subjects the regulation of which by international agreement, appears most desirable and realizable", and following consultations with governments, "to submit a report to the Council of the League on questions which appear sufficiently ripe for solution by conferences".[31]

The work of this Committee eventually resulted in the convening of the League of Nations Codification Conference in 1930, which was generally considered to be the first general codification conference.[32] It had some success, adopting a convention on the law of nationality, but progress in the other areas, including the territorial sea and State responsibility, was minimal.[33]

---

29 Ibid.

30 League of Nations, *The Records of the First Assembly, Plenary Meetings* (Meetings held from the 15th of November to the 18th of December 1920) (United Nations Library 1920) 746. The Assembly did not adopt the recommendation. In a motion, Robert Cecil (South Africa) argued that recommendation presented 'a very dangerous project at this stage in the world's history'. His concern was that the wounds of the First World War were still fresh for the world to undertake the first steps towards the codification of international law, 747.

31 League of Nations resolution adopted by the Assembly of the League of Nations on 22 September 1924 (1924), League of Nations Official Journal, Special Supplement No 21, 10, reproduced as Appendix 6, (1947) 41 AJIL Supplement 103.

32 League of Nations resolution adopted by the Assembly of the League of Nations on 27 September 1927 (1927), League of Nations Official Journal, Special Supplement No 53, 9, reproduced as Appendix 8 (1947) 41 AJIL Supplement 107. See also Manley O. Hudson 'The First Conference for the Codification of International Law' (1930) 24 AJIL 447, 448–449.

33 Ibid 450.

Despite disappointing results, the 1930 Conference was seen as an "important milestone on the road to organized and systematic codification".[34] With the outbreak of the Second World War, the League had failed in its main purpose. It reduced its operations significantly from 1938 onward and was eventually dissolved in 1947.[35]

Surprisingly, progressive development and codification of international law did not appear in early drafts of the Charter of the United Nations. The Dumbarton Oaks Proposals referred only to the power of the General Assembly to "... initiate studies and make recommendations for the purpose of promoting international co-operation in political, economic and social fields".[36] A proposal by China to extend this "to the development and revision of the rules and principles of international law"[37] triggered a discussion of whether the General Assembly should have legislative authority. The idea that the Assembly should act as a world legislature was not accepted, but there was wide agreement that it should be tasked with initiating studies and making recommendations on international law. This was enshrined in Article 13, paragraph 1(a) of the Charter.[38] There was considerable discussion of the wording of this provision, some States considering that reference only to "codification" would be too narrow because it could be read as limiting the provision to putting existing law into writing. Other States considered that adding the word "revision" would open the way for too much change and instability. Eventually, the mandate was agreed as follows: "The General Assembly shall initiate studies and make recommendations for the purpose of [...] encouraging the progressive development of international law and its codification".[39] The combination

---

34 Jose Sette-Camara, 'The International Law Commission: Discourse on Method' in Roberto Ago (ed), *International Law at the Time of its Codification: Essays in Honour of Roberto Ago* (Dott. A. Guiffré 1987) 473.

35 See 'History of the League of Nations (1919–1946)' (Library of the United Nations Office at Geneva, Records and Archives Unit)13, available at: http://www.unog.ch/80256EDD006B8954/(httpAssets)/36BC4F83BD9E4443C1257AF3004FC0AE/%24file/Historical_overview_of_the_League_of_Nations.pdf.

36 'The Dumbarton Oaks Conversations' (1946–1947) I *Yearbook of the United Nations*, 5.

37 *Documents of the United Nations Conference on International Organization* (UNCIO), *San Francisco, 1945* vol III, 25.

38 For a more detailed account of the legislative history of Article 13, see Carl-August Fleischhauer and Bruno Simma, 'Article 13' in Bruno Simma et al (eds), *The Charter of the United Nations: A Commentary* (3rd edn, OUP 2002) 528–52; Anne-Thida Norodom, 'Article 13, paragraphe 1 (a)' in Jean-Pierre Cot, Mathias Forteau, Alain Pellet (eds), *La Charte des Nations Unies: Commentaire article par article* (3rd edn, Economica 2005) 701–703.

39 Article 13 paragraph (1)(a) of the Charter of the United Nations.

of the words "progressive development" and "codification" were considered to establish "... a nice balance between stability and change".[40]

At its first session in 1946, the General Assembly established the Sixth (Legal) Committee of the Assembly, and also the Committee on the Progressive Development of International Law and its Codification (the "Committee of Seventeen").[41] The Committee of Seventeen, requested by the Assembly to consider the procedures necessary for the discharge by the Assembly of its responsibilities under Article 13, paragraph 1(a) of the Charter, recommended the establishment of the International Law Commission and prepared a first draft of its statute. In its resolution 174 (II) of 21 November 1947, the Assembly recognized that to carry out its function under Article 13, paragraph 1(a), it would need assistance from an international expert body, and accordingly approved the statute of the Commission. The Commission was thus established as a subsidiary organ of the Assembly and, in accordance with its statute,[42] it reports annually to the Assembly, through the Sixth Committee.

The Sixth Committee holds a debate on the Commission's annual report during the main session of the Assembly, traditionally in late October and early November. The debate is attended by many legal advisers of the foreign ministries of States and has become known as "International Law Week".[43] The Secretariat of both the Sixth Committee and the Commission is the Codification Division of the United Nations Office of Legal Affairs, which was itself also established in 1946, and is tasked with providing substantive support and servicing to both bodies.[44]

3 Institutional Relationship with the Sixth Committee

Given its origins and mandate, it is appropriate that the Commission began the stocktaking during its seventieth anniversary in New York, in the Sixth Committee. The Commission is a subsidiary organ of the General Assembly. Although subsidiary organs remain institutionally accountable to the parent

40 UNCIO (n 37) IX, 178; see also Herbert W Briggs, *The International Law Commission* (Cornell University Press 1965) 12.

41 UNGA Res 94 (I) (11 December 1946).

42 UNGA Res 174 (II) (21 November 1947).

43 See International Law Week and 29th Informal Meeting of Legal Advisors, 22–23 October 2018, <http://legal.un.org/ola/lc-ILW-ILAW-10-2018.aspx>.

44 UNGA Res 13(I) (13 February 1946). See also (1946–1947) I *Yearbook of the United Nations*, 630.

organ, in particular by reporting on their activities, the Commission was established to carry out its substantive functions in respect of the progressive development and codification of international law independently, and is doing so in practice. The Sixth Committee is not a subsidiary organ of the Assembly, but rather a manifestation of it – a main committee of the Assembly in which the legal officers of the Permanent Missions of the Member States in New York represent the legal and policy views of the governments they represent. The annual interaction between the two bodies on the basis of the Commission's report of its session is therefore one between independent expert subsidiary organ and its intergovernmental parent. The common endeavour of both is the progressive development of international law and its codification. As the Secretariat of both bodies, the Codification Division of the United Nations Office of Legal Affairs shares the same purpose.

The Commission's independence does not mean, however, that the views of States are not important to its functioning. In fact, the contrary is true. The statute of the Commission establishes a relationship in which the input of States is important at all stages of the Commission's work. It is important for the choice of topics. The views of States are fundamental while each topic is being considered, whether made orally during the annual Sixth Committee debate, or in writing. The Commission's work should be firmly grounded in the practice of States. Government views are particularly important during and after the stage of first reading, at which point the Commission takes a pause to allow governments time to comment in writing on a complete set of draft provisions and commentaries. Finally, government views are important on the Commission's final product, completed at second reading. If in the form of draft articles, the Sixth Committee will determine whether they should be negotiated into a treaty, either within the Sixth Committee or at a diplomatic conference convened for this purpose. If in one of the other forms discussed in subsection a) below, the Sixth Committee adopts a draft resolution[45] *inter alia* to disseminate the Commission's output and commend it to the attention of States.

These are the formal and institutional aspects of the relationship, but the quality of the relationship is crucial to the success of the Commission.[46] In this respect, some of the interventions by members of the Commission in the panel discussions at the commemorative event (Part 1 of this volume) were

45 The Sixth Committee adopts draft resolutions, which are then considered and adopted as resolutions by the plenary of the General Assembly.

46 In this regard, see the contributions in Section 2 of this volume.

critical of the current state of the relationship. In particular, some members stated that States too seldom suggest topics; too few States take part in the Sixth Committee debate on the Commission's report; an insufficient number of States otherwise offer comments in writing on the Commission's work; and such comments as are made may sometimes not have sufficient detail and substance.[47] These factors engender a risk that the Commission members may feel that States in the Sixth Committee are disinterested in their work, and give rise to a concern that the views of States cannot be fully reflected.[48] The fact that over the past two decades, the Commission has delivered nine sets of draft articles to the Sixth Committee intended as the basis for treaty negotiations, but that only one has been taken up by the Committee, is described by the Chair of the Commission's seventieth session as "deplorable" and demonstrating a reluctant attitude.[49]

The Secretariat's interactions with Sixth Committee delegates, which are frequent and take place throughout the year, do not suggest a lack of interest in the Commission's work, but rather a lack of capacity to take on board the quantity and detail of the Commission's report each year.[50] The report, which can run to hundreds of pages in length, is issued informally as an advance version in English as quickly as possible after the Commission's session, usually during the second half of August, about one week after the end of the Commission's session. It issues in the six official United Nations languages only in the second half of September.[51] In other words, delegations have about four to eight weeks in which to assimilate and develop views and comments on the Commission's very detailed analysis and outputs before the debate on the Commission's report during International Law Week.[52] The timing is such that this four to eight weeks is also the busiest time of the year for New York delegations as they prepare for the High-level segment of the General Assembly session, when their Heads of State and Government are present. This challenge is particularly difficult for smaller delegations from developing countries, who may not have a dedicated team of lawyers in capital available to assess the

47 See the contributions by François Alabrune and Ernest Petrič contained in Section 1 of this volume.
48 See the contribution by Ernest Petrič in Section 1 of this volume.
49 See the contribution by Eduardo Valencia-Ospina in Section 8 of this volume.
50 See the contribution by Angel Horna contained in Section 2 of this volume.
51 The report is compiled by members of the Codification Division, working with an editing team at the UN Office in Geneva, in the week immediately after the Commission has finished adopting it, usually in mid-August.
52 See n 43 above and accompanying text.

Commission's report.[53] The Committee has developed the practice of the first few speakers in its various debates being a delegation speaking on behalf of the regional or other group in question – by this means, the positions of many delegations are wrapped up into a common position on behalf of, for example, the African Group of States, or the Community of Latin American and Caribbean States (CELAC).[54]

The question of how to improve the capacity of States to engage meaningfully in the debate on the Commission's report, either through adjusting the timing of the respective sessions of the Commission and the Sixth Committee, and/or finding ways to make the Commission's report more accessible and digestible, are perennial subjects of discussion among delegates and the Secretariat. Ways should perhaps be found for the Commission itself to engage in this important discussion. The Secretariat, for its part, conducts briefings for delegates in New York during the year to help prepare them for the Sixth Committee debate, and is considering how these might be improved, either in terms of quantity or content.[55]

The interaction between the Commission and the Committee is restricted to a week or so of formal debate, with little interactive discussion. Further, the Special Rapporteurs for the various topics considered by the Commission and dealt with in the report may or may not be present in New York during the debate. Against the background of the worsening financial situation of the United Nations, the payment of stipends to Special Rapporteurs to assist them in obtaining sufficient research support and to travel to New York was discontinued by the Fifth Committee of the General Assembly some years ago.[56] There are funds only for the Chair of the Commission to be present throughout the debate. Many of the Special Rapporteurs and other members of the Commission do, however, fund their own travel and are present, at least for some of the debate. Those Special Rapporteurs present engage in an interactive half afternoon question and answer session on their topics with delegates,[57] and also in

53 See the contributions of François Alabrune in Section 1 and Concepción Escobar Hernández in Section 2 of this volume.

54 See e.g. UN Doc A/C.6/73/SR.20 (22 October 2018).

55 In this regard see also the suggestions by Concepción Escobar Hernández and Hussein A. Hassouna in Section 2 of this volume.

56 See also the call by Evgeny Zagaynov in Section 2 of this volume to reconsider the decision of the General Assembly, in 2002, to set the level of honoraria for members of the Commission at one dollar (see UNGA Res 56/272 of 27 March 2002).

57 The 2018 Interactive Dialogue was organized by the Permanent Missions of Austria and Sweden to the UN on 24 October 2018 (see <https://www.un.org/en/ga/sixth/73/pdfs/24_october_2018_4.pdf>).

informal meetings. These forms of informal contacts with delegates at the time of the Sixth Committee debate are considered very valuable, and do not engender the same concerns on the part of some as side events organised during the Commission's session, when it is actively considering the topics before it.[58]

A further criticism by States in the Sixth Committee has been the difficulty of preparing comments on all matters requested by the Commission (in Chapter III of its report) because of the number of topics on the Commission's programme. At the seventieth session, there were nine topics before the Commission, whereas in earlier decades, there were generally significantly fewer.[59] This is an additional reason underlying the apparent "disinterest" of States. It is a challenge even for the foreign ministries of developed country governments to prepare in-depth comments on so many topics.[60] There has also been criticism of the content of some of the topics chosen by the Commission, and suggestions that the Commission should return to consideration of more "classical" areas related to treaties and other sources of law, responsibility of States, and diplomatic and consular relations, and should revert to recommending draft articles for negotiation into treaties.[61] The suggestion is that the Commission is less able to take on more specialised topics like protection of the atmosphere.[62]

Reducing the number and variety of topics before the Commission may be counter-intuitive to Commission members at a time when the number and diversity of Member States of the United Nations, the interconnected challenges facing the international community, and the plurality of actors engaged at the international level, pull in the opposite direction. As discussed in subsections a) and d) below, the breadth of the Commission's topic choices and the variety of the forms of output may be seen as keeping up with the changing landscape of international law. The Commission may be unlikely to draw in its horns at this time of great change in international relations.

One consequence of the variety of forms of output currently produced by the Commission is worthy of particular mention for its potential impact on the role of States in the formation of international law. Where the Commission's

58 See subsection b) below on the 'Working Methods of the Commission'.

59 See, for example ILC, 'Report of the International Law Commission on the work of its twenty-first session' [1969] II ILC Ybk 203, when there were four substantive topics before the Commission; and ILC, 'Report of the International Law Commission on the work of its twenty-ninth session' [1977] II(2) ILC Ybk 4, when there were three substantive topics before the Commission.

60 See the contribution by François Alabrune contained in Section 1 of this volume.

61 Ibid.

62 Ibid.

product is either not intended to become a treaty (for example, conclusions or principles), or even where it is in a form that could become a treaty (such as the articles on the responsibility of States for internationally wrongful acts) but is not taken up by the Sixth Committee, States do not have the opportunity to renegotiate the text. The Commission, in effect, has the final word. In cases where a Commission output is considered sufficiently authoritative by the International Court of Justice, or other international courts or tribunals, it may be cited by the court in support of the court's reasoning and decision. The International Court of Justice and other courts have done this on numerous occasions, for example, in relation to the articles on State responsibility.[63] The articles on State responsibility are widely regarded, in many of their aspects, as reflecting customary international law.[64] Whilst States are also broadly relying on these articles in their practice, the same might not always be true in relation to other Commission texts.[65] In these cases, the question is whether the role of States in the formation of international law, which is primordial, is being diminished.

A final point, little discussed by the panels at the commemorative event but often aired in more informal conversations, is the question of the Sixth Committee's working methods. There is a tendency for States in the Sixth Committee debate, understandably, to focus on what States need from the Commission. It is apparent from the opening remarks of the Chair of the Commission in Section 8 of this publication,[66] however, and of the Commission members taking part in the panels,[67] that there is a certain sense of frustration on the part of the Commission at what it perceives as the lack of responsiveness of States in the Sixth Committee to the Commission's outputs – a lack of "productivity" on the part of the Sixth Committee. A brief comparison between the main features of the Commission's working methods (subsection b below) and those of the Sixth Committee would reveal no equivalent of the "engine" of the Commission (the Special Rapporteurs), nor of a subset of the membership responsible to the plenary for negotiating and referring text to it (the Drafting

63 See the reports of the compilations of decisions by international courts, tribunals and other bodies referring to the 2001 articles on the responsibility of States for internationally wrongful acts, as contained in UNGA, 'Report of the Secretary-General' UN Doc A/62/62, UN Doc A/65/76, UN Doc A/68/72, UN Doc A/71/80 and UN Doc A/74/83.

64 In this regard, the views expressed by UN Member States during the consideration of the item 'Responsibility of States for internationally wrongful acts' at the seventy-first session of the General Assembly, as contained in A/C.6/71/SR.9 (7 October 2016).

65 See the contribution by Laurence Boisson de Chazournes in Section 3 of this volume.

66 See the statement by Eduardo Valencia-Ospina in Section 8 of this volume.

67 See e.g. the contributions by Ernest Petrič in Section 1, Hussein A. Hassouna in Section 2 and Pavel Šturma in Section 3 of this volume.

Committee). Perhaps there is a case to be made for the Sixth Committee setting up its own equivalent of the Commission's Working Group on Working Methods to consider whether the Committee is realizing its full potential.

4 The Elements of the Stocktaking

The various panel discussions during the seventieth anniversary commemorative events in New York and Geneva focused on specific questions relating to the theme of "Drawing a balance for the future". This section of the Introduction separates the strands that run through those questions and discussions into five elements: a) the impact of the Commission; b) the Commission's working methods; c) progressive development and codification of international law; d) the changing landscape of international law; and e) the authority and membership of the Commission.

In practice, these five elements cannot be neatly separated. Discussion inevitably tends to overlap among them. A consideration of the Commission's impact, for example, cannot be dissociated from the question of its authority, nor from the broader changing international landscape in which international law is made and functions.

The purpose of this section of the Introduction is not to summarize the contributions of the different authors in this edited volume, nor to deal with them comprehensively. The aim is to give a flavor of the issues that are to be discussed in later Chapters – to interest the reader sufficiently that she or he is motivated to read on.

a) *The Impact of the Commission*

The sense of unease at the time of the Commission's sixtieth anniversary commemoration[68] was founded on an assessment that the most productive years of the Commission's work up to the end of the 1960s, sometimes referred to as its "golden era",[69] had passed, and that its contribution to the progressive development and codification of international law, when measured in terms of the number of international conventions adopted on the basis of its work, was dwindling.[70] If this were the sole measure of the Commission's impact, then the seventieth anniversary commemoration should have been equally sombre. Indeed, in the decade since the sixtieth anniversary, no further treaty has been

---

68 See n 7 and 8 and accompanying text.

69 See UN Doc A/CN.4/SR.3422 at 9 and 11.

70 Tomuschat (n 3).

negotiated and adopted by the General Assembly on the basis of the Commission's draft articles.

A purely numerical approach to the Commission's outputs would show that over seventy years, 23 conventions have been adopted on the basis of its drafts and 19 of these have entered into force. Of these 19, 12 conventions have been widely ratified by States. The other 7 conventions have less than 40 States parties.[71] The numbers are not staggeringly high, but the impact of these conventions is undeniable. The 1969 Vienna Convention on the Law of Treaties,[72] the 1961 Vienna Convention on Diplomatic Relations[73] and the 1963 Vienna Convention on Consular Relations[74] are at the heart of international relations among States, relied upon on a daily basis by officials in foreign ministries, diplomatic and consular missions around the world, legal practitioners, judges in international courts and tribunals, and increasingly also national judges. Additionally, States have adopted conventions on the basis of the Commission's outputs on: the law of the sea;[75] the reduction of Statelessness;[76] special missions;[77] the protection of internationally protected persons, including diplomatic agents;[78] the representation of States in their relations with international organizations of a universal character;[79] succession of

71 See the contribution by Laurence Boisson de Chazournes in Section 3 of this volume.

72 Adopted 23 May 1969, entered into force 27 January 1980, 1155 UNTS 331.

73 Adopted 18 April 1961, entered into force 24 April 1964, UNTS registration no 7310.

74 Adopted 28 August 1967, entered into force 27 September 1967, 596 UNTS 261.

75 Convention on the Territorial Sea and the Contiguous Zone, adopted 29 April 1958, entered into force 10 September 1964, 516 UNTS 205; Convention on the High Seas, adopted 29 April 1958, entered into force 30 September 1962, 450 UNTS 11; Convention on the Fishing and Conservation of the Living Resources of the High Seas, adopted 29 April 1958, entered into force 20 March 1966, 559 UNTS 285; Convention on the Continental Shelf, adopted 29 April 1958, entered into force 10 June 1964, 499 UNTS 311; Optional Protocol of Signature Concerning the Compulsory Settlement of Disputes, adopted 29 April 1958, entered into force 30 September 1962, 450 UNTS 169.

76 Convention on the Reduction of Statelessness, adopted 30 August 1961, entered into force 13 December 1975, 989 UNTS 175.

77 Convention on Special Missions, adopted by UNGA on 8 December 1969, entered into force 21 June 1985, 1400 UNTS 231; Optional Protocol Concerning the Compulsory Settlement of Disputes, adopted by UNGA on 8 December 1969, entered into force 21 June 1985, 1400 UNTS 339.

78 Convention on the Prevention and Punishment of Crimes against Internationally Protected Persons, including Diplomatic Agents, annexed to UNGA resolution 3166 (XVIII) of 14 December 1973, entered into force 20 February 1977, 1035 UNTS 167.

79 Vienna Convention on the Representation of States in their Relations with International Organizations of a Universal Character, adopted 14 March 1975 not yet in force, UN Doc A/CONF.67/16.

States;[80] non-navigational uses of international watercourses;[81] jurisdictional immunities of States and their property;[82] and international criminal law.[83] The Commission's output has also, on occasion, served as inspiration for regional agreements.[84]

The "treaty fatigue" that has seen the number of multilateral treaties adopted in recent years decline, however, is not unique to the Commission's outputs.[85] The series of initiatives by States that led to the adoption by the Sixth Committee of the Terrorist Bombing Convention,[86] the Terrorist Financing Convention,[87] the Nuclear Terrorism Convention[88] and the Protocol to the Convention the Safety of United Nations and Associated Personnel,[89] came to an end in 2005, and has not yet been repeated. This decline in treaty initiatives by States has been accompanied by a rise in their negotiation and adoption of other types of international instruments, for example, declarations by Heads of State and Government, and "global compacts". Examples

80 Vienna Convention on Succession of States in Respect of Treaties, adopted on 23 August 1978, entered into force 6 November 1996, 1946 UNTS 3; Vienna Convention on Succession of States in respect of State Property, Archives and Debts, adopted 8 April 1983, not yet in force, UN Doc A/CONF.117/14.

81 Convention on the Law of the Non-navigational Uses of International Watercourses, adopted by UNGA 21 May 1997, entered into force 17 August 2014, UNTS registration no 52106.

82 Adopted 2 December 2004, not yet in force, UN Doc A/59/508.

83 Rome Statute of the International Criminal Court, adopted 17 July 1998, entered into force 1 July 2002, 2187 UNTS 3.

84 For example, the Guaraní Aquifer Agreement, signed by Argentina, Brazil, Paraguay and Uruguay, on 2 August 2010, took into account the provisions of the articles on the law of transboundary aquifers adopted by the Commission, in 2008 (see [2008] II (2) ILC Ybk 2008 19 at para 53). Indeed, the General Assembly has on several occasions, most recently in resolution 71/150 of 13 December 2016, commended the articles "as guidance for bilateral or regional agreements and arrangements for the proper management of transboundary aquifers".

85 Joost Pauwelyn, Ramses A Wessel and Jan Wouters, 'When Structures Become Shackles: Stagnation and Dynamics in International Lawmaking' (2014) 25 EJIL 733, 734–36.

86 International Convention for the Suppression of Terrorist Bombings, adopted on 15 December 1997, entered into force 23 May 2001, 2149 UNTS 256.

87 International Convention for the Suppression of the Financing of Terrorism, adopted on 9 December 1999, entered into force 10 April 2002, 2178 UNTS 197.

88 International Convention for the Suppression of Acts of Nuclear Terrorism, adopted on 13 April 2005, entered into force 7 July 2007, 2445 UNTS 89.

89 Optional Protocol to the Convention on the Safety of United Nations and Associated Personnel, adopted 8 December 2005, entered into force on 19 August 2010, 2689 UNTS 59.

include the 2005 World Summit Outcome,[90] which contains the "Responsibility to Protect" doctrine, and the negotiation of a Global Pact for the Environment.[91] A more rounded assessment of the Commission's impact should also take account of its many 'non-treaty' outputs. The Commission's statute does not limit it to preparing draft articles intended as the basis for treaty negotiations by States.[92] Although it is a popular perception that the early decades of the Commission's existence were characterized by the preparation of draft articles, the Commission also prepared non-treaty outputs during that period, for example, the draft declaration on rights and duties of States;[93] principles of international law recognized in the Charter of the Nuremberg Tribunal and in the Judgment of the Tribunal;[94] the draft code of offences against the peace and security of mankind;[95] and model rules on arbitral procedure.[96] Draft instruments intended to have a different normative character than treaties have therefore always been, to some extent, a characteristic of the Commission's outputs.

It is in current times, however, that the Commission's focus has shifted more substantially to outputs in forms other than those intended to be negotiated by States into treaties. Of the nine topics on the Commission's programme of work at the time of the seventieth anniversary, only three were being prepared as draft articles.[97] The other six topics were being dealt with either in the form of draft conclusions,[98] draft guide or guidelines,[99] or draft principles.[100] In none of these latter cases has the Commission specified what the varying

---

90 UNGA Res 60/1 (24 October 2005).

91 UNGA Res 72/277 (10 May 2018) and UNEP, 'Towards a Global Pact for the Environment', <https://www.unenvironment.org/events/conference/towards-global-pact-environment>.

92 See the contribution by Laurence Boisson de Chazournes contained in Section 3 of the book.

93 [1949] ILC Ybk 287 at para. 46.

94 [1950] II ILC Ybk 374 at para. 97.

95 [1954] II ILC Ybk 149 at para. 50.

96 [1958] II ILC Ybk 83 at para. 22.

97 The draft articles on crimes against humanity; the draft articles on immunity of State officials from foreign criminal jurisdiction; and the draft articles on succession of States in respect of State responsibility.

98 The draft conclusions on subsequent agreements and subsequent practice in relation to the interpretation of treaties; the draft conclusions on the identification of customary international law; and the draft conclusions on peremptory norms of general international law (*jus cogens*).

99 The draft guidelines on the protection of the atmosphere; and the draft guide on the provisional application of treaties.

100 The draft principles on the protection of the environment in relation to armed conflicts.

terms mean. It is clear from the titles and the forms in which these six topics are being prepared by the Commission that they are not intended as the basis for negotiation by States – in general, they inform and guide the user. The action taken by the General Assembly on 20 December 2018 in "taking note of" the conclusions on subsequent agreements and subsequent practice in relation to the interpretation of treaties, and the draft conclusions on the identification of customary international law, signifies that these conclusions are a final product – they will not be a basis for further negotiation by States. It is also clear that the conclusions are intended for use not only by States, but also "… all who may be called on" to interpret treaties and identify customary international law, respectively.[101]

What legal value, then, do such 'non-treaty' Commission outputs have? The basic starting point of which to remind ourselves is that no outputs of the Commission, nor of the General Assembly, in whatever form, are *per se* international law. Their legally binding nature under international law, as such, depends upon conduct by States. Finalization of draft articles by the Commission and, subsequently, the conclusion on that basis of the text of a treaty by the General Assembly, depend on ratifications by a sufficient number of States for the entry into force of the treaty. Outputs of the Commission that reflect customary international law, whether in the form of draft articles, draft conclusions, or any other 'non-treaty' form, do not themselves create customary international law. Such law is created by the pre-existing (or subsequent) general practice of States that is accepted by them as law (*opinio juris*).[102]

Some argue that, even where Commission outputs have not (or not yet), through the actions of States, become part of international law, they may nevertheless have a 'soft law' character with a degree of normative legal effect.[103] Whether this argument is accepted in principle or not, it would certainly be difficult to take the view that Commission outputs that are not intended as the basis for treaty negotiations are irrelevant to the progressive development and codification of international law. The Commission's authority,[104] its persuasive force, and the thoroughness and quality of its working methods,[105] based on

101 See UNGA Res 73/202 (20 December 2018) and 73/203 (20 December 2018).

102 See the commentaries to the 'Draft Conclusions on Identification of customary international law' (2018) UN Doc A/73/10, 141 at para. 2.

103 See, for example, Elena A. Baylis, 'The International Law Commission's Soft Law Influence' (2019) 13 FIU LRev 1007. See also the contributions by Laurence Boisson de Chazournes in Section 3 and Shinya Murase in Section 4 of this volume.

104 See subsection e) below on 'Authority and membership'.

105 See subsection b) below on the 'Working methods of the Commission'.

a thorough scientific analysis of State practice and sometimes that of international organizations, are such that its pronouncements tend to be given great weight by States and by international courts and tribunals, particularly the International Court of Justice.[106] The working methods that the Commission uses in the preparation of draft conclusions, guidelines and principles do not differ from those of the preparation of draft articles.[107] Just like draft articles, they are accompanied by commentaries that set out in detail the practice that underpins them and the rationale underlying the individual provisions.[108] These 'non-treaty' outputs therefore tend to exert a persuasive force on the views of States, international courts and tribunals as to the current state of the law and State practice, and may add momentum if there is a developing trend in the law in a particular direction.

In a world where States, faced with multiple interconnected challenges and a diversity of international actors, are themselves turning to more diverse forms of international instruments to regulate their cooperation, and demand for multilateral conventions has declined, the Commission could be viewed as keeping up with the curve. Its move away from preparing draft articles as a basis for treaties to working on a range of more diverse forms of output can be seen not as a sign of weakness or as a cause for concern, but rather as responding to broader international trends.[109] In designing its products in a way that is not only aimed at States in the Sixth Committee, but also addressed to other end-users, including practitioners, international and national judges, and academics and teachers of international law, the Commission is not showing symptoms of decline, but rather a keen sense of its authority and value, and in doing so, is ensuring for itself a continuing and important role at the heart of international relations.

b) *Working Methods of the Commission*

The working methods of the Commission, and their efficiency and effectiveness, are a vital component in the Commission's functioning, and essential to

---

106 Rosalyn Higgins, 'Keynote Address by H.E. Judge Rosalyn Higgins, President of the International Court of Justice, at the Sixtieth Anniversary of the International Law Commission' (Geneva, 19 May 2008) 2, <https://www.icj-cij.org/files/press-releases/8/14488.pdf>. See also the contribution by Danae Azaria in Section 4 of this volume; and Michael Peil, 'Scholarly Writings as a Source of Law: A Survey of the Use of Doctrine by the International Court of Justice' (2012) 1 CJICL 136, 152.

107 See the contribution by Maurice Kamto in Section 4 of this volume.

108 With regard to the importance of the commentaries see the contribution by Danae Azaria in Section 4 of this volume.

109 See also the contribution of Alejandro Rodiles in Section 3 of this volume.

maintaining the quality and therefore the authority and persuasive force of its work with States and other international actors. The Commission, aware of this, keeps its working methods constantly under review through its Working Group on Methods of Work, chaired during the current quinquennium by Ambassador Hussein A. Hassouna, a long-serving member of the Commission.

To attempt to outline the working methods of the Commission in this introductory Chapter would not be possible. A full and detailed description can be found in "The Work of the International Law Commission" prepared by the Codification Division, the Secretariat of the Commission.[110] The discussion below assumes at least some knowledge of how the Commission works. A few preliminary remarks, however, may be useful.

The essential dynamic of the Commission generally depends upon three actors: the Special Rapporteur; the plenary of the Commission; and the Drafting Committee. Special Rapporteurs are the 'engine' of the Commission, producing reports each year on the topic assigned to them, which are the raw material on which the Commission feeds. The plenary debates these reports over several days and gives a sense of the views of the Commission as a whole on the topic, on the Special Rapporteur's analysis of it, and on any draft provisions that the Special Rapporteur has included in the report. The Drafting Committee, which meets once the plenary debate is completed, looks in detail at any draft provisions referred to it by the plenary, negotiating and agreeing text for referral back to the plenary. In its contemporary practice, discussed below, the Drafting Committee has on occasions taken decisions on questions of policy or approach, as part and parcel of the drafting process; a function previously more the province of Working Groups established by the Commission for this purpose.[111] The Drafting Committee is a self-selecting subset of the membership of the Commission, consisting of any members with a particular interest in the

110 United Nations, *The Work of the International Law Commission*, vol I and II (9th edn, United Nations 2017).

111 Working Groups and sub-committees were established by the Commission as early as 1949, when the Commission established sub-committees on the question of the formulation of the principles recognized in the Charter of the Nuremberg Tribunal and in the Judgment of the Tribunal, as well as on the draft declaration on the rights and duties of States. They have been resorted to more frequently in recent times. For example, the Commission established a working group for the topic draft code of crimes against the peace and security of mankind in 1990, 1992–1994 and 1996 (in the latter case to consider the inclusion of wilful and severe damage to the environment as a war crime). A working group was also established for the topic "Diplomatic protection" (to examine the scope and content of the topic) in 1997 and 1998, as well as for the topic "Unilateral acts of States" at each session from 1997 to 1999 (to consider aspects of the scope and content of the topic, and from 2004–2006 to prepare a set of draft conclusions).

topic who wish to take part. The composition of the Drafting Committee varies from topic to topic, but its Chair remains constant throughout the session.

The Commission has not developed different working methods depending on the intended outcome of the topic – whether draft articles or a 'non-treaty' form.[112] Although the statute of the Commission is premised on a distinction between the procedures for progressive development and codification,[113] in fact, the Commission has not distinguished between these two functions in its working methods. Although there is a constant need for the Commission to keep its working methods under review, it is also the case that the thoroughness and consistency of the process is a major factor underpinning the quality of the Commission's outputs, and a significant source of its authority.[114]

Perhaps the most basic of the Commission's working methods, little mentioned in the contributions in this publication, is to meet away from United Nations Headquarters. The fact that the Commission's deliberations take place at the Palais des Nations in Geneva, at a distance from the General Assembly, its political parent organ in New York, in surroundings that are calm and conducive to reflective study, work and interaction among the members, and with excellent library services, is an essential element in the Commission's working methods and its independent functioning. The dislocation of the two bodies is not accidental. The Commission itself has commented on the importance of the location of its seat in Geneva.[115] The holding of the first part of the seventieth session in New York was, therefore, exceptional.[116] It generated a lot of interest among delegates to the Sixth Committee, and a large number of informal meetings, side events and panel discussions.

There is a certain amount of support among delegates for the Commission to hold one part-session in New York each quinquennium.[117] Generating the above-mentioned informal meetings and side-events can certainly have advantages in terms of strengthening the relationship between Commission members and Sixth Committee delegates. Support, however, is not universal

112 See the contribution by Maurice Kamto in Section 4 of this volume.

113 Chapter II of the ILC Statute on the "Functions of the International Law Commission" distinguishes "A. Progressive development of international law" and "B. Codification of international law".

114 For support for this statement, see commentary to conclusion 14 of the conclusions on identification of customary international law (n 102), 151 at paras. 3 and 5; and the contribution by Danae Azaria in Section 4 of this volume.

115 See generally United Nations (n 110) 72.

116 The last occasion when this took place was during the fiftieth anniversary, in 1998.

117 See the contribution by Hussein A. Hassouna in Section 2 of this volume.

for more regular meetings of the Commission in New York. Some concerns in this regard were raised during the annual Sixth Committee debate and the negotiations on the resolution on the Commission's report. Concerns include the amount of time and energy needed for the members to attend the numerous side events, which would make it more difficult to focus on the Commission's considerable workload. A further concern is that where such side-events address topics that are currently before the Commission, direct contacts between government representatives and Commission members while their discussions and negotiations are on-going may not be ideal in terms of perceptions of the Commission's independent functioning. Diplomatic missions in Geneva generally do not hold such events.

The current Commission has large numbers of members regularly attending the Drafting Committee. Whereas twelve or so members might have been a typical Drafting Committee size during previous quinquennia, it is not uncommon now for twenty or more members to attend. This inevitably has an impact on the nature of the Drafting Committee proceedings. As the Chair of the Drafting Committee has to demonstrate a certain fairness and inclusiveness, rounds of comments by members may sometimes precede the more negotiation-oriented interventions of those most closely familiar with and interested in the text proposed. These aspects of the Drafting Committee resemble, to some extent, the plenary debate. A skilful Chair therefore has to balance a democratic approach, allowing all members wishing to do so to intervene, with a more results-oriented approach, aiming to restrict general comments to the extent possible so that textual progress can be made. An accompanying development has been a tendency for the plenary on occasions to devolve the responsibility for finding a common way forward on a policy matter to the Drafting Committee.[118] The practice in the past had been to establish a Working Group for this purpose to consider the matter and to make a recommendation to the plenary.[119]

The Commission does not have its own rules of procedure but works in accordance with the General Assembly's Rules of Procedure,[120] adapted in practice to its own specificities. Decision-making is, therefore, in principle by majority of the members present and voting. Although voting was a common

118 See e.g. the Commission's decision to refer the question of the desirability of including a provision on corporate liability in the draft articles on Crimes against humanity to the Drafting Committee in UN Doc A/CN.4/SR.3301 (19 May 2016) 11.

119 See n 111 and accompanying text.

120 Rules of Procedure of the General Assembly, UN Doc A/520/Rev.18 (as adopted on 21 February 2017).

practice in the Commission during its first two decades, this has become much less common since the 1970s. Decision-making by consensus has since become the Commission's general practice. Members make every effort to take decisions without a vote, with those in the minority on any particular issue not objecting to the decision being taken, but often reading their differing or opposing position into the record of the meeting. In addition, 'indicative votes' are occasionally taken whereby, to avoid a formal vote, the Commission members in the Drafting Committee (and sometimes in plenary) decide an issue by informal show of hands, and then proceed by consensus on the basis of the result.[121] It is only where serious and irreconcilable differences of principle arise, therefore, that formal voting now takes place. The most recent example was in 2017, in relation to draft article 7 of the draft articles on the immunity of State officials from foreign criminal jurisdiction,[122] which concerns exceptions to immunity of State officials. Voting is a valid means of taking decisions under the Rules of Procedure, and in this sense, cannot be criticized. It may well be necessary where progress cannot otherwise be made. The fact of a vote on draft article 7 was, however, criticized by a number of States in the Sixth Committee.[123] States in the Sixth Committee, of course, look to the Commission to guide them on the state of development of the law and on State practice. A visible split in the Commission on these fundamentals arguably lessens the persuasive force of the Commission in respect of the particular provision voted on.[124]

A critical aspect of the working methods of the Commission, surprisingly little discussed in the literature, is the preparation and adoption of commentaries to accompany the outputs – referred to in the Commission's statute as "explanatory report".[125] In the commentaries, the Commission explains the draft provisions by reference to State practice, judicial decisions and doctrine, and in doing so, demonstrates the thoroughness and diligence of its work. The commentaries provide States, international organizations, international courts and tribunals, and scholars, access to the sources of practice, jurisprudence, teachings and rationales that underpin its analyses and its texts. The International Court of Justice and many other international courts and tribunals

121 United Nations (n 110) 62.

122 ILC (n 1) 164 at para 74.

123 See 'Topical summary of the discussion held in the Sixth Committee of the General Assembly during its seventy-third session, prepared by the Secretariat' UN Doc A/CN.4/724 (12 February 2019), para 65.

124 See the contribution by Danae Azaria contained in Section 4 of this volume.

125 See articles 16 and 22 of the ILC statute.

have cited not only the Commission's texts, but also its commentaries in a very significant number of the cases before them.[126]

Given the importance and value of the commentaries, surprise is sometimes expressed that they are considered and adopted at the end of the Commission's session, during the adoption of the Commission's annual report in plenary.[127] There is no equivalent to the Drafting Committee process for the consideration of commentaries. On the other hand, the adoption of the commentaries by the Commission at the end of its session represents the final stage of a longer and deeper process of crafting and consideration, led by the Special Rapporteur. The draft commentaries are prepared by the Special Rapporteur for the topic after the Drafting Committee has finished its work and has provisionally adopted draft provisions. The Special Rapporteur does so taking into account all comments relevant for inclusion in the commentaries made during the Drafting Committee's deliberations on the draft provisions, and will also often circulate a draft of the commentaries to members for input before finalizing them. On occasions, when time permits, a thorough opportunity for consideration of draft commentaries has been made available through the convening of a Working Group for this purpose.[128] The draft commentaries before the Commission during the last week or so of the annual session therefore represent the culmination of a process of informal consultations by the Special Rapporteur.

For those topics considered in the first part of the Commission's session (usually May to early June), the Special Rapporteur has time to prepare commentaries during the break in the Commission's session. The commentaries are adopted along with the draft provisions that had earlier been provisionally adopted by the Drafting Committee. For those topics considered in the second part of the Commission's session (usually July to early August), there is insufficient time for the Special Rapporteur to prepare commentaries for consideration by the plenary. In these cases, the Commission does not adopt the draft provisions referred back to it by the Drafting Committee, but "takes

---

126 See e.g. the compilations of decisions by international courts, tribunals and other bodies referring to the 2001 articles on the responsibility of States for internationally wrongful acts referred to in UNGA (n 63). See also the contribution by Danae Azaria in Section 4 of this volume.

127 See the contribution by Danae Azaria in Section 4 of this volume.

128 For example, at its sixty-eighth session, in 2016, the Commission decided to establish an open-ended working group to consider the draft commentaries to the draft conclusions on the identification of customary international law. 'Report of the International Law Commission on the work of its sixty-eighth session' (2016) UN Doc A/71/10, 75 at para. 58.

note" of them. Traditionally, these texts taken note of by the Commission were not reproduced in the Commission's annual report, the principle being that the Commission's outputs should always be accompanied by the explanatory material in the commentaries. Since 2012, however, a practice has developed in some instances of placing the texts taken note of in footnotes in the relevant parts of the Commission's annual report.[129] Although there are advantages to drawing attention to the latest texts under consideration by the Commission, this practice, which has not been consistent among the various topics, has led to some confusion and criticism on the part of States in the Sixth Committee, as well as some members of the Commission.[130]

A further and related practice that has developed in recent years is to place the statement of the Chair of the Drafting Committee on the website of the Commission.[131] When the Drafting Committee has finished its work on the draft provisions for a particular topic and referred the drafts back to the plenary of the Commission, the Chair of the Drafting Committee makes a detailed oral statement to the plenary giving an account of the deliberations that took place, and the rationale underlying the particular drafts provisionally adopted by the Drafting Committee. The statement is prepared by the Chair of the Drafting Committee with the support of the Secretariat, with input from the Special Rapporteur. It is not a substitute for the commentaries, prepared later by the Special Rapporteur, but it serves the purpose of informing the Commission, States and the public in some detail and in real time of the outcome of the Drafting Committee's work and the underlying rationale.

There is insufficient space in this Introduction for further discussion of the interrelated issues surrounding the Commission's commentaries, the statement of the Chair of the Drafting Committee, and the advantages and disadvantages of reproducing texts that have been taken note of without accompanying commentaries in the Commission's annual report. This subject area is one of great importance, however, and is more fully explored in Section 4 of this publication.[132]

129 The draft articles on the protection of persons in the event of disasters provisionally adopted by the Drafting Committee were quoted in a footnote in the Commission's report. ILC, 'Report of the International Law Commission on the work of its sixty-forth session' (2012) UN Doc A/67/10, 85 at footnote 275.

130 See the contribution by Danae Azaria in Section 4 of this volume.

131 ILC, <http://legal.un.org/ilc/>. The statements are available under 'Reports of the Drafting Committee' in the Analytical Guide of the respective topic.

132 See the contribution by Danae Azaria in Section 4 of this volume.

c) *Progressive Development and Codification of International Law*

As set out in the "historical context" section above, the juxtaposition of "progressive development" of international law and its "codification" has its origins in the negotiation of Article 13, paragraph 1 (a), of the Charter of the United Nations. The words were reproduced by the Committee of Seventeen when drafting the statute of the Commission, and separate procedures were envisaged for each activity.[133] Article 15 of the statute emphasizes the distinction between these two terms by defining "for convenience": progressive development as "… the preparation of draft conventions on subjects that have not yet been regulated by international law or in relation to which the law has not yet been sufficiently developed in the practice of States"; and codification as "… the more precise formulation and systematisation of rules of international law in fields where there already has been extensive State practice, precedent and doctrine".

The notion of "codification" has a long history and has not always enjoyed a single meaning nor universal support. Bentham wrote about codification in utopian terms, postulating an international code which would create a legal foundation for eternal peace.[134] Critics, on the other hand, pointed to the nature of law as an evolutionary phenomenon, subject to constant change, with codification posing the risk of interfering with its organic growth, rendering it static.[135] The former Commission member and Chair, Alain Pellet, stated: "… all topics involve partial codification since no topic is entirely new when it is undertaken by the [Commission] … in addition, all imply an element of progressive development since, almost as a matter of definition, customary rules always comprise some elements of uncertainty calling for clarification and this is precisely one of the main purposes of codification".[136]

---

133 See also section 2 above.

134 P. J. Baker, 'The Codification of International Law' (1924) 5 BYIL 38–65. See also Jeremy Bentham, 'Principles of Judicial Procedure with the outlines of a procedure code' in *The Works of Jeremy Bentham*, published under the superintendence of his executor John Bowring (William Tait, and Simpkin, Marshall, and Company 1843) 537–540. See also Bentham's *Legislator of the World: Writings on Codification, Law, and Education*, edited by Philip Schofield and Jonathan Harris (Clarendon Press 1998).

135 Mathias Reimann 'The Historical School against Codification: Savigny, Carter, and the Defeat of the New York Civil Code' (1989) 37 AmJCompL 95–119, 98. See also 'Savigny: German Lawgiver: Commentary' (1972) 55 MarqLRev 280–295.

136 Alain Pellet, 'Responding to New Needs through Codification and Progressive Development' in Vera Gowlland-Debbas (ed), *Multilateral Treaty-making: The Current Status of Challenges to and Reforms Needed in the International Legislative Process* (Martinus Nijhoff 2000) 13, 15–16.

In other words, codification and progressive development are difficult to dissociate and lie on the same spectrum of activity. The Commission's functions inherently encapsulate both law identification (codification) and legal policy (progressive development) aspects. The notion of a neat distinction between the two has proved to be unsustainable in practice and was abandoned early on.[137] Accordingly, the Commission's outputs typically include elements of both codification and progressive development of international law.

Why then, seventy years later, are we still debating the distinction between progressive development and codification and confirming its importance? If we start from the premise that international law is an essential ingredient not only in international dispute resolution, but also as the "glue" in the everyday dealings of States with each other and, increasingly, with and within international organizations, then it is clear that knowing what international law is and in which direction it is developing are fundamental. International law provides the framework, the substance and the vocabulary for international discourse. The Commission is uniquely and authoritatively placed as the sole universal expert body tasked with analysing State practice and international law, with a direct institutional interactive connection to States. Against this background, the debate about codification and progressive development by the Commission becomes one about the balance between *lex lata* and *lex ferenda*, and therefore about stability and change in international relations.

Continuing the discussion about the distinction is therefore important because it underlies concerns about the process of international law-making and, in particular, who is undertaking it. States, and more and more also international organizations, are the primary actors, but as we have seen in subsection a) above, the Commission makes a very significant contribution to the process that leads to the formation of international law. When working at the codifying end of the spectrum, it is self-evident that the Commission must base itself in the practice of States. It is important to underline, however, that when progressively developing, the Commission should also base itself closely on State practice, to the extent that this exists, and not ignore or contradict that practice. States in the Sixth Committee can be very vocal

137 James Crawford, 'The Progressive Development of International Law: History, Theory and Practice' in Denis Alland et al (eds), *Unity and Diversity of International Law: Essays in Honour of Professor Pierre-Marie Dupuy* (Martinus Nijhoff 2014) 19 (quoting the then Secretary of the Commission, Yuen-li Liang); Alain Pellet, 'Between Codification and Progressive Development of the law' (2004) 6 International Law FORUM du droit international 15, 15.

when they consider that State practice is not reflected in the work of the Commission.[138]

Against the background of the differing forms that the Commission's outputs take (subsection a) above), knowing whether the Commission's work, or parts of it, represent codification or progressive development, *lex lata* or *lex ferenda*, can be very important for States.[139] Where the Commission's output is in the form of draft articles, intended as a basis for negotiation by States of a treaty, it is clear that the Commission's word is not intended to be the final one. On the other hand, the Commission's draft conclusions, guidelines and principles are not intended for renegotiation by States. The Commission's text is the final product. In these circumstances, States arguably have a stronger need to know whether, in the Commission's view, the text represents codification or progressive development. International courts and tribunals, which frequently rely on the Commission's outputs and commentaries as authoritative, also have a strong interest in knowing whether the Commission considers the text to represent *lex lata or lex ferenda.*

Why then does the Commission rarely identify which of these it is presenting, either for whole projects or for particular provisions of those texts? The reality is that it would be very difficult, and sometimes impossible, for the Commission to parse its work in this way consistently. As Alain Pellet analysed above, the distinction is difficult to discern. Given that the membership of the Commission is very diverse, a microcosm of the United Nations membership, representing the various legal systems of the world, it is perhaps not surprising that the Commission is unwilling or unable to attempt consistently to distinguish between codification and progressive development in its work. In reality, there are occasions when it helps the deliberations within the Commission and the Drafting Committee to agree that a particular provision is a

138 See, for example statements made by the representatives of various States on the topic of "Immunity of State officials from foreign criminal jurisdiction" during the consideration of the Report of the International Law Commission on the work of its sixty-ninth session at the seventy-second session of the Sixth Committee. The statements made by the representatives of France and Italy, UN Doc A/C.6/72/SR.18 (23 October 2017) para. 126 and 146; the representative of the Russian Federation, UN Doc A/C.6/72/SR.19 (24 October 2017) para 38; the representative of the United States of America, UN Doc A/C.6/72/SR.21 (25 October 2017) para. 21; the representatives of Switzerland, Australia, India and Japan, UN Doc A/C.6/72/SR.22 (26 October 2017) para. 86, 98, 121, and 127; the representatives of Thailand and China, UN Doc A/C.6/72/SR.23 (27 October 2017) para. 54, and 57; and the representatives of Ireland, Belarus, Spain, the United Kingdom, Iran (Islamic Republic of), Germany and Malaysia, UN Doc A/C.6/72/SR.24 (27 October 2017) para. 26, 34, 41, 57–58, 64, 90, and 119.

139 See the contribution of Sean Murphy in Section 5 of this volume.

codification of existing international law, *lex lata,* and equally there are other occasions when it helps the deliberating dynamic to agree that the provision in question represents a development of international law, *lex ferenda*. The Commission therefore proceeds pragmatically. Its practice of working collegially, predominantly without voting, may be sorely tested if it were to attempt to identify all of its outputs as either *lex lata* or *lex ferenda.*

The Commission also has a practical and pragmatic interest in getting through its workload at each session. This could be thrown into disarray if it were to stop and consider at each step whether it is codifying or progressively developing. Those who have experienced first-hand the work of the Drafting Committee, which works behind closed doors, know that there are many and divergent views on a great number of the provisions considered – differing views about relevant practice and the jurisprudence.

This, and the broader challenges facing the Commission and its relationship with the Sixth Committee, including multilateral "treaty fatigue" on the part of States, are considered further in section 3 above and subsection d) below.

d) *The Changing Landscape of International Law*

International law is a stabilizing influence in a world facing an increasingly complex and challenging set of realities. The lifetime of the Commission has marked the evolution of international law from a system that was applicable only among a relatively small number of States to a universal legal order in which 193 United Nations Member and 2 Observer States from all corners of the globe participate.[140] In addition, international law has moved toward recognizing not only the rights and obligations of States, but also responding to the needs of a plurality of actors, including international organizations, individuals, corporations and other non-State actors. The world is continuing to experience the scourge of war and its adverse impact on humanity and the environment; international terrorism and growing extremism; climate change and natural disasters; growing inequality between the rich and poor; and exponential advances in technology which bring great benefits, but also risks of cyber warfare and cyber crime.

The other aspect of the changing landscape that emanates from the various factors described above, and which bears repetition here, is that of multilateral treaty fatigue on the part of States. Historically, treaties have been used to shape new orders in the wake of major world events, including the aftermath of the Second World War, the end of the colonial period, and the end of the

140 See the keynote address by Abdulqawi A. Yusuf contained in Section 9 of this volume.

Cold War.[141] This phenomenon now seems to have declined, and as described in subsection a) of this Introduction, some States are reducing their multilateral engagement, while others are negotiating and participating in new forms of arrangement that do not amount to treaties, or may be treaties with "softer" obligations. The most prominent example of the latter is the Paris Agreement, the content of which is primarily procedural in nature, with few fixed substantive obligations. The States parties determine their own "contributions" to the reduction of greenhouse gas emissions.[142]

Given the turbulence in international relations caused by the above challenges, and the plurality of actors engaged, the Commission may seem a rather traditional organ. The institutional factors which have placed it at the centre of the progressive development and codification of international law, including in particular its status as a subsidiary organ of the General Assembly in a direct relationship with States in the Sixth Committee, also give rise to questions about its ability to adapt to such changing circumstances. To compound the challenges, the Commission now works in an environment where there has been a proliferation of other negotiating fora – where many specialized areas of international law are discussed and developed.

Faced with all of this, one of the Commission's reactions is not surprising, and carries great value and merit. Described by some as "complementary" or "annotative" codification, it consists of updating and expanding "foundational" or "architectural" codification work.[143] Both the conclusions on subsequent agreements and subsequent practice in relation to the interpretation of treaties, completed at the seventieth session, and the draft guide to provisional application of treaties, now at the First Reading stage, are examples of this. They both build on aspects of the Vienna Convention on the Law of Treaties which were not fully developed in 1969, and on which there has been fifty years of State practice. This work is of obvious utility to States and maximizes the Commission's competitive advantage as the preeminent expert body on questions of general international law. Another area of focus for the Commission has been to further its work on the other sources of international law, including customary international law and general principles of law.[144]

141 See the contribution by Laurence Boisson de Chazournes contained in Section 3 of this volume.

142 Adopted on 12 December 2015, entered into force 4 November 2016, UNTS registration no 54113.

143 See the contribution by Alejandro Rodiles, contained in Section 3 of this volume.

144 ILC (n 102) 117 at para 65; and the decision to include the topic "General principles of law", ibid at para 263.

There are, inevitably, a limited number of such topics left where the Commission is the obvious preeminent expert body. It has, therefore, not been shy in shifting its attention to new and more specialized areas of international law. These topics tend to lend themselves to forms of Commission output that are not intended for negotiation by States into treaties, and which contain a mixture of provisions containing aspirational language and provisions that state the existing law. Current examples of such topics before the Commission include the "Protection of the atmosphere" and the "Protection of the environment in armed conflict", each of which is being prepared in the form of draft principles. An example of draft articles are those on the protection of persons in the event of disasters, completed by the Commission in 2016,[145] and currently before the Sixth Committee for consideration of whether the draft should form the basis of a treaty.

It is in relation to these more specialized legal topics where the Commission members do not necessarily have the full breadth of appropriate expertise, or, as in the case of "Protection of the atmosphere", scientific evidence is useful, so that the Commission sometimes actively reaches out to external bodies.[146] The statute authorizes the Commission in article 16 (e) to "... consult with scientific institutions and individual experts" for the purpose of progressive development of international law. As the Commission's engagement with such specialized areas increases, this in turn may lead the Commission in the context of its working methods to ask how the source of such expert advice should be determined – who is to determine who are the appropriate experts? Should the Special Rapporteur make this determination, or should the Commission in plenary decide, much as the International Court of Justice has started to do when it needs input from expert witnesses that are not appointed by the parties before the Court?[147]

Inevitably, it is in the choice of such new and more specialized topics that the Commission tends to come in for most criticism from States in the Sixth Committee. There are calls for the Commission to be more attentive to the wishes of States, and not to take up topics that do not enjoy the support of States generally.[148] Having said this, it is also the case that the Sixth Committee rarely makes requests to the Commission to take up particular topics,

145 ILC, 'Draft Articles on the protection of persons in the event of disasters' (2016) UN Doc A/71/10, 13 at para 48.

146 See the contribution of Shinya Murase in Section 4 of this volume.

147 See *Maritime Delimitation in the Caribbean Sea and the Pacific Ocean* (*Costa Rica v Nicaragua*) [2016] ICJ Rep 240.

148 See the contribution by François Alabrune contained in Section 1 of this volume.

and it is even unusual for individual States to make recommendations.[149] Notably, the Commission at its seventieth session brought two new topics onto its long-term programme, and will no doubt be actively considering at future sessions whether either or both of these topics should be brought onto its programme of work: "Sea-level rise in relation to international law", and "Universal criminal jurisdiction". A positive argument in favour of the Commission involving itself in more specialized areas is that, with its generalist viewpoint, it may help to avoid "fragmentation" among different bodies of law.

The Commission has, from time to time, conducted "surveys" of international law as a means to identifying potential new topics. The first was prepared primarily by Hersch Lauterpacht in 1949 on the basis of a memorandum prepared by the Secretariat,[150] which informed the Commission's work for decades. A further survey in 1968 sought to provide a full review of the state of international law, and was conceived of as a successor to the 1949 Survey.[151] In 1996, the Commission established a general scheme of topics of international law classified under a non-exhaustive list of 13 main fields, further subdivided into topics which the Commission had already taken up, those under consideration and possible future topics.[152] Most recently, at the request of the Commission in 2014, the Secretariat prepared a survey reviewing the 1996 general scheme and submitting working papers for six potential new topics.[153]

149 For a recent example see e.g. the statement of the Pacific Small Island Developing States in the Sixth Committee requesting the International Law Commission to take up the topic of 'Legal implications of sea-level rise' into its long-term programme of work (UN Doc A/C.6/72/SR.22 (26 October 2017) para. 52). The request was supplemented by a proposal contained in a letter, dated 31 January 2018, by the Government of the Federated States of Micronesia to the International Law Commission (on file with the Secretariat of the ILC). On the selection of topics more generally see United Nations (n 110) vol 1, 34. See also the contribution by François Alabrune contained in Section 1 of this volume.

150 ILC, 'Survey of International Law in Relation to the Work of Codification of the International Law Commission: Preparatory work within the purview of article 18, paragraph 1, of the of the International Law Commission – Memorandum submitted by the Secretary-General' (10 February 1949) UN Doc A/CN.4/1/Rev.1.

151 ILC 'Review of the Commission's programme and methods of work: working paper prepared by the Secretariat' [1968] II ILC Ybk 226 (annex); and ILC, 'Review of the Commission's programme of work and of the topics recommended or suggested for inclusion in the programme: working paper prepared by the Secretariat' [1970] II ILC Ybk 247; and ILC 'Survey of international law: Working paper prepared by the Secretary-General' [1971] II (2) ILC Ybk 1.

152 ILC 'Report of the Commission to the General Assembly on the work of its forty-eighth session' [1996] II (2) ILC Ybk 97 at paras 246–248 and annex II.

153 ILC UN document A/CN.4/679 and Add 1.

An interesting approach was taken in 1962 when, pursuant to a resolution, the General Assembly decided to place on its agenda: "Future work in the field of the codification and progressive development of international law ..." "... in order to study and survey the whole field of international law and make necessary suggestions with regard to the preparation of a new list of topics for codification and for the progressive development of international law ...".[154] The resulting survey was prepared primarily on the basis of replies received from governments. If States in the Sixth Committee wish seriously to engage with the Commission on its choices of topics, repeating the 1962 experience may be one means of achieving this end.

e) *Authority and Membership*

The theme of this subsection takes in both the broader authority of the Commission, which rests on multiple foundations, and its membership, which is one such foundation among many. The Commission's outputs in the form of draft articles, draft conclusions etc. are not binding under international law – they do not carry authority in this sense, nor in the hierarchical sense. Nor, for that matter, do the outputs of the General Assembly, even where these are concluded in the form of treaties. Except to the extent that such products are statements of existing international law, they depend upon further actions by States to become law, and to carry the authority of being binding under international law.

The authority that is discussed in this subsection is, rather, the intangible authority, or persuasive force, that the Commission's work carries, and which tends to be acknowledged and respected by States, international organizations, courts and tribunals, both international and national, and publicists. Where does this kind of authority emanate from and why is it respected?

The sources of the Commission's authority in this sense relate both to its institutional characteristics and to its individual outputs on the topics before it. Institutionally, the Commission is a body carrying the authority of having been established by the General Assembly soon after the inception of the United Nations, comprising recognized experts in international law acting independently of governments, with a mandate directly related to the Assembly's responsibilities under the Charter of the United Nations, not shared by any other actor on the playing field of general international law, and enjoying a privileged and direct relationship with States through the Sixth Committee.[155]

---

154 UNGA Res 1505 (XV) of 12 December 1960.

155 See, in particular, articles 3, 16, 17(c), 18, 20, 22, 23 and 24 of the ILC statute.

No other international expert legal body is endowed with these institutional and other characteristics.

The membership of the Commission and the way in which the membership is selected form part of these institutional characteristics that buttress the Commission's inherent authority. The fact that the membership is "universal", in the sense of being representative of the full geographical spread of United Nations Member States, is essential to the Commission's credibility and legitimacy. Nomination by States and election by the General Assembly on a basis that is designed to be representative of the five United Nations regional groupings of States is a visible demonstration of the Commission's ability to represent the various legal traditions.[156] Although elections by political organs are increasingly criticized in the literature as a means of selecting individuals for international judicial and other such expert positions,[157] they remain the primary means by which the authority and legitimacy of the UN's principal plenary organ is bestowed.

At the time of the establishment of the Commission, there were 57 Member States of the United Nations. There are now 193 and 2 Observer States. In the words of Judge Yusuf, President of the International Court of Justice, this change is not only numerical: "… [i]t represents a profound societal change involving the emergence of a diverse body of actors, each with their own culture, customs and legal traditions. These changes strengthened the mission of the International Law Commission and laid the foundations for its ability to contribute to the formation of a universal international legal order."[158] In other words, the membership of the Commission, representative of the five regional groups of States and their widely diverse cultures and traditions, including legal traditions, is essential to the authority and respect that the Commission needs to carry out its mandate.

---

156 See article 8 of the ILC statute.

157 See e.g. Ruth MacKenzie et al., *Selecting International Judges: Principle, Process and Politics* (OUP 2010); Ruth Mackenzie and Philippe Sands, 'International Courts and Tribunals and the Independence of the International Judge' (2003) 44 HarvIntlLJ 271 at 278; Allison Danner and Erik Voeten, 'Who is Running the International Judicial System?' in Deborah Avant et al (eds), *Who Governs the Globe?* (CUP 2010) 35–71; Davis R. Robinson, 'The Role of Politics in the Election and the Work of Judges of the International Court of Justice' (2003) 97 ASILPROC 277 at 279; and International Service for Human Rights, 'Vote trading and sliding standards risk eroding the credibility of the Human Rights Council', (5 October 2016) <https://www.ishr.ch/news/vote-trading-and-sliding-standards-risk-eroding-credibility-human-rights-council>.

158 See the Keynote address by Abdulqawi A. Yusuf in the Section 9 of this volume.

As one panelist expresses it, the Commission would hardly be able to determine what are the "pressing concerns of the international community as a whole" if it were not itself representative of that community.[159] The number of members has therefore increased several times from the original fifteen to the current thirty-four in order to be representative of the increase in the number of United Nations members. A fixed distribution of seats has been established to ensure an equitable geographical distribution.[160] Importantly, the membership of the Commission is a microcosm of the membership of the United Nations.

Over the years, the General Assembly has elected a variety of types of members to the Commission, including judges, academics, former or current legal advisers of foreign ministries, diplomats and sometimes government ministers.[161] Legal expertise is important, but is also closely linked to the need to ensure representation of the main forms of civilization and of the principal legal systems of the world. The Commission's statute provides for a balance to be struck between regional representativeness[162] and legal expertise.[163] Some of the contributors who are Commission members remark this mix of membership in positive terms – there does not seem to be a suggestion that government legal advisers are any less valuable members of the Commission than academics or other members not, or no longer, affiliated with a government.[164] Indeed, awareness of the views of governments and the ability to take full account of State practice is an essential quality of the Commission.

A very important criticism voiced by many contributors is the lack of gender equality among the Commission members.[165] The Commission has had seven female members during its seventy-year history.[166] There are currently only four female members out of thirty-four. This is not the fault of the Commission itself. If the purpose of the Commission is to represent "the main forms of civilization and ... the principal legal systems of the world"[167] and to reflect

---

159 See contribution by Hajer Gueldich contained in Section 6 of this volume.

160 UNGA Res 1103 (XI) (18 December 1956) (increasing the number to 21); UNGA Res 1647 (XVI) (6 November 1961) (increasing the number to 25); UNGA Res 36/39 (18 November 1981) (increasing the number to 34).

161 See contribution by Ernest Petrič contained in Section 1 of this volume.

162 See article 8 of the ILC statute.

163 See article 2 of the ILC statute.

164 See the contributions by Ernest Petrič in Section 1 and by Dire Tladi in Section 7 of this volume.

165 See e.g. the contributions by Zuzana Trávníčková and Mónica Pinto and the concluding remarks of Dire Tladi to Section 7 of this volume.

166 See e.g the concluding remarks by Claudio Grossman Guiloff in Section 6 of this volume.

167 Article 8 of the ILC statute.

the international community of States, then States from all regions will need to nominate more women, and the General Assembly will need to elect more women to the Commission. Gender equality on the Commission is equally as important as other forms of diversity. As one contributor states, gender diversity would contribute to the "catalyst of reason"[168] created by the joining of diverse perspectives, just as the Commission's diversity of legal cultures and legal backgrounds does.

Turning to the authority that the Commission's individual outputs carry, these of course depend to some extent on the Commission's inherent institutional authority discussed above, but also on the care and diligence with which the Commission produces the particular output in question. In other words, the thorough and scientific working methods of the Commission as applied in the preparation of its individual outputs are critical to the reception that the outputs will receive from the Commission's primary "clients" – States, international organizations, international courts and tribunals and scholars.

This aspect of the Commission's authority is analyzed in some depth in Section 4, in which one contributor draws on the work of the late Thomas Franck to argue that rules that are developed through a process that adheres to accepted methodology are more likely to be regarded as "legitimate" and therefore to be complied with.[169] In the context of the Commission's work, adherence to the tried and tested working methods of the Commission "… operates as a restraint on the Commission's discretion: it anchors its output in State practice, *opinio juris* and international jurisprudence, rather than on mere policy preferences of the Commission's members".[170]

The Commission itself has recognized that the thoroughness and technical quality of its work is central to the authority and persuasiveness of its outputs.[171] This can be found in the Commission's work on the "Identification of customary international law".[172] The conclusions on the topic do not include a provision specifically dedicated to the Commission's own outputs, but it is stated in the introductory commentary to part five of the conclusions that the Commission's determinations "… may have particular value [flowing from, *inter alia*] the thoroughness of its procedures (including the consideration of extensive surveys of State practice and *opinio juris*); and its close relationship

168 See the concluding remarks by Claudio Grossman Guiloff in Section 6 of this volume.
169 Thomas Franck, *Fairness in International Law and Institutions* (OUP 1995) 30, 40–46.
170 See the contribution by Danae Azaria in Section 4 of this volume.
171 Ibid.
172 ILC (n 102).

with the General Assembly and States (including receiving oral and written comments from States as it proceeds with its work)."[173] It concludes that "the weight to be given to the Commission's determinations depends [...] on various factors, including the sources relied upon by the Commission, the stage reached in its work, and above all upon States' reception of its output".[174]

With these factors in mind, some contributors cast a certain degree of doubt on the Commission's capacity to examine the practice, cultures and legal traditions of 193 Member States of the United Nations,[175] particularly bearing in mind the low rate of responses by States to requests by the Commission for views and information.[176] This is a further reason why the universally representative character of the Commission is critical to its authority. Even in the absence of widespread input by governments on some topics, the Commission's diverse geographical membership and the wide backgrounds of the members, both governmental and non-governmental, helps to ensure that a spread of views is taken into account.

Regional representation infuses every aspect of the working methods of the Commission. The position of Chair rotates among the five regional groups each year, as do the other four positions in the Bureau (the two Vice-Chairs, the Chair of the Drafting Committee and the General Rapporteur). The Bureau is the organizational centre of gravity of the Commission, considering and recommending to the plenary a wide range of important matters for decision. These include the programme of work, choices of Special Rapporteur, and whether any particular topic should be brought from the Commission's long-term programme onto its current programme. The fact that each regional group of members in the Commission has a member in the Bureau eases the way for decisions to be made by the plenary on such important matters. The Commission aims, for example, for a good regional spread of Special Rapporteurs across the various topics on its programme. The visible regionally representative nature of the Commission and the fact that it works on the basis of regional rotation for the Chair and other positions in the Bureau, mirroring in this respect the working methods of the General Assembly, is an essential element in the authority that the Commission has in its relationship with the Sixth Committee.

173 See the general commentary to part five in ILC (n 102) 142 at para. 2.
174 Ibid.
175 See the contribution by François Alabrune contained in Section 1 of this volume.
176 See section 3 of this Introduction on 'Institutional Relationship with the Sixth Committee'.

5 Summaries of the Contributions

Part 1 of this volume on “Drawing a balance for the future: the New York conversation” contains the contributions of the panelists during the celebratory events in New York. In his opening remarks to *Section 1* on “The Commission and the Sixth Committee: structural changes”, *Eduardo Valencia-Ospina* notes the success of the work of the Commission, which is practice-driven, has depended as much on sustained dialogue with the Sixth Committee, as on the cooperation received from governments. He criticizes the fact that no convention has been adopted by the General Assembly, nor under its auspices, based on a final draft by the Commission since 2004. *François Alabrune* also sees the relationship between the Commission and the Committee largely as the basis for the proper functioning of Commission. He discusses the structural challenges facing the Commission and suggests possible ways of dealing with those challenges. *Mahmoud D. Hmoud* explains that the Commission plays an advisory role in relation to the international community, which may be expository in nature in many instances. He acknowledges the existence of other international law-making bodies and organs and recommends that the Commission should continue to take into account the work and processes of such bodies. *Janine Felson* argues that it may be best to look beyond the bifurcation between codification and progressive development and instead search for a practical functionality of the Commission as a progressive codifier, preserving its legitimacy and simultaneously promoting the development of international law, including in areas of common concern of humankind. According to *Ernest Petrič*, the main challenge of the Commission is the selection of topics. Noting that the Commission was established when the world was a different place, he encourages the Commission, together with States, to find ways to adapt its methodology to handle topics of modern international life and emerging needs of the international community.

In *Section 2*, the contributors discuss “The Commission and the Sixth Committee: reflections on the interaction in the past and the future”, including suggestions for improving that interaction. In his introductory remarks, *Burhan Gafoor* distinguishes between three roles in which the Sixth Committee has interacted with the Commission: first, its traditional role as a main Committee of the General Assembly that debates the Commission’s annual report; second, a forum where *inter alia* drafts prepared by the Commission are negotiated; and third, a filter and consensus-builder that uses its modalities to reach consensus on the Commission’s work. *Evgeny Zagaynov* notes that the Commission enjoys a high degree of autonomy, while the general political guidance from the Sixth Committee provides insight into the needs and expectations of States. To strike a balance between the needs of States and the Commission's independence, he suggests focusing on how to improve the existing procedure for selecting and then working on topics. *Concepción Escobar-Hernández* asks whether the current relationship model regarding the Commission and the Sixth Committee is satisfactory and effective. She discusses different aspects of the relationship such as the selection of topics, the transmission of information on the Commission's work, contributions by States, the holding of meetings between the Commission and the Sixth Committee, and the response of the Sixth Committee to the final work of the Commission. *Angel Horna* examines the ways in which the Sixth Committee and the Commission have influenced each other, formally and informally, in terms of joint achievements and difficulties. He also considers how the Commission should design its outcomes, and how the Sixth Committee should deal with them in the future. Comparing the distinct but interrelated roles of the Sixth Committee and the Commission, *Hussein A. Hassouna* concludes that the Commission's institutional knowledge, its framework within the General Assembly and its partnership with the Sixth Committee, provide it with a unique position to continue to codify and progressively develop international law in the future.

Part 2 of this volume 'Drawing the Balance for the Future: The Geneva Symposium' includes the contributions made during the celebratory events in Geneva. Introducing the symposium, *Georg Nolte* notes that the Commission seems to have overcome the sense of crisis that had prevailed during the sixtieth anniversary celebrations. He explains that the main purpose of the Geneva symposium was to produce a lasting impulse that will serve to improve and to safeguard the unique role of the Commission in progressively developing and codifying international law. In his opening remarks to *Section 3* on "The Commission and its Impact", *Pedro Comissário Afonso* observes that even sovereignty needs law: internally, to function properly and with fairness, and at the international level, to co-exist and cooperate with other competing sovereignties. *Alejandro Rodiles*, in his contribution entitled "The International Law Commission and Change: Not Tracing but Facing It", argues that the perception of the Commission's lacking capacity to cope with the changing structures of the international legal system is not accurate. Using different examples, he shows how the Commission fine-tunes the rules of international law in response to a changing and uncertain normative environment. In her contribution on "International Law Commission in a Mirror – Forms, Impact and Authority", *Laurence Boisson de Chazournes* assesses whether the progressive decrease in the number of conventions adopted based on the Commission's work is a sign of its decline, and whether the increasing diversity of instruments drafted by the Commission affects its impact. She concludes that the Commission enjoys an authority *per se*, which is of a dynamic nature and guarded by the Commission and States as its short-term and longer-term custodians. In his concluding remarks, *Pavel Šturma* observes that a better understanding of the Commission's interlocutors is needed to evaluate and propose possible modifications to its methods of work in a changing normative environment. The Commission, as an expert body and subsidiary organ, is, in fact, the place where theory may (and sometimes does) become practice, which comes with responsibilities and expectations of its different constituencies.

Section 4 discusses the "The Working Methods of the Commission". *Aleksandar V. Gajić*, in his opening remarks, explains that the Section will focus on how the International Law Commission conducts its work; in other words, on how it produces results that remain indispensable for the contemporary international community. *Danae Azaria*, in her contribution entitled "The Working Methods of the International Law Commission: Adherence to Methodology, Commentaries and Decision-Making" reflects on the importance of the Commission's working methods in preserving and enhancing the quality of its work based on an increasing number of non-binding instruments. She concludes that the Commission's working methods cannot and should not be further abbreviated but should be expanded and enhanced. In his contribution on "The Working Methods of the International Law Commission", *Maurice Kamto* asks whether the Commission has been able to take advantage of the comments and suggestions made by the participants in the colloquium held on the occasion of its fiftieth anniversary. He argues that a clarification of methodology in relation to the adoption of the Commission's products could allow it to maintain the current terminological diversity while safeguarding its authority and reputation. In his concluding remarks, *Shinya Murase* focuses on the final form of the Commission's products, but also comments on issues such as the importance of distinguishing between codification and progressive development of international law, the possibility of voting, the role of the Special Rapporteurs' reports and the Commission's commentaries, the usefulness of input from scientists and the support provided by the Secretariat.

In her introductory remarks to *Section 5* on "The Function of the Commission: How Much Identifying Existing Law, How Much Proposing New Law?", *Davinia Aziz* argues that the debate on the right balance between stability and change in the Commission's mandate remains relevant today. She notes that it enhances Member States ability to meaningfully respond to the Commission's products in a world characterized by a plurality of actors. The Commission, as the codification body of the sole universal international organization, has evolved alongside changes in multilateral treaty-making and global governance. In his contribution entitled "Between Codification and Legislation: A

Role for the International Law Commission as an Autonomous Law-Maker", *Yifeng Chen* submits that the Commission performs a dual role in the international law-making process, as both registrar and legislator, which engages in different types of legislation, namely "legislation through conceptualization", "legislation through *lex scriptum*", "legislation through codification" and "legislation through convention". Reflecting on "The Functions of the International Law Commission: Identifying Existing Law or Proposing New Law?", *Ineta Ziemele* proposes that the Commission should revise its functions and methods of work to take into account the increasing plurality of actors and sources of law. Considering the European Court of Human Rights' engagement with the work of the Commission, she encourages more openness, dialogue and communication between the various bodies involved in the making and application of international law. *Sean D. Murphy*, in his concluding remarks, offers an "insider's perspective" on the factors that push the balance within the Commission either in the direction of "codification" of international law or in the direction of "progressive development?", and he discusses when the Commission is transparent in drawing the distinction. In his view, much of what the Commission does is progressive development of the law, even if it is commonly perceived by others as codification.

Section 6 addresses "The Changing Landscape of International Law". In her opening remarks, *Elinor Hammarskjöld* notes that it is an important aspect of the interaction between the Commission and governments that the Commission does not have to restrict itself to traditional topics but should also consider issues that reflect new developments in international law. In her contribution on "Challenges of Codification for the International Law Commission in a Changing Landscape of International Law", *Hajer Gueldich* surveys the changing landscape of international law for pertinent topics. She concludes that the Commission must diversify not only the topics on its programme of work but also the dissemination of its outcomes, the way it brings in external expertise and viewpoints from developing States, and its interaction with other bodies, from regional organizations to academia. "Recalibrating the Conception of Codification in the Changing Landscape of International Law", *Keun-Gwan Lee* conducts a historical assessment of the concept of codification of international law, beginning with Jeremy Bentham's proposals, leading up to the adoption of the Commission's statute. Distinguishing between (i) mega- or total codification, (ii) foundational or architectural codification, (iii) thematic codification, and (iv) complementary or annotative codification, he suggests redressing the balance between these various categories of codification. *Claudio Grossman Guiloff*, in his concluding remarks, observes that both contributors to the Section agree on the strengths of the Commission that have allowed it to remain relevant and effective: the Commission's ability to adapt to meet the changing demands of the international community; the diversity of the Commission; and the Commission's independence. He also reflects on three additional topics, namely the lack of gender balance on the Commission, the current geopolitical environment, and the "human factor" of international law.

In his opening remarks to *Section 7* on "The Authority and the Membership of the Commission", *Djamchid Momtaz* cautions that the Commission should avoid taking up topics that are unsuitable for codification. At the same time, the selection criteria set out in 1997 should not prevent the Commission from considering topics that reflect new trends and concerns of the international community as a whole, which are the Commission's lifeblood. *Zuzana Trávníčková*, in her contribution on "The International Law Commission and the International Law Codification Market", elaborates on the codification and progressive development of international law as services offered, as well as on the International Law Commission as the leading supplier and on States as demanders. She observes that the behavior of demanders changes slowly but steadily, while the aggregate demand for codification weakens. On the side of suppliers, however, the International Law Commission still holds a unique position due to its general mandate. Focusing on the "Authority and the Commission of the Commission in the Future", *Mónica Pinto* argues that States should be encouraged to nominate and elect more women to the Commission, and that the Commission's working methods should incorporate the diversity of legal systems. If the International Law Commission is going to further develop products other than draft articles, it should consider consulting a broader field of stakeholders. *Dire Tladi*, in his concluding remarks, observes that the contributions by Zuzana Trávníčková and Mónica Pinto are complementary in offering different perspectives on the interaction between authority and membership, in particular on the issue of gender representation.

Part 3 includes "Celebratory Contributions on the Occasion of the Seventieth Anniversary of the Commission". *Section 8* contains the commemorative speeches delivered in New York. In his statement, Eduardo-Valencia Ospina, in his capacity as the *Chair of the International Law Commission at its seventy-first session*, emphasizes that the Commission has played a crucial role in laying the foundations for the proper functioning of the international community in the post-war era. Given the worrying isolationist tendencies that have recently surfaced on the world stage, there is a need, today more than ever, for it to continue its work of consolidating international law. The *President of the General Assembly at its seventy-second session*, Miroslav Lajčák, notes that the work of the Commission has made the body of international law more robust. The Commission has helped to create many key international instruments and contributed to creating avenues, *inter alia*, for the prevention, prosecution and punishment of most serious crimes. The *Under-Secretary-General for Legal Affairs and United Nations Legal Counsel*, Miguel de Serpa Soares, underlines different reasons for the Commission's success: its intergovernmental mandate, its unique composition, its sophisticated working methods, and the support provided by its Secretariat. He also observes that while the Commission faces significant challenges today, it has proven to be adaptive over the past 70 years. The *Chair of the Sixth Committee of the General Assembly at its seventy-second session*, Burhan Gafoor, points to the relationship between the Sixth Committee and the Commission as being an organic and symbiotic relationship that is based on a common objective, which is to support the progressive development and codification of international law and to strengthen the multilateral rules-based system. The *Permanent Representative of Switzerland to the United Nations*, Jürg Lauber, observes that while all efforts to enhance the dialogue between the Sixth Committee of the General Assembly and the International Law Commission are welcome, the choice to hold the meetings of the Commission in Geneva ensures the complete independence of its work. *The Legal Adviser of the Department of State of the United States of America*, Jennifer Newstead, explains that the United States has not always agreed with proposed topics or particular conclusions, but the United States recognizes the unique role that the Commission plays in advancing the rule of law in the international arena. In his keynote address, Nico Schrijver, *President of the Institut de Droit international and Professor of Public International Law*, discusses some similarities and differences between the Commission and the *Institut de Droit international*, followed by various examples where both institutions have contributed to the progressive development of international law.

Section 9 includes the commemorative speeches delivered in Geneva. Eduardo-Valencia Ospina, in his capacity as the *Chair of the International Law Commission at its seventy-first session*, elaborates on a broader concept of codification, which merges classic codification and progressive development, and notes that the final form of the Commission's work could perhaps be less important for the future than the complex process of codification and progressive development itself. The *Under-Secretary-General for Legal Affairs and United Nations Legal Counsel*, Miguel de Serpa Soares, emphasizes that the International Law Commission remains at the centre of the development and strengthening of the international legal order. Corinne Cicéron Bühler, *Director of the Directorate of International Law and Legal Advisor of the Swiss Federal Department of Foreign Affairs*, observes that the diversity of legal cultures specific to the Commission and the Sixth Committee, which complement each other, is an asset for the development of international law. Kate Gilmore, *United Nations*

Deputy High Commissioner for Human Rights, highlights the great importance of the Commission's work for the Office of the High Commissioner for Human Rights and the fulfilment of the panoply of its human rights mandates. Abdulqawi A. Yusuf, *President of the International Court of Justice*, discusses how the International Law Commission has fulfilled its mandate in light of the changes to the structure and composition of the international community that have occurred over the past 70 years. Considering in particular decolonization and the shift away from a State-centric system, he notes that the work of the Commission, as a whole, demonstrates an openness to diverse perspectives, which have left an indelible mark on the contours of contemporary international law.

PART 1

Drawing a Balance for the Future: the New York Conversation

SECTION 1

The Commission and the Sixth Committee: Structural Challenges

Introductory Remarks by Eduardo Valencia-Ospina

Chair of the International Law Commission at Its Seventieth Session

Quite appropriately, the commemoration of the seventieth anniversary of the International Law Commission includes as its main feature a conversation between the Commission and the Sixth Committee.

May I in this respect recall that, ever since its first session in 1949, the Commission has submitted annually to the General Assembly a report as the means to keep it informed of the work accomplished at its session. The consideration of the annual report of the Commission by the Sixth Committee gives rise to a substantive debate, which attracts the participation of legal advisers, not only from Permanent Missions, but also from foreign ministries, many of whom honour the Commission with their presence here today. That debate, and the ensuing resolution of the Assembly, represent the concrete manifestation of the close relationship that exists between the Commission, an expert body, and its parent organ, consisting of representatives of governments.

That relationship, recognized by its Statute, is quite central to the working methods of the Commission, and one that makes the Commission's work unique. In the course of that work, governments have an opportunity to comment on the Commission's products; this is first done annually in the Sixth Committee, where governments have an opportunity to address individual chapters of the report or the report as a whole. Governments may also, orally or in writing, provide comments and observations, including furnishing evidence of State practice on specific questions addressed to them in chapter III of the report.

Once the Commission concludes a topic on first reading, it again invites comments and observations on the text, to be taken into account during the second reading. As previous Chairpersons of the Commission have stressed, the success of the work of the Commission, which is practice-driven, has depended as much on the sustained dialogue with the Sixth Committee, as on the cooperation received from governments in the form of written comments and observations, including information on State practice. These are very valuable in the discharge of the Commission's functions, as they ensure that its work is not only based on theoretical formulations. It is my hope that our conversation today will offer us a chance to reflect further on how our relationship can be strengthened.

DOI:10.1163/9789004434271_003

The manifestation of such a relationship is particularly far-reaching when it concerns the Commission's final drafts. In this connection, it is significant that article 20 of the Commission's statute only contemplates the preparation of drafts in the form of articles. The Commission has, however, increasingly undertaken and concluded work on drafts couched in terms of principles, conclusions, guidelines or model clauses, or as the final report of a study or working group. In many instances, these will be the forms to be given to the final products on the topics currently on its agenda, including the four to be adopted on second or first reading at the present session.

It is noteworthy, that since the beginning of this millennium, and until 2014, in all final sets of draft articles submitted to the General Assembly the corresponding recommendation by the Commission, pursuant to article 23 of its statute, has been formulated in the sense that, as a first step, the Assembly take notes of the respective set of draft articles in a resolution, and reproduces the text in an annex thereto, and that at an ulterior moment the Assembly consider the possibility to elaborate a convention on the basis of the draft in question.

Significantly, the Commission reverted in 2016 to its earlier practice, when it squarely recommended to the Assembly the elaboration of a convention on the basis of its draft articles on the protection of persons in the event of disasters. By departing from its old practice, the Commission had attempted to fall in line with the – to say the least – reluctant attitude that openly and increasingly has been shown by the Assembly towards the elaboration of international conventions on the basis of the final drafts of the Commission.

Such an attitude is faithfully reflected in the fact that, starting in 2004 – that is to say, during the last 14 years – no convention has been adopted by the General Assembly, nor under its auspices, on the basis of a final draft by the International Law Commission. In the past two decades, the Commission has submitted to the Assembly nine final drafts on diverse topics, all aimed to eventually serve as the basis of international codification conventions. For its part, the Assembly has reacted systematically in resolutions, adopted periodically, in general at three-year intervals, limiting itself to implement the recommendatory formula utilized by the Commission, annexing the corresponding text, but repeatedly delaying – in one recent specific case last year almost *ad vitam aeternam* – its consideration of the Commission's recommendation to the effect that its final drafts be transformed into international conventions. This is a deplorable state of affairs, which calls for prompt and effective remedial action on the part of the General Assembly, through its Sixth Committee.

Presentation by François Alabrune

Director of Legal Affairs of the Ministry of Europe and Foreign Affairs, France

The International Law Commission is particularly important for France, given its essential mission to codify and develop international law. Respect for international law is a guiding principle of France's foreign policy and also a decisive element of our national legal system. Indeed, it was in France that "constitutional monism" was first posited, in the 1946 Constitution, at the initiative of the first French member of the Commission, Professor Georges Scelle. This explains why, since the creation of the International Law Commission, France has been determined to contribute actively to the Commission's work.

The relationship between the International Law Commission and States is undoubtedly crucial to the success of the Commission's work. In the lifetime of the Commission, this success has been due to the positive dynamic that has consistently characterized this relationship for a long time. However, in recent years some questions have been raised, including on the advisability of maintaining the Commission in existence, at least in its current form.

I shall therefore first consider the main features of the relationship between the Commission and the Member States of the United Nations, which is largely the basis for the proper functioning of the Commission and the success of its work. Second, I shall discuss the structural challenges facing the Commission, as suggested by the title of this panel. Third, I shall attempt to suggest possible ways of dealing with these challenges.

I Achievements of the Relationship between the International Law Commission and the Member States of the United Nations

The first comment to be made is that the International Law Commission has close ties to the Member States of the United Nations. The Commission resulted from the desire of States, expressed in General Assembly resolution 174 (II), to establish it as a subsidiary organ of the Assembly.[1] The goal was for States to have an expert body able to promote the codification and progressive development of international law.

1 UNGA Res 174(II) (21 November 1947), annex.

© THE UNITED NATIONS, 2021 | DOI:10.1163/9789004434271_004

Moreover, the Commission is composed of members elected by the General Assembly from a list of candidates submitted by the governments of Member States. Some members of the Commission previously represented their governments in the Sixth Committee. Others have simultaneously performed or continue to perform official functions.

Lastly, States have an opportunity to express their positions and views at many stages of the Commission's work: (i) through the General Assembly and its Sixth Committee, they may propose topics for inclusion on the agenda – something they undoubtedly still do too seldom; (ii) they state their views on the topics included in the programme of work and decide the order of priority; (iii) they submit information and observations on the items on which the Commission is working and comment on the drafts that it prepares; (iv) each year they receive the Commission's report, which is then submitted for the consideration of the Sixth Committee, offering States an opportunity to conduct an ongoing dialogue with the Commission; (v) they have the last word on the ultimate fate of the work done; and (vi) when the work involves drafting of a convention, they participate in the relevant negotiations and are expected to sign and ratify the convention.

A second comment concerns the importance of the relationship between States and the Commission for the Commission's proper functioning: meeting the expectations of States is essential to the success of the Commission's work, whether this involves the codification or the progressive development of international law.

Meeting the expectations of States is inherent to the Commission's codification mission. This requires it to examine in detail practices and viewpoints of States. As indicated in article 15 of its statute, the task of the Commission is "the more precise formulation and systematization of rules of international law in fields where there already has been extensive State practice, precedent and doctrine".[2]

The task of codification involves collecting information on the topic under study, with a view to extracting from it a synthesis reflecting, as harmoniously as possible, the practice of States in that regard. This task is complicated by the diversity of cultures and legal systems in the world. It falls mainly to the Special Rapporteurs.

Meeting the expectations of States is also crucial for the other mission of the Commission: the progressive development of international law. According to article 15 of the Statute, this concerns "subjects which have not yet been regulated by international law or in regard to which the law has not yet been sufficiently developed in the practice of States".[3]

---

2 Ibid.

3 Ibid.

As part of this process, the comments and observations provided by governments and the wishes that they express, as well as the dialogue with members of the Sixth Committee, are extremely important, although ultimately it is the General Assembly that decides the fate of the work done: whether to take no action, to take note of the report or to use it as a basis for the adoption of a convention.

The quality of the relationship between the Commission and States is thus crucial to the success of the Commission's work. It has in the past enabled the Commission to contribute to the adoption of major international conventions, thus meeting the very expectation underlying its establishment: progressive development and codification of international law. The more limited results obtained by the Commission recently can be explained partly by the challenges encountered in the relationship between the Commission and the Member States of the United Nations.

II Challenges in the Relationship between the International Law Commission and the Member States of the United Nations

Now that we are "drawing a balance for the future" of the International Law Commission, several factors can be cited to explain the questions being asked about the Commission.

A first factor is the limited means available to States to follow and participate effectively in the work of the Commission. One or more representatives must be mobilized in order to follow the Sixth Committee discussions on the Commission's report. However, it is not enough to attend the Sixth Committee's debate during the International Law Week. Preparation is also necessary and this requires significant work. It is also difficult for States to transmit to the Commission their observations on all the topics on which the Commission requests information each year under Chapter III of its report. The multiplicity of topics dealt with by the Commission makes it difficult for States and for the Commission itself to deal with them in depth.

The second factor is probably the limited means available to the Commission itself to cover the diversity of State practice, culture and opinions. The biggest risk for the Commission is that it will be inspired by a single vision, a single legal culture or even a single language. This is why an effort must be made to enable Special Rapporteurs to receive useful information on the evolution of the various legal systems.

The third factor, in view of the limited means available to States, concerns the topics dealt with by the Commission. There are undoubtedly too many topics in the Commission's programme of work: nine this year and 11 last year. The multiplicity of projects does not facilitate in-depth study of them and slows down the work. As well as their number, the content of topics may be debatable.

Moreover, the success of the Commission's work depends on topics being selected which are of specific interest to States, which do not give rise to strong objections among them and on which they are prepared to adopt a convention in a specific area. Since its establishment in 1947, the International Law Commission has done a considerable amount of work on classical branches and subjects of international law: diplomatic and consular law, law of treaties, succession, law of the sea, responsibility of States and international organizations, etc. However, in recent years, certain topics included in the Commission's programme of work seem more questionable. Work on protection of the atmosphere, for example, requires technical expertise and is probably of limited legal interest.

The fourth factor is undoubtedly the temptation for the Commission to stop proposing draft conventions and to favour the formulation of soft law rules. If the Commission and the Special Rapporteurs want their work to be the basis for adoption of an international convention, they must achieve a sufficiently consensual outcome. Substantive dialogue with the Sixth Committee and meeting the expectations of States are certainly the best way of doing this. Especially as the likelihood of a convention being signed and ratified is greater if it meets the expectations of States.

Now, however, much of the Commission's work is no longer designed to be the basis for the adoption of a convention but settles, sometimes successfully, for the status of soft law. A good example are the Commission's articles on the responsibility of States for internationally wrongful acts.[4] The question of the adoption of a convention on the topic is still being studied in the General Assembly. Yet the articles have been widely accepted in practice and are cited specifically by numerous international courts and tribunals, such as the International Court of Justice, and frequently by arbitral tribunals of the International Centre for Settlement of Investment Disputes.[5] There is also interest in the guide to practice on reservations to treaties.[6]

4 ILC, 'Draft articles on responsibility of States for internationally wrongful acts' [2001] II(2) ILC Ybk 26.

5 See United Nations, *Materials on the Responsibility of States for Internationally Wrongful Acts* (United Nations Legislative Series 2012); and United Nations, 'Responsibility of States for internationally wrongful acts. Compilation of decisions of international courts, tribunals and other bodies' (2016) UN Doc A/71/80.

6 ILC, 'Guide to practice on reservations to treaties' [2011] II(3) ILC Ybk 23.

However, this trend raises questions about the nature of the Commission's work and of international law. Is the Commission not at risk, in certain cases, of producing drafts of an academic nature, sometimes with an ideological or symbolic dimension? Is there not, in turn, a danger that States may lose interest in some outcomes of the Commission's work if they do not take into account the expectations, the wishes or the practices of States?

III Ways of Improving the Relationship between the International Law Commission and the Member States of the United Nations

Based on these comments, there are several possible ways of improving the relationship between the International Law Commission and the Member States of the United Nations.

First, it would be desirable for the Commission to refocus on its central mission: general international law. It is unrealistic to expect the Commission to work effectively and with the necessary expertise on overly specialized technical topics.

Second, reforms of a practical nature could considerably improve the way the Commission functions and enhance its working relationship with Member States. For instance, it would be useful to limit to four or five the number of topics considered each year. This would enable the Commission to make more rapid progress on each one, or at least to study them in greater depth. Above all, it would permit a genuine dialogue with States: it is impossible to imagine that all States are able to digest in two months an annual report that in recent years has covered about a dozen subjects in very diverse areas.

Third, the Commission should be able to adopt a truly universal approach, by enhancing its ability to understand the practice and the precedents of the various regions of the world and by strictly observing the rules concerning its linguistic coverage. In this connection, use of the working languages can improve the quality of the written work of the Commission, particularly in its Drafting Committee.

Fourth, States must more clearly convey their expectations regarding the Commission and its work. States should propose topics for the attention of the Commission. The topics in the Commission's current programme of work were all included on the proposal of the Commission itself. It is noteworthy, however, that Poland recently proposed the inclusion of a new topic (Non-recognition) in the Commission's work programme. In 2017, several topics were – exceptionally – proposed by States. It is to be hoped that this trend will continue.

As mentioned, States exert a decisive influence on the productivity of the Commission through the election of its members. According to the Commission's statute, they must propose candidates "of recognized competence in international law".[7] Consequently, States must ensure that all candidates are in a position to make an active and useful contribution to the Commission's work.

States must also assist the Commission in its work by means of the information which they can provide to it and the dialogue in which they must engage. This could, for example, mean collaboration with academia, as was the case recently when the Codification Division was preparing its memorandum on ways and means for making the evidence of customary law more readily available.[8]

In conclusion, it is to be hoped that dialogue between the Commission and States can once again become a strong and positive force. This undoubtedly requires an effort on the part of the Commission. It also requires an effort on the part of States. The debate on the Commission's report at the autumn session of the Sixth Committee in New York is the best place for dialogue with Member States, because of the presence of numerous legal advisers visiting from the capitals, while the Commission sessions in Geneva should be preserved to ensure that the work of the Commission can proceed optimally.

---

7 Statute of the ILC (n 1) article 2(1).

8 UN Doc A/CN.4/710.

Presentation by Mahmoud D. Hmoud

Member of the International Law Commission

The seventieth anniversary of the International Law Commission marks an important milestone in the development of international law after the Second World War and the creation of the United Nations. The Commission has played a key role in such development, in the various areas of law, whether it is the law of treaties, the law of the sea, the law of international relations, international criminal law and other areas where the work of the Commission has been instrumental in the international law-making process.

When the Commission was first conceived and Article 13, paragraph 1, of the Charter of the United Nations was drafted, it was thought that there were certain areas of international law where practice was well-established and which could thus be codified. On the other hand, the drafters of the Article and the statute of the International Law Commission also perceived that progressive development of the law is as important as codification. Consequently, they set out in the statute elaborate yet separate procedures for the initiation of progressive development and codification. Article 15 of the statute provides that:

> ... the expression 'progressive development of international law' is used for convenience as meaning the preparation of draft conventions on subjects which have not yet been regulated by international law or in regard to which the law has not yet been sufficiently developed in the practice of States. Similarly, the expression 'codification of international law' is used for convenience as meaning the more precise formulation and systematization of rules of international law in fields where there already has been extensive State practice, precedent and doctrine.[1]

The subsequent articles allowed the General Assembly, Member States, as well as other United Nations organs and other official bodies to propose topics and instruments for progressive development, while they enabled the Commission itself to survey the whole field of international law with a view to selecting topics for codification.

1 Statute of the ILC, UNGA Res 174 (II) (21 November 1947), as amended by UNGA Res 485(V) (12 December 1950); UNGA Res 984(X) (3 December 1955); UNGA Res 985(X) (3 December 1955) and UNGA Res 36/39 (18 November 1981).

Nonetheless, the process has proven to be flexible enough over the years and the projects of the Commission have been a mix of codification and progressive development. This is due, in part, to the fact that the line between the two functions is not clear, especially in light of the difficulty in identifying the relevant practice that can indeed be translated into being customary international law ripe for codification. This, together with the fact that practice sometimes is mixed and contradictory, while pronouncements that can assist in identifying the rules may not be clear on whether such a rule is customary or is in the process of formation, resulted in the flexible approach by the Commission, where no separating line exists between progressive development and codification.

Nevertheless, depending on the topic, the Commission has chosen sometimes to identify whether a certain proposition for a rule or conclusion is in fact progressive development or otherwise codification; and in other instances, it chose not to do so.

There are key elements that are taken into account in assessing the work of the Commission on any single topic to gauge the direction and nature of rules contained in the work. The Commission is composed of jurists from different legal backgrounds who approach any single topic and any proposition for a rule from different angles. Obviously, the commentary plays an important role in describing the approach of the Commission and the underlying reasons for arriving at a certain rule or conclusion, including describing the practice, the precedent and the doctrine. The commentary also points towards the logic the Commission has applied in the process.

Another element to consider is the reactions of States and other actors towards any project and the content of the work, whether during consideration in the Sixth Committee or responses to questionnaires prepared by the Commission. Another element to consider is the form of the outcome, e.g. whether it is draft articles that is suitable for adoption in the form of a treaty or other legally binding instrument. In such case, as the binding nature would arise from the conclusion of an agreement or a treaty, the line between codification and progressive development becomes less relevant. In other instances, when the outcome is a study, the underlying emphasis is on describing the state of law, the state of practice, judicial precedents and doctrine, more than on identifying what is codification and what is progressive development.

In summary, there is no single approach; it is the combination of elements mentioned above, as well as other elements, that would determine whether or not delineation between progressive development and codification is relevant. But from my experience in the Commission, it is not such a delineation which is important for the work of the Commission, but the emphasis on ensuring that any single work of the Commission receives the deserved acceptance and recognition and be of legal value and weight to the international community.

This brings me to the challenges to the progressive development of international law and its codification. I consider this issue and the mandate of the Commission to be the same. But the reality is that the process is not entirely dependent on the work of the Commission. Indeed, the Commission is an entity tasked by the General Assembly with this process. Our role is advisory to the international community and it may be, in many instances, expository in nature. However, there are other bodies and organs, both within and outside the United Nations system, which play a significant role in identifying, developing or crystalizing the rule of law or describing what the law should be. International courts and tribunals, treaty bodies, national courts and institutions, other international organizations and non-governmental organizations all play an important role. Indeed, there are other specialized bodies in certain technical areas which contribute to this process. One challenge is for the International Law Commission to take into account the work and processes of such bodies in choosing its topics and determining the nature and content of its outcomes. We have done this in the past and we will continue to do so in the future.

Another challenge is posed by the advances in areas of science and technology, as well as the sub-specializations in the various areas of law and transnational law. The Commission is well positioned to use such challenges to its benefit by concentrating its work more on the value it can add to the development and codification of any field of international law, without spreading itself to much in a manner that may undermine its outcomes. But the idea that the Commission should confine itself to areas of general international law has proven wrong, as the Commission has embarked over the years on specialized topics, in areas such as the environment, human rights and investment law. Its work has had its own authoritative value and continues to be quoted by courts, tribunals and in the practice of States and international organizations. A few years ago, there was a worry expressed in the Commission that we may "run out" of topics of general international law to consider. But since then, the Commission has included, both in its long-term programme of work and on the active agenda, topics of general international law as well as from specialized fields.

Yet another challenge is to strike a balance between being assertive in choosing topics which are relevant to the international community and to take principled legal positions on the content of our work. Obviously, we do not only speak to States but to the international community as a whole: to courts, whether national and international; to international organizations, whether governmental or non-governmental; to other expert bodies, whether official or non-official; and to individuals and persons who are the ultimate beneficiaries of our work. The well-being, security, prosperity and development of people in the world can be achieved through the respect for the rule of international law and the work of the International Law Commission goes in such a direction.

Presentation by Janine Felson

Deputy Permanent Representative of Belize to the United Nations

In this paper, I will first address the role of the International Law Commission in the multilateral legislative process and then go on to discuss future challenges to the progressive development of international law and its codification.

Clarifying the role of the Commission in an increasingly democratized international legislative process is at the heart of the debate of the challenges it faces in achieving the objectives set forth in its statute. The statute entrusts the Commission with the promotion of the progressive development of international law and its codification.[1] Scholars have debated the relevance in practice of a distinction between the progressive development of international law and its codification. That debate has provided varying perspectives of the role of the Commission.

For example, Alain Pellet has called the distinction "artificial"; while it was "intellectually attractive", the distinction has proved "practically impossible", according to Pellet.[2] Speaking about the Commission's work, he stated that:

> [a]ll topics involve partial codification since no topic is entirely new when it is undertaken by the [Commission] … in addition, all imply an element of progressive development since, almost as a matter of definition, customary rules always comprise some elements of uncertainty calling for clarification and this is precisely one of the main purposes of codification.[3]

Pellet concluded that not only is progressive development "indissociable from codification", it is part of codification.[4] The real question, he posits, should be "when is legal development 'progressive'?"[5] In his view, the extent of what can

---

1 See article 1 of the ILC statute, UNGA Res 174 (II) (21 November 1947) as amended by UNGA Res 485(V) (12 December 1950); UNGA Res 984(X) (3 December 1955); UNGA Res 985(X) (3 December 1955) and UNGA Res 36/39 (18 November 1981). See also article 15 of the statute, which further clarifies the terms "codification" and "progressive development" of international law.

2 Alain Pellet, 'Responding to New Needs through Codification and Progressive Development' in Vera Gowlland-Debbas (ed), *Multilateral Treaty-making: The Current Status of Challenges to and Reforms Needed in the International Legislative Process* (Martinus Nijhoff 2000) 13, 15–16.

3 Ibid 15.

4 Ibid 16.

5 Ibid 16.

be determined "progressive development" is completing existing law, but not changing the entire system of the law of nations. In other words, the Commission decodes the logic of existing rules and uses that logic as the framework for developing them further.

To Pellet, members of the Commission serve strictly as "codifiers" addressing (in his words) "the real needs of the international society", that is to say, "the 'constitutional law' of the international society" which means "uniform legal rules which transversally cut through all fields covered by international law".[6] But if the members of the Commission were to be confined to the role of "codifiers" focused mainly on the global constitutive process, would codification itself be confined to a procedural function?

Husain Al-Baharna, has observed that the "distinction between 'development' and 'codification' has, unwittingly, been sidelined with dismal consequences".[7] Al-Baharna argued for restoring the original intention of the drafters of the statute as regards the progressive development. In his view, the key to change was the realization of the object of the "*promotion* of development of international law".[8] Could the "codifier" go beyond the clarification of customary international law to an active engagement in *promoting* its progressive development?

The dynamic nature of international relations and likewise of international law, which is further discussed below, could justify a more progressive role for the Commission. At the same time, the legitimacy of the Commission's work cannot be diminished. It is argued that the distinction between the progressive development and codification is important in determining what issues are more appropriate for experts, as opposed to issues that are more appropriate for intergovernmental negotiations. Herein the question of the form of the Commission's work takes on significance. In this regard, Sean Murphy has pointed out that

> [a]n approach whereby the Commission blends codification with progressive development is defensible if the ultimate outcome is the adoption by States of a convention, but such blending in a situation where no further State action is envisaged, and with the expectation that the draft

6 Ibid 22.

7 Husain Al-Baharna, 'Future Topics for the Codification of International Law Viewed in Historical Perspective' in *International Law on the Eve of the Twenty-first Century: Views from the International Law Commission* (United Nations 1997) 379.

8 Ibid (emphasis added).

articles will simply be seen as "the law", potentially casts the Commission in the role of legislator.[9]

David Caron suggested that the Commission's articles on the responsibility of States for internationally wrongful acts[10] would have unwarranted influence primarily because of their form.[11] Whether or not this is by design, the test of the influence of the Commission's work is whether States and other relevant actors determine that they offer appropriate and workable solutions. Accordingly, he argued that "the [Commission's] articles should exercise such influence as they deserve. But the question of how much influence they deserve requires an appreciation of their authority and a method for applying and interpreting them." In this regard, Caron touched upon the importance of considering the user of the Commission's work. This brings me to the question posed: To whom does the Commission speak?

While the Commission is accountable and reports to States, its audience is much wider than just States. Caron pointed out that even prior to their adoption by the Commission, the articles on State responsibility had already affected legal discourse, arbitral decisions, and possibly State practice. This point marks the end user of the Commission's work. The process of the development of international law involves a wide range of actors. Myres McDougal observed that, while the nation State through its officials remains the predominant decisionmaker, a vast proliferation of non-State entities perform important decision functions in what he coined the "global constitutive process".[12] He spoke thus of international organizations serving both as participants and institutional structures for the interaction of other participants, including political parties, pressure groups, non-governmental organizations, multinational business entities, and even individuals as subjects of international law.

In light of this wider audience base, it is appropriate that the Commission has expressed a willingness not to restrict itself to traditional topics, but to consider those that reflect new developments in international law and pressing concerns of the international community as a whole. This willingness notwithstanding, the Commission's main criteria for the selection of new topics

9 Sean Murphy, 'Codification, Progressive Development, or Scholarly Analysis? The Art of Packaging the ILC's Work Product' in Maurizio Ragazzi (ed), *Responsibility of International Organizations: Essays in Memory of Sir Ian Brownlie* (Martinus Nijhoff 2013) 29, 35.

10 See UNGA Res 56/83 (12 December 2001).

11 David D. Caron, 'The ILC Articles on State Responsibility: The Paradoxical Relationship between Form and Authority' (2002) 96 AJIL 857.

12 Myres McDougal 'International Law and the Future' (1979) 50 MissLJ 259.

should focus on the needs of States, on sufficiency and advancement of State practice, on feasibility and on concreteness.

Returning to an observation made by Al-Baharna in relation to the question of future topics, he noted that "the question of the selection of topics for codification and development of international law has not been an easy one" and that "it had become all the more daunting due to the vast changes in the socio-economic and political conditions of the world society."[13] I would add to these changes (1) technological progress and invention, which have created a virtual world within which we conduct much of our day-to-day interactions; (2) growing influence of multinational entities, particularly over natural resources management; and (3) climate change and the Anthropocene, in particular the accelerated impacts of anthropogenic climate change, in the near term, for small island developing States (SIDS) and low-lying coastal States which is re-defining responsibilities for the protection of the environment. I would further propose that it is these very changes and the expanded range of participants in the contemporaneous global constitutive process that instructs a role for the Commission to go beyond the mere clarification of customary international law.

Accordingly, I would support entrusting the Commission with the promotion of the development of international law in those areas where the common concern of humankind is evident. Historically, the Commission has concluded work relating to the law of international responsibility and it is currently conducting work relating to the law of the environment. Therefore, it cannot be said that venturing into areas relating to the common concern of humankind would be revolutionary; it would be timely.

In the context of environmental law, the SIDS have advocated for the development of international law in relation to the permanent loss and damage resulting from the adverse impacts of climate change, especially sea level rise.[14] This issue has gained notoriety in the climate change context, particularly due to concerns regarding the implications for responsibility and liability. And yet it could be argued that, if the purpose of codification and the role of the codifiers is to address the needs of the international society and to instruct a societal order through institutions and law, then addressing the fundamental question

13 See Al-Baharna (n 7) 373.

14 See, *inter alia*, the statement of the Marshall Islands (on behalf of the Pacific Small Island Developing States), made in the Sixth Committee of the General Assembly under agenda item 81, 'Report of the International Law Commission on the work of its sixty-ninth session (Cluster II)' (26 October 2017) <https://papersmart.unmeetings.org/media2/16154559/marshall-islands-on-behalf-of-pacific-small-island-developing-states-.pdf>.

of the territorial integrity of a State in the face of permanent loss and damage as a result of climate change is within the expectations and interests of all States, large and small.

This brings us full circle to the question regarding the distinction of the function of progressive development vs. codification. It is fair that, as Pellet observed, the two are indissociable, though as others suggest, this warrants some caution regarding how the Commission packages its work. Perhaps it is best to look beyond the bifurcation of the role of the Commission and instead to search for a practical functionality of the Commission as a progressive codifier, preserving its legitimacy and simultaneously promoting the development of international law. And perhaps, rather than debating the boundaries that the concepts of progressive development and codification could place on the Commission, we should rather reinforce the role of the Commission in relation to the utility of its work and its contribution to what Prof. Nico Schrijver elucidated in his keynote address, that is, the preservation of the rule of law in global affairs.[15]

15 See the keynote address by Nico Schrijver in Section 8 of this book.

Presentation by Ernest Petrič

Some Remarks on Future Challenges for the International Law Commission

Member of the International Law Commission

While celebrating 70 years of work of the International Law Commission and discussing its contemporary work, its problems and its future, it is important to say a few words concerning its past. It is not necessary to speak of the past achievements of the Commission, which are generally considered a great contribution to the development of international law, in terms of codification and progressive development, but also by enhancing awareness and understanding of international law. It is however worthwhile to mention that, when 70 years ago the Commission was established and its statute was adopted,[1] the world was a different place. International law was at that time to a large extent customary, not codified and not written international law, and, compared to nowadays, limited in its scope. Important branches of contemporary international law, like human rights law and environmental law – to mention just a few – did not yet exist or were only emerging as international law *de lege ferenda*. Thus, now, in a much different world and globalised international community, the Commission, whose statute, role and functioning has remained stable and has not much changed all those 70 years, should indeed be exposed to a critical review, in spite of its great past achievements.

The victorious powers after the Second World War, while establishing the new world order and the United Nations as its institutional core, could not overlook the expectations and hopes of people throughout the world, that international relations in the future should be ruled by international law and that the international community should be a community based on collective security and cooperation regulated by international law. The ideals of the greatest thinkers of the past, that the international community should be the community of peace and of rule of law, were to become reality.

At that time, international law was to a large extent of a customary nature, with all the characteristics and challenges of customary law. Among them, in particular, is the problem of legal certainty, the problem of determining whether a norm exists and what its precise meaning, its substance, is. In other words, for customary international law – as for any customary law – the problem of "*lex certa*" was,

1 Statute of the ILC, UNGA Res 174(II) (21 November 1947).

and still is, crucial, since customary international law is not written law, unless it is codified in an international treaty. After 1945, and when in 1948 the Commission was established, most international law, with the exception of bilateral treaties and laws of war (*jus in bello*) and some other multilateral arrangements, was customary international law. There was no codified international law even on matters crucially important for regulating communications and relations among States, such as diplomatic and consular law and the law of treaties. Codification, and in its context progressive development of international law, was a must for international relations to function. Besides, many new spheres and matters of international cooperation appeared which had to be regulated by international law. Moreover, in the ideologically divided, bipolar international community during the Cold War, several legal concepts were not commonly shared. They were interpreted differently, reflecting different sets of values. To clarify the existing and binding international law, the codification was a great necessity.

Thus, the role of the Commission, as a subsidiary organ of the General Assembly of the United Nations for the codification and progressive development of international law, was exceptionally important and useful to States. Consequently, its work has attracted great attention of States, expressed in the General Assembly and its Sixth Committee. The work of the Commission was considered crucial for closing the gaps in international law and to clarify the uncertainties of its interpretation. With some simplification, it could be said that the most important parts of international law have been codified – partially also progressively developed – in the first four decades of existence and work of the Commission. It was the time of the Commission's greatest achievements in assisting States to codify and progressively develop international law, as some say, the "golden age" of the Commission. It was also the time of high interest of States for the Commission's work, which was also reflected in the respect and recognition given to the Commission and its members, whose status at that time could be compared to the International Court of Justice and its judges. However, those times have passed.

I will now turn to my contribution to the panel's discussion on the Commission's future. Due to the limited time and scope, I will not be able to consider all specific contemporary problems of the Commission. However, for today's panel let me first say that, to a large extent, I align myself with most of the critical views expressed by the former member and Chair of the Commission, Mr. Alain Pellet,[2] who served in the Commission for 22 years; his experience

2 Alain Pellet, 'The ILC Adrift? Some Reflections from Inside' in Miha Pogačnik (ed), *Challenges of Contemporary International Law and International Relations: Liber Amicorum in Honour of Ernest Petrič* (Nova Gorica 2013) 299–312.

can hardly be ignored. According to him, among the main problems of the Commission in our time are the lack of consideration and respect of States for the work of the Commission, as well as its composition and consequently the problem of its independence, also the independence of its members. They are supposed to be independent experts, but are often government officials. I must say that neither the composition of the Commission nor the independence of its members, after my 12 years on the Commission, seem to be a problem. On the contrary, the combination of academics, diplomats and practitioners seems to be productive, as is the diverse regional background of its membership. I, however, fully share the view of Alain Pellet, who, as the main problem of the contemporary Commission, exposes the selection of topics which are to be dealt with by the Commission and which should lead to codification and progressive development of international law.

I share the view that the lack of profound involvement of States in the selection of topics for the programme of work of the Commission, as well as the insufficient interest and meagre reactions of States throughout the work of the Commission on a topic, is a serious problem. The consequence of this is that practically no drafts produced by the Commission in the last few decades have been transformed into binding international treaties. No codification of international law in the last two decades has been based on the work of the Commission, except perhaps for the Rome Statute of the International Criminal Court.[3]

In my opinion, the problems of the Commission may be summarized as insufficient interest of States for its work, i.e. for the choice of its topics, for its work on a topic and use of its products. Contrary to the present situation, the Commission should in the future be given more guidance by States in the selection of topics and more input by States, including critical feedback, during the work on a topic. It is unfortunate when in most cases less than 30 States react to the Commission's proposal of a topic, or to subsequent reports on the work on it. Not to mention that often there are no reactions at all, or just a few from some regional groups or specific continents, and that many reactions are poorly elaborated, inconcrete and superficial. As a probable consequence of this not very productive relationship between the General Assembly's Sixth Committee and the International Law Commission, when States express their views they are superficially considered and sometimes even ignored in the Commission. To conclude, the relationship between States and the Commission should be more intense, more productive in contributing to the common

3 Adopted 17 July 1998, entered into force 1 July 2002, 2187 UNTS 3.

task: codification and progressive development of international law. Without improvement of this relationship the Commission might in the future find itself less relevant for States.

Let me add in this context that the decision to hold the first part of the Commission's seventieth session at the United Nations Headquarters in New York was part of the Commission's endeavour to improve the creative relationship between States and the Commission. I have, however, my doubts that this move of the session of the Commission to New York, even if repeated in some future years, will significantly improve the interest of States for the work the Commission and raise awareness among States that the Commission is their organ which should assist them in codifying and developing international law, in fact to establish the rule of law in international relations.

Let me say just a few words concerning the selection of topics in the Commission. According to its still valid statute, the Commission's work has two components: progressive development and codification of international law.[4] In the work of the Commission, it soon became evident that the division of these two components does not work in practice. In most cases, now as in the past, codification and progressive development go hand in hand, depending on the topic. It will remain so in the future. In most topics both components are present, progressive development and codification. It would be unacceptable and probably impossible in the Commission's drafts to formally distinguish the two and indicate which elements, according to the Commission's view, are supposed to be codification and which elements are progressive development. However, for users of the Commission's products, in particular draft articles that might in the future become binding conventions, it is important to know what the Commission considers already to be existing customary law *de lege lata* and what might only by a future codification or by future practice of States crystalize from *de lege ferenda* into binding international law *de lege lata*. It is thus important that commentaries to proposed drafts indicate what the Commission considers codification of already existing international law *de lege lata* and what the Commission proposes as progressive development. It is logical to expect that States and other users wish to know what the Commission considers already existing international law and what it only suggests to States as progressive development. The existence or non-existence of relevant and consistent State practice should be crucial in the Commission's consideration and assessment.

It might also be said that in the future work of the Commission on "contemporary" topics, not already covered by abundant State practice, the component

4 Article 1 of the ILC statute.

of progressive development might grow. In any case, and in line with the statute of the Commission, the General Assembly and its Sixth Committee should have an important, indeed decisive role in the selection of topics if they are indeed to be relevant and thus of interest for States. Not the personal considerations, ambitions, or wishes of members of the Commission – as relevant as they may be – but the needs and proposals of States should be the most relevant in the selection of topics. The Commission is an independent body of experts in international law that serves and helps States in their endeavours to codify and progressively develop international law. The States should, via the General Assembly and its Sixth Committee, submit to the Commission their proposals and recommendations of topics, and the Commission should, according to article 18 of its statute, "give priority to request of the General Assembly to deal with any question." Of course, this assumes that such requests would be made at all. In reality, "requests" from States in the General Assembly and its Sixth Committee very rarely appear. In the majority of cases, the Commission proposes and selects its own topics.

The topics selected by the Commission for its work are supposed to reflect the needs and interest of States. But even when the Commission's proposals of new topics are presented to States, through the Sixth Committee, the reactions of States rarely exceed the level of formal and not much elaborated remarks. Any topic suggested by the Commission is very formalistically endorsed or some reservations to it are expressed. But even in case of reservations of States, the Commission usually proceeds with the topic.

In the last three decades, the General Assembly has not suggested topics for inclusion on the agenda of the Commission and very rarely a State has proposed a topic. There are some exceptions, like in the case of the statute of the International Criminal Court,[5] which later via negotiations among States became the Rome Statute, establishing the International Criminal Court. It is also worth to mention the suggestion to the Commission of a group of small island States in 2017 to put on its agenda the international legal aspects of rising sea level.[6] It seems this will soon become a topic of the Commission.

---

5 See 'Draft Code of Offences against the Peace and Security of Mankind', UNGA Res 36/106 (10 December 1981), para 2; 'International criminal responsibility of individuals and entities engaged in illicit trafficking in narcotic drugs across national frontiers and other transnational criminal activities: establishment of an international criminal court with jurisdiction over such crimes', UNGA Res 44/39 (4 December 1989) para 1.

6 See statement of the Marshall Islands (on behalf of the Pacific Small Island Developing States), made in the Sixth Committee of the General Assembly under agenda item 81, 'Report of the International Law Commission on the work of its sixty-ninth session (Cluster II)' (26

Since the work of the Commission should first and foremost reflect the needs and wishes of States, additional endeavours should be made to improve the relationship between the Commission and States (i.e. the General Assembly and the Sixth Committee), in particular in the choice of topics to be dealt with by the Commission. It might be useful for this purpose to hold in the Sixth Committee each year, in the framework of the International Law Week, a separate debate focused only on the choice and relevance of future topics of the Commission, those suggested by the Commission and its members and those suggested or preferred by States.

General international law establishes the framework of foreign policy for all States, while it is also being used by States as a means of foreign policy. It is thus important for States what kind of international law is being codified and/or progressively developed. The future codification and progressive development of international law, and *mutatis mutandis* of other relevant instruments like "guidelines", "conclusions" and "principles" in the Commission is very important for all States. It is particularly important for those States which might not possess power and other means of foreign policy except international law. They would be expected to be most interested in the future development of international law, its codification and progressive development. It is difficult to understand the passive attitude of many States towards the work of the Commission and to the selection of its topics. I believe that separately organised debate on the Commission's new topics in the Sixth Committee might contribute to more engagement between the Commission and States concerning the development of international law and consequently the rule of law in international community. Also, a special and well-prepared topical and concrete debate in the Sixth Committee on its relationship with the Commission would be useful, whereby revision of the Commission's statute should not *a priori* be excluded.

There have been critical remarks in the past concerning the choice of some specific topics. Generally, I believe the choice of topics in the Commission has been appropriate, including its work on clarifying important aspects of the law of treaties, which were not sufficiently clarified by the Vienna Convention of 1969[7] (reservations, subsequent practice and subsequent agreement in interpretation of treaties, provisional application of treaties, *jus cogens*, and also the impact of armed conflicts on treaties). The clarification of those

---

October 2017) <https://papersmart.unmeetings.org/media2/16154559/marshall-islands-on-behalf-of-pacific-small-island-developing-states-.pdf>.

7 Vienna Convention on the Law of Treaties, adopted 23 May 1969, entered into force 27 January 1980, 1155 UNTS 331.

important matters of the law of treaties is a great contribution in the last few decades of the Commission to the development and understanding of international law.

In many cases the Commission has opted for the final form of its product not to be draft articles for a future convention, but other forms (guidelines, conclusions principles etc.). In several cases, these forms suit the topic better and also better reflect the development of relevant State practice. Also, the fact that, in the last two decades or more, no draft convention proposed by the Commission was considered by States as capable of becoming a convention probably contributed to preference of other forms of the Commission's products. These guidelines, conclusions and principles can have, and often do have, an important impact on development and interpretation of international law. Often, they might be "stronger" than a non-ratified draft convention not entering into force, which might be *a contrario* understood as proof that the majority of States does not consider the draft convention to reflect existing international law. States, but also courts and other users of international law may, and often do, in their claims and decisions use the guidelines, conclusions and principles adopted by the Commission as means of proof or as explanation. There seems to be no legal basis for not giving the views of the Commission, even when expressed in non-binding products, similar value and importance as the explanations of decisions of the International Court of Justice and other international courts. Moreover, the role and importance of the Commission, as a subsidiary organ of the General Assembly, entrusted by States to progressively develop and codify international law, should not be equated with private institutions, while important and knowledgeable, like the *Institut de Droit international* and the International Law Association.

Reflecting on the contemporary development and expansion of international relations, in the future there will be more topics which will require specific, scientific and technical knowledge. The Commission, together with States, will have to find ways to adapt its methodology to handle such topics, for which a general knowledge of international law does not suffice. One can foresee many such topics, since developments of international law in matters such as environmental law, information technology and communications will require it. In the long run, the Commission and States cannot ignore topics that are the result of modern international life and novel needs of the international community. Also, though in the past the ambitious development of international human rights law took part mostly outside the Commission, this does not mean that the Commission should avoid human rights topics. The successful work on the topic of protection of persons in the event of disasters is a valuable example. However, in case of human rights topics – and the same is true for topics of international environmental law – the Commission should find a way to involve civil society. This is certainly a difficult and sensitive matter, but also a necessary one, and one that is unavoidable in the contemporary world.

In the past, the Commission has been hesitant to deal with highly political topics. It is true, however, that several topics in the past have had profound political implications, like the responsibility of States (as well as the responsibility of international organizations), topics concerning State succession, the law of the sea, among others. In fact, every topic of international law is *ultima ratio* also more or less politically relevant. The question, however, is to what extent the Commission, in the future, should avoid "politically sensitive topics" that have important legal connotations and which are now left completely in the hands of States and their political considerations and interpretations. The right of peoples to self-determination, established in the most authoritative international legal instrument, the Charter of the United Nations, and thus a *jus cogens* norm to some, with all its contradictions, has never attracted the interest of the Commission or States for its interpretation in international law. Questions have been raised, *inter alia*, regarding its limitations and its relationship to the Charter's principle of sovereign equality of States, as well as regarding the right of States to exist and their territorial integrity to be respected. The question is, who if not the Commission, with its authority, knowledge and mission, should clarify contradictions of this and other similarly important though controversial principles and rules of international law.

In my statement, I have tried to address the questions posed to the panel. I have yet to answer the last: to whom does the Commission speak; only to States or also to courts and other actors? It speaks and should speak first of all to States, and States should speak back to it more. Dialogue between the Commission and States is crucial for both in their common endeavour: the codification and progressive development of international law. It is also clear that the Commission, with its authority, knowledge and wisdom, speaks to courts, international organizations and to all involved and interested in international law. It does so in our times not only through draft articles but also with its several contemporary products, including guidelines, conclusions and principles. Personally, I wish the Commission would, besides to States, speak more to the general public, to all who believe in a future world based on the rule of law. However, its basic role remains helping States to codify and progressively develop international law. It does so as an independent expert body. As an independent expert body in its work, in its conclusions, in its views. But also bound to States to help them, to support them, to listen to their comments, and views to serve them. Independence of the Commission from States in its work and in its conclusions is crucial for its successful work and its authority. At the same time, working on topics that are academically interesting but lack relevance to States would not enhance the Commission's independence but could lead to its irrelevance.

SECTION 2

The Commission and the Sixth Committee: Reflections on the Interaction in the Past and the Future

Introductory Remarks by Burhan Gafoor

Chair of the Sixth Committee of the General Assembly at Its Seventy-Second Session

The relationship between the Sixth Committee and the Commission is an organic and symbiotic one. The Sixth Committee has an important role to play and I would like to identify three roles that are important from my point of view. First, it continues to function in the *traditional* role, of being one of the main Committees of the General Assembly, as a forum for debate, and as a forum for legal matters to be debated by policy makers. This role, which can be called a policy-making role, is manifested ultimately in the draft resolutions adopted by the Sixth Committee. The draft resolutions are a result of very careful, deliberate and wide-ranging consultations and negotiations. There is considerable interaction between representatives of the Sixth Committee and legal advisers from capitals, especially when it comes to discussing the report of the International Law Commission. The Sixth Committee's debate on this particular report is also an occasion that demonstrates the very close relationship between the Commission and the Committee. The interaction is one of the unique features of International Law Week, held during the annual General Assembly sessions. The debate on the report and the negotiation on the resolution are intended to provide clear policy guidance and decisions on matters relating to the work of the Commission.

The second role played by the Committee is as a *negotiating forum*. Through its working groups and subsidiary bodies, over the years, the Committee has concluded a number of important instruments, including on drafts based on the Commission's works. Indeed, the Convention on the Law of the Non-Navigational Uses of International Watercourses[1] was negotiated in the framework of the Working Group of the whole of the Sixth Committee, on the basis of draft articles prepared by the Commission.[2] The last time that the Sixth Committee proposed the convening of a diplomatic conference, the traditional form of concluding and adopting such instruments, was with respect to the Rome Conference on the establishment of the International Criminal Court, which was inspired by a text that was prepared by the Commission[3] and was

1 Adopted 21 May 1997, entered into force 17 August 2014, UNTS registration no. 52106.

2 ILC, 'Draft articles on the law of the non-navigational uses of international watercourses' [1994] II(2) ILC Ybk 89.

3 ILC, 'Draft Statute for an International Criminal Court, with commentaries' [1994] II(2) ILC Ybk 26; 'Draft code of crimes against the peace and security of mankind' [1996] II(2) ILC Ybk 15.

 | DOI:10.1163/9789004434271_008

further the subject of negotiations in the context of *ad hoc* and preparatory committees established on the recommendation of the Sixth Committee prior to the convening of the Conference.

The third role of the Committee that we have also witnessed is the Committee serving as a *filter and consensus builder*. For instance, through the use of informal consultations, the Committee has facilitated the reaching of a generally acceptable decision in the case of the draft articles on the status of the diplomatic courier and the diplomatic bag not accompanied by the diplomatic courier.[4] Today, the Committee continues to utilise modalities such as working groups and informal consultations in order to help build consensus on particular issues.

Over the last 10 to 15 years, the Commission has presented to the Sixth Committee eight completed works,[5] which remain in the Committee at various levels of discussion. The task that faces the Sixth Committee is to bring these various discussions and processes to a successful closure. To do this, the Committee will have to navigate and address the legal, policy and other considerations in order to build consensus and reach political agreement. This is no easy task, but I believe that by working collectively within the framework of the Committee, and by continuing to perform the role of building consensus and finding political agreement, the Committee can make an important contribution to reaching agreement on some of the most important issues before it. The last thing that I would say is that within the Committee, there is a degree of professionalism and congeniality that I find remarkable. There is a very positive spirit of cooperation that prevails among all members. I think that this too is a very important asset for the work of the Committee as it works together with the Commission to help build consensus on important issues of international law.

4 See UNGA decision 50/416 (11 December 1995) UN Doc A/50/49 (vol I) 351.

5 These are: (a) ILC, 'Draft articles on responsibility of States for internationally wrongful acts' [2001] II(2) ILC Ybk 26; see also UNGA Res 56/83 (12 December 2001), annex; (b) ILC, 'Draft articles on prevention of transboundary harm from hazardous activities' [2001] II(2) ILC Ybk 146; (c) ILC, 'Draft principles on the allocation of loss in the case of transboundary harm arising out of hazardous activities' [2006] II(2) ILC Ybk 58; (d) ILC, 'Draft articles on diplomatic protection' [2006] II(2) ILC Ybk 24; (e) ILC, 'Draft articles on the law of transboundary aquifers' [2008] II(2) ILC Ybk 19; (f) ILC, 'Draft articles on the responsibility of international organizations' [2011] II(2) ILC Ybk 40; (g) ILC, 'Draft articles on the expulsion of aliens' (2014) UN Doc A/69/10, 11; and (h) ILC, 'Draft articles on the protection of persons in the event of disasters' (2016) UN Doc A/71/10, 13.

Presentation by Evgeny Zagaynov

Director of the Legal Department of the Ministry of Foreign Affairs, Russian Federation

It is a great honour and pleasure to be back in New York and to take part in today's discussion. I wish to thank the organizers of this event for giving me the chance to address this meeting. After I received the invitation, a major event took place in my life; I would like to take this opportunity to express my sincere gratitude to the members of the International Law Commission for the trust that they have placed in me by electing me to join their ranks. I will endeavour to live up to that trust.

Today, however, I intend to follow my original plan and to speak in my capacity as Director of the Legal Service of the Ministry of Foreign Affairs of the Russian Federation, particularly since I have yet to commence work as a member of the Commission.

This year marks the seventieth anniversary of the Commission. The idea of codifying international law, however, is much older and dates back centuries. Although it has evolved over that time, its goal has always been to create a more just world order and to prevent war and conflict.

As the representative of the Russian Federation, I would like to say a few words about the contribution that has been made to the Commission's work by eminent international jurists from my country: Vladimir Mikhailovich Koretsky, Grigory Ivanovich Tunkin, Nikolai Aleksandrovich Ushakov and Roman Anatolyevich Kolodkin. The latter prepared three reports on the immunity of State officials from foreign criminal jurisdiction when he was Special Rapporteur for the topic, prior to Escobar Hernández.[1]

The Commission's achievements would not have been possible without the professionalism and dedication of the Secretariat. Today, we pay tribute to the efforts of many generations of colleagues who have participated in that work.

The relationship between the Commission and the Sixth Committee is a subject of paramount importance. The Commission, although a subsidiary body of the General Assembly, enjoys a high degree of autonomy, while the general political guidance from the Sixth Committee provides insight into the

1 Roman A. Kolodkin, 'Preliminary report on immunity of State officials from foreign criminal jurisdiction' [2008] II(1) ILC Ybk 157; 'Second report on immunity of State officials from foreign criminal jurisdiction' [2010] II(1) ILC Ybk 395; and 'Third report on immunity of State officials from foreign criminal jurisdiction' [2011] II(1) ILC Ybk 223.

needs of States and what they expect from the Commission's work and helps to set the necessary benchmarks.

When recalling the Commission's achievements, we often evoke the 1960s and 1970s. At that time, the Commission produced texts and reports that would become the basis for a number of key international legal instruments. Those successes were, in part, a result of its having set the bar high from the outset in the choice of topics for its long-term programme of work.

The Commission examined the most important and topical issues of international law in the first decades of its existence. As a result, in later years, the number of conventions adopted on the basis of its work substantially declined.

Does that mean that there is less demand for its work? I do not believe so; the Commission is currently considering a number of important topics. It is true, however, that the formulation of its programme of work is taking on growing significance. How a topic is formulated will determine the final outcome of the Commission's work, whether or not its conclusions are favourably received and supported by States and, subsequently, whether or not a decision is made to draft a convention. In precisely that regard, a balance must be struck between the demands of States and the independence of the Commission's members.

How can the Commission avoid working on topics that subsequently turn out not to reflect the needs of States? It is well known that the procedure for selecting topics has undergone changes. Since 1992, a mechanism has been in place for designating members of the Commission to write short outlines and explanatory summaries on topics included in a pre-selected list.[2] Under article 17 of the Commission's statute, Member States, the General Assembly and other organs of the United Nations may submit proposals to the Commission regarding the progressive development of international law and its codification. In its early years, the Commission received numerous proposals and special tasks from the General Assembly, but in more recent times they have become fewer in number. It might be worthwhile trying to revive that practice.

Consideration should be given to how to make more effective use of the available mechanisms for including topics in the Commission's programme of work. Perhaps a special discussion should be held on how to improve the existing procedure for selecting and then working on topics. One option, in our view, could be to set up a mechanism under which topics for consideration by the Commission would be agreed upon and endorsed by the Sixth Committee.

Igor Ivanovich Lukashuk, a former member of the Commission, once remarked that it was a victim of its own early success: having codified the

2 See ILC, 'Report of the International Law Commission on the work of its forty-fourth session' [1992] II(2) ILC Ybk 1, 54 at para 369.

principal areas of international law through global conventions, it went on to study complex but marginal topics, which can result only in the generation of doctrinal material.

That said, many of the texts produced by the Commission in recent years, such as those on the responsibility of States for internationally wrongful acts,[3] the responsibility of international organizations,[4] and diplomatic protection,[5] are highly relevant. That they are held up for years before the Sixth Committee or emerge from it without being followed up is not the Commission's doing. Rather, the responsibility lies with the Committee, in other words, with States. For one reason or another, they prefer not to have conventions in those areas. One result of this passivity is that, even without the "blessing" of States, courts are nevertheless beginning to invoke these texts, which they view as a part of customary law.[6] They are even referring to texts that the Commission has yet to finalize.[7]

On occasion, one hears the view that a particular text produced by the Commission is so good that the input of States would only spoil it. I do not believe that is the right approach. If States cannot reach a decision on a given topic, one must assume that, unfortunately, the work on it is not yet complete.

In today's difficult circumstances, the Sixth Committee is one of the few United Nations organs to remain faithful to the principle of consensus. That is very valuable. One can hardly expect unanimity in the Committee regarding issues on which members of the Commission have been unable to reach agreement. Such situations should be avoided.

With regard to the important issue of the pace of the Commission's work, speed should not be a goal unto itself. It is well known that many of the Commission's landmark texts have been worked on for decades. For example, where a text has not elicited many responses from States after the first reading, it has at times been advisable to defer discussion on it for a year or two in order to gather more views. Not all governments are able to respond rapidly to the Commission's texts, but that does not mean that their views are unimportant.

---

3 UNGA Res 56/83 (12 December 2001).

4 ILC, 'Draft articles on the responsibility of international organizations' [2011] II(2) ILC YBK 40.

5 ILC, 'Draft articles on diplomatic protection' [2006] II(2) ILC YBK 24 .

6 See, for example, and United Nations, 'Responsibility of States for internationally wrongful acts. Compilation of decisions of international courts, tribunals and other bodies' (2016) UN Doc A/71/80.

7 See, e.g. *Gabcikovo-Nagymaros Project (Hungary/Slovakia)* (Merits) [1997] ICJ Rep 7, paras 47, 50, 52, 79 and 83.

I should like to draw attention to another practical problem: the honoraria of Special Rapporteurs. The preparation of reports is a time-consuming process that also requires considerable intellectual effort. As you know, the Chair of the Commission and Special Rapporteurs used to receive honoraria. Then, in 2002, the General Assembly fundamentally changed the system, setting the level of honoraria for members of the Commission at one dollar.[8] That decision was taken without consulting the Commission. Since then, the Commission has on more than one occasion called upon the General Assembly to revisit the issue.[9] From the outset, our delegation has maintained that the matter must be resolved. We trust that dialogue between the General Assembly and the Commission will continue and that a practical solution will be found.

The work of codifying and progressively developing international law is an ongoing process. As long as humanity pursues its endeavours in different areas and strives for excellence and harmony, that work will continue to be vital and beneficial to the international community.

8 UNGA Res 56/272 (27 March 2002).

9 ILC, 'Report of the International Law Commission on the work of its fifty-fourth session' [2002] II(2) ILC Ybk 1, 102 at para 525–531; 'Report of the International Law Commission on the work of its fifty-fifth session' [2003] II(2) ILC Ybk 1, 101 at para 447; 'Report of the International Law Commission on the work of its fifty-sixth session' [2004] II(2) ILC Ybk 1, 120 at para 369; 'Report of the International Law Commission on the work of its fifty-seventh session' [2005] II(2) ILC Ybk 1, 92 at para 501; 'Report of the International Law Commission on the work of its fifty-eighth session' [2006] II(2) ILC Ybk 1, 187 at para 269; 'Report of the International Law Commission on the work of its fifty-ninth session' [2007] II(2) ILC Ybk 1, 100 at para 379; 'Report of the International Law Commission on the work of its sixtieth session' [2008] II(2) ILC Ybk 1, 148 at para 358; 'Report of the International Law Commission on the work of its sixty-first session' [2009] II(2) ILC Ybk 1, 151 at para 240; 'Report of the International Law Commission on the work of its sixty-second session' [2010] II(2) ILC Ybk 1, 203 at para 396; 'Report of the International Law Commission on the work of its sixty-third session' [2011] II(2) ILC Ybk 1, 178 at para 399; 'Report of the International Law Commission on the work of its sixty-fourth session' [2012] II(2) ILC Ybk 1, 87 at para 280; 'Report of the International Law Commission on the work of its sixty-fifth session' [2013] II(2) ILC Ybk 1, 79 at para 181; 'Report of the International Law Commission on the work of its sixty-sixth session' (2014) UN Doc A/69/10, para 281; 'Report of the International Law Commission on the work of its sixty-seventh session' (2015) UN Doc A/70/10, para 299; 'Report of the International Law Commission on the work of its sixty-eighth session' (2016) UN Doc A/71/10, para 333; 'Report of the International Law Commission on the work of its sixty-ninth session' (2017) UN Doc A/72/10, para 282; and 'Report of the International Law Commission on the work of its seventieth session' (2018) UN Doc A/73/10, para 382.

Presentation by Concepción Escobar-Hernández

The Relationship between the International Law Commission and the Sixth Committee of the General Assembly: Some Methodological Reflections and Proposals

Member of the International Law Commission

1 Some Introductory Remarks

The celebration of the seventieth session of the International Law Commission offers an extraordinary opportunity to reflect, once again, upon the relationship between the Commission and the Sixth Committee of the General Assembly. This topic is not new and it is, in itself, an omnipresent element in the collective reflection upon the role to be played by the International Law Commission in the process of building the international legal order.

However, this topic calls for special attention at a moment when the Commission reaches "old age" in an international social environment in which, on the one hand, new organs and fora have emerged with whom to share the task of promoting the progressive development and codification of international law and, on the other hand, where there is a new, ongoing debate on the role of international law in the general framework of international relations, a debate driven to a great extent by the United Nations' objective of strengthening of the rule of law at the national and international levels. From this perspective, one cannot but confirm that the Commission has arrived at this moment in good shape, that in these seven decades it has fulfilled a great deal of its objectives, and that it continues to be at the centre of the international legal system. Nevertheless, it should not be forgotten that the Commission is today facing new challenges and that, in order to confront them, it must internally reflect on multiple issues, among which reconsideration of its working methods and the strengthening of its relationship with the Sixth Committee must be central. Both issues are closely intertwined and this brief contribution is devoted to them.

Indeed, the essential nature of the relationship between the International Law Commission and the Sixth Committee of the General Assembly cannot be put into question, because the fulfilment of one of the mandates given by the Charter of the United Nations to the General Assembly, namely contributing to the promotion of the progressive development of international law and its codification, depends on the existence of a fluent, constructive and efficient relationship between the two bodies. Such a relationship has been in place

DOI:10.1163/9789004434271_010

continuously due to their common character as subsidiary organs of the General Assembly, without neglecting their different nature and functions. Thus, whereas the Sixth Committee is an intergovernmental body responsible for implementing that mandate, by debating and making decisions that will later be formally adopted by the General Assembly, the International Law Commission is an expert body responsible for preparing, from a technical and legal perspective, the studies and drafts to be considered by the Sixth Committee at a later stage. Each of these bodies, it is obvious, exercises its functions autonomously, but it is also evident that the effective fulfilment of their respective mandates concerning the progressive development and codification of international law depends on an adequate relationship and interaction between them.

II An Assessment of the Current Practice

That such relationship and interaction exist is a reality. However, one could wonder whether the current relationship model is satisfactory and whether the best means to attain an effective interaction are being used. To answer these questions, one must first analyze the International Law Commission's own activity and the reaction thereto of the Sixth Committee. This approach necessitates, in particular, not so much a substantive examination of the work of both bodies as it does, above all, an examination of the means and tools they use to entertain an effective relationship. Such means and tools can relate to multiple issues but, for the sake of brevity, I will only refer to those relating to issues of particular relevance, namely: i) the selection of topics to be included in the programme of work of the International Law Commission; ii) the transmission of information (reporting) on the work of the Commission to the Sixth Committee and to States; iii) the contribution of States to the work of the Commission; iv) the holding of meetings between the International Law Commission and the Sixth Committee; and v) the response of the Sixth Committee to the final work of the International Law Commission.

i) **Selection of topics.** Although some of the first topics of the programme of the International Law Commission were referred to it by the General Assembly,[1] the use of this way to proceed has been exceptional. On the other hand, even though the statute of the Commission allows States to submit topics directly to the Commission, this possibility has been absent from the practice of the Commission until the current session, when a State proposed the conduct of a study

1 These topics were fundamental rights and duties of States, UNGA Res 178 (II) (21 November 1947); formulation of the Nuremberg Principles, UNGA Res 177 (II) (21 November 1947); a

on the implications of sea-level rise.[2] Therefore, the initiative in the selection of topics has been in the hands of the Commission, even though States have made comments (with varying degrees of intensity) on the proposals of topics included in the long-term programme of work. At any rate, this lack of participation of States in the selection of topics has at times resulted, and could result in the future, in an estrangement between the topics that are more interesting for States and the topics actually included in the active program of the Commission.

ii) **Report on the work of the International Law Commission.** The Commission reports on its work to States and to the Sixth Committee, essentially through the annual report, the reports of the Special Rapporteurs and the summary records of its debates. This is supplemented by the presentation of the annual report by the Chair of the Commission on the occasion of the discussion of the corresponding item on the agenda of the Sixth Committee. A recent addition to this is the audio-recording of the plenary meetings of the Commission, which are available on the conference website of the United Nations Office at Geneva.[3] Beyond these tools there is no other channel of information relating to the ongoing session and even though States can benefit from the complete information available on the Commission's website, this is not, strictly speaking, a tool permitting the interaction between the International Law Commission and the Sixth Committee. On the other hand, it must also be stressed that there are no formal channels for the Special Rapporteurs to interact with the Sixth Committee, except – when that is possible – on the occasion of their presence in the debates during the International Law Week and the very brief intervention they may make at the end of the debate. This is somehow alleviated by the initiative of the Interactive Dialogue (see below), which is nonetheless very limited in scope.

iii) **Contribution of States to the work of the International Law Commission.** Substantially speaking, the most important way of interaction between the Commission and the Sixth Committee is the contribution of States to the work of the Commission on each of the topics included in its programme, which essentially takes place along three avenues: a) the declarations during

draft code of crimes against the peace and security of mankind, UNGA Res 177 (II) (21 November 1947); and the question of international criminal jurisdiction, UNGA Res 260 B (III) (9 December 1948).

2 See statement of the Marshall Islands (on behalf of the Pacific Small Island Developing States), made in the Sixth Committee of the General Assembly under agenda item 81: Report of the International Law Commission on the work of its sixty-ninth session (Cluster II), on 26 October 2017, available at <https://papersmart.unmeetings.org/media2/16154559/marshall-islands-on-behalf-of-pacific-small-island-developing-states-.pdf>.

3 UNOG Digital Recordings Portal < https://conf.unog.ch/digitalrecordings/#>.

the debate of the Sixth Committee; b) the written answers to the questions annually included in the report of the Commission; and c) the written comments on the different drafts approved in first reading by the Commission. These contributions are essential for the work of the Commission as they give it the possibility of benefiting from a sort of substantive interaction with States regarding each of the topics under its consideration. However, in practice, there is a tendency towards a decrease in the number of State contributions, especially written contributions, both with regard to answers to the questions in chapter three of the annual report and with regard to comments on the drafts adopted on first reading.[4] Although the reasons for this may be various and difficult to assess, the material difficulties faced by the legal services of States in charge of preparing such answers must be taken into account. This problem is aggravated in the case of States with small legal services. In these cases, one cannot disregard the fact that the increase in the number of questions included in the annual reports, and the simultaneous completion of several topics on first reading, complicate the task of collaborating with the Commission. At any rate, whatever the reasons may be, it must be acknowledged that this tendency deprives the Commission of certain information that cannot always be obtained through other channels and, at the same time, creates an estrangement effect between the Commission and the Sixth Committee that could reduce the effectiveness of their respective work.

iv) **Meetings between the International Law Commission and the Sixth Committee.** Direct contact between the two bodies only takes place in the framework of the debate of the report of the Commission within the Sixth Committee, and such contact is limited given that the Commission participates in the debate only through its Chair. Although it is increasingly frequent that other members of the Commission, in particular Special Rapporteurs, attend the meetings of the Sixth Committee during the International Law Week, they do so on their own initiative and under no specific mandate of the Sixth Committee. On the other hand, it is also relevant that, as reiterated by members of the Commission and delegates to the Sixth Committee, the debate on the report of the Commission is excessively formal and does not permit real interaction. These shortcomings can somehow be remedied by the Interactive Dialogue that takes place on the occasion of the International Law Week, and by the initiative of a group of delegations (the "Friends of the International Law Commission") that have organized round tables and meetings with members

4 In 2018, for example, the topics which States have commented on received between three and eleven written submissions.

of the Commission who, for one reason or another, happen to be in New York. Nevertheless, in spite of their great value, these initiatives are not enough. In the first case, only three hours (one afternoon session) are allocated to the Interactive Dialogue, and in the second case, the initiative is informal and limited, essentially reliant on mere opportunity and lacking a systematic character.

v) **The response of the Sixth Committee to the final work of the International Law Commission.** Since the Commission is a subsidiary organ of the General Assembly, it is clear that how the Sixth Committee reacts to the final product of the work of the Commission is of particular importance. In this regard, it should be stressed, first, that the response of the General Assembly to the drafts submitted by the Commission has been remarkably uneven. Suffice it to recall that there was a first phase when drafts on central topics of international law were completed and then systematically transformed into conventions. Since the completion of this phase, the response of the Sixth Committee has been more modulated. Particularly during the last two decades, decision-making on the projects prepared by the Commission has slowed down, which has resulted, in practice, in the lack of transformation of such drafts into treaties. The United Nations Convention on the Jurisdictional Immunity of States and their Property[5] is the last draft to have been transformed into a convention which, moreover, has not entered into force yet. This turnaround in the practice of the General Assembly has taken place essentially after the adoption of the articles on the responsibility of States for internationally wrongful acts,[6] and has been maintained, with slight variations, to the present day. This change has ushered in an interesting debate on the decline in interest in the work of the Commission on the part of the Sixth Committee and States, and on the loss of relevance of the work itself. The Commission seems to have reacted by replacing draft articles as the principal model for its work, and by progressively reinforcing other models for the final presentation of its works, such as guides to practice, draft conclusions, recommendations or principles, and even studies on a given issue. Although the claim that the work of the Commission has lost interest and relevance cannot be sustained if practice is analyzed in detail, the truth is that this change in the response of the Sixth Committee and States to the final work of the Commission reveals a worrying distance between the approach of the Sixth Committee and that of the Commission to the process of progressive development of international law and its codification. This estrangement is no doubt worthy of serious thought, both from the substantive

5 Adopted 2 December 2004, not yet in force, UNGA Res 59/38 (2 December 2004), annex.
6 See UNGA Res 56/83 (12 December 2001), annex.

and methodological perspective, on the premise that the existing means and tools of collaboration have apparently not been sufficiently effective.

III Envisaging for the Future: Some Thoughts and Proposals

From this critical analysis of the practice and the means of collaboration used thus far by the International Law Commission and the Sixth Committee, one can derive a set of needs that must be met in order to ensure an effective relationship between both bodies. They can be summarized as follows:

i) To promote active participation of States and the General Assembly in the proposal of new topics to be included in the program of work of the Commission;

ii) To promote new mechanisms that might help to transmit more rapidly and efficiently the work of the Commission to States and to the Sixth Committee, reinforcing the principle of transparency;

iii) To promote methods ensuring that States can actively and substantially contribute to the work of the International Law Commission, in particular enabling a large number of States to overcome the challenges they face due to their level of development, or to their limited operational capacity in legal terms; and

iv) To promote and strengthen an actual, interactive dialogue between the Commission and States in the framework, and under the umbrella, of the Sixth Committee, with a view to encouraging the Commission to take into account the concerns and legitimate interests of States while preserving its technical autonomy.

Meeting these needs would constitute an effective way of contributing to the reinforcement of cooperation and mutual trust between the International Law Commission and the Sixth Committee, and it would enable both bodies to better fulfil their respective mandates with regard to the progressive development and codification of international law. This last objective is of particular importance at present, given that the needs and interests of States are undergoing significant changes that require consistent and systematic legal responses, which the Commission is in a fairly good position to offer.

However, attaining these objectives and providing an effective response to the previous list of needs can only take place through the use of useful mechanisms and working methods that reinforce the actual interaction between the Commission and the Sixth Committee. The existing mechanisms have already been mentioned and, although their limits and shortcomings have been laid bare, it must be recognized that they have made a remarkable contribution to the interaction between the two bodies through the years. Keeping and improving them must therefore be the starting point for establishing any future model of relationship and cooperation. Nevertheless, practice has shown that they do not suffice for ensuring a fluent, interactive relationship, so it could be useful to explore new ways to enable the two bodies to deepen their relationship and somehow remedy the shortcomings detected in the current mechanisms. With that in mind, two suggestions aimed at facilitating a more efficient flow of information between the Commission and Member States and at favouring a more intense, interactive debate could be made at this juncture:

i) **A collaborative space on the website of the Commission.** The website of the Commission has been remarkably improved in recent years, an achievement for which the Codification Division must be complimented. Its content and structure, extremely comprehensive, continues to follow the pattern of an informative site. Since this website is by now consolidated, it would be possible to explore the chance of opening a "collaborative space" on the site, modelled on those already existing on other websites of other international bodies specialized in international law (see, for example, the website of the Committee of Legal Advisers on Public International Law of the Council of Europe (CAHDI)).[7] This could lead to the creation of a tool for communication between States, the Commission and the Secretariat that would enable them to share information, observations and comments in a direct, flexible manner, as well as receive proposals on issues of interest to States. This flexible formula could expedite communication between States and the Commission, extend it all through the year, and facilitate the participation of States lacking the capacity to submit written comments but able to provide the Commission with information in a simpler, more direct manner.

ii) **Topical workshops.** One of the principal demands on the part of the delegates of the Sixth Committee is to increase direct contact with the International Law Commission, which has materialized in the request that the Commission meet in New York for the first part of its seventieth session. Although holding the sessions in New York does not automatically result in greater participation of the legal advisers of the Missions in the meetings of the Commission, the experience of the seventieth session, during which the Commission has held part of the meetings in New York, is a good example of how interaction between members of the Commission and delegates can be reinforced, especially through the open "side events" model. This experience is no doubt remarkable, but it does not permit the Commission and the

7 See <https://www.coe.int/en/web/cahdi>.

legal advisers to discuss in-depth, and in an interactive fashion, the topics on which the Commission is working. This concern could be addressed by convening topical workshops, dedicated to specific items on the Commission's programme of work. For them to be effective, workshops should last no longer than a week, they could be scheduled to take place during weeks of less intense work in New York, and they should be formally included in the programme of the General Assembly. The programme of the workshops could be agreed upon by the Chair of the Commission and the Chair of the Sixth Committee, with the support of the Secretariat.

These two methodological proposals require that changes be introduced in the working methods of the Commission and the Sixth Committee and, as a result, their practical value needs to be studied. Nevertheless, adding this new approach to the consolidated working and collaborating methods may result in a remarkable improvement in the relations between the International Law Commission and the Sixth Committee, thus contributing to fulfil the mandate to promote international law given to both bodies.

I am certain that both the International Law Commission and the Sixth Committee will benefit from a debate on these and other methodological issues in the coming years

Presentation by Angel Horna

Legal Adviser, Permanent Mission of Peru to the United Nations

One of the mandates of the United Nations General Assembly, contained in Article 13 of the Charter of the United Nations, refers to the initiation of studies and the making of recommendations to encourage the progressive development of international law and its codification. Subsequent practice has interpreted this provision as an authorization to elaborate new international conventions on a wide range of issues – in particular, through the work of the International Law Commission, which is later considered by the General Assembly, through its Sixth (Legal) Committee. This should contribute to establishing "conditions under which justice and respect for the obligations arising from treaties and other sources of international law can be maintained".[1] Against this backdrop, this article reflects on the relationship between those two bodies.

In what ways have the Sixth Committee and the International Law Commission interacted, formally and informally, to advance the progressive development of international law and its codification?

The contribution of the International Law Commission to the progressive development of international law and its codification depends to a large extent on the dialogue and cooperation with the Sixth Committee. Due account must be taken of the necessary definition and distinction of their respective roles.[2] The International Law Commission, composed of legal experts, plays a scientific role. In turn, the Sixth Committee offers policy guidance to the Commission through comments by government representatives with strong legal backgrounds, who are also mindful of political sensitivities.[3]

With respect to cooperation between the two bodies, responsiveness is sometimes insufficient. Indeed, there has been criticism regarding governments' failure to answer questionnaires or submit comments and observations requested by the Commission. However, a lack of response does not necessarily

1 Charter of the United Nations, preamble.

2 One author would say "complementarity, not identification", see Alain Pellet, 'Between Codification and Progressive Development of the Law: Some Reflections from the ILC' (2004) International Law FORUM du droit international 15.

3 For early reflections on "hombres de estado" versus "juristas eminentes" regarding codification, see Alberto Ulloa, *Derecho Internacional Público*, vol 1 (4th edn, Ediciones Iberoamericanas 1957) 88.

indicate disinterest. Instead, there are often logistical challenges, including difficulties in obtaining pertinent information from national authorities within the time frame allotted by the Commission.

Regarding formal interactions, the annual presentation of the report of the Commission to the Sixth Committee is to be highlighted, in particular within the framework of the International Law Week.[4] This interaction serves in some way to institutionalize the dialogue between the two bodies, which is followed by a debate and the adoption of the annual resolution of the Sixth Committee.[5] To this, one should add the formal submissions of comments and observations on the outcomes of the Commission, especially between first and second readings.

An important informal element of the dialogue and interaction between the International Law Commission and the Sixth Committee are side events organized by Permanent Missions to the United Nations in New York. They provide an opportunity for Special Rapporteurs, as well as other members of the Commission, to make informal presentations about topics of interest, to facilitate exchanges of views and sometimes a substantial informal discussion, which strengthens the interaction between Member States and the Commission.

How Have the Bodies Influenced Each Other? What Have Been the Joint Achievements and the Difficulties?

Concerning mutual influence, some members of the Commission are former delegates to the Sixth Committee, which shows the existence of "common views". Although less frequent, there are also instances in which a member of the Commission subsequently became a representative in the Sixth Committee.[6]

Another example of mutual influence is that some outcomes of the Commission have been taken up by the Sixth Committee or, even, by intergovernmental conferences, for codification. As joint achievements, several

4 The so-called "high level week" of the General Assembly's Sixth Committee, when principal legal advisers based in capitals journey to New York, coincides with the first week of the presentation of the annual report of the International Law Commission to the Sixth Committee, as well as the reports from the President of the International Court of Justice, the President of the International Residual Mechanism for Criminal Tribunals, and the President of the International Criminal Court to the General Assembly. Note that during that week there is also an annual briefing of the President of the ICJ to the Security Council, in the format of a "closed session", as well as an address of the ICJ President to the Sixth Committee.

5 Note that the author, as delegate to the Sixth Committee, was the facilitator of that annual resolution from the sixty-ninth to the seventy-third session of the General Assembly.

6 While not directly linked to the relationship between the Sixth Committee and the International Law Commission, it may be worth mentioning that since the inception of the Commission it has been possible to observe, in some cases, a "flow" between members of the Commission and judges of the International Court of Justice.

conventions based on drafts prepared by the Commission could be identified. They include: the Vienna Convention on Diplomatic Relations (1961),[7] the Vienna Convention on Consular Relations (1963),[8] the Vienna Convention on the Law of Treaties (1969),[9] the Convention on the Prevention and Punishment of Crimes Against Internationally Protected Persons, including Diplomatic Agents (1973),[10] as well as the Convention on the Law of Non-Navigational Uses of International Water Courses (1997).[11] It is noteworthy that the draft statute for an international criminal court was also elaborated by the Commission.[12]

In the same vein, reference can be made to the 1958 Geneva Conventions on the Law of the Sea.[13] Even though not currently the applicable law on the subject-matter, they contain several provisions, including on maritime delimitation, that prevailed until their incorporation in the 1982 United Nations Convention on the Law of the Sea.[14]

On the other hand, there have been instances in which the work of the Commission on a given topic extended for several decades, as was the case with the draft articles on responsibility of States for internationally wrongful acts (2001).[15] Another – far from ideal – example is that of the Convention on the Jurisdictional Immunities of States and Their Property:[16] the Commission worked on a text between 1978 and 1991,[17] but the General Assembly only adopted the Convention in 2004 and it has not yet entered into force.

Notwithstanding the foregoing, the success of the Commission cannot be assessed by considering only whether its final outcomes ever came into force, or by the number of ratifications of the conventions it has produced. In fact, other factors may play an important role. For instance, the impact of the draft articles on State responsibility, even when they were in the making, has been remarkable.

---

7 Adopted 18 April 1961, entered into force 24 April 1964, 500 UNTS 95.

8 Adopted 24 April 1963, entered into force 19 March 1967, 596 UNTS 261.

9 Adopted 23 May 1969, entered into force 27 January 1980, 1155 UNTS 331.

10 Adopted 14 December 1973, entered into force 20 February 1977, 1035 UNTS 167.

11 Adopted 21 May 1997, entered into force on 17 August 2014, UNTS registration no 52106.

12 [1994] II(2) ILC Ybk 1, 26.

13 Convention on the Territorial Sea and the Contiguous Zone, adopted 29 April 1958, entered into force 10 September 1964, 516 UNTS 205; Convention on the Continental Shelf, adopted 29 April 1958, entered into force 10 June 1964, 499 UNTS 311; Convention on the High Seas; Convention on Fishing and Conservation of Living Resources of the High Seas, adopted 29 April 1958, entered into force 20 March 1966, 559 UNTS 285.

14 Adopted 10 December 1982, entered into force 16 November 1994, 1833 UNTS 3.

15 UNGA Res 56/83 (12 December 2001), annex.

16 Adopted 2 December 2004, not yet in force, UN Doc A/59/508.

17 ILC, 'Draft articles on jurisdictional immunities of States and their property and commentaries thereto' [1991] II(2) ILC Ybk 13.

At present, it would be hard to challenge the authority of the draft articles, even though not all of their provisions reflect customary international law.

As for the difficulties facing the interaction between the two bodies, in recent years the Sixth Committee has not taken a concrete decision on the final outcomes of the Commission. There are plenty of examples of situations where – irrespective of carefully crafted recommendations by the Commission – the Sixth Committee simply decides to "take note" of such outcomes and then to consider at a later stage the question of the elaboration of a convention ("technical roll-overs"). These situations should be avoided.

Indeed, in the last 14 years, no convention has been adopted by the General Assembly, or under its auspices, on any of the topics on which the Commission had produced draft articles for codification. It is my hope that this trend will be reversed, including with the final outcome of the Commission's work on the topic crimes against humanity.

The Sixth Committee should also not turn into a forum for continuing the debates within the Commission, given that the Committee discussions should be more of a political nature and provide some guidance to the Commission.

An enhanced interaction between the two bodies could improve the chances of the International Law Commission producing outcomes that are useful to the Sixth Committee. At the same time, the Sixth Committee, through its guidance reflected in comments and observations, would also enable the Commission to produce the desired outcomes.

It would also be desirable that the Sixth Committee more actively request the Commission to include topics directly relevant to the interests of States in its programme of work.[18] While this type of specific request should be

18 It should be noted, however, that in some cases issues referred by the Sixth Committee had political implications (e.g.: the question of the definition of aggression and the code of offenses against the peace and security of humanity); see, in this regard: Ian Sinclair, *The International Law Commission* (Grotius Publications 1987). On the other hand, the General Assembly requested the Commission, by resolution 2780 (XXVI) of 3 December 1971, "to study as soon as possible, in the light of the comments of Member States, the question of the protection and inviolability of diplomatic agents and other persons entitled to special protection under international law, with a view to preparing a set of draft articles dealing with offences committed against diplomats and other persons entitled to special protection under international law for submission to the General Assembly at the earliest date which the Commission considers appropriate". This culminated in the adoption of the Convention on the Prevention and Punishment of Crimes against Internationally Protected Persons, including Diplomatic Agents (n 10). Other examples include requests made, in accordance with article 17 of the ILC statute, through ECOSOC resolutions, such as resolution 304 D (XI) of 17 July 1950 and resolution 319 B (XI) of 11 August 1950.

encouraged, the Sixth Committee, on some occasions, has chosen to establish other subsidiary bodies, such as ad-hoc committees (which were the framework in which, for instance, the sectoral counter-terrorism conventions were drafted),[19] special committees[20] and even working groups.[21]

In light of the above, there are a number of practical measures that may improve the relationship between the Sixth Committee and the International Law Commission:

1. Encourage the Sixth Committee not only to endorse topics it deems appropriate for the Commission to consider (given the independent role of the Commission, pursuant to its statute),[22] but to actually suggest topics. This could increase the credibility, authority and relevance of the International Law Commission.
2. In this regard, carefully consider the manner in which the Sixth Committee puts forward a request for a topic ("referral" or "terms of reference") to the Commission.
3. Consider an informal meeting between the Chair of the Commission and the Chair of the Sixth Committee, at the beginning of each session, to review the issues to be considered by the Sixth Committee, with the idea of sensitizing States.
4. Stimulate informal dialogue between States and the International Law Commission – in particular with the Special Rapporteurs – and, as far as possible, with members of academia.
5. In connection with the foregoing, consider holding a part of the Commission's session in New York from time to time, perhaps once every quinquennium, taking due account of article 12 of its statute.

---

19 International Convention for the Suppression of Terrorist Bombings, adopted 15 December 1997, entered into force 23 May 2001, 2149 UNTS 256; International Convention for the Suppression of the Financing of Terrorism, adopted 9 December 1999, entered into force 10 April 2002, 2178 UNTS 197; and International Convention for the Suppression of Acts of Nuclear Terrorism, adopted 13 April 2005, entered into force 7 July 2007, 2445 UNTS 89.

20 See, e.g., the Special Committee of the Charter of the United Nations and of the Strengthening of the Role of the Organization, established in accordance with UNGA Res 3499 (XXX) (15 December 1975).

21 For instance, a Working Group was formed in preparation of the 1997 Convention on the Law of the Non-Navigational Uses of International Watercourses (n 10), based on draft articles by the International Law Commission ([1994] II(2) ILC Ybk 89).

22 Statute of the ILC, UNGA Res 174(II) (21 November 1947) as amended by UNGA Res 485(V) (12 December 1950); UNGA Res. 984(X) (3 December 1955); UNGA Res 985(X) (3 December 1955) and UNGA Res 36/39 (18 November 1981).

6. Encourage timely preparation of comments and observations from States on the work of the Commission, in the framework of the debates in the Sixth Committee, which could integrate, as appropriate, the contributions not only from the ministries of foreign affairs, but also other ministries, such as justice, economy, trade, environment, trade etc.

How should the International Law Commission design outcomes, and how should the Sixth Committee deal with them?

When the International Law Commission selects a topic *motu proprio*, it must exercise flexibility in the format of the final products (draft guidelines, draft conclusions etc.) and be guided by the Sixth Committee on what product it desires, if any. Similarly, when the Sixth Committee requests a topic, it should also define, in the request and in a precise manner, what it expects from the Commission.

What should the Commission look like in ten years?

As a body comprising members of recognized competence in international law, reflecting the main legal systems, and representing all geographic regions, the 2030 Commission, while maintaining the global vision of international law that it has, should continue taking into account the increasing output of other specialized forums (e.g. human rights treaty bodies, the Human Rights Council, the United Nations Commission on International Trade Law (UNCITRAL), and other intergovernmental processes). In this sense, its role should be more focused on specific areas, bearing in mind that other institutions are also taking part in international law-making.

For instance, the Arms Trade Treaty[23] was negotiated in the First Committee of the General Assembly, as was the case with the Nuclear Ban Treaty.[24] The Paris Agreement[25] was negotiated in the framework of the Conference of the Parties of the United Nations Framework Convention on Climate Change,[26] and the possibility of a Global Pact for the Environment is being considered in an *ad hoc* open-ended working group under the auspices

23 Adopted 2 April 2013, entered into force 24 December 2014, UNTS registration no 52373.

24 Comprehensive Nuclear-Test-Ban Treaty, adopted 10 September 1996, not yet in force, UN Doc A/50/1027 (1996).

25 Adopted 12 December 2015, entered into force 4 November 2016, UNTS Registration no 54113.

26 United Nations Framework Convention on Climate Change, adopted 9 May 1992, entered into force 21 March 1994, 1771 UNTS 107.

of the General Assembly.[27] The future treaty on the conservation and sustainable use of marine biological diversity of areas beyond national jurisdiction is being negotiated within the framework of an intergovernmental conference, following the model of the Third United Nations Conference of the Law of the Sea.[28]

Furthermore, at the 2018 Munich Security Conference, the United Nations Secretary-General called for the need to regulate cyber space suggesting it could entail the competence of the First Committee of the General Assembly.[29] Conversely, the compelling issue of the governance of artificial intelligence, in light of its ethics component, could be considered by the International Law Commission.

In addition, the 2030 Commission should continue to review its working methods, including aspects related to the frequency of its meetings and decision-making (usually by consensus), in order to make its outcomes as relevant as possible for governments.

Other improvements could include an increase in the number of women elected as members and a move towards gender balance. Furthermore, a Commission that works effectively in the six official United Nations languages and encourages multilingualism would be desirable. The Commission should also take into account the diversity of legal systems throughout the different stages of the codification process.

To conclude, the International Law Commission – a body in which Peru has been represented three times, currently by Professor Juan José Ruda Santolaria – has played a fundamental role in the development and clarification of the scope of international law. As the international community continues to evolve, despite threats to multilateralism, and as legal relations continue to become more complex, the work of the Commission will remain a mainstay in the efforts to achieve a rules-based order and a world where the unrestricted respect for international law and, specifically, the Charter of the United Nations, is ensured.

---

27 The Secretary-General recently issued a report on gaps in international environmental law and environment-related instruments. See UN Doc A/73/419 (2018).

28 UNGA Res 72/249 (24 December 2017).

29 'Secretary-General's address at the Opening Ceremony of the Munich Security Conference [as delivered]' (16 February 2018) <www.un.org/sg/en/content/sg/statement/2018-02-16/secretary-general%E2%80%99s-address-opening-ceremony-munich-security>.

Presentation by Hussein A. Hassouna

Member of the International Law Commission

It is an honour for me to participate in this panel organized on the occasion of the seventieth anniversary of the International Law Commission. Our panel has addressed the topic of interaction between the Commission and the Sixth Committee. As a former member of the Sixth Committee and a current member of the Commission, this subject is of particular interest to me, having been involved in the work of both bodies and having witnessed their joint achievements in the field of codification and progressive development of international law. As the last speaker on this panel, I confirm that I agree with most of what has been said by the previous speakers. Allow me, however, to add my own perspective on some aspects of the subject matter.

I will begin by stating that the Commission's relationship with the Sixth Committee of the General Assembly is central to the Commission's work. In fact, the Commission has been able to have such an impact on international law because of its unique relationship with the Sixth Committee, a relationship which is both reactive and proactive, but at its roots, firmly founded upon interaction and communication.

The Commission proposes topics for the benefit of making the law more visible and more readily available for States, as well as presents reports on its work which serve as the basis for the Sixth Committee debates on the various topics. In turn, the Sixth Committee comments, provides data, and advises the Commission on how topics can be improved, and which topics should be prioritized. It is this relationship that has enabled States, developed and developing, to provide their input on the formulation of international law, and to help develop a truly transnational conception of international law.

Whereas the presentation by the Chair of the Commission of its annual report to the Sixth Committee has traditionally been the formal procedure leading to interaction between the two bodies, various activities have contributed in recent years to promote their relationships. Thus, in addition to the Chair of the Commission, a number of Commission members have been present during the Sixth Committee's debate on the report. An Interactive Dialogue has been held between Special Rapporteurs and interested delegates of the Sixth Committee on the margins of that debate. Informal briefings at other times of the year were provided by Commission members whenever they were present in New York, for interested Sixth Committee members.

The current meeting of the Commission in New York during the first part of its seventieth session was also designed, in large part, to allow for greater formal and informal interaction between members of the Commission and of the Sixth Committee. Such interaction has enabled the Commission to discuss its work with the members of the Sixth Committee so as to allow the Commission to develop its activities, including the choice of its topics, in response to the needs and concerns of States. In addition, the current session in New York has been an opportunity for Commission members to explain their views on the Commission's topics at the numerous side events that were scheduled almost daily. Finally, the current session has further allowed another body, the Security Council, to be reminded of the achievements of the Commission. It was during its open debate held last week on the role of the Security Council in upholding international law that mention was made of the need to recognize the work of the principal legal organ to the United Nations, the International Law Commission, and its invaluable contributions over the years. Let us hope that such debate will lead the Security Council to ensuring that international law is applied and respected worldwide.

The success of the current meeting of the Commission in New York should encourage us to hold at least one part of its annual session each quinquennium in New York, so as to continue benefiting from greater formal and informal interaction between the Commission and the Sixth Committee. But let me reassure the Federal Government of Switzerland that the Commission will otherwise continue holding its annual sessions in Geneva and enjoy Swiss hospitality.

The Commission is generally autonomous with regard to its relationship with the Sixth Committee. The view of the General Assembly and the Sixth Committee has been that the Commission should have a substantial degree of autonomy and should not be subject to detailed directives from either the Sixth Committee or the General Assembly. Overall, the dependence of the Commission on the Sixth Committee and the General Assembly is based upon the guidance and information those two bodies can give to the Commission in its pursuit of the formation of international law and making it more clear and accessible. Otherwise, the Commission has great autonomy in deciding how to make this possible.

One must recognize, however, that although both the Commission and the Sixth Committee deal with issues pertaining to the codification and progressive development of international law, they differ in how they approach these issues, and one of the reasons for that lies in the composition of those bodies. Let us remember that the Commission is composed of independent experts who avoid politics in their discussions and in their selection of topics.

Although they normally agree on most issues by consensus, on controversial issues they sometimes have to resort to voting. The Sixth Committee, on the other hand, is composed of State representatives who bring a political background and perspective to discussions. The independence of the Commission's experts encourages impartiality and objectiveness in approaching a certain subject, although they are often also influenced by their legal background and national experience.

On the other hand, the Sixth Committee members serve more as advocates for their individual States' interests. Indeed, the election by the General Assembly of the members of the Commission is regretfully always influenced by political considerations and is not mainly based on the qualifications of the candidates. In spite of this different dual approach, it is certain that both the objective perspective of the Commission members and the subjective perspective of the State representatives are required to address the codification of international law. Both perspectives are needed to get the full scope of international practice regarding a topic, but also to make sure that the codification of such a topic is relevant and useful to States. Without further collaboration, the work of the Commission is in danger of becoming academic and irrelevant, and the Sixth Committee is in danger of losing objective expertise on cutting edge issues in international law, an expertise that is greatly needed for a fruitful collaboration of the two bodies in the codification and development of international law.

In seeking to enhance its relationship with the Sixth Committee and other bodies, the Commission has dealt with that issue in the context of reviewing its methods of work. This process has been periodically undertaken by the Commission, at the request of the General Assembly at times, and more recently in 2011 and 2017 upon its own initiative.[1] That review, aimed at expediting and streamlining the Commission's procedures, had an internal dimension covering how the Commission organizes its work, and an external dimension, as to how the work and the final product of the Commission is communicated to the General Assembly and its Member States, in particular, the Commission's relationship with the Sixth Committee and with governments regarding information on the State practice crucial to the Commission's work. The work of the Working Group on Methods of Work, which I have the honour of chairing, is still in progress and will resume at the upcoming Geneva part of the session

1 See ILC, 'Report of the International Law Commission on the work of its sixty-third session' [2011] II(2) ILC Ybk 176 at para 370. 'Report of the International Law Commission on the work of its sixty-ninth session' (2017) UN Doc A/72/10, 218 at para 283.

in July. In my view, the experience learned through the Commission's interaction with the Sixth Committee at the current session in New York will certainly enrich the Working Group's debate on ways and means to enhance the Commission's relationship with the Sixth Committee. I do hope, however, that the Sixth Committee would undertake a similar review of its methods of work.

With regard to the outcome of the Commission's work products, we may notice its increasing practice of formulating "principles," "guidelines," "conclusions" or "report of study groups", rather than draft treaties or conventions. This development is likely a reaction to States' diminished support for creating binding obligations through treaties. In spite of that, the legal authority of such texts has been recognized through decisions of courts, organizations and in academia.

In addition, although the Commission's statute envisages full cooperation with governments in its deliberation process through reporting to the Sixth Committee and exchanging documents throughout the Commission's work on a document, in practice, there seems to be a disconnect between the expectations of the Commission and States. Even in some of the most recent successful work products by the Commission, the articles on responsibility of States for internationally wrongful acts[2] and the articles on the expulsion of aliens,[3] the Sixth Committee continues to postpone consideration of their final form to future sessions. While the Sixth Committee does not explain its decisions regarding the final outcome of the Commission's work products, it cites States' hesitation about certain aspects and often requests further comments from governments. This was the case, for instance, with the topics "Consideration of prevention of transboundary harm from hazardous activities" and "Allocation of loss in the case of such harm[4] and Diplomatic protection".[5] On such a problem, there must be room for improvement in the communication between the Commission and the Sixth Committee. One suggestion to prevent stalling of a final product of the Commission would be for States to submit preferences for the final outcome of a given topic in their comments throughout the deliberation process. This would allow the Special Rapporteur and the Commission members to learn where States stand, and what they expect out of the topic and how they value the work generally. Another suggestion to face that

2 UNGA Res 56/83 (12 December 2001), annex.

3 ILC, 'Draft articles on the expulsion of aliens' (2014) UN Doc A/69/10, 11.

4 See UNGA Res 56/82 (12 December 2001), 61/36 (4 December 2006), 62/68 (6 December 2007), 65/28 (6 December 2010), 68/114 (16 December 2013) and 71/143 (13 December 2016).

5 See UNGA Res 61/35 (4 December 2006), 62/67 (6 December 2007), 65/27 (6 December 2010), 68/113 (16 December 2013) and 71/142 (13 December 2016).

problem would be to encourage the General Assembly and the Sixth Committee to recommend to the Commission topics for codification. This procedure resulted in the successful Rome Statute of the International Criminal Court,[6] and could be replicated to ensure that the Commission is focusing on topics that are ripe for codification and have the necessary political support by the General Assembly.

In proceeding with the analysis of topics on its agenda, the Commission always seeks the opinion of States through their written comments or oral views expressed during the Sixth Committee debates. It is noteworthy that the number of States that submit comments has consistently been limited. Moreover, the commenting States do not reflect the diverse views held by Member States, and the African and Asian perspectives are particularly underrepresented. Despite continuous calls by Commission members for States to submit comments on a given topic, comments from under-represented States remain disproportionately low. This has resulted in the absence of their perspectives in the process of formulating universal rules of international law. In my view, the solution lies in encouraging their participation through regional United Nations procedures, as well as regional organizations. This has inspired, for instance, the members of the Commission from States belonging to the African Group to plan a meeting this week with the African legal advisers of the Sixth Committee, to coordinate the African position on the various topics of the Commission's agenda and encourage African participation in the work of the Commission. In addition, an organization like the Asian-African Legal Consultative Organization (AALCO) can play an important role in coordinating the position of its members towards the work of the Commission and induce them to submit their views on the various topics on its agenda.

It is occasionally argued that the Commission has completed the bulk of its work and faces an identity crisis during a time of fragmentation of international law. While the creation in the Commission of the Working Group on the Long-term Programme of Work has ensured a steady flow of practical and worthwhile suggestions for the Commission's future work, it is generally recognized that the Commission may not be the proper institution to address emerging technical areas of international law. Indeed, the proliferation of specialized bodies to codify certain fields of international law, such as the law of outer space[7] and the law of economic relations,[8] has reduced the scope

6 Adopted 17 July 1998, entered into force 1 July 2002, 2187 UNTS 3.

7 For instance, the Committee on the Peaceful Uses of Outer Space <http://www.unoosa.org/oosa/en/ourwork/copuos/index.html>.

8 For instance, the United Nations Commission on International Trade Law (UNCITRAL) <https://uncitral.un.org/>.

of the Commission's work. However, I am convinced that the Commission could address more complex and specialized topics. For example, the Special Rapporteur for the topic of protection of the atmosphere proactively brought scientists to earlier Commission sessions to inform members of the scientific nuances of the law of the atmosphere.[9] In my view, the Commission should explore more specialized areas of international law, and by doing so, it could benefit from outside consultations, either with scientists or experts in the relevant field, or with specialized international institutions.

In conclusion, I would assert that, although the future of the Commission has been claimed by some commentators to be uncertain, its institutional knowledge, its framework within the General Assembly and its partnership with the Sixth Committee, make it uniquely positioned to continue to codify and progressively develop international law. Indeed, the Commission plays a greater role and assumes a more important responsibility when States fail to agree on the development of international law. The International Law Commission has always adjusted to the needs of the international community. Now, as the Commission ventures into areas of international law that are not as settled as the topics it addressed seventy years ago, it should be attuned to how it can serve its mandate while responding to the needs of all States.

9 See ILC, 'Report of the International Law Commission on the work of its sixty-fifth session' (2015) UN Doc A/70/10 22 at para 49.

PART 2

Drawing a Balance for the Future: the Geneva Symposium

Introductory Remarks by Georg Nolte

Chair of the International Law Commission at Its Sixty-Ninth Session

Our program indicates that the speeches before the coffee break were part of a "solemn meeting". Now it is my duty to introduce you to what may be a less solemn, but which is an equally important part of our anniversary celebration events. In fact, the five panel discussions which follow are the core of what the Commission envisaged when it conceived a series of events with the aim of "Drawing a balance for the future".

"Drawing a balance for the future" signals an ambition. The ambition is to commemorate, on the occasion of the anniversary, but not to simply do so in a self-congratulatory manner. Rather the ambition is to use the occasion for reflections to prepare the Commission for challenges which lie ahead. Such challenges may have their roots in the past and the present.

When I joined the Commission eleven years ago, the Commission was facing its sixtieth anniversary. A sixtieth anniversary is not as important as a fiftieth or a seventieth anniversary, simply because of the magic of the numbers. This lesser character of the anniversary may have been the reason why the Commission, at the time, only organized a small official event, here in Geneva, which has left no traces in the form an official publication.[1] But there may have been deeper reasons for this lesser form of celebration than just the magic of the numbers. In fact, at the time, there was a certain sense of crisis. This sense of crisis was well expressed in the title of an academic article, which read: "The International Law Commission – An Outdated Institution?".[2] The author of the article was Christian Tomuschat, our former colleague. I am particularly happy that he has joined us today. In this article, Tomuschat expressed skepticism about the future role of the Commission. He wondered what was left for the Commission to do after the most important areas of general rules of international law had been more or less successfully progressively developed and codified by the Commission. This article reflected well the mood which prevailed at the time. There was then a certain sense of stagnation and a crisis of self-confidence of the Commission.

1 However, an unofficial colloquium among the members of the Commission, together with invited academics, has also taken place on that occasion, in Munich, whose proceedings are published in Georg Nolte (ed), *Peace through International Law – The Role of the International Law Commission. A Colloquium at the Occasion of its Sixtieth Anniversary* (Springer 2009).

2 Christian Tomuschat, 'The International Law Commission – an Outdated Institution?' (2006) 49 GYIL 77.

Today, the situation seems to be very different. The Commission is dealing with so many topics that it can hardly manage. Even the once holy coffee breaks have this year been canceled for weeks. The Commission is dealing with important topics, and it is dealing with them at a higher speed than in previous times. The number of proposed new topics exceeds the capacity of the Commission. If I am not mistaken, the members of the Commission are more active on average than ten years ago, at least if we compare the degree of participation in the Drafting Committee on the various topics. And it is perhaps also an important sign that the Commission attracts more young people than ever before who are interested to work as assistants of the members.

So, is the Commission in a better condition at age seventy than it was at age sixty? Maybe, but we should not be too certain. One of the purposes of our colloquium today is to diagnose the state of health of the Commission and the situation in which it is. As any reasonable seventy-year-old, the Commission has decided that it should not try to perform a self-diagnosis, but rather go to recognized experts and have itself and its situation checked by them. The Commission has therefore invited reputed academics, some long established and some more recently established, to provide it with in-depth analyses of different aspects of its work. And the Commission wishes to have these analyses discussed and probed by our most important constituents, which are the Legal Advisers of States and international organizations.

The purpose of our discussions today thus goes beyond an exchange of views, and beyond having pleasant meetings during the coffee breaks and the receptions. The main purpose of our discussions is to produce a lasting impulse which will serve to improve and to safeguard the role of the Commission in its unique role of progressively developing and codifying international law. We will try to turn today's colloquium into a lasting impulse by two follow-up activities: First, a report of our discussions here will be produced and presented later this year in New York, during the International Law Week, to the delegates in the Sixth Committee, to stimulate further discussion. Even more importantly, the written contributions of our speakers and the proceedings of our discussion will be published as a book. This book will provide an important reference point for further debates in broader circles about the performance of the Commission in achieving its mandate, perhaps even playing a role in the context of the future eightieth or hundredth anniversaries of the Commission.

There are, of course, limits to what we can do as a Commission. The international political context is currently quite turbulent. Some even say that that this context bodes ill for the progressive development and the codification of international law. These turbulences may affect the Commission, directly as well as in more subtle and indirect ways. It is thus possible that an increased activity of the Commission is not met with a corresponding receptivity on the part of States, their courts, international organizations and other actors. The only means by which the Commission can respond to broader challenges for the international rule of law, it seems to me, is to base its work on authoritative sources, to present its work in a transparent and well-argued fashion, and to maintain its cohesion as a voice, which reminds States and other actors that there is a common basis from which peaceful and fruitful international relations need to be conducted in the common interest of all.

The titles of the five panels are focused on questions of immediate interest for the Commission, but each of those topics is affected by broader political and other developments. This is certainly true for the first panel, "The Commission and its impact", which squarely forces us to look beyond the Commission itself, and to reflect on its role in relation to its addressees and international law as a whole. The second panel on "The working methods of the Commission" seems to focus on more technical matters, but I suppose that it will turn out that the working methods are also mirrors, or symptoms, of more general principles and developments. The third panel on "The function of the Commission: How much identifying existing law, how much proposing new law" addresses one of the classic questions for the Commission, a question which has acquired a new significance in the face of the fact that the products of the work of the Commission are today more frequently used by national and regional courts. The fourth panel on "The changing landscape of international law" also addresses matters which are currently high on the agenda of the Commission, which is how to prioritize among the multitude of possible areas in which the Commission might contribute. The title of the fifth panel on "The authority and the membership of the Commission" may be read as suggesting that there is a connection between the authority of the Commission and its membership, but the panelists should, of course, feel free to question whether and how far this is actually the case.

I wish us all instructive and stimulating debates. And with this may I invite the Chair of the first panel, our former colleague and good friend, Ambassador Comissario Afonso, to take the floor together with his fellow panelists!

SECTION 3

The Commission and Its Impact

Opening Remarks by Pedro Comissário Afonso

A most warm welcome to the first panel of the event celebrating the seventieth anniversary of the International Law Commission. I was given this rare privilege and responsibility of presiding over the first panel of a total of five, to be held under the theme: "Seventy Years of the International Law Commission: Drawing a Balance for the Future". I wholeheartedly thank the members of the Commission and, in particular, Professor Georg Nolte, Chair of the International Law Commission at its sixty-ninth session, for this honour bestowed upon me and for their trust.

In these brief remarks, I would like to recognize and introduce my distinguished colleagues in the panel, namely, Alejandro Rodiles, Professor of International Law and Global Governance at the Instituto Tecnológico Autónomo de Mexico, School of Law, in Mexico City; Laurence Boisson de Chazournes, Professor of International Law at the University of Geneva; and Mr. Pavel Šturma, Professor of International Law and member of the International Law Commission.

The topic of panel 1 is "The Commission and its impact". The members of the panel will discuss issues that are well known. Among those issues are the following: 1) What happens to the final products of the International Law Commission?; 2) What has been the impact of the work of the Commission on State practice, jurisprudence of international courts and tribunals and legal scholarship?; 3) To what extent does the form of the work of the Commission affect its impact?

After having heard many important and inspiring statements at the solemn meeting, we are very fortunate to have these three speakers with us today. Professor Rodiles will speak on the topic "The International Law Commission and change: Not tracing but facing it". Professor Boisson de Chazournes will expound on the theme "The International Law Commission in a Mirror – Forms, Impact and Authority".

The celebration of the sevenieth anniversary of the International Law Commission is a momentous event. It is an opportunity for us to pause and reflect on the centrality of international law in today's international relations. In this chamber, we have come from different walks of life. For some of us, who have been following law and diplomacy for almost 40 years, there is an obvious lesson that we can draw from the Charter of the United Nations. It is the notion that even sovereignty needs law; internally, to function properly and with fairness, and at the international level, to co-exist and cooperate with other competing sovereignties.

This is to say that law, and for that matter, international law, is an important source of order of international order and justice. This has been shown very clearly in a fine book entitled "Peace through International Law – the Role of the International Law Commission", edited by Professor Georg Nolte as a result of a colloquium marking the sixtieth anniversary of the International Law Commission.[1]

I am convinced that many of the insights and conclusions from that book are as relevant today as they were ten years ago. The world will continue to need, for many years to come, this important body that we call the International Law Commission and that is at the core of today's international rule of law. It is my sincere hope that all of us in this room will offer an active and constructive participation in the debate of the topics of our panel.

1 Georg Nolte (ed), *Peace through International Law: The Role of the International Law Commission. A Colloquium at the Occasion of its Sixtieth Anniversary* (Springer 2009).

The International Law Commission and Change: Not Tracing but Facing It

Alejandro Rodiles

Turn and face the strange.[1]

I Introduction

International law is undergoing profound transformations. This affirmation has become a commonplace nowadays, but as most commonplaces, it reflects reality. But then again, the reality underlying commonplaces tends to be more complex than what the latter is able to tell us on its own, and this complexity can only be grasped through differentiation. This is also the case when one tries to understand what international law's transformations are actually about. In an initial step, one has to differentiate between changes *in* and *of* international law. In the first case, we are in the presence of international law's contents and how they evolve over time. The second concerns the changing ways in which contents are made.

Changes in the law do not transform a legal system into something else, at least not from a formal, systemic point of view. Debates about the increasing juridification of international affairs are about changes *in* the law. As Hans Kelsen already observed, there are no fixed material boundaries to international law because it can deal with any subject-matter States agree to regulate on the international plane.[2]

The International Law Commission is a privileged witness of the genesis, transformation, and decay of international legal materials due to its place within the United Nations Organization, the assistance it receives from the United Nations Office of Legal Affairs, the institutionalized communication with States, especially through the channel of the General Assembly's Sixth Committee,[3] the legitimacy it enjoys because of its multi-regional

1 David Bowie, 'Changes' in David Bowie, *Hunky Dory* (RCA 1971).
2 Hans Kelsen, *Principles of International Law* (Rinehart & Company, Inc. 1952) 190–192.
3 Articles 16, 17 and 18 of the ILC statute, UNGA Res 174 (II) (21 November 1947), as amended by UNGA Res 485(V) (12 December 1950); UNGA Res 984(X) (3 December 1955); UNGA Res 985(X) (3 December 1955) and UNGA Res 36/39 (18 November 1981).

DOI:10.1163/9789004434271_015

composition,[4] as well as the balance between academic expertise and diplomatic experience.[5] However, it is important to clarify that just as a prime witness contributes through her testimony to the construction of legal truth, so too is the Commission's work crucial in the identification, existence, and evolution of international law.

To summarize, when it comes to changes in the system, the Commission helps to make them visible in the beginning, already articulating the law-to-be, which is then used in the further positivization of the law. In a way, this is nothing but the old story of the codification and progressive development of international law, but explained by means of the idea of construction through re-construction.[6] The added value of this explanation lies in that it helps to unpack the complex value-chains of international legal production,[7] while it also highlights the vital role of change in the endurance of the system over time. The Commission is a key player in this kind of norm-production dynamics that have been able to achieve a delicate balance between stability and change,[8] thus allowing for a successful evolution of international law, despite its decentralized architecture.

However, when changes *of* the system are concerned, the risk of destabilization is acute. Here, we are not in the presence of evolving contents, but of moving structures. Thus, the issue is not about international law dealing with the protection of the atmosphere[9] or crimes against humanity,[10] but about the ways in which these and other issues are dealt with. These changes entail the questions of whether the factory of international law

4 Ibid Article 8.

5 Christian Tomuschat, "The International Law Commission – An Outdated Institution" (2006) 49 GYIL 77.

6 This passage owes much to Wouter Werner, 'Restating Restatements: Repetition in the ILC Report on the Identification of Customary Law' (unpublished paper, on file with the author).

7 The ILC member Sean Murphy has previously resorted to the 'factory' metaphorical structure to describe the work of the Commission, see Sean D. Murphy, 'Codification, Progressive Development, or Scholarly Analysis? The Art of Packaging the ILC's Work Product' in Maurizio Ragazzi (ed), *The Responsibility of International Organizations: Essays in Memory of Sir Ian Brownlie* (Martinus Nijhoff 2013) 29.

8 The topic of "treaties over time", as initially proposed by Georg Nolte, is framed in precisely those terms in relation to treaties, see ILC, 'Report of the International Law Commission on the work of its sixtieth session' [2008] II(2) ILC Ybk 1, 365–384.

9 ILC, 'Report of the International Law Commission on the work of its seventieth session' (2018) UN Doc A/73/10, 157–200.

10 ILC, 'Report of the International Commission on the work of its Sixty-ninth Session' (2017) UN Doc A/72/10, 9–127.

operates differently today, and whether the shifts in operation are transforming the factory into a site of variegated and innovative global norm production.

Whereas the role of the Commission regarding changes in the system is undisputed, its capacity to deal with changes of the international legal order cannot be taken for granted. One might even say that the same circumstances that make this organ so privileged in the former case are the ones which put its adaptive aptitude to changing structures under strain. Its place within the United Nations, its State-focused work and its rather formalistic working methods[11] make us think of the Commission as quite an orthodox institution,[12] which would resist rather than face change.

In this chapter, I argue that the perception of a deficient capacity of the Commission to cope with the changing structures of the international legal system is not accurate.[13] A way of showing this is by recalling another 'crisis' that the Commission has faced in the past. An underlying preoccupation about the Commission's impact has been its decreasing role in the codification of international law. But the nostalgia about the Commission's "golden age",[14] when it used to draft great codification projects that resulted in hallmark multilateral

---

11 See the contribution of Danae Azaria in Section 4 of this book.

12 In this sense, see Matthias Forteau, 'Comparative International Law Within, Not Against, International Law' in Anthea Roberts et al (eds.), *Comparative International Law* (OUP 2018) 161 at 166; and Georg Nolte, 'The International Law Commission and Community Interests' in Eyal Benvenisti and Georg Nolte (eds), *Community Interests Across International Law* (OUP 2018) 101 at 117.

13 Understanding a set of norms in terms of a system means that those norms are not unconnected, but tied through a relationship. In other words, it means that explaining a set of norms *plus* a relationship (which can be very complex, indeed) is a mental representation of a legal order as a system that provides the criteria for the identification and unity of that order. It is, in this sense, that I use the notions 'legal order' and 'legal system' interchangeably. In doing this, I am highlighting the systemic understanding of the international legal order. On this, see Ricardo Caracciolo, 'Sistema Jurídico' in Ernesto Garzón Valdés and Francisco J. Laporta, *El Derecho y la Justicia* (Trotta, 2nd edition, 2000) 161; id., 'Rechtsordnung, System und Voraussagen des Rechts' in Ernesto Garzón Valdés and Eugenio Bulygin, *Argentinische Rechtstheorie und Rechtsphilosophie heute* (Duncker & Humboldt 1987) 117.

14 This was very present in the ILC's sixtieth anniversary, and already during the fiftieth session; see ILC, 'Report of the International Law Commission on the work of its sixtieth session' [2008] II(2) ILC Ybk 1, 348–350 (referring to the commemoration of the sixtieth anniversary of the Commission and the following meeting with legal advisers of member states under the theme *The International Law Commission: Sixty Years...And Now?*); and the various contributions in *The International Law Commission Fifty Years After: An Evaluation* (United Nations 2000).

treaties, some arguably even of "world order",[15] actually reveals the adaptability of the Commission's work to changing circumstances. Commission members and others have mentioned this on the occasion of past anniversaries of the International Law Commission and elsewhere.[16] While they acknowledged the fading scope of possible topics to be codified, given what the Commission had already covered by 1997 or 2007, they also asserted that this should not be regretted because there is still much to be clarified with regard to the basic rules of general international law.[17]

Indeed, what may be perceived as the vanishing importance of the Commission actually shows its resilience, i.e. the Commission's ability to cope with the changing structures of international law. As mentioned by Georg Nolte, there is a need to "reaffirm and continue developing the general rules of the game".[18] I would add that this continued requirement is driven today by moves that threaten to change the game altogether. Thus, this necessity is not only and not even primarily about elucidating the meaning and scope of legal concepts (such as permissible reservations and interpretive declarations to treaties),[19] but about facing the means of production which seem to stem from a different site than the factory of international law.

In the following section, I will refer to these new normative products or "trends", to use Neil Walker's eloquent description.[20] It is important to clarify, however, that I do not think that it is for the Commission to codify and progressively develop these trends. This is what I mean in alluding to the lyrics of David Bowie's 1971 "Changes": not tracing, but facing change. The way that these trends can be faced by the Commission may be described as the fine-tuning of the rules of the game so that these can respond to a changing and uncertain normative environment.

---

15 See Christian Tomuschat, 'Obligations Arising for States Without or Against Their Will' (1993) 241 RdC 269.

16 See Vaughan Lowe, 'Future Topics and Problems of the International Legislative Process – Presentation by Vaughan Lowe' in *The International Law Commission Fifty Years After: An Evaluation* (United Nations 2000) 122–137; Christian Tomuschat, 'The International Law Commission – An Outdated Institution?' (2006) 49 GYIL 77; Georg Nolte, 'The International Law Commission Facing the Second Decade of the Twenty-First Century' in Ulrich Fastenrath et al (eds), *From Bilateralism to Community Interests: Essays in Honour of Judge Bruno Simma* (OUP 2011) 781 at 789–792.

17 Ibid.

18 Nolte (n 16) 792.

19 See ILC, 'Guide to practice on reservations to treaties' [2011] II(3) ILC Ybk 26–38.

20 Neil Walker, *Intimations of Global Law* (CUP 2015) 166–169.

In the third section, I will show this fine-tuning by resorting to the work of the Commission on "Fragmentation of international law: difficulties arising from the diversification and expansion of international law",[21] and to the conclusions on subsequent agreements and practice in relation to interpretation of treaties.[22] While the former represents a watershed in the Commission's work, facing for the first time and comprehensively the structural transformations of international law, the latter provides endogenous means from the law of treaties to cope with trends that cannot easily be accommodated within the usual means of international law production.

In the fourth and concluding section, I will come back to the notion of the Commission's and international law's resilience. It will then become clear, I hope, that this resilience is not about grasping at straws, nor an academic obsession with international law's purity, but a rather fundamental struggle for the political ideas that inform the rule of law at the international level.

II A Bit on 'Trend-spotting'

International legal scholarship has been dealing with international law's profound transformations for quite some time now, approaching them through different lenses. Writings on global administrative law (GAL),[23] informal international law-making (IN-Law),[24] the interplay between formality and informality,[25] transnational legal orders,[26] the decay of State consent,[27] global legal pluralism,[28]

---

21 ILC, 'Fragmentation of international law: difficulties arising from the diversification and expansion of International Law' [2006] II(2) ILC Ybk 175; see also 'Fragmentation of international law: difficulties arising from the diversification and expansion of international law - Report of the Study Group of the International Law Commission' (2006) UN Doc A/CN.4/L.682 (hereinafter, "Report of the Study Group on Fragmentation").

22 ILC (n 9) 11–116.

23 See Benedict Kingsbury, Nico Krisch and Richard B. Stewart, 'The Emergence of Global Administrative Law' (2005) 68 Law&ContempProbs 15.

24 See Joost Pauwelyn et al (eds), *Informal International Lawmaking* (OUP 2012).

25 See Alejandro Rodiles, *Coalitions of the Willing and International Law – The Interplay between Formality and Informality* (CUP 2018).

26 See Terence C. Halliday and Gregory Shaffer (eds), *Transnational Legal Orders* (CUP 2015).

27 See Nico Krisch, 'The Decay of Consent: International Law in an Age of Global Public Goods' (2014) 108 AJIL 1.

28 See Paul Schiff Berman, *Global Legal Pluralism – A Jurisprudence of Law Beyond Borders* (CUP 2012).

and global law more broadly,[29] are all motivated by the growing perception among scholars of the changing structures of international law. Even the question retaken by Anthea Roberts of whether international law is international, and the broader comparative international law project of which Roberts' book is a part,[30] are closely interlinked with the issue of the structural transformations of the international legal order. In the end, an emphasis on observing and acknowledging how international law functions differently in different places cannot but affect the classical post-war conception (or aspiration) of international law *qua* universal legal system.[31]

The possible objection, consisting in that these approaches and observations are of a predominantly academic nature, should be addressed here. This is so since the Commission is, for very good reasons, perceived as a practice-oriented body and not an academic institution. But these observations are made with regard to new practices of what is going on out there when States, alone or in concert with other actors, address climate change, migration, or international security issues like terrorism, piracy, weapons of mass destruction, or cyber attacks. As I have argued elsewhere,[32] it would be quite anachronistic to teach today a course on the law of the sea without engaging with coalitions of the willing like the Proliferation Security Initiative (PSI), or on international environmental law without paying due regard to the several players (from the private sector to cities) involved in "the transnational regime complex for climate change".[33] So, it would be problematic, if not self-defeating, for international lawyers, including for the Commission, to ignore these trends.

The normative products that result from the new practices are manifold and do not easily fit within the classical sources of international law,[34] i.e. with those principles and rules identified in the Statute of the International Court of Justice.[35] Best practices, indicators, standards, recommendations, and

29 See Anne-Marie Slaughter, 'Filling Power Vacuums in the New Global Legal Order' (2013) 54 BCLRev 919; for a comprehensive and distanced analysis, see Walker (n 20).

30 See Anthea Roberts, *Is International Law International?* (OUP 2017); Anthea Roberts et al (eds) (n 12). The importance of this question was previously emphasized by Martti Koskenniemi, 'The Case for Comparative International Law' (2009) 20 FinnishYBIL 1.

31 See also Forteau (n 12).

32 See Rodiles (n 25) p. 252.

33 Kenneth Abbott, 'Strengthening the transnational regime complex for climate change' (2014) 3 *Transnational Environmental Law* 57.

34 See Benedict Kingsbury, 'The Concept of 'Law' in Global Administrative Law' (2009) 20 EJIL 23.

35 See Article 38 of the Statute of the International Court of Justice.

pledges are the types of global normative trends most commonly known, but this list is only indicative of the burgeoning tendency to regulate and coordinate behavior through unorthodox ruling devices. What these products have in common is that they are non-legally binding. But it is important to underline that they are not just policies. No matter how much those products claim not to produce legal obligations, they are at least directing behaviour in the global realm. More often than usually acknowledged, they are attached to legal norms and processes in an intense and mutually defining interplay.[36]

It is true that a crucial factor spurring these normative trends is the prominent role of non-state actors in the various fields of global governance. Just think of the impact of the self-regulatory practices of Facebook, Google, and Twitter on content moderation,[37] internet governance more broadly, and what all of this actually means for public law issues on the global scale, like freedom of expression, data protection, security, and democracy indeed.[38] Subnational entities, mostly cities, are today undisputable global actors on topics such as climate change, security, and human rights, and their role in the most ambitious United Nations programme, i.e., the 2030 Sustainable Development Agenda,[39] is literally ubiquitous, going clearly beyond Sustainable Development Goal 11 which expressly deals with safe, resilient, and sustainable cities.[40] These evolutions have led one to posit the question on the possible character of cities as new (old) subjects of international law,[41] a question that has been taken up as one of the objectives of the new study group on "The role of cities in international law" of the International Law Association (ILA).[42]

Given that the Commission is a creature of the United Nations General Assembly and that its main audience is that of United Nations Member States, one may be inclined to think that the Commission is not the proper organ to assess what these other global actors do. That is already a problematic assumption in itself. However, the bigger problem is to think that the conduct

36 See Rodiles (n 25).

37 See, for instance, Facebook Community Standards, <https://www.facebook.com/communitystandards//> (as of 18 February 2019).

38 See Eyal Benvenisti, 'EJIL Foreword: Upholding Democracy Amid the Challenges of New Technology: What Role for the Law of Global Governance' (2018) 29 EJIL 9.

39 UNGA Res 70/1 (21 October 2015).

40 See the various contributions in Helmut Philipp Aust and Anél du Plessis (eds), *The Globalisation of Urban Governance – Legal Perspectives on Sustainable Development Goal 11* (Routledge 2019).

41 Particularly illustrative on this, see Helmut Philipp Aust, *Das Recht der globalen Stadt* (Mohr Siebeck 2017), 141–194.

42 See <http://www.ila-hq.org/index.php/study-groups>.

of States does not contribute to the new normative trends, or, in other words, that the structural changes of international law are solely spurred by non-state actors and subnational entities. States are themselves behaving in unorthodox ways when it comes to global action and regulation. There is now a well-settled inclination of these traditional subjects of international law to gather in informal coalitions of the willing and to coordinate actions and decision-making through networks, often circumventing classical international organizations, and law-making.[43] These alternative forms of cooperation frequently serve to shape the work of intergovernmental organizations, through orchestration tactics performed by a few member States of the latter that participate in the former.[44] 'Participating States parties' is an emerging category of this interplay between informal coalitions and formal international organizations. Note, for instance, the case in which participating States to a coalition agree to provisionally apply amendments to a treaty of which they are parties, and which have not entered into force.[45] It is difficult not to think here of the current work of the Commission on provisional application of treaties, led by the Special Rapporteur Juan Manuel Gómez Robledo,[46] and of the utility of fine-tuning article 25 of the Vienna Convention on the Law of Treaties[47] vis-à-vis these evolutions.

The interplay between formality and informality that States entertain also affects the evolution of other international legal obligations like United Nations Security Council resolutions. The design and implementation of the United Nations sanctions today cannot be understood without studying what States do, not only in the Security Council and within their national jurisdictions, but also as participants in a selective club like the Financial Action Task Force.[48] This interplay eventually leads to a contemporary reading of traditional concepts of treaty law, especially subsequent practice and agreements, in their recognized *mutatis mutandis* application to Security Council resolutions.[49]

43 See Rodiles (n 25).

44 Ibid 202–209.

45 This has been the case, e.g., of the participating States of the Nuclear Security Summit which are parties to the Convention on Physical Protection of Nuclear Material, see ibid 192–193.

46 ILC (n 9) 201–223.

47 Vienna Convention on the Law of Treaties, adopted 23 May 1969, entered into force 27 January 1980, 1155 UNTS 331.

48 See Alejandro Rodiles, 'The Design of UN Sanctions through the Interplay with Informal Arrangements' in Larissa van den Herik (ed), *Research Handbook on UN Sanctions and International Law* (Edward Elgar 2017) 177–193.

49 See *Accordance with International Law of the Unilateral Declaration of Independence in Respect of Kosovo* (Advisory Opinion) [2010] ICJ Rep 403; see also Michael Wood, 'The

The above-mentioned examples are but a snapshot of the many new global normative trends. These examples show, nonetheless, why international lawyers need to – and do – engage in "trend-spotting"[50] more and more often, borrowing again from Neil Walker. In the ensuing pages, I will argue that today the Commission may have one of its most important impacts by explaining the new normative global trends from within the international legal system. This means that these normative trends, however at odds they may are with classical international law, its doctrine of sources, and its formal rationality indeed, have to be taken very seriously by the people and institutions that devote their work to international law as we know it.

In my view, however, it is not the task of the Commission to identify such new normative trends in the sense of declaring whether certain informal norms should be considered as part of international law (whether there is something as IN-law,[51] for instance), thus broadening the sources and the concept of international law. This would push the Commission to its institutional limits and put its legitimacy in jeopardy.

III The Role of the Commission in Facing the Strange

The Commission cannot afford to ignore new and unorthodox normative trends if it wants to retain its relevance in the contemporary global legal landscape. However, it is not the Commission's custom to explicitly address these trends in the sense of codifying and progressively develop them; nor should this be the case. Instead, the way of dealing with new, alien products consists in the identification, explanation, and elaboration of the existing tools of the system, which will then help to assess these extra-systemic normative devices as they operate in connection with international law.

Analytically, this means that the kind of work of the Commission that is most likely to unfold a significant impact today is the one that is systemic in nature, concerning secondary and not primary rules. From the point of view of the Commission's professional ethic, this requires a self-comprehension that is conscious of its institutional constraints, respectful of its historical purpose, while being increasingly sensitive to context. In this section, I will refer to the

Interpretation of Security Council Resolutions' (1998) 2 MaxPlanckUNYB 73; see also Michael Wood, 'The Interpretation of Security Council Resolutions, Revisited' (2017) 20 MaxPlanckUNYB Online 1.

50 Walker (n 20) 159–161.

51 See Pauwelyn et al (n 24).

role of the Commission in elaborating on "the general rules of the game"[52] in the face of big transformations. Since the professional ethic of the Commission is strictly related to the struggle for the international rule of law, I will return to it in the concluding remarks.

The work of the Study Group on the "Fragmentation of international law" constitutes a watershed in the work of the Commission, which faced for the first time straightforwardly international law's structural transformations and signalled to a great extent the way ahead. It is true that its focus on the diversification of international legal regimes and the collision and harmonization of norms from within international law represent, *prima facie*, an analysis of major changes in the system – provided that the different fields of international law are part of a single and unified legal order, which was a major question back in the beginning of the millennium when the Commission decided to include the topic "risks ensuing from fragmentation of international law" on its long-term programme of work, based on the feasibility and already very illustrative study presented by Gerhard Hafner.[53]

Nonetheless, in dealing explicitly with the systemic question par excellence, namely with the nature of "international law as a legal system",[54] it sets the basis for understanding the interactions within and across normative complexes. Such complexes involve not only recognized legal regimes but also flexible, emerging and informal frameworks, i.e. the new global regulatory trends that present the most serious challenge to the coherence of the international legal order. This becomes clear in the report of the Study Group finalized by Martti Koskenniemi:

> A discussion of the extent to which new types of "global law" might be emerging outside the scope of traditional, State-centric international law would require a different type of exercise. This is not to say, however, that the Vienna Convention or indeed international law could not be used so as to channel and control these patterns of informal, often private interest-drawn types of regulation as well. The more complex and flexible the ways in which treaty law allows the use of framework treaties, of clusters of treaties and regimes consisting of many types of normative materials, the more such decentralized, private regulation may be grasped within the scope of international law.[55]

52 See Nolte (n 16) 792.
53 ILC, 'Report on the Work of its Fifty-Second Session' [2000] II (2) ILC Ybk 2.
54 See the Conclusions of the work of the Study Group (n 21) 177–178.
55 See Report of the Study Group on Fragmentation (n 21) 248.

This paragraph reflects the need for international lawyers to engage with normative trends from outside the system, "the new types of 'global law'", which may derive from private actors, public-private partnerships, "or other types of informal regulation of transnational activities",[56] like the trends discussed in the previous section of this chapter. The request to take these trends seriously is addressed to the Commission itself, since it figures in the section on "The perspective of this Study",[57] which is framed as suggestions for the Commission to deal with "[t]he whole complex of inter-regime relations [which] is presently a legal black hole".[58] Importantly, it makes clear that this engagement should not be a sort of trend-spotting. Instead, it should be about applying the existing tools of international law (i.e. the 1969 Vienna Convention on the Law of Treaties and general international law) to these trends in order to understand "their effects on traditional law-making".[59]

In light of the context of the section in which this paragraph figures and of the whole report indeed, it also becomes clear that the need to face these trends is most acute in regard to the interactions they entertain with traditional international law, public and private, within and across international and transnational regime complexes. This reflects, in my view, an early warning of the risks that result from the enmeshment of traditional and non-traditional normative clusters. Such enmeshment jeopardizes the coherence and certainty aspirations of international law *qua* legal system. As Koskenniemi developed in his academic writings on the deformalization of international law, such a development undermines the idea that the "world can – or should – be governed through a single international law".[60]

According to the Study Group's report, the tools of international law which serve to understand and ultimately "channel and control these patterns of informal [...] regulation"[61] are secondary rules, coming mainly from the law of treaties as well as from general international law. In this sense, it can be said that this report picks up and builds upon the calls that were made on the occasion of the fiftieth and sixtieth anniversaries of the Commission, which were quite clear on the need to concentrate on the systemic components of international law, i.e. on the "general rules of the game".[62] The report finalized

---

56 Ibid.

57 Ibid paras 245ff.

58 Ibid 253.

59 Ibid 248.

60 Most clearly on this, see Martti Koskenniemi, 'Global Governance and Public International Law' (2004) 37 *Kritische Justiz* 241, 243.

61 See Report of the Study Group on Fragmentation (n 21) 248.

62 See Nolte (n 16) 792.

by Koskenniemi makes no bones out of this: "there is a limit to what can be obtained in terms of codification and progressive development of universal rules".[63]

Given the object of this study, the specific norms that are commented and elaborated on are collision rules as those known from private international law. Actually, one of the main proposals is to understand and use the Vienna Convention on the Law of Treaties "as a basis of an 'international law of conflicts' ".[64] Similarly, those 'general principles as recognized by civilized nations' that are drawn upon, i.e. *lex specialis, lex prior, lex posterior*,[65] serve the main function of overcoming collisions of rules that stem from the different and increasingly specialized fields of international law.

It must be clarified that contrary to the articles on the responsibility of States for internationally wrongful acts,[66] which identify, develop, and systematize secondary rules on attribution, legal consequences, exceptions, invocation, etc., the Report of the Study Group on Fragmentation does not codify and progressively develop, but comments and elaborates on already well-established secondary rules of change,[67] like those on interpretation of, derogation from, and suspension of rules of international law. Hence, the report of the Fragmentation Study Group suggests to the Commission a turn to restatements of international law:

> Thus, it is proposed that the Commission should increasingly look for the avenue of "restatement" of general international law in forms other than codification and progressive development – not as a substitute but as supplement to the latter.[68]

---

63 See Report of the Study Group on Fragmentation (n 21) 256.

64 Ibid 250. Here, the influence of Gunther Teubner and Andreas Fischer-Lescano is quite clear; see Andreas Fischer-Lescano and Gunther Teubner, *Regime-Kollisionen* (Suhrkamp 2006).

65 These principles are derived from the medieval *glossae* of the Code of Justinian made by the Bologna school in the twelfth and thirteenth centuries. Back then, they already served as collision-rules in a highly pluralistic legal environment. They have become part of the general principles of several national legal systems across the globe, especially in those influenced by the Roman-German-Canonical legal tradition; see Harold J. Berman, *Law and Revolution: The Formation of the Western Legal Tradition* (Harvard University Press, 1983); see also Rolando Tamayo Y Salmorán, *La Ciencia del Derecho y la Formación del Ideal Político* (UNAM 1989).

66 ILC, 'Draft articles on responsibility of States for internationally wrongful acts' [2001] II(2) ILC Ybk 26.

67 See H.L.A. Hart, *The Concept of Law* (Clarendon Press/OUP 1994) 95–96.

68 See Report of the Study Group on Fragmentation (n 21) 256.

Since then, it can fairly be said that repetition and explanation have become recurrent activities of the Commission,[69] such as the completed work on subsequent agreements and subsequent practice in relation to the interpretation of treaties[70] and the identification of customary international law,[71] and the ongoing study on provisional application of treaties[72] demonstrate. This tendency is quite inevitable, and contrary to what some may think, it is well-suited for dealing with a changing normative environment.

Indeed, a good example of a recent Commission's restatement that faces structural changes in the way outlined in the report of the Study Group on fragmentation is the work on subsequent practice and agreements. The conclusions on this topic and their commentaries can help explain much of what is going on out there in terms of normative evolutions that are not strictly part of classical international law, but that are tied to international legal materials, especially treaties (bilateral and multilateral), and other normative instruments such as United Nations Security Council resolutions.[73]

Let us take, for instance, the proliferation of 'best practices', as identified and developed by, *inter alia*, expert treaty bodies in relation to the implementation of treaties, and how these informal norms, as well as other trends, like typologies and indicators, can spur the practice of States parties in the application of a treaty norm. The potentially relevant role of the former in treaty interpretation is something which becomes much clearer in light of the Commission's clarification and contextualization of the meaning and scope of article 31, paragraph 3 (b) of the Vienna Convention on the Law of Treaties. To be clear, the technocratic trend in the management of multilateral treaties through best practices and other informal norms is not spotted by the Commission in the conclusions of this topic. The latter constrain themselves to identifying, recalling, and fine-tuning the tools offered by positive international law in order to face the new trends of treaty-management from within the law of treaties. Thus, we are not in presence of a sort of surrender to "expert rule",[74] quite to the contrary: the work of the Commission on

69 In this sense, although grounding it on different theoretical frameworks and taking different positions, see: Matthias Forteau, 'Comparative International Law Within, Not Against, International Law' in Anthea Roberts (n 12) 161 at 166; and Werner (n 6).

70 ILC (n 9) 11–116.

71 ILC (n 9) 117–156.

72 ILC (n 9) 201–223.

73 See n 49 and accompanying text.

74 David Kennedy, 'Challenging Expert Rule: The Politics of Global Governance' (2005) 27 SydneyLR 1.

subsequent agreements and practice can be described as making clear(er) what the legal conditions are for best practices, indicators, and typologies to become relevant in the interpretation of treaties and their evolution over time. The agreement, i.e. the common understanding of the parties to the treaty, concerning the normative content that may or may not result from the practice in its application, is unambiguously emphasized in draft conclusion 10 as a *sine qua non* condition for any authentic interpretation to arise.[75] In case this condition of a common understanding regarding the interpretation is not met, the practice based on these non-binding trends may still play a role, but only as a subsidiary means of interpretation according to article 32 Vienna Convention of the Law of Treaties (draft conclusion 4.3).[76] Best practices and the like may not necessarily spur future developments, but they can also serve an evidentiary role regarding existing subsequent practice ("assessing such practices",[77] in the words of the Commission). The commentaries to the conclusions elucidate this possible role of guidelines or handbooks of international organizations and agencies.[78]

Laurence Boisson de Chauzournes argues that best practices and other "major trends" form part of what she calls "family practices", that is the kinds and species of conduct, traditional and non-traditional, State-centred or not, that "have legal relevance under today's treaties".[79] Understanding how those practices function and become relevant for the life of treaties, i.e., for their interpretation, application, and evolution, requires the sort of 'contextual sensitivity' highlighted in the report of the Study Group on fragmentation,[80] which in this case "embeds subsequent practice in its proximate operative milieu".[81] Thereby, the wide-open texture of the concept of 'practice' in international law is also acknowledged. Accordingly, there is a complex interplay among many species of practices that relate to a given treaty norm, and that can only be ignored at the peril of reducing the role of subsequent practice as a means of interpretation to its minimalist expression, something which could have very little to do, in the end, with the actual meaning, scope, and efficacy of the treaty norm. Such a minimalist version would waste the great potential of the rules

75 ILC (n 9) 75–77.
76 Ibid 33.
77 Ibid 40.
78 Ibid 40–41.
79 Laurence Boisson de Chazournes, '"Subsequent Practice", and "Family-Resemblance": Towards Embedding Subsequent Practice in its Operative Milieu' in Georg Nolte (ed), *Treaties and Subsequent Practice* (OUP 2013) 53, 55 and 62.
80 See Report of the Study Group on Fragmentation (n 21) 248–250.
81 See Boisson de Chazournes (n 79) 62.

of the Vienna Convention on the Law of Treaties to comprehend increasingly complex treaty regimes.[82]

The restatements of the Commission, like that on subsequent agreements and practice, remind us and clarify the potential of existing rules, fulfilling thus also an important pedagogical function in regard to the confusions caused by the shifting normative environment.[83] This pedagogical function is widely accepted because of the legitimacy that the Commission enjoys. However, it should not be overstretched. Actually, its strength also resides in recognizing that in certain cases it can only provide the legal frames of reference for ongoing debates about unclear normative developments. The Paris Agreement on Climate Change may serve to explain this.[84] The innovative architecture of this treaty, which imported several governance techniques,[85] has become a puzzle for international lawyers in many respects. Suffice it here to briefly refer to the national determined contributions (NDCs). Scholars have classified them as unilateral declarations,[86] but their non-binding nature makes this rather doubtful. More convincing is the attempt to explain them as a potential case of subsequent practice.[87] Indeed, every party is to communicate in its NDC how it intends to apply the treaty. The problem is that the common understanding which is required to emerge from such eventual practice, as expressed in the words the "agreement of the parties regarding its interpretation" in article 31, paragraph 3(a) of the Vienna Convention on the Law of Treaties, is extremely unlikely to arise through this highly decentralized implementation design.[88]

In my view, the Paris Agreement is designed to foreclose any common understanding regarding its interpretation, precisely because that is part of the *quo* for having a nominally legal instrument. If my argument is correct, it shows that subsequent practice cannot be restated so as to explain what is not

82 See also Nele Matz-Lück, 'Norm Interpretation Across International Regimes: Competences and Legitimacy' in Margaret A. Young (ed), *Regime Interaction in International Law: Facing Fragmentation* (CUP 2012) 201–234.

83 On this "educational function" of restatements, see also Werner (n 6).

84 Paris Agreement, adopted 12 December 2015, entered into force 4 November 2016, UNTS registration no 54113.

85 See, e.g., Charles F. Sabel and David G. Victor, 'Making the Paris Process more Effective: A New Approach to Policy Coordination on Global Climate Change', *Policy Analysis Brief* (The Stanley Foundation, February 2016).

86 See Jorge E. Viñuales, 'The Paris Agreement: An Initial Examination (Part II of III)' (EJIL: Talk!, 8 February 2016) <https://www.ejiltalk.org/the-paris-climate-agreement-an-initial-examination-part-ii-of-iii/>.

87 See Annalisa Savaresi, 'The Paris Agreement: A Rejoinder' (EJIL: Talk!, 16 February 2016) <https://www.ejiltalk.org/the-paris-agreement-a-rejoinder/>.

88 See Rodiles (n 25) 201–202.

within the reach of article 31, paragraph 3 (b) of the Vienna Convention on the Law of Treaties, and, in doing this, it also shows that the NDCs remain a puzzle for the law of treaties as we know it. But as my argument is but an argument, it also illustrates, that the restatement performed by the Commission recasts the attention to a very useful frame of reference, enabling it to function "as part of an ongoing, future-oriented discussion".[89]

IV Conclusion

The current and future impact of the Commission should be assessed in light of the structural transformations that international law as a legal system is going through, i.e. the changes of, not in, the system. The challenge for the Commission should not be underestimated: if it wants to retain a meaningful role, it has to face these changes. Ignoring them comes at the peril of shrinking its significance and influence concerning the manifold ways the world is being ruled today. At the same time, however, the Commission is not well-suited for adventures. Being a fundamental institution of the system, its strength lies in the privileged position it has within that system, the knowledge it has acquired of its sources and institutions, the assistance it receives from the United Nations Office of Legal Affairs, and the mixture of scholarly expertise, regional representation, and diplomatic experience that exists nowhere else. An essential component of this strength is the legitimacy that the Commission enjoys, precisely because it is a key part of the system. The Commission has to remain faithful to its principal audience, and the expectations that States place in it, the most important one arguably being the defence of the classical post-war international legal system, which it has helped to build over seven decades.

But this defence should not be understood as being for the sake of this legal order's integrity only. There are very strong meta-systemic reasons for defending international law as a legal system, reasons which are based on the political ideas that inform the rule of law at the international level. These have to do with the control of sheer power, the containment, to some extent, of asymmetries in international relations, and the construction of possibilities for the less powerful to articulate their views and demands. The new global normative trends challenge the conception of international law as a legal system, because they are not easily, if at all, traceable to a valid a source of law, and they are not usually, if ever, made according to the means (i.e. formal processes) that international law recognizes

89 Werner (n 6).

with the "authoritative mark" that unifies the international legal system.[90] If one translates these challenges for the systemic understanding of international law into threats to the political ideal of the international rule of law, it means, quite simply, that the new ruling devices of global governance are not transparent: it is not always clear who makes them; they foreclose predictability, since they do not claim to impose legal obligations but are highly efficient ruling devices; and they do not aspire to equal participation, because they circumvent State consent through international clubs, transnational networks, and global coalitions.[91]

That is, in my view, the reason why the report of the Study Group on Fragmentation is clear about the need "to channel and control these patterns of informal [...] regulation".[92] The International Law Commission faces the dilemma of finding ways of ensuring that its work retains a meaningful impact in the complex global environment of fragmentation, governance, and informality, while remaining faithful to its mandate, expertise, and the expectations placed on it by the international community; expectations which come quite close to a conception of the Commission as "the priesthood of international legal formalism".[93]

Matthias Forteau's careful argument in relation to the role of the Commission with regard to the project on comparative international law (CIL) is revealing.[94] CIL can be explained as a major project aimed at studying the similarities and differences in the ways that international law is approached and functions in different places.[95] It postulates that this, in principle, universal body of law may actually be about many particular versions of it. In a way, the project is another global normative trend since it takes the premise seriously that in an increasingly complex world characterized by non-polarity and a highly unstable political environment, international law is more prone to diversity than ever before. For Forteau, in the end, the Commission's work is a case in point for how developments that are not easily captured, conceptually

---

90 See Hart (n 67) 95.

91 On the meta-systemic value of the conception of the international legal system, see also Eyal Benvenisti, 'The Conception of International Law as a Legal System' (2007) 50 GYIL 393.

92 See Report of the Study Group on Fragmentation, (n 21) 248.

93 Forteau (n 12) 166 (quoting Kristen David Adams, 'Blaming the Mirror: The Restatement and the Common Law' (2007) 40 Indiana LR 205, 244, who describes in this vein the American Law Institute's Restatements on US law; Forteau says that the same can be said of the ILC's work in relation to international law).

94 Ibid.

95 Anthea Roberts et al, 'Conceptualizing Comparative International Law' in Anthea Roberts et al (eds) (n 12) 3–31.

and operationally, as part of classical international law, may nonetheless be addressed – and resorted to – from "within international law (thus avoiding undermining it) in the process of establishing what international is or should be".[96] The diplomatic sensitivities of the Commission and the support provided to it by the United Nations Secretariat makes the former particularly attentive to the many State practices, the identification of similarities and differences, and the careful conclusions that can be drawn from this convergence in diversity in terms of the status of international law on any given issue area. Accordingly, the Commission has learned to use " 'accommodating' tools which permit common agreement on the drafting of an international rule while simultaneously preserving diversity".[97] This explains, for instance, the resort to more flexible normative outcomes of the Commission,[98] which are hence not to be viewed as a sign of its weakness (the lament of the glorious past expressed in the grand codification projects), but as a show of the skills it has developed in order to cope with drastic change.

One of the most efficient means for the Commission to face these changes from within the system is by resorting to restatements of the law, in particular of secondary, that is systemic, rules.[99] The report of the Study Group on fragmentation quite explicitly signals this working method as the way ahead,[100] and recent outcomes of the Commission's work confirm this tendency.

In particular, the conclusions on subsequent agreements and practice and their commentaries show that it is possible to analytically and normatively intervene in the interstices where international legal and global non-legal materials converge by exclusively relying on the existing tools of the system, the rules of the game. The Report of the Study Group on Fragmentation paved this way by making visible the built-in-flexibility of international law as a resilient system, capable of coping with external stress without renouncing its essential qualities and "relative autonomy".[101] One can expect that the major impact of the International Law Commission on the contemporary global legal landscape will increasingly consist in unravelling these capabilities to "turn and face the strange."[102]

96 Forteau, (n 12) 164.

97 Ibid 173.

98 See the contribution of Laurence Boisson de Chazournes in this Section.

99 Forteau also talks about the ILC's contemporary work in terms of restatements, see Forteau (n 12).

100 See Report of the Study Group on Fragmentation (n 21) 256.

101 Jan Klabbers 'The Relative Autonomy of International Law or the Forgotten Politics of Interdisciplinarity' (2004 – 2005) 1 JIntlLIntlRel 35.

102 Bowie (n 1).

The International Law Commission in a Mirror—Forms, Impact and Authority

Laurence Boisson de Chazournes

1 Introduction*

Since the early 19th century, the codification and development of international law have been on the international diplomatic agenda. The Final Act of the Congress of Vienna of 1815, which contains the treaties and declarations negotiated in Vienna, includes several provisions codifying practices in the fields of freedom of navigation on rivers and the precedence of diplomatic agents.[1] This phenomenon continued with nearly a hundred international conferences or congresses that were held until 1914.[2] Following the First World War, attempts were made to systematize the codification and development of international law. By a resolution of 22 September 1924, the Assembly of the League of Nations established a Committee of Experts for the Progressive Codification of International Law to draw up a list of subjects "sufficiently ripe" for codification.[3] Three topics were considered to meet the criterion of ripeness, and as a result, a codification conference was convened in 1930.[4] Despite its meagre results, the conference was seen as an "important milestone on the road to organized and systematic codification".[5]

---

* The author wishes to thank Guillaume Guez for his very helpful assistance in the preparation of this contribution.

1 'Regulations concerning the Relative Rank of Diplomatic Agents of 19 March 1815' and 'Regulations respecting the free navigation on rivers of 29 March 1815' in Georg Friedrich de Martens, *Nouveau Recueil de Traités d'Alliance, de Paix, de Trêve, de Neutralité, de commerce, de limites, d'échange etc. et de plusieurs autres actes servant à la connaissance des relations étrangères des Puissances et États d'Europe* (De Dieterich 1818) 449–50, 434–49.

2 United Nations Secretariat, 'The Progressive Development of International Law' (1947) 41 AJIL Supp. Official Documents 32, 32.

3 League of Nations, 'Resolution adopted by the League of Nations Assembly on 22 September 1924' (1924) League of Nations Official Journal Spec Supp 21, 10.

4 League of Nations, 'Resolution adopted by the League of Nations Assembly on 27 September 1927' (1927) League of Nations Official Journal Spec Supp 53, 9. The three topics were nationality, territorial waters and responsibility of States for damage done in their territory to the person or property of foreigners.

5 Jose Sette-Camara, 'The International Law Commission: Discourse on Method' in Roberto Ago (ed), *International Law at the Time of its Codification: Essays in Honour of Roberto Ago* (Dott. A. Guiffré 1987) 473.

However, and quite surprisingly, the question of codification and progressive development of international law was absent from the early drafts of the Charter of the United Nations. Initially, the Dumbarton Oaks Proposals for a United Nations charter only conferred on the General Assembly the power to "initiate studies and make recommendations for the purpose of promoting international co-operation in political, economic and social fields".[6] Following a Chinese proposal to extend this power "to the development and revision of the rules and principles of international law",[7] States discussed at length the question of the legislative power of the General Assembly. While the idea of turning the General Assembly into a world legislature was finally rejected, there was wide agreement that the General Assembly should be charged with initiating studies and making recommendations on international law. This consensus was enshrined in the Charter of the United Nations in its Article 13, paragraph 1(a).[8] However, there was much discussion about the wording of the provision. For some States, codification alone would be too narrow because it would be limited to putting existing law in writing. On the contrary, for others, adding the word revision would suggest too much change. In the end, the juxtaposition of the words "progressive development" and "codification" was retained. According to Committee II/2, these words would "establish a nice balance between stability and change".[9] The mandate of the General Assembly thus reads as follows: "The General Assembly shall initiate studies and make recommendations for the purpose of [...] encouraging the progressive development of international law and its codification".[10]

To give effect to Article 13, the General Assembly established the Committee on the Progressive Development of International Law and its Codification

6 'Dumbarton Oaks Proposals' Washington Conversations on International Peace and Security Organization (Washington DC 21 August – 7 October 1944) Chapter V (B) at para 6.

7 United Nations Conference on International Organization (UNCIO) (San Francisco 25 April – 26 June 1945) III, 1.

8 For a more detailed account of the legislative history of Article 13, see Carl-August Fleischhauer and Bruno Simma, 'Article 13' in Bruno Simma et al (eds), *The Charter of the United Nations: A Commentary* (3rd edn, OUP 2002) 528–52; Anne-Thida Norodom, 'Article 13, paragraphe 1 (a)' in Jean-Pierre Cot, Mathias Forteau, Alain Pellet (eds), *La Charte des Nations Unies: Commentaire article par article* (3rd edn, Economica, 2005) 701–703.

9 UNCIO (n 7) IX, 179; see also Herbert W Briggs, *The International Law Commission* (Cornell University Press, 1965) 12.

10 Charter of the United Nations, adopted 24 October 1945, 1 UNTS XVI, Article 13 paragraph (1)(a).

(also known as the "Committee of Seventeen"). The latter recommended the establishment of the International Law Commission and prepared a first draft of its statute. By resolution 174 (II) of 21 November 1947, the General Assembly recognized the need for assistance from an international body and approved the statute of the International Law Commission. However, the establishment of the International Law Commission did not exhaust the General Assembly's function in the progressive development and codification of international law. Faced with the emergence of new areas of international law and the need for regulation, it has established other bodies over time. Examples include the United Nations Commission on International Trade Law, the Legal Sub-Committee of the Outer Space Committee or the various ad hoc committees established by the Sixth Committee such as the Ad Hoc Committee on International Terrorism or the Special Committee on the Charter of the United Nations and on the Strengthening of the Role of the Organization. In this context of multiple "law-making" bodies, the International Law Commission has retained its pre-eminent status.

In its 70 years of existence, the Commission has accomplished sterling work in many respects. Much of its output is considered to be the cornerstone of the contemporary international legal order. It is only necessary to refer to the 1969 Vienna Convention on the Law of Treaties[11] or the articles on responsibility of States for internationally wrongful acts.[12] However, this positive note should not distract attention from the challenges facing the Commission. Among these, the end of the "golden era" of codification,[13] and the phenomenon of treaty fatigue call into question the relatively comfortable position of the International Law Commission. Questions arise: Is the progressive reduction in the number of conventions adopted as a result of the Commission's work a sign of its decline? Is the increasing diversity of instruments used by the Commission a problem in terms of impact?

To answer these questions, this contribution will first deal with the diversity of forms of the final products and the questions this diversity raises in terms of legal effects (II.). Once this framework for analyzing the Commission's work has been established, its various impacts will be examined (III.). The present contribution will then focus on the users of the Commission's work (IV.), and will also shed light on its authority (V.).

---

11 Adopted 23 May 1969, entered into force 27 January 1980, 1155 UNTS 331.

12 UNGA Res 56/83 (12 December 2001), annex.

13 Patricia Galvao Teles, 'The work of the International Law Commission in the Present Quinquennium (2012–2016) and Possible Future Topics: How to Remain Relevant in the 21st Century' (2014) ABDI 215, 215.

II The Commission's Final Products in Their Diversity

Despite the Commission's early practice marked by a plurality of outputs, it has long been believed that its work should lead to conventions. Yet, the statute never envisaged that this would be the only outcome (A). The diversity of final products raises the question of assessing their impact. Should we consider that in the many cases where the Commission's work has not resulted in the adoption of a convention, they have little or no impact? The answer to this question involves addressing the issue of the legal effects of non-binding instruments (B).

A *A Diversity of Forms*

When drafting the statute of the International Law Commission, the Committee of Seventeen decided to create separate procedures for 'progressive development' and 'codification' as the tasks "vary in their nature".[14] This distinction was supposed to have some impact on the form of the final product, since in the case of progressive development, only a convention was expected.[15] However, this distinction proved to be unsustainable in practice and "hardly defensible scientifically",[16] which led the International Law Commission to abandon it altogether. Thus, as early as 1953, the Commission stressed in its report on the draft convention on arbitral procedure that the latter contained both elements of codification and progressive development.[17] In the end, this dual working approach was replaced by a "functional hybrid between codification and progressive development but proceeding under the rubric of codification alone".[18] This results in final products adopted by the Commission under the codification procedure, including both elements of codification and progressive development of international law.

14 UNGA Sixth Committee (2nd session) GAOR, Annex 1, 175.

15 Ibid; Statute of the ILC, UNGA Res 174 (II) (21 November 1947) as amended by UNGA Res 485(V) (12 December 1950) article 15 (ILC statute); see Santiago Villalpando, 'Codification Light: A New Trend in the Codification of International Law at the United Nations' (2013) 8 ABDI 117, 125.

16 James Crawford, 'The progressive development of international law: history, theory and practice' in Denis Alland et al (eds), *Unity and Diversity of International Law: Essays in Honour of Professor Pierre-Marie Dupuy* (Martinus Nijhoff 2014) 19 (quoting the then Secretary of the Commission, Yuen-li Liang); Alain Pellet, 'Between Codification and Progressive Development of the law' (2004) 6 International Law FORUM du droit international 15, 15.

17 ILC, 'Report of the International Law Commission on the work of its fifth session' [1953] II ILC Ybk 200, 201–202 at para 15.

18 Crawford (n 16) 19.

Under the codification procedure, the work of the Commission need not necessarily be concluded by conventions. Article 23(1) of the Commission's statute provides for other possibilities such as the publication of a report or the adoption of a resolution by the General Assembly.[19] Over time, the Commission has diversified the forms of its work products. It has adopted "draft conventions" (such as the draft convention on the elimination of future statelessness),[20] "draft articles" (such as the draft articles on responsibility of States for internationally wrongful acts),[21] "draft principles" (such as the draft principles on the allocation of loss in the case of transboundary harm arising out of hazardous activities),[22] "draft guidelines" (such as the guide to practice on reservations to treaties),[23] "reports" (such as the final report of the Study Group on the Most-Favoured-Nation Clause),[24] "model rules" (such as the model rules on arbitral procedure),[25] "draft declarations" (such as the draft declaration on rights and duties of states),[26] "resolutions" (such as the resolution on confined transboundary groundwater)[27] or "conclusions of the work of the Study Group" (such as the conclusions of the Study Group on the Fragmentation of International Law: Difficulties arising from the diversification and expansion of international law).[28]

The choice of form is a good indicator of the Commission's intention regarding the future of a final product. A report or guide is not intended to become a conventional instrument. Another indicator is the type of referral to the General Assembly. In accordance with article 23 of its statute, the Commission may recommend the convening of an international conference to conclude a convention, or simply that the General Assembly take note of the final product.[29]

19 ILC statute, article 23 paragraph 1.

20 ILC, 'Report of the International Law Commission on the work of its sixth session' [1954] II ILC Ybk 140, 143–47.

21 ILC, 'Report of the International Law Commission on the work of its fifty-third session' [2001] II(2) ILC Ybk 1.

22 ILC, [2006] II(2) ILC Ybk 59.

23 ILC, [2011] II(3) ILC Ybk 23.

24 ILC, (2015) UN Doc A/70/10.

25 ILC, [1958] II ILC Ybk 83.

26 ILC, [1949] I ILC Ybk 287.

27 ILC, [1994] II(2) ILC Ybk 135.

28 ILC, [2006] II(2) ILC Ybk 177 at para 251.

29 See for instance, the draft articles on the law of treaties where the International Law Commission recommended the convening of an international conference of plenipotentiaries be convened: ILC, [1966] II ILC Ybk 177 at para 36; see also the draft articles on responsibility of States for internationally wrongful acts where it recommended that the General Assembly take note of the report: ILC, [2001] II(2) ILC Ybk 25 at para 72.

Not all final products of this "wide palette of results"[30] are thus destined to become conventional instruments.[31] Their impacts may vary. Therefore, the focus should not be limited to products that have given rise to conventions; that would ignore much of the Commission's work.

B *Hard and Soft, Soft and Hard: the Law in All Its Forms*

The Commission's impact has long been assessed in the light of the conventions resulting from its work.[32] In the absence of conventions in force, it is argued that the Commission's final products have little or no impact since they are not binding. Behind this prism lies the division between hard law and soft law, or binding law and non-binding law.

To conceive the distinction between binding law and non-binding law in the "Big Bang way"[33] – i.e. that what is not binding has no legal effect[34] – is highly simplistic. Rules can have limited normative value, "either because the instruments containing them are not legally binding, or because the provisions in question, although contained in a binding instrument, do not create an obligation under positive law, or create only loosely binding obligations."[35] Although they have a limited normative value, these rules, which form what is called soft law, are not without effect. They can expand the "Law's Empire"[36] by clearing unexplored normative fields. In doing so, it may incentivize States to put these newly explored issues on the international negotiating agenda. Soft law instruments can also be a first step towards the conclusion of legally binding instruments. As such, they can serve as a basis for work. They can also aim at clarifying the law and proposing new developments. All these roles see soft

---

30 Villalpando (n 15) 125.

31 Yves Daudet, 'Sujets futurs et problèmes du processus législatif international' in *International Law Commission Fifty Years After: An Evaluation* (United Nations 2000) 119–20; Vaughan Lowe, 'Future Topics and Problems of the International Legislative Process' in *International Law Commission Fifty Years After: An Evaluation* (United Nations 2000) 128.

32 See, for instance, Christian Tomuschat, 'The International Law Commission – An outdated institution?' (2006) 49 GYIL 77, 84.

33 Georges Abi-Saab, 'Cours général de droit international public' (1987) 207 RdC 204; Laurence Boisson de Chazournes and Sandrine Maljean-Dubois, 'Normes parajuridiques, système concurrent ou complémentaire: le rôle des ONG internationales et de la soft law' in Brigitte Feuillet-Le Mintier (ed), *Normativité et biomédecine* (Economica 2003) 217.

34 Prosper Weil, 'Vers une normativité relative en droit international?' (1982) 86 RGDIP 5.

35 'soft law' in Jean Salmon (ed), *Dictionnaire de droit international public* (Bruylant 2001).

36 Georges Abi-Saab, 'Éloge du "droit assourdi" Quelques réflexions sur le rôle de la *soft law* en droit international contemporain' in *Nouveaux itinéraires en droit: Hommage à François Rigaux* (Bruylant 1993) 64.

law as transitional law. But there are other cases where soft law instruments can be final products and not just intermediate steps. The best-known case is where a soft law instrument aspires to serve as a model for other instruments. In these cases, it has all the characteristics of a hard law instrument, except that it is not binding. A striking example is the United Nations Commission on International Trade Law Model Law on International Commercial Arbitration.[37] Very often, States integrate the Model Law into their national systems without change. In the case of technical regulations, soft law instruments are often resorted to due to their evolving nature and high degree of technicality. These soft law instruments act as law in a specific sector.[38] This is the case, for instance, of norms of the International Organization for Standardization (ISO) in the field of global industrial production and distribution or the *Codex Alimentarius* on food, food production, and food safety.

As we have just seen, soft law instruments blur the limits of the threshold of what constitutes law since the absence of a binding character does not exclude the existence of legal effects.[39] There is therefore a normative gradation. The final products of the International Law Commission fit into this context and run on the entire scale of normativity.[40]

III The Numerous Impacts of the Commission's Final Products

The impact of the Commission, i.e. the consequences of its work, is multifaceted. In some instances, the Commission's final products constitute reference materials that serve as sources of inspiration or models (B.). In others, they provide practical tools to resolve or clarify legal issues (C.). The Commission also plays an important role in making State practice available (D.). However, the most well-known impact is undoubtedly its contribution to the codification and progressive development of international law. Over the decades, the Commission's work has transposed many rules of customary international law into easily accessible pronouncements, thus providing legal certainty

37 UNCITRAL Model Law on International Commercial Arbitration, UN Doc A/40/17, 24 ILM 1302 (1985), with amendments adopted on 7 July 2006.

38 Laurence Boisson de Chazournes, 'Standards et normes techniques dans l'ordre juridique contemporain: quelques réflexions' in Laurence Boisson de Chazournes and Marcelo Kohen (eds), *International Law and the Quest for Its Implementation – Le droit international et la quête de sa mise en œuvre: Liber Amicorum Vera Gowlland-Debbas* (Brill 2010) 351–76.

39 Boisson de Chazournes and Maljean-Dubois (n 33) 217.

40 Ibid.

and predictability. It has also resulted in the establishment of numerous new rules (A.).

A *The Commission's Contribution to the Codification and Progressive Development of International Law*

According to article 1 of its statute, "[t]he International Law Commission shall have for its object the promotion of the progressive development of international law and its codification". The implementation of this object has yielded different results. In some cases, it has taken a formal turn with the conclusion of treaties (1.). In others, however, it has remained in the form of soft law instruments. This has a number of implications, particularly for the elements of progressive development (2.).

1 Formal Codification and Progressive Development of International Law

A number of treaties have resulted from the International Law Commission's work. A quantitative overview sheds light on this impact. Of the 41 topics dealt with by the Commission, three of which were the subject of a dual examination,[41] 23 conventions were adopted. For some, this may not seem like much. For others, this may be satisfactory. If the analysis is taken a little further, however, the picture is more nuanced. Indeed, of the 23 conventions produced, 19 have entered into force. Of these, 7 have been ratified by less than forty parties.[42] Ultimately, only 12 conventions have been widely ratified. These figures are indicative of the relative impact these treaties may have in terms of coverage and binding character.

However, the analysis cannot be limited to a sole quantitative approach. Despite their relatively small number, these conventions are of material importance. Many of them can be considered amongst the most important treaties ever concluded.[43] They are the cornerstone of the international legal order. Examples include the 1969 Vienna Convention on the Law of Treaties, the 1961 Vienna Convention on Diplomatic Relations[44] and the 1963 Vienna Convention on Consular Relations.[45] In addition, these conventions cover a wide range of

41 These three topics are the question of international criminal jurisdiction (1949–50 and 1994), the draft code of offences against the peace and security of mankind (1954 and 1996) and on the most-favoured-nation clause (1978 and 2015).

42 Anne-Thida Norodom, 'CDI' in Hervé Ascensio et al (eds), *Dictionnaire des idées reçues en droit international* (Pedone 2017) 65–66.

43 Pellet (n 16) 21; Galvao Teles (n 13) 215.

44 Adopted 18 April 1961, entered into force 24 April 1964, 500 UNTS 95.

45 Adopted 28 August 1967, entered into force 27 September 1967, 596 UNTS 261.

areas of international law, ranging from diplomatic and consular relations to the law of the sea, the use of international watercourses and the succession of States. They also widely codify customary international law. Therefore, limiting the analysis to a quantitative point of view would not account for the importance of these conventions in international life. Even though they are not widely ratified, they reflect norms that are opposable to a large number of States.

That said, over the past two decades, only two conventions have been concluded on the basis of the Commission's work, namely the 1997 Convention on the Law of the Non-Navigational Uses of International Watercourses[46] and the 2004 Convention on Jurisdictional Immunities of States and their Property.[47] Does this reveal the existence of a crisis? Not necessarily. One of the reasons given for this situation is the exhaustion of subjects suitable for codification by convention. The topics under consideration by the Commission may prove otherwise.[48] Besides, as mentioned above, conventions are not the only outcome to be achieved by the Commission. Indeed, not all topics placed on the agenda of the Commission are conducive to the adoption of treaties.

In fact, this interest or disinterest in adopting treaties should be placed in a broader context. The decline in the number of treaties adopted in recent years is not unique to the International Law Commission. Treaty fatigue is becoming more prevalent, at least in some areas of international law.[49] More generally, there is less of an appetite for the adoption of multilateral treaties and, when multilateral conventions are adopted, they often do not attract a large number of ratifications. A historical explanation can be given for this phenomenon. After the Second World War, treaties were used as a means to shape a new order. Similarly, in the post-colonial period, treaties were used to make international law more inclusive. During the Cold War, treaties ensured that all key stakeholders were bound by the same rules. And in the aftermath of the fall of the Berlin Wall, a number of treaties were intended to craft a so-called new legal, political and economic order. That period now seems to be over.

Today, in the alternative, other types of multilateral instruments are adopted, including G20 declarations, memoranda of understanding and Heads of State declarations, amongst others. A striking example is the Global Compact on Safe,

---

46 Adopted 21 May 1997, entered into force 17 August 2014, UNTS registration no 52106.

47 Adopted 2 December 2004, not yet in force; UNGA Res A/59/508 (30 November 2004).

48 See for instance, the topic on "Crimes against humanity".

49 Joost Pauwelyn, Ramses A Wessel and Jan Wouters, 'When Structures Become Shackles: Stagnation and Dynamics in International Lawmaking' (2014) 25 EJIL 733, 734–36.

Orderly and Regular Migration, adopted under the aegis of the United Nations on 11 July 2018, which constitutes a "non-legally binding, cooperative framework".[50] And when multilateral treaties are adopted, their form and content may vary. A good example is the Paris Agreement, the content of which is essentially procedural in nature with hardly any substantive obligations.[51] It is notable that the Paris Agreement was negotiated together with a decision of the Contracting Parties to the United Nations Framework Convention on Climate Change in which substantive commitments were integrated.[52] Hard and soft, soft and hard, it is hard to keep track.

In the end, the International Law Commission's final products are in line with these normative fluctuations. The Commission is not "Lost in Translation". One may wonder whether the Commission itself should not suggest to the General Assembly that other types of instruments than conventions be adopted for some of its final products.

2 Informal Codification and Progressive Development of International Law

Final products that do not result in conventions also contribute to this effort to codify and progressively develop international law. However, the soft form of these instruments has some consequences. It thus becomes important to distinguish between rules that codify international law and those that progressively develop it. Indeed, only those reflecting customary law can be directly used, even in the absence of treaties. In practice, however, the distinction is not always made. This is particularly so "when there is a legal vacuum of authority relevant to an issue".[53] In such cases, whatever is available is used without paying much attention to its legal status. The articles on responsibility of States for internationally wrongful acts constitute a prime example. Many international courts and tribunals rely on them as if they were a treaty.[54] They

---

50 'Final draft of 11 July 2018', Intergovernmental Conference to Adopt the Global Compact on Safe, Orderly and Regular Migration, Preamble, Recital 7.

51 Adopted on 12 December 2015, entered into force 4 November 2016, UNTS registration no 54113.

52 Laurence Boisson de Chazournes, 'Regards sur l'Accord de Paris – Un accord qui bâtit le futur' in Marta Torre-Schaub and Mireille Delmas-Marty (eds), *Bilan et perspectives de l'Accord de Paris (COP 21) – Regards croisés* (Paris, IRJS Editions 2017) 97–106; Pieter Jan Kuijper, 'Acceptance speech of the Maastricht Prize for International Law' (2016) (on file with the author).

53 David D. Caron, 'The ILC Articles on State Responsibility: The Paradoxical Relationship between Form and Authority' (2002) 96 AJIL 857, 866–69.

54 Ibid.

make no distinction between articles codifying international law and those progressively developing it. This may prove problematic. As indeed acknowledged by the Commission in the commentaries, some articles "reflect the progressive development of international law".[55]

In this context, the Commission has a role to play in clarifying or recalling that its projects constitute both codification and progressive development of international law. Where possible, the Commission should specify the category in which a provision falls. This would provide valuable assistance to users of its final products and would also allay the concerns of some States that the Commission's pronouncements are given too much authority on the assumption that they reflect existing law.[56] This is what it did, for example, with article 48, paragraph 2, of the articles on responsibility of State for internationally wrongful acts. In the accompanying commentary, it stated that the paragraph "involves a measure of progressive development, which is justified since it provides a means of protecting the community or collective interest at stake."[57]

However, this level of detail is not always possible. As the Commission admitted, some drafts "it has formulated contain elements of both progressive development as well as of codification of the law and, as in the case of several previous drafts, it is not practicable to determine into which category each provision falls".[58] Ultimately, it is important to assess what the International Law Commission's approach has been on a particular point and to bear in mind that it is not always possible to draw a fine line between existing law and progressive development.

B *The Commission's Final Products as Sources of Inspiration or Models*

The final products of the Commission have often played an important role as sources of inspiration or models. The United Nations Convention on the Non-Navigational Uses of International Watercourses is illustrative. Even before its late entry into force on 17 August 2014, this instrument had a considerable impact on State practice. A number of agreements have been concluded on

55 ILC, 'Report of the International Law Commission on the work of its fifty-third session' [2001] II(2) ILC Ybk 1, 114 at para 3, 141 at para 1.

56 See in that regard Danae Azaria in Section 4 of this volume.

57 ILC (n 55) 127 at para 12; see also 'Guide to practice on reservations to treaties', [2011] III(3) ILC Ybk 73.

58 ILC, 'Report of the International Law Commission on the work of its twenty-sixth session' [1974] II(1) ILC Ybk 174; For a comprehensive account of the Commission's practice, see Donald M McRae, 'The Interrelationship of Codification and Progressive Development in the Work of the International Law Commission' (2013) 111 JILD 75, 81–86.

the basis of its provisions. For example, the Revised Protocol on Shared Watercourses in the Southern African Development Community of 7 August 2000[59] largely copied parts of the United Nations Watercourses Convention. Similarly, the Convention greatly influenced the Charter of Senegal River Waters,[60] the Niger Basin Water Charter,[61] the Agreement on the Nile River Basin Cooperative Framework[62] and the Water Charter for Lake Chad Basin.[63] Even more interesting, certain agreements have been concluded on the basis of the Commission's articles on the law of the non-navigational uses of international watercourses. Examples include the 1992 Helsinki Convention on the Protection and Use of Transboundary Watercourses and International Lakes[64] and the 1995 Cooperation Agreement for the Sustainable Development of the Mekong River Basin.[65] The principles and rules codified and developed by the Commission have therefore served as a reference tool for the negotiations of a set of treaty instruments.[66]

Likewise, the articles on the law of transboundary aquifers are another example of that impact.[67] Upon completion of its work, the Commission recommended that the States concerned make appropriate bilateral or regional arrangements for the proper management of their transboundary aquifers on the basis of the principles enunciated in the articles.[68] Building on these articles, Argentina, Brazil, Paraguay and Uruguay concluded the Guarani Aquifer Agreement on 2 August 2010.[69]

Finally, special mention should be made of the draft statute for an international criminal court and its marked influence on the Rome Statute of the

---

59 Adopted 7 August 2000, entered into force 22 September 2003.

60 Adopted 28 May 2002.

61 Adopted 30 April 2008.

62 Adopted 14 May 2010, not yet in force.

63 Adopted April 2012.

64 Adopted 17 March 1992, entered into force, 6 October 1996, 1936 UNTS 269.

65 Adopted 5 April 1995.

66 See Laurence Boisson de Chazournes, *Fresh Water in International Law* (1st edn, OUP 2015) 7–53.

67 ILC, 'Report of the International Law Commission on the work of its sixtieth session' [2008] II(2) ILC Ybk 1, 22–43. For a critical assessment of the inclusion of an article dealing with "Sovereignty of aquifer States" (Article 3), see Stephen C. McCaffrey, 'The International Law Commission Adopts Draft Articles on Transboundary Aquifers', (2009) 103(2) AJIL 272.

68 Ibid.

69 Adopted 2 August 2010, not yet in force, preamble, Recital 3; see Lilian del Castillo Laborde, 'The Rio de la Plata River Basin: The Path Towards Basin Institutions' in Laurence Boisson de Chazournes and Mara Tignino (eds), *International Water Law* (Edward Elgar 2015) 388–411.

International Criminal Court.[70] It acted as a catalyst for the establishment of the International Criminal Court. Welcoming the report of the Commission on the statute of a criminal court, the General Assembly in its resolution 49/53[71] decided to initiate the procedure for the establishment of the International Criminal Court. Although the Commission's draft statute was not ultimately adopted, it enabled the prompt adoption of the Rome Statute on 17 July 1998 by framing the discussions.

C *The Commission's Final Products as Clarifying Tools*

In some cases, the Commission's final products aim at clarifying previous work. The Commission's final products are the result of compromises and negotiations, which can lead to a broad formulation of certain principles or rules. Over time, there may be a need to clarify these principles or rules so that they can be easily used in practice. Several treaty-related projects fall within this context such as the project on subsequent agreements and subsequent practice in relation to interpretation of treaties[72] and that on reservations to treaties.[73] In particular, with regard to the latter, the Commission noted that the provisions concerning reservations in the 1969 Vienna Convention on the Law of Treaties, the 1978 Vienna Convention on Succession of States in Respect of Treaties[74] and the 1986 Vienna Convention on the Law of Treaties between States and International Organizations or between International Organizations[75] could be clarified and developed as they "were too general to act as a guide for State practice and left a number of important matters in the dark".[76] This resulted in the adoption of a guide to practice on reservations to treaties.[77]

Other work has also aimed at developing legal techniques to resolve conflicts that may arise in the interpretation and application of international law. This is the case, for instance, of the report entitled "Fragmentation of international

---

70 ILC, 'Report of the International Law Commission on the work of its forty-sixth session' [1994] II(2) ILC Ybk 1, 26–75.

71 UNGA Res 49/53 (17 February 1995).

72 ILC, 'Draft conclusions on subsequent agreements and subsequent practice in relation to the interpretation of treaties' (2018) UN Doc A/73/10, 12; the International Law Commission at its seventieth session, in 2018, submitted the draft conclusions to the General Assembly (UN Doc A/73/10, para 49).

73 UNGA Res 68/111 (16 December 2013).

74 Adopted on 23 August 1978, entered into force 6 November 1996, 1946 UNTS 3.

75 Adopted 21 March 1986, not yet in force, A/CONF.129/15.

76 ILC, 'Report of the International Law Commission on the work of its forty-fifth session' [1993] II(2) ILC Ybk 427.

77 ILC, 'Report of the International Law Commission on the work of its sixty-third session' [2011] II(2) ILC Ybk 1, 26–38; see also ILC (n 54).

law: difficulties arising from the diversification and expansion of international law". Its purpose was to "provide a toolbox with the help of which lawyers dealing with that problem (or any other comparable issue) may be able to proceed to a reasoned decision".[78] Four types of "collision rules" and a "user manual" have thus been developed by the Commission to deal with regime conflicts. This report has proved useful in addressing the difficulties raised by Article 103 of the Charter of the United Nations as well as in other contexts.[79]

D *The Commission's Contribution to the Availability of State Practice*

The practical usefulness of the Commission's work is not limited to the final products. As part of the codification and progressive development process, the Commission carries out an in-depth study of State practice. This results in compendia of State practices for each topic addressed. This is undoubtedly a major contribution from the Commission.[80]

Article 24 of the statute also entrusts the International Law Commission with the task of exploring "ways and means for making the evidence of customary international law more readily available".[81] The objective at the time was to "remed[y] the present unsatisfactory state of documentation".[82] Under that provision, the Commission adopted in 1950 a Report on Ways and Means for Making the Evidence of Customary International Law more readily available.[83] This report has proved extremely useful both for practitioners and for the Commission itself. It led to the emergence of new legal publications[84] and "provided clues as to where State practice related to international law could be found".[85]

---

78 ILC, 'Fragmentation of international law: Difficulties arising from the diversification and expansion of international law – Report of the Study Group of the International Law Commission' (2006) UN Doc A/CN.4/L.682, 17.

79 *Al-Jedda v The United Kingdom*, App no. 27021/08 (ECtHR, 7 July 2011), para 57.

80 For an example of the use of these compendia, see *Jurisdictional Immunities of the State (Germany v Italy: Greece intervening)* (Merits) [2012] ICJ Rep 99, 134–135 at para 77.

81 ILC statute, article 24.

82 ILC, 'Ways and means of making the evidence of customary international law more readily available: Preparatory work within the purview of article 24 of the Statute of the International Law Commission – Memorandum submitted by the Secretary-General' (1949) UN Doc A/CN.4/6, 5.

83 ILC, 'Report of the International Law Commission on the work of its second session' [1950] II ILC Ybk 364, 367–74.

84 ILC, 'Identification of customary international law – Ways and means of making the evidence of customary international law more readily available – Memorandum submitted by the Secretary-General' (2018) UN Doc A/CN.4/710,3 at para 5.

85 Mathias Forteau, 'Comparative International Law Within, Not Against, International Law: Lessons from the International Law Commission' in Anthea Roberts et al (eds), *Comparative International Law* (OUP 2018) 169.

With the advent of the Internet and the emergence of a multitude of new States, an update was necessary. It is therefore welcome that the 1950 Report has finally been updated by the Secretariat. It is regrettable, however, that this memorandum prepared by the Secretariat has not been more widely advertised and disseminated.[86]

More generally, the work of the Commission has had an impact on the way international law is taught. The careful study of State practice and the Commission's pronouncements codifying and progressively developing international law have made it possible to lay down a large number of rules in writing. As a result, doctrine and case analysis have been replaced by written law.[87] This unintended impact has led to a wider dissemination of this legal corpus.

In summary, the Commission's impacts are varied. Whether by serving as a source of inspiration, providing clarifying tools or resulting in treaties, the Commission's work has proved very valuable. These impacts are also indicative of the predominant place that this body still occupies today, particularly for the users of its work.

That said, this positive picture must not mask the failures that the Commission has experienced. The reasons for these failures are diverse. For some, such as the draft articles on the status of the diplomatic courier and the diplomatic bag not accompanied by diplomatic courier,[88] or the 1975 Vienna Convention on the Representation of States in their Relations with International Organizations of a Universal Character,[89] it was a lack of balance that led to their downfall.[90] For others, such as the 1986 Vienna Convention on the Law of Treaties between States and International Organizations or between International Organizations, it was the lack of interest of the recipients that undermined them. Likewise, faced with very little interest from States in the

---

86 This situation could change. In referring the work on 'Identification of customary international law' to the General Assembly in accordance with article 23 of its statute, the Commission recommended to the General Assembly that it take note of the memorandum of the Secretariat and follow up on its suggestions (see ILC, 'Report of the International Law Commission on the work of its seventieth session' (2018) UN Doc A/73/10, at para. 63). In this regard, see UNGA Res 73/203 (20 December 2018).

87 Georges Abi-Saab, 'Uses and Perils of Codification' in *International Law Commission Fifty Years After: An Evaluation* (United Nations 2000) 168.

88 ILC, 'Report of the International Law Commission on the work of its forty-first session' [1989] II(2) ILC Ybk 1, 14–49.

89 Adopted 14 March 1975, not yet in force, UN Doc A/CONF.67/16.

90 Tomuschat (n 32) 86–87.

Declaration on Rights and Duties of States, the General Assembly decided to defer consideration of the draft indefinitely.[91] There are also certain final products such as the 1983 Vienna Convention on Succession of States in respect of State Property, Archives and Debts[92] which are the mark of a certain historical period. In yet other cases, the study of certain topics did not lead to the production of a final product. This was the case for shared natural resources (oil and gas). The Commission decided not to develop it, particularly because of its political sensitivity.[93]

IV The "regard des autres" on the Commission

As the artist Marcel Duchamp once stated, "the painting is made as much by the viewer as by the artist".[94] This idea is reflected in Marc Chagall's magnificent work entitled "The visit of the self-portrait". In this canvas, the painter faces his portrait. While the right eye of the portrait is uncovered, the head of the painter contemplating his portrait covers the left eye. This captures the idea of a dual perspective. The right eye represents the perception of the artist producing the work while the covered left eye represents the external perspective, that of the viewer.

The external perspective on the Commission is held by many actors. They include courts and tribunals, international organizations, jurisconsults, negotiators of international agreements, diplomats, counsels pleading before international courts and tribunals, non-governmental organizations and academics. Interestingly, this great diversity of "external" viewers reveals a relatively uniform perception of the Commission: that of a body with great authority.

International courts and tribunals have often referred to the Commission's work, whatever its form and status. Amongst these jurisdictions, the International Court of Justice holds a special place. As Dame Rosalyn Higgins noted during the Commission's sixtieth anniversary celebrations, "it is remarkable to note the high percentage in which reference has been made to the work of the

91 UNGA Res 596 (VI) (7 December 1951).

92 Adopted on 8 April 1983, not yet in force, UN Doc A/CONF.117/16.

93 ILC, 'Report of the International Law Commission on the work of its sixty-second session' [2010] II(2) ILC Ybk 1, 200–201 at paras 374–84.

94 Georges Charbonnier, Entretiens avec Marcel Duchamp [réalisés en 1960], André Dimanche, 1994, 81–82: "Je crois sincèrement que le tableau est autant fait par le regardeur que par l'artiste" (author's translation).

International Law Commission".[95] This still holds true today.[96] In general, the Court refers to the work of the Commission in determining the customary status of particular rules. While in theory the Court should survey State practice and *opinio juris* on its own, "in practice, [it] has never found it necessary to undertake such an inquiry ... and instead has made use of the best and most expedient evidence available".[97] The work of the Commission has fulfilled that role. Thus, for example, in the *North Sea Continental Shelf* case, the Court decided that, on the basis of the extensive discussions contained in the reports of the International Law Commission, article 6 of the 1958 Geneva Convention on the Continental Shelf was not customary law.[98] This is only one of many examples where the Court has used the work of the Commission to establish the customary character of a rule. This use by the International Court of Justice of the work of the Commission is of great importance and it is a testament to the Court's respect and recognition for the expertise of the International Law Commission

This relationship between the International Court of Justice and the International Law Commission is not one-way. The Commission has relied heavily on the decisions and judgments issued by the International Court of Justice in its work. This has been the case, for example, in the areas of the law of treaties, the law of the sea and State responsibility. Sometimes the Commission has even paused its work pending a decision by the Court. This was the case with guarantees and promises of non-repetition when these issues were at play in the *LaGrand* case.[99] Besides, membership in these two institutions is often linked. Many judges of the International Court of Justice are former members of the Commission. Of these, nine served as President of the Court.[100] Currently, seven judges have previously served as members of the Commission. These two institutions are thus intrinsically linked, which explains their trust in each other's work.

---

95 Rosalyn Higgins, 'Keynote Address by H.E. Judge Rosalyn Higgins, President of the International Court of Justice, at the Sixtieth Anniversary of the International Law Commission' (Geneva, 19 May 2008) 2.

96 See the contribution by Danae Azaria in Section 4 of this volume. See also Michael Peil, 'Scholarly Writings as a Source of Law: A Survey of the Use of Doctrine by the International Court of Justice' (2012) 1(3) CJICL 136, 152.

97 Peter Tomka, 'Custom and the International Court of Justice' (2013) 12 LPICT 195, 197.

98 *North Sea Continental Shelf* (Merits) [1969] ICJ Rep 3, 33–51; *Jurisdictional Immunities* (n 80) 127 at para 64.

99 Higgins (n 95) 2; *LaGrand* (*Germany v United States of America*) (Merits) [2001] ICJ Rep 466.

100 In chronological order: Manfred Lachs, Eduardo Jiménez de Aréchaga, Sir Humphrey Waldock, Taslim Elias, Nagendra Singh, Mohammed Bedjaoui, Stephen Schwebel, Shi Jiuyong, and Peter Tomka.

Other international courts and tribunals have also referred to the work of the Commission but in a less systematic manner, which is sometimes even questionable. In this regard, reference can be made to the use of the articles on the responsibility of international organizations[101] by the European Court of Human Rights in the *Behrami v France* and *Saramati v France, Germany and Norway* cases.[102] Interestingly, the references made by these jurisdictions to the work of the Commission are rarely accompanied by explanations. As if invoking the Commission were sufficient on its own: references to its work are perceived as an argument of authority. Examples include references made to the articles on State responsibility by numerous courts, such as the Inter-American Court of Human Rights,[103] the International Tribunal for the Law of the Sea[104] and arbitral tribunals.[105]

However, this use of the work of the Commission is not always without its problems. Unlike the International Court of Justice, few other international jurisdictions distinguish between existing law and progressive development.[106] This may lead to the application of rules that have not yet been accepted as binding by the international community. In other cases, projects were used despite the fact that their scope did not cover the legal issue at stake. In this regard, one can mention the references made by investment tribunals to the "Guiding principles applicable to unilateral declarations of States capable of

101 ILC, 'Draft articles on the responsibility of international organizations' [2011] II(2) ILC Ybk 40.

102 *Behrami v France* and *Saramati v France, Germany and Norway* App no. 71412/01 and 78166/01 (ECtHR, 2 May 2007), paras 28–34; see for critique, Laurence Boisson de Chazournes and Vassilis Pergantis, 'A propos de l'arrêt Behrami et Saramati: un jeu d'ombre et de lumière dans les relations entre l'ONU et les organisations régionales' in Marcelo Kohen, Robert Kolb and Djacoba Liva Tehindrazanarivelo (eds), *Perspectives of International Law in the 21st Century: Liber Amicorum Christian Dominicé in Honour of its 80th Birthday* (Martinus Nijhoff 2012) 191–223.

103 *Gutiérrez and Family v Argentina* (Merits, Reparations and Costs Judgment) Inter-American Court of Human Rights Series C No 271 (25 November 2013), para 78, note 163.

104 *M/V 'Saiga' (No 2) (Saint Vincent and the Grenadines v Guinea)* (Judgment of 1 July 1999) ITLOS Reports 1999, 41 at para 82, 45 at para 98.

105 *Jan de Nul NV and Dredging International NV v Egypt* (Award, 2008) ICSID Case No ARB/04/13, [155]-[173]; *ConocoPhillips Petrozuata B.V., and others v Bolivarian Republic of Venezuela* (Decision on Jurisdiction and Merits, 2013) ICSID Case No ARB/07/30, [339]. For a detailed account of the decisions of international courts, tribunals and other bodies referring to the State responsibility articles, see UNGA, 'Report of the Secretary-General', UN Doc A/62/62,UN Doc A/65/76, UN Doc A/68/72 and UN Doc A/71/80.

106 Marija Dordeska, 'The Process of International Law-Making: The Relationship between the International Court of Justice and the International Law Commission' (2015) 15 ILCR 7, 37.

creating legal obligations" when dealing with consent to jurisdiction through domestic legislation.[107] These various examples, although sometimes problematic, are nevertheless indicative of the authority enjoyed by the Commission.

This perception of authority is not just that of international courts and tribunals. Other actors similarly perceive the Commission as authoritative. This is the case of the General Assembly and other United Nations bodies that have submitted topics to the International Law Commission. These proposals are a mark of recognition of the expertise and authority enjoyed by the Commission. This was made clear when the United Nations Environment Programme recommended in 2009 that the International Law Commission "examine the existing international law for protecting the environment during armed conflict and recommend how it can be clarified, codified and expanded" as "the leading body with expertise in international law".[108] Finally, the numerous – but difficult to measure – uses made by professors, diplomats, legal advisers, non-governmental organizations, and counsels also bear testament to the authority of this body.

The "*regard des autres*" helps to illuminate the authority of the International Law Commission. Many actors refer deferentially to the work of the Commission. Sometimes this deference goes too far and the work is relied upon almost blindly. The use of the final products must be done with care. The Commission has a role to play in facilitating the appropriation of its final products by users.

V Concluding Remarks: the Authority of the International Law Commission

As we have seen, the International Law Commission enjoys an authority *per se*. The notion of "authority" refers to a voluntary submission,[109] grounded in

107 *Tidewater Inc. v Venezuela* (Decision on Jurisdiction, 2008) ICSID Case No ARB/10/5, [92]; *Mobil v Venezuela* (Decision on Jurisdiction, 2010) ICSID Case No ARB/07/27, [89]; Laurence Boisson de Chazournes, 'Rules of Interpretation and Investment Arbitration' in Meg Kinnear, Geraldine Fischer, Jara Minguez Almeida, Luisa Fernanda Torres, Mairée Uran Bidegain (eds), *Building International Investment Law, The First 50 Years of ICSID* (Kluwer Law International 2015) 18–23.

108 UNEP, *Protecting the Environment During Armed Conflict – An Inventory and Analysis of International Law* (UNEP, 2009) 53, Recommendation 3; see also ILC, 'Report of the International Law Commission on the work of its sixty-third session' [2011] II(2) ILC Ybk 1, 211–21, 219 at para 23.

109 Max Weber, *The Theory of Social and Economic Organization* (1st edn, The Free Press 1964) 324.

recognition.[110] Put simply, the person or institution treated as an authority is recognized as having "the right to speak credibly".[111] There is no hierarchical relationship between an authority holder and the subjects. In other words, a pronouncement is accepted as authoritative, "not because of a threat of sanction […], or through persuasion, but because it emanates from a particular person".[112] As defined, the notion of 'authority' therefore excludes coercion and persuasion. This is well illustrated by Hannah Arendt's parable of the father: "[a] father can lose his authority by beating his child or by starting to argue with him".[113]

The authority of the Commission rests on multiple foundations. Its universal character, composition and working methods have played a major role in the establishment of this authority. The Commission was established by the United Nations General Assembly as a subsidiary organ with universal membership. Its statute provided for a balance to be struck between regional representativeness[114] and legal expertise.[115] Over the years, States have appointed academics, former or current legal advisers, diplomats and sometimes ministers, as members of the Commission. Legal expertise is important but closely linked to the need to ensure representation of the main forms of civilization and of the principal legal systems of the world. In this regard, the number of members has increased from fifteen to thirty-four in order to accompany the increase in the number of United Nations members.[116] At the same time, a fixed distribution of seats was established to ensure equitable geographical distribution. Such universal composition is important in explaining the authority of the Commission. So are the working methods. They include the nomination of Special Rapporteurs and Working Groups, the issuance of reports, the use of questionnaires, dialogue with States and other stakeholders, as well as dialogue with the Sixth Committee. The working methods aim at ensuring that

110 Fuad Zarbiyev, 'Saying Credibly What the Law Is: On Marks of Authority in International Law' (2018) 9 JIDS 291, 297; Richard B Friedman, 'On the Concept of Authority in Political Philosophy' in Joseph Raz (ed), *Authority* (New York University Press 1990) 68.

111 Michael Barnett and Martha Finnemore, *Rules For The World: International Organizations in Global Politics* (1st edn, Cornell University Press 2004) 20.

112 Zarbiyev (n 110) 294–95; see also Joseph Raz, *The Morality of Freedom* (Clarendon Press 1986) 35–37.

113 Hannah Arendt, *On Violence* (Harcourt, Brace & World 1970) 45.

114 ILC statute, article 8.

115 ILC statute, article 2.

116 UNGA Res 1103 (XI) (18 December 1956) (increasing the number to 21); UNGA Res 1647 (XVI) (6 November 1961) (increasing the number to 25); UNGA Res 36/39 (18 November 1981) (increasing the number to 34).

the projects are thoroughly researched and carefully worded.[117] Further, as the only United Nations organ with general competence in the progressive development of international law and its codification, it is the only one capable of addressing a topic in a comprehensive and cross-cutting manner.[118] Another factor is the involvement of other stakeholders, as foreseen in the statute of the International Law Commission.[119] Like Matisse's Dance, the Commission is an integral part of a choreography in which various actors play a role. If one of them were to fail, the whole would be weakened. This is particularly true for States. Their participation is essential. Through their comments or lack of comments, as well as their proposals for topics, they can strengthen or weaken the final products of the Commission and, ultimately, the Commission itself. Finally, in addition to this institutional authority, each final product has its own authority, which varies depending on the form chosen, recommendations made to the General Assembly under article 23 of the statute of the International Law Commission, interactions with the Sixth Committee, comments by States, or cooperation with other stakeholders.

The International Law Commission is socially recognized as "the leading body with expertise in international law".[120] Its final products are often qualified as falling under article 38, paragraph 1 (d) of the Statute of the International Court of Justice, i.e. "highly qualified publicists".[121] However, authority is dynamic in nature. It can be gained, it can be lost. It can increase, it can decrease over time. Nothing is set in stone. The Commission and States are the custodians of this authority, in the short-term but also in the longer term.

117 John Dugard, 'How effective is the International Law Commission in the development of international law?' (1998) 23 SAfrYIL 34, 38.

118 Yves Daudet, 'Actualités de la codification du droit international' (2003) 303 RdC 110.

119 ILC statute, articles 16, 17, 21, 25 and 26.

120 UNEP (n 108); see also UNGA Res 36/39 (18 November 1981), Recital 1.

121 Caron (n 53) 867; Bertrand G Ramcharan, *The International Law Commission: its Approach to The Codification and Progressive Development of International Law* (Martinus Nijhoff 1977) 25.

Concluding Remarks by Pavel Šturma

The International Law Commission and Its Impact: Some Comments

1 Introduction

It is an ambivalent feeling of honour and anxiety for an author to be called to comment on two excellent papers by Laurence Boisson de Chazournes[1] and Alejandro Rodiles,[2] both dealing with the Commission and its impact, yet from different perspectives. The task seems to be even more difficult for someone who is, despite his background in the academia and long-dated practice to follow and comment the work of the International Law Commission, an insider of this body. Being a member of the Commission is a great privilege and a source of the invaluable experience and information. However, after almost seven years in the Commission, the author pays a price for his membership: he cannot pretend to be a mirror or to express "le regard des autres". To put it simply, one can see oneself in the mirror but and be the mirror at the same time.

It is still possible to criticize the mirror for giving a false picture of the object, the Commission in this case. However, this option would not work either in the present case. I mostly agree with the papers presented by the cited authors. What remains is to try to take a certain distance from both the defense of the institution and the views of the commentators.

This paper will be divided in two parts that do not follow closely the structure but rather the nature and underlying ideas of the papers. The first focuses on the changing forms and consequently impact and authority of the works of the Commission. In other words, it considers how the methods of work and outcomes of the International Law Commission have evolved over time (70 years is a sufficient time for evaluation) and what this means for its authority. The second one concerns rather the factors external to the Commission; it discusses its role in new global normative trends. In other words, the Commission does not live in clinical isolation from new developments in international law, as driven by States and other actors, in particular international organizations, and reflected in the doctrine(s) of international law.

1 See the contribution by Laurence Boisson de Chazournes in this Section.
2 See the contribution by Alejandro Rodiles in this Section.

True, these two aspects are not exclusive but rather complementary, they can be viewed as two sides of the same coins. Nevertheless, it may be useful to analyze them separately before arriving at some general conclusions. To present my views as an insider to the work of the Commission with regard to the third-party perspectives of Laurence Boisson de Chazournes and Alejandro Rodiles, I will borrow the eyes (optique) of two well-known and provocative intellectuals, namely Woody Allen and Martti Koskenniemi. The latter is a former member of the International Law Commission and greatly contributed to one of its best-known outcomes.

II Looking Back to the "Golden Era"

Indeed, Woody Allen did not produce any play or movie about the Commission. However, his film "Midnight in Paris" nicely recalls that it is probably part of human nature that we always look back to a "belle époque" or another kind of golden era.

It is generally accepted and probably true that, if we focus on the number of codification conventions resulting from its work, the "golden era" of codification by the International Law Commission lies in the past, approximately between the end of the 1950s and the first half of 1970s. In other words, one can also speak about the miraculous decade of codification, delimited by 1958 and 1969, i.e. from the adoption of four Geneva Conventions on the Law of Sea,[3] going through the codification of diplomatic and consular relations,[4] to the Vienna Convention on the Law of Treaties.[5] Many of the instruments adopted during this period still belong to the cornerstones of the contemporary international law. Indeed, the Commission can be proud and refer to such highlights of its codification work.

It is also true that the number of binding instruments adopted on the basis of draft articles from the International Law Commission has dropped in

3 Convention on the Territorial Sea and the Contiguous Zone, adopted 29 April 1958, entered into force 10 September 1964, 516 UNTS 205; Convention on the Continental Shelf, adopted 29 April 1958, entered into force 10 June 1964, 499 UNTS 311; Convention on the High Seas, adopted 29 April 1958, entered into force 30 September 1962, 40 UNTS 11; Convention on Fishing and Conservation of Living Resources of the High Seas, adopted 29 April 1958, entered into force 20 March 1966, 559 UNTS 285.

4 Vienna Convention on Diplomatic Relations, adopted 18 April 1961, entered into force 24 April 1964, 500 UNTS 95; Vienna Convention on Consular Relations, adopted 24 April 1963, entered into force 19 March 1967, 596 UNTS 261.

5 Adopted 23 May 1969, entered into force 27 January 1980, 1155 UNTS 331.

number since that time. The reasons for this development depend only partly on the work of the Commission itself. On the one hand, it is an undeniable fact that most parts of general international law have been already codified. Therefore, the Commission more and more often selects new, non-traditional topics that bear on progressive development of international law and even produces outcomes that differ from both codification and progressive development (for example, studies, interpretative guides).[6] No doubt, different topics require different forms, the International Law Commission thus may use more forms other than the traditional draft articles.

On the other hand, States seem to be less interested in binding treaties today, in particular the general codification conventions elaborated by the expert body, such as the International Law Commission, instead of intergovernmental negotiations. This may push the Commission, in turn, to search for and adopt new, non-traditional topics and methods of work. The role of States and other factors external to the Commission will be addressed in the second part of this contribution.

To be fair, one must acknowledge that the Commission has diversified the forms of its final products. Some of the most authoritative and frequently relied upon instruments that resulted from the work of the Commission are in the form of texts that have not, so far, become multilateral treaties or were never intended to be. The guide to practice on reservations to treaties issued in 2011,[7] for instance, is a significant example of such a non-binding document. It seems that it may be followed by another, though much shorter document, the guide to provisional application of treaties, provisionally adopted by the Commission on first reading in 2018.[8]

The variety of forms of codification does not imply that the Commission does not intend to contribute to the adoption of new multilateral treaties. In recent years, it has recommended to the General Assembly the adoption of conventions on the basis of its draft articles. This was the case with the topic "Protection of persons in the event of disasters",[9] for which the Commission adopted draft articles in 2016 that were taken note of by the General

6 See, for instance, reports of study groups such as 'Fragmentation of international law: difficulties arising from the diversification and expansion of international law – Report of the Study Group of the International Law Commission' (2006) UN Doc A/CN.4/L.682 (hereinafter, "Fragmentation report").

7 ILC, [2011] II(2) ILC Ybk 1, 26.

8 ILC, (2018) UN Doc A/CN.4/L.920 and Add.1.

9 ILC, (2016) UN Doc A/71/10, para 48.

Assembly,[10] and it may be the case in relation to the topic "Crimes against humanity" that were adopted on second reading in 2019.[11]

It is true that the last example of the International Law Commission's draft articles that was transformed into a multilateral treaty dates back to 2004 when the United Nations Convention on Jurisdictional Immunities of States and their Property was adopted.[12] It still took no less than 13 years from 1991 when the Commission had adopted the final text of draft articles on the topic, with commentaries, to the adoption of the Convention.[13] In accordance with article 23 of its statute,[14] the International Law Commission submitted the draft articles to the General Assembly, together with a recommendation that the General Assembly convene an international conference of plenipotentiaries to examine them and to conclude a convention on the subject.[15] The years between 1991 and 2004 were devoted to extensive negotiations conducted first in the open-ended working group of the Sixth Committee, then, on the invitation of the General Assembly,[16] also within the International Law Commission's Working Group on Jurisdictional Immunities of States and their Property (1999),[17] and finally in the Ad Hoc Committee on Jurisdictional Immunities of States and their Property (2000–2003).[18] Although the General Assembly adopted the text of the Convention in December 2004,[19] this Convention has not yet entered into force.[20]

Why to recall this example? First, it seems that it is not only the community of international lawyers of today (inside or outside the Commission) who have looked back at previous codification efforts. Most likely, our predecessors one or two decades ago also dreamed about the "golden era" of codification in the 1960s. The era when almost all final products of the International

---

10 UNGA Res 71/141 (13 December 2016).

11 ILC, 'Report of the International Law Commission on the work of its seventy-first session' (2019) UN doc A/74/10, 10 at paras 39–41.

12 United Nations Convention on Jurisdictional Immunities of States and their Property (adopted on 2 December 2004, not yet in force) UN Doc A/59/508.

13 ILC, [1991] II(2) ILC Ybk, paras 23 and 28.

14 Statute of the ILC, UNGA Res 174 (II) (21 November 1947) as amended by UNGA Res 485(V) (12 December 1950).

15 ILC, [1991] II(2) ILC Ybk, para 25.

16 UNGA Res 53/98 (8 December 1998).

17 UNGA Res 54/101 (9 December 1999).

18 UNGA Res 55/150 (12 December 2000); UNGA Res 56/78 (12 December 2001); UNGA Res 57/16 (19 November 2002); UNGA Res 58/74 (9 December 2003).

19 UNGA Res 59/38 (2 December 2004).

20 It requires 30 ratifications; as of 1 October 2018, just 22 instruments of ratification have been deposited.

Law Commission became codification conventions within few years from the submission of the adopted draft articles to the General Assembly. On balance, not all conventions have entered into force and, if so, it also took quite some years.

The second and more important reason is that the experience of the negotiation of the Convention on Jurisdictional Immunities of States may repeat itself with respect to the 2001 articles on responsibility of States for internationally wrongful acts.[21] Recent debates in the Sixth Committee and several side events organized in New York (such as the one that took place in May 2018, at the margin of the first part of the International Law Commission's seventieth session) have shown that some States would like to have a convention while others continue to be rather reluctant. Members of the Commission also seem divided on the question of a convention.[22] In principle, once the Commission submitted its final product (for example, draft articles) and made a corresponding recommendation to the General Assembly, it is no longer the master of the product that it passed to the hands of States. However, as the example of the Convention on Jurisdictional Immunities shows, the Commission may be asked by the General Assembly to resume its work and to contribute to clarification of certain issues in the final stage of codification process.

Nevertheless, the impact or authority of the International Law Commission's products does not only depend on the binding nature of a document. Even a non-binding document, resolution or anther soft law product, including the final draft articles with commentaries, may serve the needs of the international community.

One of the best examples has been already mentioned. The codification of the law of State responsibility belongs, together with the law of treaties achieved in the 1969 Vienna Convention on the Law of Treaties, to the most important results of the International Law Commission's codification work.[23] Unlike the 1969 Vienna Convention, however, the articles on responsibility of States for internationally wrongful acts still remain in a non-binding form. Although proposals to convoke a diplomatic conference have been made more often in recent years, there are still some strong arguments in favour of the *status quo*. On the request of the Secretary-General, some States responded to the

21 UNGA Res 56/83 (12 December 2001), annex.

22 One of such side events took place already in 2014; see Pavel Šturma, 'Responsibility of States: State of play and the way forward' (2014) Anuario Português de Direito Internacional 2013, 93.

23 Pierre-Marie Dupuy, 'Quarante ans de codification du droit de la responsabilité internationale des Etats. Un bilan' (2003) 107 RGDIP 305, 306.

question of the final form of the articles. Some of them showed reservations towards the idea of a convention. For example, according to the comments of the United Kingdom,

> it is difficult to see what would be gained by the adoption of a convention ... The draft articles are already providing their worth and are entering the fabric of international law through State practice, decisions of courts and tribunals and writings. They are referred to consistently in the work of foreign ministries and other Government departments. The impact of the draft articles on international law will only increase with time, as is demonstrated by the growing number of references to the draft articles in recent years. ... Our view remains that any move at this point towards the crystallization of the draft articles in a treaty text would raise a significant risk of undermining the currently broad consensus on the scope and content of the draft articles.[24]

Arguably, the articles on responsibility of States for internationally wrongful acts are one of the outcomes of the Commission's codification work the impact of which does not depend so much on their form, as both practice and writings refer to the content of the draft articles as an expression of customary international law. Clearly, the level of acceptance of the customary nature of the articles is not the same for all rules contained therein. At the same time, the articles as a whole form a balanced document, covering all the consequences of an internationally wrongful act, at least from the point of view of the Commission.[25]

From this perspective, a convention would be advantageous only if certain conditions were present (and certain risks avoided),[26] and mostly with respect to some rules in the articles for which their customary nature may be questioned.

This brings the debate to the well-known issue of codification and progressive development of international law. The mandate of the United Nations General Assembly under Article 13, paragraph 1 (a), of the Charter of the United Nations clearly includes the "progressive development of international law

24 United Kingdom (2006) UN Doc A/62/63, 6.

25 Cf. Alain Pellet, 'The ILC's Articles on State Responsibility for Internationally Wrongful Acts and Related Texts' in James Crawford, Alain Pellet, Simon Olleson (eds), *The Law of International Responsibility* (OUP 2010) 86.

26 Šturma (n 17).

and its codification".[27] This mandate was specified in article 15 of the Statute of the International Law Commission which provides a definition of these terms. It is clear that the qualification of the topic has an effect on the methods of work to be used by the Commission and also on the form in which progressive development or codification will take place.[28]

As an example, contrary to the articles on responsibility of States for internationally wrongful acts, the draft articles on crimes against humanity (adopted on second reading in 2019) were prepared with a view of a future convention.[29] Otherwise they could hardly have an expected impact. This does not deny the customary nature of the definition of crimes against humanity, taken over from article 7 of the Rome Statute of the International Criminal Court.[30] The main added value of the topic lies in the provisions on horizontal (inter-state) cooperation in criminal matters, including criminalization of acts under national law, extradition etc., which may become binding on States only by way of a treaty. It seems that the distinction between codification and progressive development, or even treaty law-making is useful in some cases.

However, this distinction in its strict form proved to be unsustainable in the practice of the Commission and was quickly abandoned.[31] As pointed out by some eminent commentators and former members of the Commission, the distinction "was hardly defensible scientifically".[32] Although the actual share may differ from topic to topic, the final products of the Commission comprise elements of both the codification of general international law and of its progressive development.

27 Charter of the United Nations, adopted 24 October 1945, 1 UNTS XVI, Article 13 paragraph (1)(a).

28 Boisson de Chazournes (n 1).

29 In the original proposal it was noted by Sean D Murphy that "[a]s such, a global convention on crimes against humanity appears to be a key missing piece in the current framework of international humanitarian law, international criminal law, and international human rights law. The objective of the International Law Commission on this topic, therefore, would be to draft articles for what would become a Convention on the Prevention and Punishment of Crimes against Humanity (Crimes against Humanity Convention)." See ILC, 'Report of the International Law Commission on the work of its sixty-eight session' (2016) UN Doc A/68/10, 140 at para 3.

30 Adopted 17 July 1998, entered into force 1 July 2002, 2187 UNTS 38544.

31 Boisson de Chazournes (n 1).

32 See James Crawford, 'The Progressive Development of International Law' in Denis Alland, *Unity and Diversity of International Law: Essays in Honour of Professor Pierre-Marie Dupuy* (Brill 2014) 19; Alain Pellet, 'Between Codification and Progressive Development of the Law' (2004) 6 International Law FORUM du droit international 15.

That is why the revival of the debate on this distinction within the Commission during past few years may appear surprising. One may ask whether this is a sign of uncertainty or a lack of confidence of the International Law Commission, or due to the lack of the traditional topics of general international law that still need codification or a crisis of codification.

The argument of transparency in the work of the International Law Commission has certain merits. There are also some situations where a consensus of the members may depend on the "labeling" of a specific provision (draft article, principle or conclusion) in terms of codification or progressive development.[33] However, such practice should remain rather exceptional. The generalization or over-use of such qualifications also entails a risk which is not negligible.

Apart from the above-mentioned difficulties to draw a scientifically precise dividing line between "codification" and "progressive development", at least two other problems should be noted. First, the distinction bears a risk for the dynamic process of interrelation between codification and development, or custom and treaty (or other forms of the final product). As is well known, a treaty provision may codify (or be *declaratory* of) a pre-existing rule of customary international law, or lead to the *crystallization* of a rule of customary international law, or give rise to (or *generating*) a new rule of customary international law.[34]

Indeed, this is a dynamic process. It happens quite often that a rule which had not yet been established in its customary form before the adoption of a convention has evolved subsequently into a rule of customary international law. However, the strict labeling of each and every provision (either as codification or progressive development of law) may sometimes downgrade the status of "development" rules and freeze them in this quality.

The most famous product of the International Law Commission, the 1969 Vienna Convention on the Law of Treaties, seems to be the best example of how wise it may be not to overburden individual provisions with such a qualification. Not all articles of the 1966 draft articles that became the 1969 Vienna Convention, including the rules on treaty interpretation, were of a customary nature at that time. Nevertheless, today, they are considered part of customary international law and also applied by those States that did not ratify the 1969 Vienna Convention.

---

33 See in that regard the contribution by Sean Murphy in Section 5 of this volume.

34 Cf. *North Sea Continental Shelf* (Merits) [1969] ICJ Rep 3, 38–41. See also draft conclusion 11 in the 'Draft conclusions on identification of customary international law' (2018) UN Doc A/73/10, 122.

The second problem relates to the changing character of the work of the Commission and of its products. Some new topics and the forms of their presentation hardly obey the dichotomy between progressive development and codification. In particular, studies and conclusions such as that on "Fragmentation of international law" (as the most typical example),[35] but also more recently adopted conclusions on "Subsequent agreements and subsequent practice"[36] or the "Identification of customary international law",[37] can be qualified neither as codification nor progressive development of international law. Instead, they have mostly explanatory or interpretative character.

The question if and how the new kinds of final products of the Commission correspond to new normative trends in international law and doctrinal streams is to be addressed in the second part.

III Responding to New Challenges, Crisis of Codification and Backlash to International Law

The "golden era" (and Woody Allen) is over, and it is a time to take the perspective of Martti Koskenniemi who, as an academic, greatly contributed to the articulation of critical studies and a "deconstruction" of international law. It is a kind of paradox that he, as a member of the Commission, also elaborated on the fragmentation of international law and ways how to respond to this phenomenon. As the chair of the Study Group on the topic "Fragmentation of international law: difficulties arising from the diversification and expansion of international law", he contributed, by means of the final report of that Study Group,[38] to the efforts to counter the fragmentation and work towards the integration of general international law.

According to some commentators, the work of the International Law Commission should change in response to the new normative trends in international law. Such trends also include a preference for informal ways of law-making, diluting its frontiers to related fields, mostly international politics, and thus compromising "international law's relative autonomy".[39] For instance,

---

35 ILC (n 6) 174.

36 ILC, 'Draft conclusions on subsequent agreements and subsequent practice in relation to the interpretation of treaties' (2018) UN Doc A/73/10, 12.

37 ILC (n 35) 118.

38 ILC (n 6) 174.

39 See Jan Klabbers, 'The Relative Autonomy of International Law or The Forgotten Politics of Interdisciplinarity' (2004) 1 JILIR 35.

Alejandro Rodiles argues that the trends are of a structural nature.[40] In other words, he pointed out that the Commission moved, in its study on the fragmentation, from "an analysis of major changes *in* the system" to the question of the nature of "international law as a legal system".[41]

It seems to me that it is not possible to disconnect the issue of the end of codification in the traditional sense (the above-discussed crisis of codification or the end of its "golden era"), which also concerns the search for suitable topics, from the pure question of methods (how to perform the tasks) of the Commission. After all, the examples of the new and good practice of the Commission, named by Alejandro Rodiles, are two of the recent topics, namely "Subsequent agreements and subsequent practice" and "Identification of customary international law", which cannot be easily labeled as codification or progressive development of international law.

Indeed, the Commission needs both the new topics, such as the studies on "Fragmentation of international law" or "Subsequent agreements and subsequent practice", and more traditional topics, which continue to be present in its programme of work. The two above-mentioned examples can be best described as interpretative restatements of the relevant areas of international law. Of course, such products have a great potential to contribute to the stability and integration of international law. This seems to be compatible with the mandate of the Commission.[42] It is clear that a greater variety of topics may require and explain the use of different methods to elaborate and forms to adopt the final products of the Commission. However, the International Law Commission should not cease to pursue its original mandate of codifying and progressively developing international law to the extent that suitable topics are available.

As pointed out by Matthias Forteau, who knows the International Law Commission well from the inside and outside, the Commission may be perceived or criticized as being too "old-fashioned", especially "in a time of deformalization in international law".[43] Given its nature as a subsidiary body of

40 Rodiles (n 2).

41 Ibid.

42 This seems to result already from the Fragmentation report (ILC (n 6)), and Michael Wood and Arnold Pronto, *The International law Commission 1999–2009. Volume IV: Treaties, Final Draft Articles and Other Materials* (OUP 2010), 814 ("Thus, it is proposed that the Commission should increasingly look for the avenue of 'restatement' of general international law in forms other than codification and progressive development – not as a substitute but as supplement to the latter.")

43 Mathias Forteau, 'Comparative International Law Within, Not Against, International Law' in Anthea Roberts et al (eds), *Comparative International Law* (OUP 2018) 166–167.

the United Nations General Assembly, "the ILC operates in a specific context, driven mainly by orthodox attitudes toward international law".[44] Indeed, this is true. One cannot but agree that the Commission's objective is the preservation of the relative autonomy of international law. Both the composition and the institutional link to the General Assembly makes the Commission a unique organ to fulfill this task.

However, what is not possible to take for granted is the belief of some authors that "deformalization" is the only or main trend in contemporary international law. With due respect, this seems to be highly exaggerated. The evolution and/or changing structures of international law are not an entirely new phenomenon but are one of its features. One should always distinguish between new challenges arising from the practice of States (or other actors) and those produced by the doctrine.

First, considering practice, which is not only but still predominantly State practice, one can discern a trend towards a certain appetite of States for informal instruments. Such informal instruments are concluded, somewhere and sometimes, depending on the areas of international law and politics concerned. At the same time, however, many treaties are still negotiated and concluded in full form, subject to ratification or another expression of the will of the parties to be bound. Maybe States prefer both formal and informal instruments that are results of their political negotiations (where they can advance their priorities) rather than general codification conventions drafted by an expert body.

Another challenge which cannot be well explained by new normative trends (such as deformalization) is the fact that some States prefer bilateralism to multilateral negotiations, which does not speak in favour of the codification or development of general international law. Last but not least, international lawyers, including the Commission, also have to face the recent backlash to international law in general or to some treaty regimes, in areas such as human rights, the International Criminal Court, free trade agreements or investment treaty arbitration. How to respond to such challenges? It seems that the Commission is better prepared to do so by reaffirming the traditional (formalist) legal approach than by embracing new normative trends, in particular if they are still unsettled and sometimes even contradictory.[45]

44 Ibid.

45 According to one view, there exists a so-called autoimmunity symptom by which the Commission itself re-prioritises the priviledged over the unprivileged in the name of democracy. See Yota Negishi, 'The International Law Commission Celebrating its 70th Anniversary: Dresser le bilan pour l'avenir 'à venir' (2018) 7(8) ESIL Reflections.

Second, considering doctrine, an infinite variety of theoretical approaches and concepts exists in international law scholarship today. Unlike in the past, there is no single predominant school of thought, which could claim authority in the interpretation of law and in legal discourse. If a term could describe the situation in scholarly writings, it would be "theoretical pluralism" or "eclecticism". In such a situation, it would be unlikely (and not advisable) if the Commission took the position of one of the many doctrinal streams. Its place is rather in the mainstream, which is traditional formalism.

However, this does not mean in any way that the Commission cannot and should not be aware of the recent doctrinal trends or open to relevant debates. To the contrary, the International Law Commission is an expert organ, consisting of mostly generalists in international law, coming from both academia and practice. Its expertise and authority would increase rather than decrease if it also took into account, critically and where appropriate, the newest doctrinal streams and projects. As a matter of example, the topic "Succession of States in respect of State responsibility", though only recently put on the Commission's programme of work, refers to two traditional areas of general international law, State succession and international responsibility. While the Special Rapporteur considers the topic to belong to the category of those topics that require progressive development and codification (in the traditional sense), he also looks at and would like to explore the new doctrinal project on "Shared responsibility".[46] The project certainly merits closer examination before deciding whether it may or may not help the Commission in its work.[47]

IV Conclusions

In order to evaluate the impact of the Commission and to propose possible changes in its methods of work, it is important to ask ourselves who we, as the International Law Commission, are and to whom we should speak. In the new circumstances and changing structures of international law, the answer to those questions would be very helpful.

On the one hand, the Commission is an independent expert body. It is not a diplomatic organ although its membership also includes some current or former diplomats, legal advisors, and other categories of government officials.

46 See André Nollkaemper and Ilias Plakokefalos (eds), *Principles of Shared Responsibility in International Law* (CUP 2014).

47 See Pavel Šturma, 'First report on succession of States in respect of State responsibility' (2017) UN Doc A/CN.4/708, para 133.

Many members are professors or researchers but this does not make the Commission a purely academic institution. Neither is the International Law Commission a kind of bar associated with the International Court of Justice despite the fact that several members have represented governments as advocates before the Court and some eventually became judges of the Court. To best describe the Commission and its outcomes, I would say that it is a part (maybe a more visible part) of the "invisible college of international lawyers".[48] This also means that the products of the International Law Commission can generally be characterized as writings, unless they are transformed into binding instruments.

On the other hand, the International Law Commission is an official organ of the United Nations and has a large audience. Being a subsidiary organ of the General Assembly, the Commission has to speak to States, mainly through the Sixth (Legal) Committee. In other words, it addresses mostly legal advisors of States. But the audience of the Commission is much larger and includes international courts and tribunals, intergovernmental organizations but also non-governmental organizations and academia. Of course, all of those constituencies do not have the same but quite different perspectives on international law and expectations of the International Law Commission. This brings to mind Koskenniemi's critical analysis of the different forms of commitment and different professions in international law: the judge, the advisor, the activist and the academic.[49] Indeed, as he put it, "international law is what international lawyers do and how they think".[50]

The Commission is in fact the place where theory may (and sometimes does) become practice. This brings about a high level of responsibility and expectations. Indeed, the Commission is not able to meet the expectations of all of its constituencies at the same time. What is too much for a legal advisor of a given State would probably not be enough (and too old-fashioned or conservative) for an activist. It is a natural fate of the Commission (and its members) that it cannot make all of them happy. The Commission could and should be aware of different political agendas and different theories, without giving

48 See Oscar Schachter, 'The Invisible College of International Lawyers' (1977) 72 NULR 217. See also Santiago Villalpando, 'The 'Invisible College of International Lawyers' Forty Years Later' (2013) ESIL 5th Research Forum: International Law as a Profession Conference Paper No. 5/2013.

49 See Marti Koskenniemi, 'Between Commitment and Cynicism: Outline for a Theory of International Law as Practice' in United Nations Office of Legal Affairs, *Collection of Essays by Legal Advisors of States, Legal Advisors of International Organizations and Practitioners in the Field of International Law* (United Nations 1999) 512–523.

50 Ibid 523.

preference to one of them. It may also adopt new topics and methods where appropriate. What matters, however, is to make a best effort and to speak in a language that is understood by all professions and actors of international law. After all, this is what the Commission must do if it wishes to keep its relevance and authority.

SECTION 4

The Working Methods of the Commission

Opening Remarks by Aleksandar V. Gajić

It is a great honour to chair the panel dedicated to the working methods of the Commission, on the occasion of the celebration of 70 years of the International Law Commission.

In the field of international public law, two institutions are indispensable: the International Court of Justice, as the principal judicial organ of the United Nations, and the International Law Commission, as the principal institution of the United Nations for codification and progressive development of international law.

The reputation of the International Law Commission seems indisputable. Its impact is visible in the academic field, in foreign policy and in international jurisprudence. No serious academic work in the field of international law can disregard the results of the work of the International Law Commission, whether it concerns the Commission's outcomes, its commentaries or the records of its deliberations. Similarly, no reasonable foreign policy decision could be made without paying due regard to positions taken by the International Law Commission. In turn, the International Court of Justice and other international judicial bodies also continue to rely on the work of the International Law Commission.

The reputation and authority of the International Law Commission, certainly, lies in the fact that it has proven to be a highly competent body, composed of persons acting in their personal capacity, driven by professionalism and acting in the best interests of the international legal system. Its contribution to fundamental fields of international law, including the law of treaties, State responsibility, international criminal law and many others, has demonstrated that the Commission is capable of dealing with the most important and the most sensitive issues of international law.

The reputation, authority and quality of the products of the International Law Commission are, to a large extent, due to its working methods. Accordingly, this panel will focus on how the International Law Commission conducts its work; in other words, on how this highly reputable institution produces results that remain indispensable for the contemporary international community.

The Working Methods of the International Law Commission: Adherence to Methodology, Commentaries and Decision-Making

Danae Azaria

1 Introduction

In the twenty-first century, the International Law Commission has increasingly moved away from its "codification by convention" paradigm to the preparation of instruments that remain non-binding.[1] A combination of factors may encourage governments, national courts and international courts and tribunals to rely on the Commission's non-binding outputs.[2] The Commission's composition is geographically representative of the world's legal systems; the Commission is institutionally required to interact with governments, whose comments find reflection in the Commission's final output; and the quality of the Commission's work addresses a frequent challenge that governments and national and international courts face: collecting and assessing State practice for the purpose of interpreting treaties or identifying rules of customary international law.

This last aspect, the *quality* of the Commission's work, is inextricably linked with its working methods. Today, the Commission faces numerous challenges that are different from those that existed at the time when the Commission was established. The number of States has almost tripled compared to 70 years ago. The Commission's composition has been enlarged.[3] More multilateral treaties have been concluded, covering many areas of international law. International courts and tribunals have proliferated and often apply rules of

1 See also Jacob Katz Cogan, 'The Changing Form of the International Law Commission's Work' in Robert Virzo and Ivan Ingravallo (eds), *Evolutions in The Law of International Organizations* (Martinus Nijhoff 2015), 275; Frank Berman, 'The ILC within the UN's Legal Framework: Its Relationship with the Sixth Committee' (2006) 49 GYIL 107; David D. Caron, 'The ILC Articles on State Responsibility: The Paradoxical Relationship between Form and Authority' (2002) 96 AJIL 857.

2 See also the Commission's own understanding of these factors: ILC, 'Draft conclusions on the identification of customary international law, with commentaries' (2018) UN Doc A/73/10, 122 at 142 (general commentary to part five, para 2).

3 Since 1981, the Commission's statute provides that the Commission is to be composed of 34 members, see UNGA Res 36/39 (18 November 1981).

general international law. More national courts engage with international law.[4] At present, an increasing number of States seem keen to retreat from international law, especially multilateralism.

All of these challenges call for further reflection on the Commission's working methods, in order to preserve and enhance the quality of its work. The following analysis will comment on three issues, taking into account some recent developments. First, the Commission's adherence to methodology will be discussed. Second, the role and preparation of commentaries will be examined. Third, the method of decision-making will be analyzed.

Before embarking on the main discussion, some preliminary comments about the Commission's functions and procedures are warranted. First, the Commission has not developed different procedures depending on the outcome of the topic (a convention or a non-binding instrument)[5] or depending on the nature of the rules concerned (rules of general scope, such as secondary rules on sources and on State responsibility, or rules that deal with a specific issue, e.g. the protection of the environment in relation to armed conflict). The Commission has instead followed a process that does not turn upon any such differences, and has deviated from this process only on an *ad hoc* basis. Second, the statute of the Commission is structured upon a distinction between progressive development and codification. Chapter II of the statute contains two separate parts: Part A on the progressive development of international law, and Part B on the codification of international law.[6] These provide for two distinct procedures for each function.[7] However, in practice the Commission has mostly not distinguished between these two functions, including in its

4 Eyal Benvenisti, 'Reclaiming Democracy: The Strategic Uses of Foreign and International Law by National Courts' (2008) 102 AJIL 241.

5 See in that regard see the contribution of Maurice Kamto in this Section.

6 Statute of the ILC, UNGA Res 174(II) (21 November 1947) as amended by: UNGA Res 485(V) (12 December 1950); UNGA Res 984(X) (3 December 1955); UNGA Res 985(X) (3 December 1955); and UNGA Res 36/39 (18 November 1981).

7 Compare articles 16 and 17 (on progressive development) to articles 18–24 (on codification). For instance, according to its statute, the Commission lacks the initiative to consider topics on progressive development. The General Assembly, pursuant to article 16 of the Commission's statute, and United Nations Members, the principal organs of the United Nations other than the General Assembly, specialized agencies, or official bodies established by intergovernmental agreement, pursuant to article 17 of the Commission's statute, may refer to the Commission a proposal for progressive development. In relation to codification, the Commission shares the initiative with the General Assembly (article 18), United Nations Members, the principal organs of the United Nations other than the General Assembly, specialized agencies, or official bodies established by intergovernmental agreement (article 17, paragraph 1). In relation to progressive development, the statute expressly

procedures, because any topic may include both instances of codification and of progressive development to varying degrees.

II Consistent Adherence to Methodology

As mentioned above, the Commission has developed a practice whereby it does not usually classify its output on a topic as either progressive development or codification. Sometimes, the Commission indicates in the introduction to its commentary that there are instances of both in the topic.[8] Occasionally, it clarifies in the commentary to a specific provision that it represents *lex lata*[9] or *lex ferenda*, and the extent of *lex ferenda*.[10]

Today, States at times express concern that the lack of differentiation gives the Commission's pronouncements too much authority, since international courts and tribunals assume that all of its pronouncements reflect existing law.[11] So far, this criticism has not encouraged the Commission to be more expressive in identifying whether its pronouncements fall within codification or progressive development. Perhaps this is because until recent years the Commission has worked on the assumption that most of its work may lead to negotiations for a future convention; and negotiations operate as a "safety net" for States, which can influence the final language of a treaty and are only bound by their consent.

---

foresees the appointment of a Rapporteur (article 16(a)). However, the statute does not provide for the appointment of a Rapporteur concerning codification. See also analysis by Shabtai Rosenne, 'The International Law Commission, 1949–1959' (1960) 36 BYIL 104.

8 ILC, 'Draft articles concerning the law of the sea, with commentaries' [1956] II ILC Ybk 254, 255–256 at paras 25–26; ILC, 'Draft articles on responsibility of States for internationally wrongful acts with commentaries thereto' [2001] II(2) ILC Ybk 30, 31(general commentary, para 1).

9 See, for instance, ILC, 'Draft articles on the law of treaties with commentaries' [1966] II ILC Ybk 177, 246 (commentary to article 49, para 1) ("The Commission considers that these developments justify the conclusion that the invalidity of a treaty procured by the illegal threat or use of force is a principle which is *lex lata* in the international law of today.").

10 See, for instance, ILC, 'Draft articles on responsibility of States for internationally wrongful acts with commentaries thereto' (n 8) 137 (commentary to article 54, para 3) concerning measures taken by States other than the injured State ("Practice on this subject is limited and rather embryonic").

11 See for instance the comments of the following governments in the Sixth Committee concerning the draft articles on immunity of State officials from foreign criminal jurisdiction as provisionally adopted by the Commission in 2017: China (UN Doc A/C.6/72/SR.23, 9), Spain (UN Doc A/C.6/72/SR.24, 7), Switzerland (UN Doc A/C.6/72/SR.22, 12).

However, in an era where codification through non-binding instruments becomes the main paradigm,[12] such concerns,[13] especially from States, may become more pronounced. The Commission may thus be encouraged to demonstrate a consistent adherence to methodology.[14] It may also be encouraged to be more expressive about the results of the application of such methodology.

Thomas Franck argued that rules that are legitimate are more likely to be complied with, and one of the factors that make rules legitimate is their adherence to methodology: in other words, adherence to secondary rules of international law for identifying and interpreting primary rules.[15] Consistent "adherence" to such secondary rules is an important basis on which the Commission's work is and will be relied upon. This is because adherence to such methodology operates as a restraint on the Commission's discretion: it anchors its output in State practice, *opinio juris* and international jurisprudence, rather than on mere policy preferences of the Commission's members.

Evidence that the Commission is cognizant that adherence to secondary rules is important for the persuasion of its own work can be found in the Commission's work on customary international law. In 2018, the Commission adopted on second and final reading 16 draft conclusions on the identification of customary international law.[16] The General Assembly took note of the conclusions, annexed them to a resolution, brought them 'to the attention of States and all who may be called upon to identify rules of customary international law, and encourage[d] their widest possible dissemination'.[17] These do not include a draft conclusion specifically dedicated to the Commission's own outputs. Some members of the Commission had suggested including such a conclusion.[18] However, it was decided not to insert one, but rather to make reference to the Commission in the introductory commentary to part five of the

12 See account of trend in Laurence R Helfer and Timothy Meyer, 'The Evolution of Codification: A Principal-Agent Theory of the International Law Commission's Influence' in Curtis Bradley (ed), *Custom's Future: International Law in A Changing World* (CUP 2016) 305.

13 Michael Wood, "Weighing' the Articles on Responsibility of International Organizations' in Maurizio Ragazzi (ed), *The Responsibility of International Organizations. Essays in Memory of Sir Ian Brownlie* (Brill 2013) 55 at 65–66.

14 Laurence R Helfer and Timothy Meyer, 'The Evolution of Codification: A Principal-Agent Theory of the International Law Commission's Influence' (n 12) 305.

15 Thomas Franck, *Fairness in International Law and Institutions* (OUP 1995) 30, 40–46.

16 ILC, 'Draft conclusions on identification of customary international law, with commentaries' (n 2).

17 UNGA Res 73/203 (20 December 2018).

18 ILC, 'Report of the International Law Commission on the work of its sixty-seventh session' (2015) UN Doc A/70/10, 47 at para 104.

conclusions entitled "Significance of certain materials for the identification of customary international law". That commentary introduces some qualitative criteria for the reliance on the Commission's work. It states that the Commission's determinations "may have particular value [flowing from, *inter alia*] *the thoroughness of its procedures* (including the consideration of extensive surveys of State practice and *opinio juris*); and its close relationship with the General Assembly and States (including receiving oral and written comments from States as it proceeds with its work)."[19] It concludes that "the weight to be given to the Commission's determinations depends [...] on various factors, *including the sources relied upon by the Commission, the stage reached in its work, and above all upon States' reception of its output*".[20]

Further, conclusion 14, entitled "Teachings", recognizes that teachings may constitute a subsidiary means for determining rules of customary international law. The commentary to conclusion 14 introduces some crucial criteria for teachings to be used as a subsidiary means for determining rules of customary international law. The Commission states that "assessing the authority of a given work is essential [...]"[21] for it to be a subsidiary means for the determination of rules of law. "The value of each output [of an international expert body] needs to be carefully assessed in the light of the mandate and expertise of the body concerned, the extent to which the output seeks to state existing law, *the care and objectivity with which it works on a particular issue*, the support a particular output enjoys within the body, and the reception of the output by States and others".[22] These criteria apply to outputs by the Commission as well.[23] What the Commission calls "care and objectivity" in this topic, Thomas Franck called "adherence".

19 ILC, 'Draft conclusions on the identification of customary international law, with commentaries' (n 2) 142 (general commentary to part five, para 2) (emphasis added).

20 Ibid (emphasis added).

21 Ibid 151 (commentary to draft conclusion 14 para (3)).

22 Ibid (commentary to conclusion 14, para 5) (emphasis added).

23 The commentary to draft conclusion 14 does not refer to the Commission, but to "international expert bodies". As examples of such bodies, it mentions the *Institut de Droit international* and the International Law Association. These bodies differ from the Commission, which is a subsidiary organ of an international organisation and has a direct relationship with governments. Footnote 774 of the Commission's report in the commentary to conclusion 14 states that "[t]he special consideration to be given to the output of the International Law Commission is described in paragraph (2) of the general commentary to the present Part (Part Five) above." This does not mean that the general requirements for other collective expert bodies would not apply to the Commission's determinations. As indicated above, paragraph (2) of the commentary to part five also refers to some (non-exhaustive) qualitative criteria, which overlap with the "care and objectivity" referred in the commentary to conclusion 14: e.g. "the sources relied upon".

The Commission's recent work on how international law may be identified and interpreted, whether in the context of the law of treaties, customary international law, or *jus cogens*, and in the future with respect to general principles of law,[24] should be consistently used by the Commission not only for codification, but also for progressive development: as the method for determining the existence or non-existence of rules and their content, as well as the stage of their development. The secondary rules systematized by the Commission for those topics are invaluable for the Commission itself: they should consciously guide the Commission's work, if the Commission is to maintain and even enhance its influence.

III Commentaries

In the commentaries, the Commission explains the draft text, such as draft articles, draft conclusions, draft guidelines or draft principles, with references to practice, judicial decisions and doctrine. This is important because in doing so, the Commission provides evidence of the "care and objectivity" in its reasoning. For instance, the commentaries to the 2011 guide to practice on reservations to treaties[25] and to the 2018 conclusions on subsequent agreements and subsequent practice in relation to the interpretation of treaties[26] are indicative of the methodology that the Commission employs when it interprets the Vienna Convention on the Law of Treaties.[27] Adherence to the rules on treaty interpretation may persuade States to entertain the Commission's interpretative pronouncements.

However, commentaries are also crucial for the identification and interpretation of rules, particularly by judicial actors. The following analysis demonstrates the role and importance of commentaries in judicial practice. In order to be methodologically thorough and comprehensive, the analysis focuses on the decisions of the International Court of Justice. It shows that the Court

24 ILC, 'Report of the International Law Commission on the work of its seventieth session' (2018) UN Doc A/73/10, 299 at para 363.

25 ILC, 'Guide to practice on reservations to treaties, comprising an introduction, the guidelines and commentaries thereto, an annex on the reservations dialogue and a bibliography' [2011] II(3) ILC Ybk 23.

26 ILC, 'Draft conclusions on subsequent agreements and subsequent practice in relation to the interpretation of treaties and commentaries thereto' (2018) UN Doc A/73/10, 12.

27 See detailed analysis in Danae Azaria, *'Codification by Interpretation': The International Law Commission's Interpretative Activity and Method* (forthcoming).

relies heavily on the commentaries adopted by the Commission (section 1). In light of these findings, it is surprising how very little (if any) literature exists on the significance of commentaries and on the method of their preparation and adoption. For this reason, the analysis then moves on to the manner in which commentaries are prepared and adopted; it reflects on and assesses some contemporary methods of preparing commentaries; and makes some suggestions for improving the method of preparation of commentaries that are adopted by the Commission (section 2).

1 *The Significance of Commentaries in the Decisions of the International Court of Justice*

Commentaries have considerable legal significance, which is demonstrated by the number of instances in which international courts and tribunals have relied on them. Research in this regard focused on the decisions of the International Court of Justice is quite telling.

As of 30 August 2018, the International Court of Justice has relied expressly on the Commission's work in 22 cases (19 decisions in contentious proceedings and 3 advisory opinions).[28] In each case, the Court relies on the Commission's

28 Contentious Proceedings: *North Sea Continental Shelf Cases* (*Federal Republic of Germany/Denmark; Federal Republic of Germany/The Netherlands*) [1969] ICJ Rep 3, paras 48–50, 54–55, 95; *Continental Shelf* (*Tunisia v Libya*) [1982] ICJ Rep 18, paras 41, 100, 119; *Military and Paramilitary Activities in and against Nicaragua* (*Nicaragua v United States*) (Merits) [1986] ICJ Rep 14, 100 at para 190; *Gabčíkovo-Nagymaros Project* (*Hungary/Slovakia*) [1997] ICJ Rep 7, paras 47, 50–54, 58, 123; *Land and Maritime Boundary between Cameroon and Nigeria* (*Cameroon v Nigeria*) (Preliminary Objections) [1998] ICJ Rep 275, para 31; *Kasikili/Sedudu Island* (*Botswana v Namibia*) (Merits) [1999] ICJ Rep 1045, para 49; *Maritime Delimitation and Territorial Questions between Qatar and Bahrain* (*Qatar v Bahrain*) (Merits) [2001] ICJ Rep 40, para 113; *Land and Maritime Boundary between Cameroon and Nigeria* (*Cameroon v Nigeria; Equatorial Guinea intervening*) (Merits) [2002] ICJ Rep 303, para 265; *Armed Activities on the Territory of the Congo* (*Democratic Republic of Congo v Uganda*) (Merits) [2005] ICJ Rep 168, paras 160, 293; *Application of the Convention on the Prevention and Punishment of the Crime of Genocide* (*Bosnia and Herzegovina v Serbia and Montenegro*) (Merits) [2007] ICJ Rep 43, paras 173, 186, 199, 344, 385, 398, 420, 431; *Territorial and Maritime Dispute between Nicaragua and Honduras in the Caribbean Sea* (*Nicaragua v Honduras*) (Merits) [2007] ICJ Rep 659, para 280; *Ahmadou Sadio Diallo* (*Guinea v Democratic Republic of Congo*) (Preliminary Objections) [2007] ICJ Rep 582, paras 39, 64, 84, 91, 93; *Maritime Delimitation in the Black Sea* (*Romania v Ukraine*) (Merits) [2009] ICJ Rep 61, para 134; *Pulp Mills on the River Uruguay* (*Argentina v Uruguay*) [2010] ICJ Rep 14, para 273; *Maritime Dispute* (*Peru v Chile*) [2014] ICJ Rep 3, paras 112–117; *Jurisdictional Immunities of the State* (*Germany v Italy; Greece intervening*) (Merits) [2012] ICJ Rep 24, paras 56, 69, 89, 137; *Obligations concerning Negotiations relating to Cessation of the Nuclear Arms Race and to Nuclear Disarmament* (*Marshall Island v India*) (Jurisdiction and Admissibility) [2016] ICJ Rep 255, para 42; *Obligations*

work to address a range of legal questions, and may also use more than one document for each legal question. All told, the Court has relied on Commission documents in relation to 39 different legal questions. Among these, it relied on the commentaries in 13 cases (out of 22)[29] and in relation to 21 legal questions (out of 39). Of these 21 legal questions, the Court relied exclusively on the commentary in 11 instances.

---

concerning Negotiations relating to Cessation of the Nuclear Arms Race and to Nuclear Disarmament (*Marshall Islands v United Kingdom*) (Preliminary Objections) [2016] ICJ Rep 833, para 45; *Certain Activities carried out by Nicaragua in the Border Area* (*Costa Rica v Nicaragua*) (Compensation owed by the Republic of Nicaragua to the Republic of Costa Rica) 2 February 2018 <https://www.icj-cij.org/en/case/150/judgments>, para 151. Advisory Opinions: *Interpretation of the Agreement of 25 March 1951 between the WHO and Egypt* (Advisory Opinion) [1980] ICJ Rep 73, paras 47, 49–50; *Differences Relating to Immunity from Legal Process of a Special Rapporteur of the Commission on Human Rights* (Advisory Opinion) [1999] ICJ Rep 62, para 62; *Legal Consequences of the Construction of a Wall in the Occupied Palestinian Territory* (Advisory Opinion) [2004] ICJ Rep 136, 175, 176, 195 at para 140.

29 *Military and Paramilitary Activities in and against Nicaragua* (*Nicaragua v United States*) (n 28) 100 at para 190; *Gabčíkovo-Nagymaros Project* (*Hungary/Slovakia*) (n 28) paras 50–54, 123; *Land and Maritime Boundary between Cameroon and Nigeria* (*Cameroon v Nigeria*) (n 28) para 31; *Kasikili/Sedudu Island* (*Botswana v Namibia*) (n 28) para 49; *Land and Maritime Boundary between Cameroon and Nigeria* (*Cameroon v. Nigeria; Equatorial Guinea intervening*) (n 28) para 265; *Armed Activities on the Territory of the Congo* (*Democratic Republic of Congo v Uganda*) (n 28) para 293; *Application of the Convention on the Prevention and Punishment of the Crime of Genocide* (*Bosnia and Herzegovina v Serbia and Montenegro*) (n 28) paras 173, 186, 199, 344; *Territorial and Maritime Dispute between Nicaragua and Honduras in the Caribbean Sea* (*Nicaragua v Honduras*) (n 28) para 280; *Maritime Delimitation in the Black Sea* (*Romania v Ukraine*) (n 28) para 134; *Jurisdictional Immunities of the State* (*Germany v Italy; Greece intervening*) (n 28) paras 56, 69; *Obligations concerning Negotiations relating to Cessation of the Nuclear Arms Race and to Nuclear Disarmament* (*Marshall Island v India*) (n 28) para 42; *Obligations concerning Negotiations relating to Cessation of the Nuclear Arms Race and to Nuclear Disarmament* (*Marshall Islands v United Kingdom*) (n 28) para 45; *Certain Activities carried out by Nicaragua in the Border Area* (*Costa Rica v Nicaragua*) (n 28) para 151. *Bosnia and Herzegovina v Serbia and Montenegro* and *Germany v Italy* include instances where the Court relied on the commentary to identify customary international law, and on separate occasions as a supplementary means of treaty interpretation. They are not counted twice among the 13 cases referred. However, in the breakdown below they appear in relation to instances where the Court used the Commission's commentary in relation to treaty interpretation and to custom identification. *Marshall Islands v India* and *Marshall Islands v United Kingdom* are the two cases that do not fall within these two classifications; but within the instances where the Court has used the Commission's commentary in order to interpret the draft provision without taking a position about customary international law or using it for treaty interpretation.

In seven cases the Court treated the commentaries as a supplementary means of treaty interpretation. In six of these cases, it relied on them as preparatory works of a treaty.[30] In one case, *Application of the Convention on the Prevention and Punishment of the Crime of Genocide* (*Bosnia and Herzegovina v Serbia and Montenegro*), the Court relied on the commentary of the 1996 Draft Code of Crimes against the Peace and Security of Mankind in order to interpret the 1948 Genocide Convention, a treaty which had been concluded almost 50 years earlier and in whose drafting the Commission had not been involved.[31] In six cases, the Court relied on the commentaries in order to identify a rule of customary international law.[32]

As a separate matter, as Judge Gaja has persuasively argued, since the Commission adopts draft provisions together with commentaries, the commentaries constitute the context in which draft provisions are to be interpreted.[33] This can be important in practice. In *Marshall Islands v India,* and *Marshall Islands v United Kingdom* (2016), India and the United Kingdom objected to the Court's jurisdiction. They both argued that article 43 of the 2001 articles on the responsibility of States for internationally wrongful acts requires the injured State (and by analogy States other than the injured State) to give notice of its claim to the allegedly responsible State. Since the Marshall Islands had not done so, the respondents argued that there was no dispute and as a result the Court lacked jurisdiction.[34] The Court rejected this argument. By relying

30 *Land and Maritime Boundary between Cameroon and Nigeria* (*Cameroon v Nigeria*) (n 28) para 31; *Kasikili/Sedudu Island* (*Botswana v Namibia*) (n 28) para 49; *Land and Maritime Boundary between Cameroon and Nigeria* (*Cameroon v Nigeria; Equatorial Guinea intervening*) (n 28) para 265; *Territorial and Maritime Dispute between Nicaragua and Honduras in the Caribbean Sea* (*Nicaragua v Honduras*) (n 28) para 280; *Maritime Delimitation in the Black Sea* (*Romania v Ukraine*) (n 28) para 134; *Jurisdictional Immunities of the State* (*Germany v Italy; Greece intervening*) (n 28) para 69.

31 *Application of the Convention on the Prevention and Punishment of the Crime of Genocide* (*Bosnia and Herzegovina v Serbia and Montenegro*) (n 28) para 186.

32 *Military and Paramilitary Activities in and against Nicaragua* (*Nicaragua v United States*) (n 28) para 190; *Gabčíkovo-Nagymaros Project* (*Hungary/Slovakia*) (n 28) paras 50–54, 58, and 123; *Armed Activities on the Territory of the Congo* (*Democratic Republic of Congo v Uganda*) (n 28) para 293; *Application of the Convention on the Prevention and Punishment of the Crime of Genocide* (*Bosnia and Herzegovina v Serbia and Montenegro*) (n 28) para 173; *Jurisdictional Immunities of the State* (*Germany v Italy; Greece intervening*) (n 28) para 56; *Certain Activities carried out by Nicaragua in the Border Area* (*Costa Rica v Nicaragua*) (n 28) para 151.

33 Giorgio Gaja, 'Interpreting Articles Adopted by the International Law Commission' (2016) 85 BYIL 10.

34 *Obligations concerning Negotiations relating to Cessation of the Nuclear Arms Race and to Nuclear Disarmament* (*Marshall Island v India*) (n 28) para 32; *Obligations concerning*

on the commentary to article 44, the Court found that the articles are not concerned with issues of jurisdiction or admissibility of claims.[35] In other words, the Court *interpreted* article 43 *in the context of* the commentary to article 44.

The significance of the commentaries cannot be greater than that of the draft articles, draft guidelines, draft conclusions or draft principles adopted by the Commission, though commentaries may shed important light on them. However, the fact that the Court has relied on the commentaries in more than half of the decisions where it has relied on the Commission's work overall shows that commentaries play a crucial role in judicial practice. In light of these findings, the method of their preparation and adoption deserves close scrutiny.

2 *Preparation and Adoption of Commentaries*

This section briefly describes the Commission's usual working methods and its interaction with governments through the Sixth (Legal) Committee of the United Nations General Assembly focusing on the consideration and preparation of commentaries (section a). Then, it provides some reasons for which the Commission ought to reconsider its current approaches to the preparation of commentaries and makes some proposals that may assist the Commission in drafting commentaries in a timely fashion. More specifically, it discusses the time at which the Commission considers and adopts commentaries (section b), the usefulness of working groups on commentaries (section c), and the implications of publicising the Drafting Committee's draft articles that are not accompanied by commentaries (section d). It touches on a recent development which involves the preparation of commentaries only after the Drafting Committee has adopted provisionally a complete set of draft provisions over a number of years (section e), before summarizing some suggestions about the approach that the Commission may wish to adopt vis-à-vis the preparation of commentaries (section f).

(a) Overview of Working Methods Concerning the Preparation and Adoption of Commentaries

The procedures of the Commission have changed over the years, but currently they usually take the following form. When introducing a topic in its

---

Negotiations relating to Cessation of the Nuclear Arms Race and to Nuclear Disarmament (*Marshall Islands v United Kingdom*) (n 28) paras 27–28.

35 *Obligations concerning Negotiations relating to Cessation of the Nuclear Arms Race and to Nuclear Disarmament* (*Marshall Island v India*) (n 28) para 42; *Obligations concerning Negotiations relating to Cessation of the Nuclear Arms Race and to Nuclear Disarmament* (*Marshall Islands v United Kingdom*) (n 28) para 45.

programme of work, the Commission decides whether to appoint a Special Rapporteur. Once appointed, the Special Rapporteur prepares and submits her or his report(s), which include her or his proposals backed by her or his analysis, to be considered by the Commission's plenary, where proceedings are public. In plenary, members of the Commission comment on the Special Rapporteur's report. The Commission in plenary decides whether the proposals are to be referred to the Drafting Committee. If so, the Drafting Committee meets (in closed session) in order to prepare and provisionally adopt draft texts (being draft articles, conclusions, guidelines or principles), which it then submits to plenary for approval, along with draft commentaries prepared by the Special Rapporteur. At each session the Commission (in plenary) provisionally adopts on first reading the draft texts proposed by the Drafting Committee, although it only does so when commentaries on the draft texts are available at that session. Otherwise it only takes note of the draft texts prepared by the Drafting Committee. This process repeats itself in subsequent years based on subsequent reports of the Special Rapporteur, until such time as a complete set of draft articles (or conclusions, guidelines or principles) is completed, at which point they are adopted as a whole on first reading.

The Commission's progress on the topics it considers annually is recorded in its annual report, which is submitted to the General Assembly. The General Assembly considers the Commission's annual report each year in the Sixth Committee, which is composed of delegates of all United Nations Member States, who may comment on the Commission's annual report. The Special Rapporteur and the Commission take into account governments' comments in the following sessions of the Commission. Usually oral comments on first reading draft texts and commentaries are only taken into account (along with written comments made to the first reading) in preparation of the second reading.

If and when a full set of draft articles (or conclusion, guidelines or principles) is adopted on first reading by the Commission (in plenary), the Commission submits it along with commentaries to the General Assembly. The Commission also invites written comments from governments, usually providing about fifteen months for submissions. After the written submissions are received, the Special Rapporteur produces a final report that revisits the draft articles and commentaries adopted on first reading, taking into account the comments of governments making proposals for changes. The proposed changes are then debated in the plenary, which may refer them to the Drafting Committee. When the Commission in plenary finally adopts the draft articles on second reading along with commentaries, the Commission concludes its work on the topic. It submits the draft articles together with commentaries to the General Assembly, making a recommendation concerning the future treatment of the document.[36]

The reports of Special Rapporteurs are the prime tool by which the Commission develops its work in plenary and the Drafting Committee. They are also, together with the comments in plenary and the discussions in the Drafting Committee, a springboard for the preparation of the commentaries. The Special Rapporteur, and the quality of her or his report are central to the progress of a topic. The Special Rapporteur *offers a service* to the Commission and to the Commission's *collegiate* output.

The Drafting Committee, owing to its function, informality and limited composition,[37] also makes an important contribution. The negotiations are painstakingly detailed and may revolve around technical drafting, legal substance or material that may support the one or the other possible formulation. Ideally, the Drafting Committee should be involved in the preparation of the commentary to a provision in parallel with the draft provision, because very often language in the commentaries may ease agreement about the formulation of a particular draft provision. However, because of its workload, the Drafting Committee does not produce commentaries.[38] Rather, the usual practice is that the Special Rapporteur prepares and revises the commentary after the Drafting Committee provisionally adopts draft texts. In doing so, he or she takes account of what has been said in the Drafting Committee. In some instances, commentaries have been prepared on the basis of consideration in a separate working group.

Usually the Commission (in plenary) considers commentaries at the end of its session (in August). For those topics considered in the first part of the

---

36 Following adoption by the Commission of a document on second (and final) reading, governments are invited to make comments in the Sixth Committee, which also prepares a General Assembly resolution about the handling of the text and which may decide to reconsider this issue at a future session.

37 In 1992, the Commission recommended that in order for the Drafting Committee to operate efficiently, it should not have more than 14 members, taking into account representative composition. Other members may observe, but should exercise constraint in their comments, see [1992] II(2) ILC Ybk paras 371 and 373. However, members of the Commission can be part of the Drafting Committee on any topic. The Drafting Committee's composition for some topics is up to 25 members. See 'Report of the International Law Commission on the work of its sixty-ninth session' (2017) UN Doc A/72/10, 2 at para 6.

38 ILC, 'Report of the International Law Commission on the work of its forty-eighth session' [1996] II(2) ILC Ybk 1, 92 at para 199.

Commission's session (usually in May), the Special Rapporteur has time to prepare commentaries (to the draft articles provisionally adopted by the Drafting Committee) during the break in the Commission's session and submit them for consideration and adoption in the second half of the Commission's session. However, for those topics that are considered in the second part of the Commission's session (in July), there is usually insufficient time for the Special Rapporteur to prepare the commentaries and for the plenary to consider them on time. As explained above, the Commission does not adopt draft texts (articles, conclusions, guidelines or principles) without commentaries. In such cases, the Commission merely takes note of draft texts provisionally adopted by the Drafting Committee. However, since 2012, the Drafting Committee's report that is presented by its Chair in plenary and contains these draft texts becomes publicly available.[39] This development has encouraged governments in the Sixth Committee to react to the Drafting Committee's provisionally adopted draft texts (without there being commentaries on them).

Building on these trends, in relation to some topics, a new approach has occasionally been followed: draft texts are kept in the Drafting Committee annually, and the Special Rapporteur prepares the commentary, once the Drafting Committee has adopted all draft texts on a topic. All draft texts and commentaries are then adopted by the plenary on first reading. The conclusions on identification of customary international law were prepared in this way (over a two-year period without adopting commentaries) and adopted on first reading (2016). In this particular case, the approach was followed owing to time constraints and on an exceptional basis, and with the consideration of commentaries by a working group before their consideration and adoption in plenary.[40] However, the approach of preparing and adopting commentaries only

39 The first quotation of draft provisions adopted provisionally by the Drafting Committee appeared in 2012: The draft articles on the protection of persons in the event of disasters provisionally adopted by the Drafting Committee were quoted in a footnote in the Commission's report. ILC, 'Report of the International Law Commission on the work of its sixty-forth session' (2012) UN Doc A/67/10, 85 at footnote 275.

40 The Commission considered the first report of the Special Rapporteur (UN Doc A/CN.4/663) in 2013. The Special Rapporteur only proposed draft conclusions in his second report (UN Doc A/CN.4/672) (2014) and his third report (UN Doc A/CN.4/682) (2015), and proposed amendments to the conclusions provisionally adopted by the Drafting Committee in his fourth report (UN Doc A/CN.4/695 and Add.1) (2016). In 2014, the Commission only dealt with the report of the Special Rapporteur in the second half of its session which meant that the Drafting Committee dealt with this topic late in the Commission's session leaving no time for commentaries to be prepared and adopted by the Commission. ILC, 'Report of the International Law Commission on the work of its sixty-sixth session' (2014) UN Doc A/69/10, 238 at paras 135–136. In 2015, the discussion

once the whole set of draft texts is prepared and adopted has been proposed for other topics as a matter of preference. In relation to the topic peremptory norms of general international law (*jus cogens*), the Special Rapporteur has indicated his preference not to draft commentaries before the whole set of draft conclusions is provisionally adopted by the Drafting Committee.[41] No commentaries have been considered by the Commission on this topic for three years while draft provisions have been provisionally adopted by the Drafting Committee.[42]

---

of the topic began in the first part of the Commission's session, but owing to the importance of commentaries in general, the Special Rapporteur proposed that "if the Drafting Committee was able to complete its work this session, and provisionally adopt a complete set of draft conclusions [...], [he] could then prepare draft commentaries on all the conclusions in time for the beginning of the 2016 session. Members would then have adequate time to consider the draft commentaries carefully," so that the full set of first reading draft conclusions and commentaries could be adopted by the Commission by the end of its 2016 session. ILC report 2015 (n 24), p. 48 at para 107. In 2016, the commentary was discussed in a Working Group early in the first half of the Commission's session (May 2016). ILC, 'Report of the International Law Commission on the work of its sixty-eighth session' (2016) UN Doc A/71/10, p 75 at para 58.

41 Dire Tladi, 'Third report on peremptory norms of general international law (*jus cogens*)' (2018) UN Doc A/CN.4/714, 4 at para 11 ("The Special Rapporteur has indicated his *preference* that the draft conclusions remain with the Drafting Committee and, for that reason, they have not been referred to the plenary"; emphasis added). The statement of the Chair of the Drafting Committee (14 May 2018) also indicates that "[i]n line with the Special Rapporteur's recommendation, made in 2016, the draft conclusions remain in the Drafting Committee until the full set has been adopted so that the Commission will be presented with a full set of draft conclusions before taking action." Peremptory norms of general international law (*jus cogens*), Statement of the Chairperson of the Drafting Committee, Oral interim report, Mr. Charles Chernor Jalloh, 14 May 2018, p 1, available at: http://legal.un.org/docs/?path=../ilc/documentation/english/statements/2018_dc_chairman_statement_jc.pdf&lang=E. Upon the concerns expressed by some Commission members, the Special Rapporteur recounted that "[t]he topic had always been considered in the second part of the Commission's annual session" thus making it impossible to have commentaries considered in plenary. See UN Doc A/CN.4/SR.3425, 3.

42 The Commission considered the first report of the Special Rapporteur (UN Doc A/CN.4/693) (2016) in the second half of its session, and the Drafting Committee provisionally adopted three draft conclusions. ILC Report 2016 (n 40), 297 at paras 98–101. In his second report (2017), the Special Rapporteur proposed six more draft conclusions (UN Doc A/CN.4/706) (2017) and the Drafting Committee provisionally adopted draft conclusions in the second half of the Commission's session. ILC Report 2017 (n 37), 192 at paras 144–147. In 2018, in the first half of the Commission's seventieth session (2018), the Drafting Committee provisionally adopted draft conclusions 8 and 9, which had been proposed by the Special Rapporteur in his second report that the Drafting Committee considered in the previous session (2017). The Commission also considered in the first and second

Having set out the Commission's main working methods and latest developments, the following sections further assess some of the practices vis-à-vis commentaries.

(b) The Time of Consideration of Commentaries

As noted above, the Commission adopts commentaries in plenary usually at the end of its session. Considering commentaries so late during the session introduces considerable time pressure and little opportunity for debate. It could be argued that Commission members have ample opportunity to consider commentaries in detail before they are adopted on second reading. However, courts and tribunals have relied upon draft articles and commentaries adopted on first reading. A paradigmatic example is the reliance of the International Court of Justice in *Gabčíkovo-Nagymaros Project* (1997) on the Commission's draft articles on responsibility of States for internationally wrongful acts adopted on first reading.[43] Further, even on second reading, commentaries are usually considered at the end of the Commission's session and adopted under time pressure.

If the Commission decreased the number of topics on its programme of work, there would be more time for Commission members to consider commentaries in further detail prior to the consideration in plenary as well as in plenary. As a separate matter, the use of working groups dedicated to the drafting of commentaries may allow for more thorough consideration by Commission members prior to the debate in plenary. This issue is further discussed below (section c).

(c) Working Groups on Commentaries

Working groups have occasionally assisted in the preparation of commentaries. For instance, the commentaries to the articles on responsibility of States for internationally wrongful acts were prepared on second reading by the Special Rapporteur and were commented on by a number of members in a working group.[44] A recent example is the working group for the commentary to

half of its session the third report of the Special Rapporteur (UN Doc A/CN.4/714 and Corr.1), who proposed 13 additional draft conclusions. ILC Report 2018 (n 24), 224–227 at paras 94–97.

43 *Gabčíkovo-Nagymaros Project* (*Hungary/Slovakia*) (n 28) paras 47, 50–54, 58. Domestic courts have also done so. For instance, the English Court of Appeal in *The Freedom and Justice Party and Ors v The Secretary of State for Foreign and Commonwealth Affairs* referred to the draft conclusions on the identification of customary international law adopted on first reading: [2018] EWCA Civ 1719, 19 September 2018, para. 18.

44 ILC, 'Report of the International Law Commission on the work of its fifty-third session' [2001] II(2) ILC Ybk 1, 21 at para 43.

the conclusions on the identification of customary international law, which worked in the first part of the Commission's session in 2016 and assisted the Special Rapporteur to prepare a commentary to the whole set of conclusions. The commentary was prepared in time for and was adopted in the second half of the Commission's session that year.

Such a working group format does not negotiate or prepare commentaries. It assists the Special Rapporteur in light of the enormous amount of material to be assessed. It also allows members of the Commission to thoroughly examine drafts of the commentaries and have some ownership over them. In this way, it enables consensus and saves time in plenary. For these reasons, it may be worth using this process further. However, the working group procedure does not necessarily entail and should not be understood as preventing members of the Commission that participate in the working group from scrutinising the commentaries in plenary,[45] where discussions are public, allowing for further clarification of the commentaries.

(d) Publicizing the Report of the Drafting Committee Without Commentaries

As explained above, since 2012, the statements of the Chair of the Drafting Committee, which summarize the debate of the Drafting Committee and present the draft provisions that the Drafting Committee has provisionally adopted, are made publicly available. This publicity has encouraged governments to read the Drafting Committee's adopted texts and react to them in the Sixth Committee. In light of these reactions, the Special Rapporteur and the Drafting Committee may make further changes before draft texts and commentaries are adopted on first reading.

On the other hand, the texts that are provisionally adopted by the Drafting Committee are currently referred to in the annual reports of the Commission in an inconsistent manner. At times the annual report quotes in a footnote the text provisionally adopted by the Drafting Committee.[46] On other occasions,

45 See the concern voiced by Shinya Murase in his contribution to this Section that members may not be willing to repeat in plenary the views they expressed in a working group.

46 For example, in the 2015 report, the draft articles on immunities of State officials from foreign criminal jurisdiction and the draft principles on the protection of the environment in times of armed conflict, both provisionally adopted by the Drafting Committee, are quoted verbatim (ILC report 2015 (n 18) 116 at footnotes 389–390 and 105 at footnotes 377–378, respectively). In the 2016 report, the draft principles on the protection of the environment in relation to armed conflict and the draft guidelines on provisional application of treaties, provisionally adopted by the Drafting Committee, are also quoted verbatim (ILC report 2016 (n 40), 308 at footnote 1309 and 365 at footnote 1454, respectively).

the annual report only cites the Commission's webpage without quoting the draft text and without citing the precise webpage where the specific document is located. Rather the reader must look for the document in the website of the Commission.[47] This inconsistency takes place not only from annual report to annual report, but also within the same annual report.[48]

This is not merely an editorial point or only a point about making more easily accessible the documents cited in the annual report of the Commission. It indicates that it is unclear whether States in the Sixth Committee comment on the Drafting Committee's output, which may be quoted verbatim in a footnote in the report or cross-referred to, or whether they only respond to the provisions proposed by the Special Rapporteur, which are usually also quoted in the Commission's report.[49] If States comment on the Special Rapporteur's report, time is lost, because the Drafting Committee often has revised the Special Rapporteur's proposals. If instead they comment on draft provisions of the Drafting Committee without reference to commentaries, States fail to consider the commentaries of these draft provisions, which give explanations and evidence of State practice and authorities, and which constitute the context in which draft provisions are to be interpreted, as explained in section 1

47 As an example, the 2017 report does not quote the draft conclusions on peremptory norms of general international law (*jus cogens*) or draft articles on succession of States in respect of State responsibility, provisionally adopted by the Drafting Committee, but it cites the Commission's webpage, which means that in order to find the statement of the Chair of the Drafting Committee appending them one needs to look for the page of a particular topic and find the list of reports of the Drafting Committee. (ILC report 2017 (n 37) 193 at footnote 809, and 203 at footnote 817, respectively).

48 The 2015 report of the Commission cites the webpage of the Commission, thus directing the reader to look for the statement of the Drafting Committee's Chair, which appends the provisionally adopted draft conclusions on identification of customary international law and the provisionally adopted draft guidelines on provisional application (ILC report 2015 (n 18) 40 at footnote 76 and 131 at footnote 395, respectively). However, in the same report, the draft articles on immunities of State officials from foreign criminal jurisdiction and the draft principles on the protection of the environment in times of armed conflict, both provisionally adopted by the Drafting Committee, are quoted verbatim (ILC report 2015 (n 18) 116 at footnotes 389–390 and 105 at footnotes 377–378, respectively). The 2016 report of the Commission quotes verbatim the draft principles on the protection of the environment in relation to armed conflict and the draft guidelines on provisional application of treaties, provisionally adopted by the Drafting Committee (ILC report 2016 (n 40), 308 at footnote 1309 and 365 at footnote 1454, respectively). However, it only cites the the webpage of the Commission, thus directing the reader to look for the statement of the Drafting Committee's Chair, which appends the draft conclusions on *jus cogens* provisionally adopted by the Drafting Committee (ibid 297 at footnote 1289).

49 ILC report 2015 (n 18) 39 at footnote 75; ILC report 2017 (n 37) 192–193 at footnote 808.

above. Their comments do not reflect on the Commission's expert analysis, and may be abstract, politicized and unhelpful. This may also result in further political considerations being introduced in the Commission's work and in further politicising the internal work and output of the Commission before the Commission has even formulated its detailed expert analysis in commentaries.[50]

(e) Preparing Commentaries Only Once the Drafting Committee Provisionally Adopts a Complete Set of Draft Provisions

As explained above (section a), there seems to be some interest in adopting a policy of preparing commentaries only once a complete set of draft articles (or conclusions, guidelines, principles) is adopted. Such an approach builds on some practices of the Commission (sections a to d). For instance, it is coupled with the practice of making publicly available the Drafting Committee's provisionally adopted draft articles. The advantages of and concerns about such practice (explained in section d) apply equally to preparing commentaries only once the whole set of draft articles have been prepared. Although it facilitates the updating of draft articles and commentaries by taking into account governments' comments prior to adoption of the draft articles on first reading, the comments of governments may be politicized and unhelpful, because governments have not considered the commentary, which is the context of the draft articles.

The Commission's statute requires that when the Commission submits to the General Assembly draft texts it must do so with commentaries. In relation to progressive development, article 16(g) of the Commission's statute, which deals with the preliminary work before governments submit comments, refers to "explanations and supporting material". In relation to codification, article 20, which deals with the stage before governments submit comments, refers to "commentary"; article 21(1), which is also relevant to the stage prior to the comments of governments, refers to "explanations and supporting material"; and article 22, which deals with the stage after governments have given comments, refers to "explanatory report". This terminology does not entail documents that are different in substance to what in the Commission's practice is called "commentary".

One way of interpreting these provisions is that the Commission is required to prepare commentaries only once the Commission has adopted the whole

50 For an empirical assessment of how world politics affect the Commission's function: Jeffrey Morton, *The International Law Commission of the United Nations* (University of South Carolina Press 2000) 74–101.

set of draft texts on a topic on first reading. Pursuant to this interpretation, making available for information only the Drafting Committee's provisionally adopted texts without commentaries is compatible with the statute, because the Commission has not yet adopted any text (on first or second reading). However, it may be argued that such an interpretation may not be consistent with the spirit of the statute. The statute establishes two aspects whose interaction leads to the progressive development of international law and its codification. The Commission represents the scientific/expert aspect of progressive development of international law and its codification. The governments, through the General Assembly, represent the political aspect. The statute requires the Commission (the expert aspect) to submit draft texts to the General Assembly together with commentaries, so that governments (the political aspect) reflect and comment on the outputs and reasoning of the expert aspect. Thus, when the General Assembly has sight of draft texts, whenever that may be, it should be with commentary on the draft text.

In addition, if commentaries are considered at the end of the Commission's work on a topic after numerous years, the preparation of commentaries may be too distant from, and they may not be given a role in the drafting process in the Drafting Committee. They cannot assist consensus through explanation of a draft provision. Further, nuances expressed when the draft provisions are adopted may be lost, owing to a significant passage of time between the adoption of a draft provision by the Drafting Committee and when the commentaries are written and adopted perhaps years later.[51] Additionally, if the Special Rapporteur changes (or indeed other Commission members change), either within the same quinquennium or between quinquennia, the memory of the details of the reasoning of the Drafting Committee that were meant to be reflected in the commentaries may be lost. Moreover, when the Commission, after a few years of considering a topic, does consider the commentaries (under time pressure in the end of the Commission's session), Commission members will have insufficient time thoroughly to consider, reflect and comment on the commentary. Finally, when the Commission adopts commentaries on first reading (after the passage of a considerable period of time), States will face a large amount of material in the commentary. Normally, they will have just over a year to give written comments. This may be challenging, even for States with a large legal staff in their ministries of foreign affairs, let alone those States that do not have such capacity.[52]

---

51 See also statement by Mr. Murase in plenary, UN Doc A/CN.4/SR.3418, 14.

52 Similar concern expressed in the Commission by Mr. Nolte, UN Doc A/CN.4/SR.3417, 15.

(f) Interim Conclusions

The Commission ought to consider systemically the role, preparation and adoption of commentaries as a matter of priority, given their importance in judicial practice, and their importance for the Commission itself.

It is of paramount importance to provide conditions for a meaningful review of commentaries by Commission members. The basic condition for such meaningful scrutiny is to give members of the Commission sufficient time to consider the commentaries before the debate and adoption in plenary, and to allow sufficient time for a debate in plenary specifically dedicated to commentaries.

Further, working groups for the consideration of commentaries is a useful practice: it assists the Special Rapporteur in their preparation, it allows Commission members to be thoroughly involved in the consideration of commentaries, and it enables consensus and saves time in plenary. However, it should not be understood or employed as a practice that pre-empts the scrutiny of commentaries in plenary.

Finally, the Commission occasionally takes note of the Drafting Committee's report for topics considered in the second half of its session for which commentaries have not yet been prepared. The report of the Drafting Committee is presented and is made public annexing the draft texts provisionally adopted by the Drafting Committee but without commentaries. This should remain an exceptional practice, and may be addressed by re-evaluating the number of topics on which the Commission works during its annual sessions.

The Commission ought to avoid establishing, as a matter of new policy, a practice whereby commentaries are only prepared at the end of its consideration of a topic on first reading. A systematic practice that follows such an approach for numerous years (or between quinquennia, when the Commission's composition changes) may deprive commentaries of their role in enabling consensus, runs the risk of losing the detailed context that the Drafting Committee intended to give to a draft text (be that a draft article, conclusion, guideline or principle), and does not facilitate the genuine interaction of the Sixth Committee with the Commission, since governments react to draft texts without considering the explanations of such provisions in the commentary, which constitutes the context of such draft provisions. If the Commission requires more time for the drafting of commentaries, it may be better to reconsider the number of topics it works on during its annual sessions, rather than considering and preparing the commentaries at the end of the drafting process. If nonetheless the Commission follows such an approach, it will be essential that the commentaries are considered in a working group so as to ensure that

Commission members have sufficient opportunity to consider the significant amount of material in the commentary.

IV Method of Decision-Making: between Vote and Consensus

Rule 125 of the rules of procedure of the General Assembly provides that decisions of committees shall be made by majority of the members present and voting. It applies equally to the International Law Commission, and governs decisions of the Commission in plenary to refer texts to the Drafting Committee, the decisions in the Drafting Committee, and the decisions to adopt texts in plenary on first and second reading.

In the early years of the Commission's life, decisions were often taken by vote. Since the 1970s, however, the Commission has predominantly taken decisions by consensus; only exceptionally has it resorted to a vote. It should not come as a surprise that the Commission moved to consensual decision-making in the 1970s, in the aftermath of the *North Sea Continental Shelf* case in 1969. In its judgment in this case, the International Court of Justice had found that the "status of the rule [set forth in Article 6] of the [Geneva] Convention [as customary or not] depended mainly on the *processes* that led the Commission to propose it".[53] The Court noted that some doubts had been voiced in the Commission about whether the equidistance principle was a customary rule, and concluded that Article 6 of the Geneva Convention had not crystallized into rule of customary international law.[54]

The latest example where the Commission resorted to a vote was in 2017, in relation to draft article 7 of the draft articles on the "immunity of State officials from foreign criminal jurisdiction",[55] which concerns exceptions to immunity of State officials. Before then, some instances from 1981 to 2017 where the Commission resorted to vote are the following: (a) in 2009 two indicative votes took place in plenary in relation to reservations to treaties (on first reading);[56] (b) in

53 *North Sea Continental Shelf Cases (Federal Republic of Germany/Denmark; Federal Republic of Germany/The Netherlands)* (n 28) para 62 (emphasis added).

54 Ibid.

55 ILC report 2017 (n 37) 164 at para 74.

56 The first vote was taken before referring to the Drafting Committee the proposals of the Special Rapporteur concerning a draft guideline on the statement of reasons for interpretative declarations. The Special Rapporteur had requested the vote and it was decided not to include such a guideline. The second indicative vote was after the Drafting Committee's work on that topic during that session; on the basis of the vote it was decided not to include in draft guideline 3.4.2 a provision concerning *jus cogens* in relation to

2008, a vote was taken in plenary on the topic of reservations to treaties concerning the amendment of a guideline on the procedure for communication of reservations (on first reading);[57] (c) in 1981, a vote was taken about the definition of "State debt" in article 30 of the draft articles on succession of States in respect of State property, archives and debts (on second reading).[58]

Consensus and voting are valid ways of decision-making. However, both come with consequences concerning the Commission's process, its documentation, as well as more generally the authority (the persuasive force) of the adopted output.

In case of a decision on the basis of a vote, a question may arise as to whether the views of the majority and the minority will be reflected in the Commission's documents, and especially the commentaries. Article 20(b) of the Commission's statute determines the content of the commentaries on first reading, and paragraph (b) expressly includes "divergencies and disagreements which exist, as well as arguments invoked in favour of one or another solution". Article 22 of the Commission's statute, which is concerned with the second reading, requires the Commission to submit to governments "a final draft and explanatory report" taking into account the comments of governments on the documents submitted by the Commission on first reading pursuant to article 20. The Secretariat has suggested that while article 20 of the Commission's statute indicates that commentaries shall contain *inter alia* "divergencies and disagreements which exist, as well as arguments invoked in favour of one or another solution", different views are only recorded in the commentaries on first reading but not on second reading, "which reflect only the decisions and positions taken by the Commission as a whole".[59] However,

the permissibility of objections to reservations. ILC, 'Report of the International Law Commission on the work of its sixty-first session' [2009] II(2) ILC Ybk, 80 at paras 58 and 60.

57 ILC, 'Report of the International Law Commission on the work of its sixtieth session' [2008] II(2) ILC Ybk, 77 at footnote 234.

58 The Commentary on second reading explains that there was a vote and summarises the different views of the members. ILC, 'Draft articles on succession of States in respect of State property, archives and debts, with commentaries' [1981] II(2) ILC Ybk 20, 72 at footnote 319, 79–80 (commentary to article 31, paras 45 and 46).

59 United Nations, *The Work of the International Law Commission*, vol I (9th edn, United Nations 2017) 50 at footnote 212; United Nations, *The Work of the International Law Commission* (8th edn, United Nations 2012), 48 at footnote 202. See also Mr. Dire Tladi (Member of the Commission): Response to his blog post 'Is the International Law Commission Elevating Subsequent Agreements and Subsequent Practice?' (EJIL:Talk!, 31 August 2018) <www.ejiltalk.org/is-the-international-law-commission-elevating-subsequent-agreements-and-subsequent-practice/#comments>.

first, the text of article 20(b) does not necessarily refer to divergences and disagreements expressed within the Commission (as opposed to those in State practice, jurisprudence or doctrine). Second, it does not necessarily follow that because article 22 refers to "explanatory report" without expressly referring to differing views, as article 20 does, differing views cannot be recorded in the commentary on second reading; article 22 may be listing the common content of a commentary or explanatory report and no need for repetition was seen fit. Third, there are occasional instances in the Commission's practice where majority and minority views have been discussed in the commentary on second reading. For instance, the commentary to article 47 on the right of hot pursuit of the draft articles concerning the law of the sea, adopted by the Commission on second reading in 1956, records the majority and minority views of members (without recording specifically the names of members taking each view, and without explaining whether a vote had been taken).[60] Another example is the 1981 vote on second reading concerning the definition of "State debt" in draft article 30 of the draft articles on succession of States in respect of State property, archives and debts: the commentary on second reading explains that there was a vote and summarizes the different views of the members.[61]

As a separate matter, there is a question as to whether a commentary adopted on second reading that demonstrates differences of opinion between members of the Commission may be sufficiently useful to States. In response, it could be said that when differences of opinion persist among members of the Commission, it is likely that these reflect different assessments of State practice, jurisprudence and doctrine and the state of the law. In such situations, the commentary on second reading should reflect these circumstances.

More generally, on the one hand, a vote enables things to move forward. On the other hand, unanimity and consensus indicate common understanding. Indeed, the Commission's widely perceived success story – the 1966 draft articles on the law of treaties – were adopted as a whole by vote. The important detail, however, is that they were adopted by vote *unanimously*.[62]

The outputs of the Commission are not binding *per se*. As is the case of the non-binding outputs of expert bodies that have a direct relationship with States, the Commission's non-binding outputs may be influential, because they

60 ILC, 'Articles concerning the Law of the Sea with commentaries' (n 8) 285 (commentary to article 47, para 2(a)).

61 ILC, 'Draft articles on succession of States in respect of State property, archives and debts, with commentaries' (n 58) 72 at footnote 319 and 79–80 (commentary to article 31, paras 45 and 46).

62 ILC, [1966] I(2) ILC Ybk 335 at para 138.

enjoy some "perceived authority" partly owing to the Commission's consistent adherence to methodology and partly owing to the fact that its decisions reflect the *common understanding* of experts representing the principal legal systems of the world. The *common understanding* among experts is especially important when it comes to identifying existing rules. But even when the Commission deals with progressive development, its output may be more convincing if it reflects the common understanding of experts as to the development of the law or the most appropriate and harmonious fit with existing rules.

It is perhaps the overt lack of common understanding and disagreement by reference to secondary rules on identifying rules of customary international law that may explain why numerous governments in the Sixth Committee in 2017 expressed a concern about the use of voting by the Commission in relation to a topic as important as exceptions to immunity of State officials from foreign criminal jurisdiction. Of the 61 States that made oral statements concerning the Commission's work, 45 States commented on the draft articles on immunity of State officials from foreign criminal jurisdiction. Of these 45 States, 25 States (more than half of those that made a statement) commented negatively on the use of a vote in the Commission or encouraged the Commission to seek consensus.[63] Two States took note of the "unusual" method of decision,[64] and 10 States mentioned the vote without criticizing it.[65] No State reflected positively on the use of voting.

63 Australia (UN Doc A/C.6/72/SR.22, 13–14 at para 88), China (UN Doc A/C.6/72/SR.23, 9 at para 56), France (UN Doc A/C.6/72/SR.23, 7 at para 42), Germany (UN Doc A/C.6/72/SR.24, 13 at para 89), Indonesia (UN Doc A/C.6/72/SR.24, 19 at para 130), Iran (UN Doc A/C.6/72/SR.24, 10 at para 63), Ireland (written statement, 27 October 2017 <www.papersmart.unmeetings.org/media2/16154683/ireland.pdf> para 3), Israel (UN Doc A/C.6/72/SR.24, 16 at para 111), Japan (UN Doc A/C.6/72/SR.22, 17 at para 126), Republic of Korea (UN Doc A/C.6/72/SR.24, 15 at para 102), Malawi (UN Doc A/C.6/72/SR.26, 19 at para 136), Norway on behalf of the Nordic Countries (i.e. Finland, Denmark, Iceland and Sweden) (UN Doc A/C.6/72/SR.22, 10 at para 67), Singapore (UN Doc A/C.6/72/SR.22, 15 at para 109), Slovakia (UN Doc A/C.6/72/SR.23, 6 at para 34), Slovenia (UN Doc A/C.6/72/SR.22, 17 at para 129), Spain (UN Doc A/C.6/72/SR.24, 8 at para 42), Sri Lanka (UN Doc A/C.6/72/SR.23, 8 at para 45), United Kingdom (UN Doc A/C.6/72/SR.24, 10 at paras 57–58), United States (UN Doc A/C.6/72/SR.21, 5 at para 25). Greece (UN Doc A/C.6/72/SR.23, 12 at para 75) did not specifically criticize the method but implicitly considered that the method reflected division in the Commission.

64 Austria (written statement, 26 October 2017 <www.papersmart.unmeetings.org/media2/16154565/austria.pdf> 3), Poland (UN Doc A/C.6/72/SR.24, 2 at para 4).

65 Chile (UN Doc A/C.6/72/SR.23, 14), Cuba (UN Doc A/C.6/72/SR.24, 11), Czech Republic (UN Doc A/C.6/72/SR.20, 5), El Salvador (UN Doc A/C.6/72/SR.25, 2), Mexico (UN Doc A/C.6/72/SR.22, 13), Malaysia (written statement, 26 October 2018 <www.papersmart.unmeetings.org/media2/16154686/malaysia.pdf> 4 at para 8), the Netherlands (UN Doc

In 1996, the Commission had reviewed its working methods, and had recommended that every effort to achieve consensus should be made, especially in relation to ultimate decisions. It proposed that a vote may be an option if consensus has not been achieved, but after a cooling-off period that allows for more informal deliberation among members of the Commission.[66] Since then, the Commission has at times established a working group to allow for some progress in cases of disagreement on issues of substance. An example is the Working Group established in relation to the topic "expulsion of aliens" (2008) to consider the issues raised by the expulsion of persons having dual or multiple nationality and by denationalization in relation to expulsion. The Working Group concluded that the commentary should include that for the purpose of the draft articles on expulsion of aliens the principle of non-expulsion of nationals applies also to persons who have legally acquired one or several other nationalities and that wording be inserted to make clear that States should not use denationalization as a means of circumventing their obligation under the principle of non-expulsion of nationals.[67] The Commission subsequently approved the Working Group's report, and instructed the Drafting Committee to take the conclusions of the Working Group into account.

Such an approach may be wise to ensure that a constructive cooling-off phase is available and that all efforts to achieve a common understanding have been exhausted.[68] However, disagreement should not freeze the Commission's work. If after a constructive cooling-off period, such as through a working group, disagreement persists, "a vote may be a better indication of the Commission's view than 'a false consensus'".[69]

V Conclusion

The Commission's working methods cannot and should not be further abbreviated. They should be expanded and enhanced. The Commission's seventieth anniversary marks a challenging time for international law: when more States

A/C.6/72/SR.24, 5), Peru (UN Doc A/C.6/72/SR.22, 15), Portugal (UN Doc A/C.6/72/SR.22, 12), South Africa (UN Doc A/C.6/72/SR.24, 3).

66 ILC report 1996 (n 38), 93 at para 210.

67 ILC report 2008 (n 57) 125 at para 171.

68 In 2017, France, in its statement in the Sixth Committee, encouraged the Commission to establish a working group in relation to article 7 of the draft articles on immunities of state officials from foreign criminal jurisdiction. UN Doc A/C.6/72/SR.23, 8 at para 43.

69 ILC report 1996 (n 38) 93 at para 210.

seem keen to retreat from international law; and when the challenges for international law as a legal order are new and many: more actors interpret and apply international law with the risk of different pronouncements as to the content of general international law, which may undermine certainty, clarity and predictability.[70] It is also a time when the Commission's own role might be questioned.[71] The *quality* of the Commission's outputs that reflect the *common understanding* of experts should allow States and international courts and tribunals to continue to rely on the Commission's work. Most importantly, this quality will enable the Commission to fulfil a real and long-term vision: to convince States to continue to use international law as a significant medium by which they regulate their international affairs.

70 Georg Nolte, 'The International Law Commission Facing the Second Decade of the Twenty-First Century' in Ulrich Fastenrath et al (eds), *From Bilateralism to Community Interest: Essays in honour of Judge Bruno Simma* (OUP 2011) 781.

71 Christian Tomuschat, 'The International Law Commission – An Outdated Institution?' (2006) 49 GYIL 77.

The Working Methods of the International Law Commission

Maurice Kamto

I Introduction

The working methods of the Commission are an area of old concern. From 1986, the General Assembly repeatedly emphasized that the Commission should re-examine the way it selects the topics it wishes to deal with, as well as the methods and procedures it uses to conduct its work.[1] On the occasion of its fiftieth anniversary, in 1998, the Commission organized a major colloquium in New York around the general theme "Making Better International Law: The International Law Commission at 50" (hereinafter the "1998 colloquium"), an important part of which dealt with the choice of topics and the working methods of the Commission.[2] The issues at the heart of the matter have not changed since then. The question is whether the Commission has been able to take advantage of the comments and suggestions made by the participants in the 1998 colloquium, most of whom have become members of this august institution. To answer this question, I will endeavour to review the various questions on the part of the programme of this colloquium devoted to the working methods of the Commission, notably: Should the Commission adapt its working methods to the outcomes of its work? How has the communication with other bodies and persons changed and how could it be improved? The role of Special Rapporteurs; the role of the Drafting Committee; the role of commentaries; the role of the Codification Division; and other support.

I will not engage in a theoretical appraisal of these different points. I will examine the issues raised in the light of my almost two decades of practical experience in the Commission, as a member, Special Rapporteur and Chair of the

1 UNGA Res 41/81 (3 December 1986); Res 42/156 (7 December 1987); Res 43/169 (9 December 1988); Res 44/35 (4 December 1989); Res 45/41 (28 November 1990); Res 46/54 (9 December 1991); Res 47/33 (25 November 1992); Res 48/31 (9 December 1993); Res 49/51 (9 December 1994); and Res 50/45 (11 December 1995).

2 United Nations, *Making Better International Law: The International Law Commission at 50. Proceedings of the United Nations Colloquium on Progressive Development and Codification of International Law* (United Nations 1998) 101 et seq.

DOI:10.1163/9789004434271_020

Commission, focusing on three topics: the working methods in relation to the outcomes of work (II), the role of Special Rapporteurs and of the Codification Division (III) and the role of the Drafting Committee (IV).

II On the Working Methods in Relation to the Outcomes of Work

A *Adaptation of the Working Methods and the Commission's Final Product*

The question of whether the Commission should adapt its working methods to the outcomes of its work did not arise in the past, and, in any case, was not a matter of major concern. This is because, until recent years, the outcomes of the work of the Commission almost exclusively took the form of draft articles. The Commission did not devote much discussion on the issue, even after the introduction of new products in its practice, like guidelines, principles, conclusions and reports of study groups.[3]

Some people think that the form of the final product of the Commission's work does not affect its methods of work. The practice of the Commission tends to validate such an assertion, simply because the Commission has never really considered the matter. The consequence is that we find ourselves in a situation where the same methods of work lead to different products. The Commission would benefit from clarifying the situation and adapting its working methods to the type of final product it intends to adopt. This requires that the type of product to be elaborated be chosen early enough, if possible within the framework of the discussions on the topic in the working group on the long-term programme of work, and in any case no later than in the preliminary or first report of the Special Rapporteur on the topic. The plenary debates of the Commission on this report should focus not only on the substantive orientation of the topic, but also on its final product; this way, the Sixth Committee has an opportunity to express its views on the choice of the expected product at the same time as it comments on a particular topic.

Although the choice of the type of final product cannot be considered immutable, it is desirable that it not be called into question once Special Rapporteurs have embarked on their treatment of the topic, because, in my opinion, the method chosen will have to depend on the expected final product. In fact, contrary to current practice, it seems to me that it would be judicious

3 See, respectively, n 9, n 10 and n 11.

to introduce a methodological differentiation between the elaboration of draft articles and the elaboration of guidelines, principles and conclusions, let alone reports of study groups. For example, while the language of draft articles should be imperative, even when engaging in progressive development of international law, the formulation of guidelines, principles or conclusions may be a little looser. Indeed, in the context of the draft articles, rules formulated by way of progressive development are typically drafted in terms of legal obligation. These provisions have the same firmness as rules falling within the ambit of codification in the strict sense of the word, that is, the formulation and systemization of rules of customary international law. On the other hand, the enunciation of a legal norm in the framework of guidelines, principles or conclusions is often done in the subjunctive in French or in aspirational terms in English, which does not imply a legal obligation but rather indicates what is desirable. Admittedly, it might exceptionally be the case that an aspirational provision, indicating to States what is desirable, is included in a draft article. A good example is article 19 of the draft articles on diplomatic protection, which offers guidance as to "recommended practice" with regard to the exercise of diplomatic protection.[4] But draft article 19, introduced at the last minute in the draft articles by the Special Rapporteur and without debate in plenary, was the result of a compromise, and the Commission rarely uses this approach in the context of draft articles to further the progressive development of international law. Fundamentally, the advantage of distinguishing working methods according to the envisaged final product is that such a distinction makes it possible, in certain cases, to introduce a degree of normative flexibility in the Commission's output. Granted, the risk that this methodological differentiation may lead to the production of depreciated by-products is not negligible. But in the absence of such a methodological differentiation, it would be difficult to explain why the Commission's unique working methods lead to the development of different products from the point of view of both the final form and the legal authority of the Commission's work.

B *Final Form of the Work*

As to the final form of the work, divergent views have been expressed in the Commission and in debates in the Sixth Committee. That was particularly the case when some Special Rapporteurs suggested that the final form of the work on their topic should be draft articles.[5]

---

4 ILC, 'Draft articles on diplomatic protection' [2006] II(2) ILC Ybk 24.

5 See, for instance, Maurice Kamto, 'Eighth report on the expulsion of aliens' (2012) UN Doc A/CN.4/651 15, para 55–57; Shinya Murase, 'Annex II. Protection of the atmosphere'

While reports of study groups more closely resemble an academic project than an exercise in progressive development and codification of international law, the nature of guidelines, principles and conclusions is more difficult to clarify. These categories of final products of the work of the Commission have gained ground within the Commission in recent years. Since 1998, the Commission's work on three topics on its agenda has taken the form of guidelines,[6] three that of principles (including guiding principles)[7] and five that of conclusions (two of which were formulated by study groups).[8] These forms, which seem to be well-established both within the Commission and the Sixth Committee of the General Assembly, and even outside it, raise theoretical, methodological and legal questions. These questions concern, first, the distinction between guidelines, principles and conclusions (including reports of

---

[2011] II(2) ILC Ybk 189 (proposing that the topic result in draft articles) and ILC, 'Other decisions and conclusions of the Commission' (2013) UN Doc A/68/10 para 168 (recording the "understanding" of the Commission that "[t]he outcome of the work on the topic will be draft guidelines that do not seek to impose on current treaty regimes legal rules or legal principles not already contained therein"); and Marie G. Jacobsson, 'Third report on the protection of the environment in relation to armed conflicts' (2016) UN Doc A/CN.4/700 para 24 and 51.

6 See ILC, 'Guide to practice on reservations to treaties'[2011] II(3) ILC Ybk 23; ILC, 'Draft guidelines on the protection of the atmosphere, together with preamble, adopted by the Commission on first reading' (2018) UN Doc A/73/10, 158; ILC, 'Draft guide to provisional application of treaties, adopted by the Commission on first reading' (2018) UN Doc A/73/10, 203.

7 ILC, 'Draft principles on the allocation of loss in the case of transboundary harm arising out of hazardous activities' [2006] II(2) ILC Ybk 58 ; ILC, 'Guiding principles applicable to unilateral declarations of States capable of creating legal obligations' [2006] II(2) ILC Ybk 160; ILC, 'Draft principles on protection of the environment in relation to armed conflicts provisionally adopted so far by the Commission' (2018) UN Doc A/73/10, 246 (currently under consideration).

8 ILC, 'Conclusions of the work of the Study Group on the Fragmentation of International Law: difficulties arising from the diversification and expansion of international law' [2006] II(2) ILC Ybk 177. 'The Most-Favoured-Nations clause' (2015) UN Doc A/70/10, 17, 19 (listing the summary conclusions adopted); 'Draft conclusions on subsequent agreements and subsequent practice in relation to the interpretation of treaties' (2018) UN Doc A/73/10, 12; 'Draft conclusions on identification of customary international law' (2018) UN Doc A/73/10, 119; Conclusions on peremptory norms of international law (*jus cogens*) (currently under consideration, see UN Doc A/73/10, 224); Conclusions on general principles of law (currently under consideration, see ILC, 'Annex A. General principles of law' (2017) UN Doc A/72/10, 224). The members proposing the topic "Sea-level rise in relation to international law", included in the long-term programme of work in 2018, envisage a set of "conclusions" to be worked out by a Study Group, if added to the agenda of the Commission; see ILC, 'Annex B. Sea-level rise in relation to international law' (2018) UN Doc A/73/10, 326, 331 at para 26.

study groups); and, second, the distinction between draft articles and other outcomes.

a) Distinction between Guidelines, Principles and Conclusions

From a theoretical perspective, the search for a criterion of distinction between guidelines, principles and conclusions may be in vain. Since none of them are draft articles, we are inclined to think that they are intended to guide States or to give them guidance or even guidelines on what international law would or could be in a specific area. But if so, why use different terms? Does this mean that there could be a difference in the level of authority between these types of products? For example, would a conclusion be firmer than a guideline, or vice versa? A principle more authoritative than a guideline? What then about "guiding principles"?

From a methodological perspective, the Commission follows the same working methods for guidelines, principles and conclusions, consisting of the designation of a Special Rapporteur, who produces draft provisions. These then go through the same process of plenary debates, followed by the drafting of normative statements by the Drafting Committee, and then the report of the Drafting Committee to the plenary, which adopts the final text of the guidelines, principles or conclusions. The Special Rapporteur produces successive reports according to the same requirements of quality and recourse to treaties, State practice and international jurisprudence. The Commission has, so far, not established precise and objective criteria to determine whether the final product of its work on a topic should be draft guidelines, principles or conclusions. This could be considered arbitrary, inspired by the impression, whether founded or not, of a hierarchy of importance between topics, an impression that is even more pronounced when the terminological distinction is between draft articles, on the one hand, and draft guidelines, principles or conclusions, on the other. If the same working methods and the same scientific and methodological requirements apply to the development of these different final products, what would really justify the terminological distinction between them? The Commission should answer this question, in order to help the Special Rapporteurs in the approach to be followed according to the expected final result, and the users of its work to see clearly the respective status of these legal products.

From a legal point of view, it is not easy to determine the respective authority of the guidelines, principles and conclusions, or to say how the authority of the one would be different from that of the others. An example of the confusion that this creates can be found in the debate concerning the Commission's work on the draft guidelines contained in the Guide to practice on reservations to treaties.[9] Would guidelines, principles or conclusions constitute legal advice – and nothing more – whose appreciation of whether to resort to it would be at the discretion of States? What is the added value of such outcomes? And how do they relate to binding rules of international law, contained in treaties or customary international law?

b) Distinction between Draft Articles, on the One Hand, and Guidelines, Principles and Conclusions, on the Other

In theoretical terms, my experience in the Commission leads me to suggest that draft articles are considered as the consummate expression of the current state of international law on the given topic. They would include, on the one hand, the crystallization of the rules of customary international law through codification and, on the other hand, the rules that the Commission considers to be emerging, on the basis of a thorough study of State practice by the Special Rapporteur for a long enough period of time and supported by the research and advice of the Codification Division of the United Nations Office of Legal Affairs, the comments and criticisms of other codification bodies with or without cooperation arrangements with the Commission, international organizations, non-governmental organizations specialized in the relevant field, as well as academic experts. The Commission thus appears both as an indicator of the law, in this case customary international law, which it reveals in a well-tested manner (even if its methodology is not without criticism), and as a quasi-legislator, because of the power it is given to formulate rules on the basis of often scattered material. Nowhere does it say that the guidelines, principles and conclusions relate to another type of exercise or that they are different products. However, it seems that this is the perception that the official recipients (United Nations Member States) and the Commission's unofficial audience (the different users of the Commission's work) have.

On the methodological side, however, the elaboration of draft articles, guidelines, principles and conclusions strictly follows the same working methods within the Commission, as described in the preceding paragraph: appointment of a Special Rapporteur on the topic, production of reports and formulation of draft provisions, which go through the same process of plenary debates followed by the elaboration of a provisional text by the Drafting Committee, and then the report of the latter to the plenary that adopts the final text of the draft articles, guidelines, principles or conclusions.

9 ILC, 'Reservations to treaties' [1997] II(2) ILC Ybk 46, 52–53.

From the point of view of legal scope, could the idea underlying the diversification of categories relate to the distinction between progressive development and codification, so that the draft articles would be the expression of the *lex lata*, while the guidelines, principles and conclusions would reflect *lex ferenda*? Such a distinction would not be well-founded, since draft articles may also contain *lex ferenda* as part of the progressive development of international law. However, the terminological differentiation leads to the feeling that with draft articles, we are dealing with a kind of quasi-treaty whose provisions might be binding on States, even if the draft articles themselves have no binding force. The development of a practice of recourse by international or even national courts to the draft articles of the Commission, which the General Assembly has taken note of, and sometimes even before the Assembly does so, tends to make States wary of the special or *ad hoc* legal status of the Commission's draft articles. Moreover, it inclines them to consider draft articles with circumspection and to caution their support. It is not uncommon for some States to express, in their statements during the debates of the Sixth Committee, real reservations with regard to draft articles submitted by the Commission. On the other hand, States would appear to be more comfortable with products such as guidelines, principles and conclusions, the naming of which seems to diminish their legal significance. This is undoubtedly why some members of the Commission, anxious to see the final products of the Commission accepted more easily by States, pushed the Commission, perhaps even unconsciously, towards these substitute products. The idea must be that powerful States could accept them more easily, these States being typically inclined to reject draft articles that could be invoked against them without their signature or ratification, thus without their formal consent, perhaps even against their will. Thus, when these States do not want international rules on a topic, they may demand that, if the topic is not abandoned, it be dealt with in the form of guidelines, principles or conclusions. It does not matter that international law provides material for codification, let alone progressive development in the relevant field. The work of the Commission on the expulsion of aliens is emblematic in this respect. While the Sixth Committee had itself approved the inclusion of the topic on the Commission's agenda for the preparation of draft articles,[10] a handful of powerful States, with influential connections within the Commission, did their best, first to defeat the codification of the topic, and then, facing the failure of this objective, to impose the abandonment of the form of draft articles in favour of draft principles, general principles or guiding principles. As I have said

10 See UNGA Res 59/41 (2 December 2004) para 4.

on several occasions, it is up to the Commission, which is an expert body, to do the technical work of codification and progressive development, in short to say on every topic on its programme of work what the established or relevant rules of international law are. The General Assembly must do legal policy, among other things by choosing the final form to give to the work of the Commission. Each body should stick to its own responsibilities and competencies.

The diversity of terms for the final products of the Commission's work is puzzling to some users of this work. In particular, it does not make it easier for judges, especially national judges, who may not know what to think of outcomes whose scope may seem merely clarificatory, particularly as regards conclusions. Although it may be thought that guidelines and principles are more prescriptive, the fact remains that they are no more than what their name says: guidelines or principles whose purpose is to guide the legal practice of States, without, however, having to consider the exact scope of legal obligations. It is doubtful whether teachers and researchers are more comfortable with these terminologies.

There is a danger that conclusions, including the reports of study groups, or even guidelines and principles, could lead to the classification of the products of the Commission's work as doctrine of the most qualified publicists of different nations, within the meaning of paragraph 1(d) of Article 38 of the Statute of the International Court of Justice. However, it must be maintained that, when the outcome takes the form of draft articles, the work of the Commission cannot fall into this category; in this form they are more than doctrine, but constitute *lex ferenda* from the formal point of view (*instrumentum*), comprising, on the substantive level (*negotium*), *lex lata* rules as declaratory of customary law. Moreover, whether the rules contained in draft articles of the Commission are *lex lata* or *lex ferenda*, they enjoy a high authority, in no way comparable to the doctrine of publicists, even if they are the most qualified of the different nations. After all, the Commission's power of enunciation or formulation of the law of the community of States is exercised through the United Nations General Assembly, of which it is a subsidiary body. According to article 1 of its statute, it should be recalled that the Commission "shall have for its object the promotion of the progressive development of international law and its codification". It is undoubtedly this assessment of the nature and level of legal authority of the Commission's work that explains why various international jurisdictions, in particular the International Court of Justice, do not hesitate to rely with confidence on the work of the Commission in the motivation of their decisions. The exchange between the Commission and the Court is from this point of view exemplary and revealing of the mutual respect which the two institutions have for each other and attach to their respective work.

Will the Court rely on the Commission's other outcomes with the same confidence and legal certainty as draft articles? It is clear that in the case of the former, there is less certainty about their legal status. States and international courts may not be willing to accept these outcomes of the Commission's work in the same way as draft articles. They will have to distinguish between what falls under the Commission's normative power (draft articles) and what flows from its doctrinal capacity (conclusions, reports of study groups, even guidelines and principles).

It is not a question of saying that the Commission should only produce draft articles. The diversification of the Commission products makes it possible to enrich its work by dealing with topics that it would be unable to address, if it were to be limited exclusively to the production of draft articles. However, the Commission must not unduly dilute what constitutes its singular identity as the highest-level technical codification body in the international system. Codification, which may include elements of the progressive development of international law, is a normative process, not merely a doctrinal one. What is feared is that, with the proliferation of doctrinal products, to the detriment of those of codification and the progressive development of international law, the work of the Commission will be assimilated – as some authors wrongly do – to doctrine. The so-called "new" products created by the Commission should be limited to a few topics of major importance to the international community and where there is a real need for legal clarification, but which does not offer a sufficient degree of maturity to proceed with codification, or even progressive development based on significant trends in State practice.

The conclusions and recommendations of the 1998 colloquium of the Commission show that

> the distinction between codification and progressive development is difficult if not impossible to draw in practice; the Commission has proceeded on the basis of a composite idea of codification and progressive development. Distinctions drawn in its Statute between the two processes have proved unworkable and could be eliminated in any review of the Statute (…).[11]

On this basis, it might also be considered that the distinction between draft articles, guidelines, principles and conclusions is not entirely relevant and that the Commission should stick to its good old practice of elaborating draft

11 United Nations (n 2) 376.

articles, a product known and appreciated by the community of States and international lawyers. However, since the diversification of outcomes may have been a condition for the survival of the Commission, there is reason to believe that a total reversal of the course of recent Commission practice may not be easy. As we have explained above, a clarification of methodology in relation to the final products developed by the Commission could allow it to maintain the current terminological diversity while avoiding the confusion it creates in people's minds.

III The Role of the Special Rapporteur and the Codification Division

A *The Central Role of the Special Rapporteur in the Treatment of the Topic*

The 1998 colloquium offered an opportunity to reflect extensively on the role of a Special Rapporteur. The statute does not seem to envisage the appointment of a Special Rapporteur for all topics, or for all aspects of a topic. It

> only expressly envisages such an appointment in the case of projects for progressive development. But from the very first, the practice of the Commission has been to appoint a Special Rapporteur very early in the consideration of a project and to do so without regard to whether the project might be classified as one of codification or progressive development.[12]

The practice of distributing rapporteurships among members from different regions should be preserved, although it is crucial that the competence and ability to perform the work expected of a Special Rapporteur be the decisive criterion in the selection of the Commission. This regional diversification in the designation of Special Rapporteurs has many advantages, "in particular in that it helps to ensure that different approaches and different legal cultures are brought to bear in the formulation of reports and proposals. "[13]

It has been noted in the past "that Special Rapporteurs have tended, or even been expected, to operate in isolation from the Commission, with little guidance during the preparation of reports on the direction of future work."[14] I do not think that this is the case now. Most of the recommendations made during the 1998 colloquium concerning the work of the Special Rapporteurs have been

12 Ibid at 386–387. See also article 16 of the statute of the ILC.

13 Ibid at 387.

14 Ibid.

implemented, and practice in recent years shows that Special Rapporteurs are aware that they are serving the Commission for the topics for which they have been designated. Even though Special Rapporteurs may want to maintain a certain degree of intellectual independence in the treatment of their topics, they tend to seek the Commission's approval of their reports and generally take the utmost account of the majority's observations and opinions within the Commission. However, there have been occasional sensitivities of some Special Rapporteurs to certain views outside the Commission, the obvious purpose of which is to influence the course of the topic's treatment. As long as such opinions are based on a thorough analysis of the prevailing state of international law, there is no reason to complain. On the other hand, it would be unfortunate and damaging to the work and image of the Commission as an expert body, if some actors would use this body to advance a social or ideological cause, or to achieve their own legal policy agenda. The Commission is not meant to enunciate primary rules, aimed at constraining the sovereign power of States; the Commission's mandate is to codify and progressively develop secondary rules, providing the foundation and basic structure of the international legal framework.

Regarding the reports of Special Rapporteurs and the timetable of work for a given topic, it seems important that the guidance or instruction to Special Rapporteurs should be provided very early, if necessary after the first report or preliminary report. In this respect, while the need for some independence of Special Rapporteurs is understandable, impartiality ought to be the rule, and it is essential that future reports of the Rapporteurs should meet the needs of the Commission as a whole. The first report, which should enable Special Rapporteurs to present in a substantial way their understanding of the topic, the direction they intend to give to their treatment and the methodological approach, is an opportunity for the Commission to set out the necessary framework for the treatment of the topic. It is at this stage that the "consultative group", advocated in the recommendations of the 1998 colloquium,[15] should be brought in, or a working group established, if necessary, to help Special Rapporteurs to get on with their topic. Indeed, in 1998, it appeared that "in most cases the practice has been for the Special Rapporteur to work largely in isolation in preparing reports. In other words, in the period between sessions a Special Rapporteur has no formal contact with other members of the Commission."[16] Other bodies, such as the International Law Association and the *Institut de*

15 Ibid at 388.
16 Ibid.

Droit International, work differently and with undeniable effectiveness, thanks to the ongoing exchanges between the members of the commissions created for each topic during the intersessional period. Indeed, in these bodies,

> [v]arious members are chosen to act as a consultative group so that, between sessions, the Rapporteur may consult over the best and most acceptable approach to be taken, and over the essential elements to the next report. Through questionnaires, the circulation of reports or exceptionally the holding of interim meetings, the group's advice is available. Although the report remains that of the Rapporteur, it is likely that the input obtained will ensure that it is acceptable to the membership of the committee and by extension to the membership of the body as a whole.[17]

This practice could also be implemented within the Commission, on the one hand, without drawing a distinction between codification and progressive development as the statute suggests, and, on the other hand, without any formalism, which makes it possible to adapt it on a case-by-case basis. The Commission may not have to exactly reproduce the practice of the above-mentioned institutions. For example, it is doubtful whether it is advisable to set up an advisory group for the duration of a session, or even the treatment of a topic. The current practice of the Commission seems more suitable for its flexibility in determining its duration and the variation of its composition, which are always determined in consultation with the Special Rapporteur. The possibility of consultations outside the session should also be considered, excluding organising physical meetings, which would necessarily entail financial costs that the budget of the Commission may not be able to bear. It worth recalling and stressing that, even with such a consultative or working group, the report will remain the responsibility of the Special Rapporteur, rather than of the group. It is not the function of the group to approve the Special Rapporteur's report, but to provide input on its general direction and on any particular issues the Special Rapporteur wishes to raise.

The topic's treatment plan should be presented in the first report of the Special Rapporteur, to enable the Commission to have an overview and to ensure that important aspects of the topic are not lost sight of. Of course, a work plan is never engraved in marble and must be adjusted if necessary, without the Special Rapporteur being able to bear the blame.

---

17 Ibid.

Special Rapporteurs should make their reports available before the beginning of the session. The experience has shown that the practice is not uniform: some reports are circulated in advance of the session, some are not; and more so, some have even been circulated only days before of their scheduled consideration, even though this has been an exception. This is not caused only by delays in translation and circulation due to financial constraints on the United Nations or to its rules for documentation, which are, of course, beyond the control of a Special Rapporteur, but sometimes by the latter themselves. This is very detrimental to the work of the Commission, as these delays do not allow proper consideration of the report by its members. It is highly desirable that all reports should be available to Commission before, or at the latest at, the beginning of the session.

B *The Valuable Support of the Codification Division*

While the Special Rapporteurs play a central role in dealing with the topics on the agenda of the Commission, the Codification Division, as its secretariat, is the linchpin of the Commission's work. In addition to its role in reminding the Commission of its rules and practices, and in suggesting solutions to thorny procedural problems, the Codification Division is making a vital contribution in two areas: its memoranda on subjects studied, and its assistance to Special Rapporteurs in the preparation of comments on draft articles, guidelines, principles or conclusions.

Regarding its memoranda, upon the appointment of a Special Rapporteur on a topic on the Commission's agenda, the Codification Division prepares a study on the subject, generally as comprehensive as possible. This highly informed research, both on the prevailing state of international law (conventional and customary) and on jurisprudence, State practice and doctrine, is invaluable. Of course, it hardly exempts the Special Rapporteurs from their own research on the subject. However, in many ways, it complements the Special Rapporteurs' research, helps them to orient themselves better in their topic and provides them with material that they would have a hard time bringing together for themselves: State practice. It is important that this research assistance provided by the Codification Division be maintained, especially since some Special Rapporteurs do not have the means to afford the assistance of a team of young university researchers. For some members of the Commission from developing countries, particularly those in Africa, the difficulty in securing the assistance of a research team is a reason for reluctance to seek the office of Special Rapporteur. In my experience, the Secretariat's studies can help them at least partially overcome this obstacle.

With regard to the preparation of comments on draft articles, guidelines, principles or conclusions, the assistance of the Secretariat is also crucial. The experience gained in this area greatly facilitates the task of the Special Rapporteurs, who, without such assistance, or that of teams of academics who may assist Special Rapporteurs from developed countries or working in those countries, would devote a much longer time, and would delay the progress of the Commission's work.

The commentaries also form a valuable part of the *travaux préparatoires* of any treaty provision that may be adopted on the basis of the proposed text. The main function of a commentary is to explain the text itself, with appropriate references to key decisions, doctrine and State practice, so that the reader can see the extent to which the Commission's text reflects or, as the case may be, develops or extends the law. According to the practice of the Commission, it is not the function of the commentaries to reflect disagreements on the text as adopted on second reading; this can be done in plenary at the time of final adoption of the text and will then be appropriately reflected in the report of the Commission to the General Assembly. As the Statute makes clear, draft articles should not be considered finally adopted without the Commission having approved the commentaries before it.

IV The Role of the Drafting Committee

The Drafting Committee is a crucial forum within the Commission. It is, as its name indicates, the place where the final product of the Commission is drafted, where the draft texts of the Special Rapporteur and the suggestions made by the members of the Commission during the plenary debates are used to formulate draft articles, guidelines, principles or conclusions. Whereas the plenary has the general policy power of the Commission, the Drafting Committee has the technical power, which in practice is binding on the plenary; because, except in the event of disagreement between the Drafting Committee and the plenary on a major question, the plenary usually approves the report of the Drafting Committee. This is to say that the Drafting Committee is the decisive place of preparation of the products of the Commission. Members of the Commission who want to influence the development of the final product of the Commission sit on it systematically. It is significant in this respect that the members of the Commission from the major world powers sit on the Drafting Committee for all topics. On the other hand, members of developing countries are, unfortunately, barely present in the work of the Drafting Committee and tend to limit their participation in the work of the Commission to plenary meetings. It is therefore not surprising that their impact on the final products of the Commission is extremely low. They are absent from the place where the provisional statements of the Special Rapporteur take their final form, and where the proposals made in plenary are shaped into concrete provisions. Here the absentees are in the wrong.

The Chair of the Drafting Committee plays a major role in the conduct of the work of the Committee. Not only does the Chair maintain the speakers list and manage the time, he or she also has to sniff out the direction in which the discussions are going, in order to quickly summarize the debates and to propose, if necessary, compromise formulas. In good practice, Chairs must ensure that their proposals are in keeping with the Special Rapporteur's position, or that the latter is not strongly opposed to it. Occasionally, some Chairs overwhelm the Drafting Committee's work with their personality, or are so directive that they come to impose their personal position. However, in general, the Chair knows how to advance the Committee's work by ensuring the fair consideration of the initial drafts of the Special Rapporteur, any new proposals by the Special Rapporteur made following the discussions in the plenary, and drafting proposals and other suggestions made by members of the Commission in plenary.

The Drafting Committee is, equally, where the independent voice of the Special Rapporteur has to be harmonized with the range of views within the Commission. The demands of particular topics, and the approach of particular Special Rapporteurs, will always produce some diversity of practice. It is in the Drafting Committee that divergent views on a topic are most clearly expressed and have to be reconciled. The Special Rapporteur must accept the view of the Drafting Committee as a whole, even if it is contrary to his or her own views, and, as necessary, reflect the view of the Drafting Committee in revised articles and commentaries. In performing his or her function, the Special Rapporteur should act as servant of the Commission rather than a defender of any personal views. In practice, the Drafting Committee amends, redrafts, splits or merges the draft articles, guidelines, principles or conclusions proposed by the Special Rapporteur. It generally adopts the new draft by consensus; only in rare cases does it do so by a vote among the members present. As was explained in 1998,

> [o]f course, a Special Rapporteur who disagrees with the eventual views of the Drafting Committee has every right to explain the disagreement in plenary when the report of the Drafting Committee is presented. It is open to the plenary to prefer the views of the Special Rapporteur to those of the Drafting Committee in such a case. Having regard to the size of the Drafting Committee and to its role vis-à-vis the plenary, however, there are likely to be few such cases. Moreover, it is better for major disagreements which cannot be resolved in the Drafting Committee to

> be reported at an earlier stage to the plenary, with the possibility of an indicative vote to settle the matter (…).[18]

Contrary to the earlier practice of the Commission, it is now not unusual for draft articles to be referred to the Drafting Committee without commentaries having been prepared. More so, draft articles are sometimes presented for final consideration by the Commission without commentaries, and the commentaries are only adopted, with little time for consideration, in the final stages of a session. It can be argued that, since the draft articles are likely to be changed substantially in the Drafting Committee, the provision of commentaries by a Special Rapporteur in advance is premature. On the other hand, it has been suggested that the Drafting Committee is in a much better position if it has available to it at the same time both draft articles and commentaries (or at least an outline of what the commentaries will contain). However, not only is it difficult for the Special Rapporteur to provide both at the same time, due to the burden of work that it implies; it also seems to me that the reports of the Special Rapporteur provide at this stage sufficient information that can help both the plenary and the Drafting Committee to understand the scope and purpose of the draft articles, guidelines, principles or conclusions. Indeed, the commentaries help to explain the purpose of the draft articles and to clarify their scope and effect. From my own experience, I do not share the view that the provision of draft articles alone precludes flexibility in resolving disagreement over some aspect of a draft, by the transfer of some provision from the text to the commentary or vice versa. The Drafting Committee will ask the Special Rapporteur to proceed that way and the Chair of the Drafting Committee will include such a request in the Committee's report to the plenary.

V Conclusion

An examination of the Commission's current practice shows that it took into account most of the recommendations made at the end of the Commission's 1998 colloquium, marking its fiftieth anniversary. One of the important issues that the Commission would benefit from clarifying is the form of the final product of the Commission's work. In the absence of such clarification, the proliferation of products without differentiation of their status could seriously affect the authority and reputation of the Commission. At a time when it

18 Ibid at 390.

attracts external criticism, mostly unjustified, the Commission must make the occasion of its seventieth anniversary the starting point of a new *aggiornamento* of its methods of work, the contribution it intends to make to international law and the type of outcomes it intends to discuss with the Sixth Committee and the General Assembly. It is very worrying that no more draft articles of the Commission have led to the convening of a diplomatic conference for their transformation into an international convention. The importance of the International Law Commission should be reaffirmed through the choice of topics and the quality of its work.

Concluding Remarks by Shinya Murase

Comments on the Working Methods of the International Law Commission: Some Issues

The International Law Commission has been reviewing its working methods through the "Working Group on Methods of Work of the Commission", currently chaired by Hussein A. Hassouna, where a discussion is in progress on a wide range of issues.[1] The present paper discusses some of the outstanding questions on the working methods, with a particular focus on the final form of the Commission's products. It also discusses briefly other issues relating to the working methods, including its decision-making procedure, study groups, Special Rapporteurs' reports, commentaries and input from scientists.

I Final Forms of the International Law Commission's Products

Article 20 of the statute of the Commission envisages that the final outcome of its work should primarily be draft articles, on the basis of which binding treaties are to be worked out.[2] Since the beginning of the 2000s, the Sixth Committee does not seem to be interested any longer in turning the Commission's draft articles into treaties,[3] and they are merely "taken note of" and shelved indefinitely. Though the Commission has continued to elaborate draft articles on some topics, there seems to be no prospect for them to become treaties.[4] In parallel, there

1 See ILC, 'Report of the International Law Commission on the work of its seventieth session' (2018) UN Doc A/73/10, para. 371.

2 Statute of the ILC, UNGA Res 174(II) (21 November 1947) as amended by UNGA Res 485(V) (12 December 1950); UNGA Res. 984(X) (3 December 1955); UNGA Res 985(X) (3 December 1955) and UNGA Res 36/39 (18 November 1981).

3 The United Nations Convention on Jurisdictional Immunities of States and Their Property (adopted 2 December 2004, not yet in force) UN Doc A/59/508, annex, was the last convention adopted on the basis of draft articles prepared by the Commission.

4 ILC, 'Draft articles on responsibility of States for internationally wrongful acts' [2001] II(2) ILC Ybk 26; 'Draft articles on diplomatic protection' [2006] II(2) ILC Ybk 24 ; 'Draft articles on the law of transboundary aquifers' [2008] II(2) ILC Ybk 19; 'Draft articles on the responsibility of international organizations' [2011] II(2) ILC Ybk 40; 'Draft articles on the effects of armed conflicts on treaties' [2011] II(2) ILC Ybk 108; 'Draft articles on the expulsion of aliens' (2014) UN Doc A/69/10, 11; 'Draft articles on the protection of persons

 | DOI:10.1163/9789004434271_021

has also been the notable tendency in recent years that the final products of the Commission take the form of draft principles,[5] draft guidelines,[6] draft conclusions,[7] or model rules.[8] In addition, there are reports of study groups[9] and working groups,[10] which are not envisaged to become binding treaties in the future.[11] Particularly noteworthy may be the increasing proliferation of "conclusions", a title that conveys little normative nuance, and may thus not be considered appropriate as a designation for the final form of the Commission's work.

---

in the event of disasters' (2016) UN Doc A/71/10, 13; Draft articles on the immunity of state officials from foreign criminal jurisdiction (currently under consideration); Draft articles on crimes against humanity (currently under consideration); Draft articles succession of states in respect of state succession (currently under consideration).

5 ILC, 'Guiding Principles applicable to unilateral declarations of States capable of creating legal obligations' [2006] II(2) ILC Ybk 160; 'Draft principles on the allocation of loss in the case of transboundary harm arising out of hazardous activities' [2006] II(2) ILC Ybk 58; Draft principles on the protection of the environment in relation to armed conflicts (currently under consideration).

6 ILC, 'Guide to practice on reservation to treaties' (2011) [2011] II(3) ILC Ybk 23; guide to practice on provisional application of treaties (currently under consideration); protection of the atmosphere (currently under consideration).

7 ILC, 'Conclusions of the work of the Study Group on the Fragmentation of International Law: Difficulties arising from the diversification and expansion of international law' [2006] II(2) ILC Ybk 177; 'Summary Conclusions on the Most-Favoured-Nation Clause' (2015) UN Doc A/70/10, 19 at para 42; 'Draft conclusions on identification of customary international law' (2018) UN Doc A/73/10, 119; 'Draft conclusions on subsequent agreement and subsequent practice in relation to the interpretation of treaties' (2018) UN Doc A/73/10, 12; Draft conclusions on peremptory norms of international law (*jus cogens*) (currently under consideration); Draft conclusions on general principles of law (currently under consideration). The topic on "Sea-level rise in relation to international law", included in the long-term programme of work in 2018, envisages a set of "conclusions" to be worked out by a Study Group, if added to the agenda of the Commission. ILC, 'Report of the International Law Commission on the work of its seventieth session' (2018) UN Doc A/73/10, 331 at para 26.

8 The 'Model Rules of Arbitral Procedure' [1958] II ILC Ybk 83 are so far the only precedent. The topic on "Evidence before international courts and tribunals", included in the long-term programme of work in 2017, may take the form of Model Rules, if adopted as an active agenda of the Commission. ILC, 'Report of the International Law Commission on the work of its sixty-ninth session' (2017) UN Doc A/72/10, 248 at para 18.

9 See the Study Groups' conclusions on fragmentation of international law and on the MFN clause (n 8).

10 ILC, 'Final Report of the Working Group on the Obligation to Extradite or Prosecute (*aut dedere aut judicare*)' (2014) UN Doc A/69/10, 140.

11 Jacob Katz Cogan, 'The Changing Form of the International Law Commission's Work' (University of Cincinnati College of Law Public Law & Legal Theory Research Paper Series, No. 15-04) in Roberto Virzo and Ivan Ingravallo (eds), *Evolutions in the Law of International Organizations* (Brill Nijhoff 2015) 275.

As Professor Kamto remarked in his paper,[12] there is currently no difference in the working methods of the Commission, whether the final form is draft articles, draft guidelines or draft conclusions.[13] Since the members of the Commission and of the Sixth Committee are now so used to the term "conclusions", they may not see any problem in calling the final products "conclusions". However, it should be borne in mind that the outside world often characterizes and evaluates the role of the Commission by its products, in particular by the forms of its products. To many outsiders, academics and law students, and possibly national judges, the term "conclusions" may sound very strange. In the ordinary meaning of the term, "conclusions" probably refers to an *internal* understanding of a group that has conducted a study. However, the International Law Commission is not an academic institution, but a normative organ, which should produce documents with certain *external* effects of normativity.

It is feared that such a proliferation of these "soft" instruments may ultimately lead to a weakening of the international legal system by incorporating "bad" norms, as encapsulated in Gresham's rule that "bad money drives out good money". The first question is what the causes are for such a proliferation of non-binding instruments at the Commission. There may be external causes and internal ones.

Causes outside the Commission may include the fact that the international community, and in particular the General Assembly, no longer show interest in holding "big" diplomatic conferences for adopting multilateral conventions on topics of general international law. Conversely, the number of conventions on special regime topics (such as human rights, the environment, trade and investment) is increasing rapidly, driven by the respective specialized organs in charge of those topics.

Causes internal to the Commission are, among others: (1) a shift from traditional topics to new topics, (2) a change in the methods of decision-making in the Commission, and (3) a change in the composition of its members.

First, having exhausted most of the traditional topics for "codification" of international law, the Commission has had to shift to new topics of "progressive development" of international law. While codification is mainly an objective, scientific and non-political exercise of determination of "established" rules of customary international law, the work for progressive development based on "emerging" rules of customary international law is likely to be more controversial due to the political and policy implications involved. Thus, for the latter,

12 See the contribution of Maurice Kamto in this Section.

13 Ibid.

precise formulation of provisions is often difficult, which tends to lead to the adoption of more flexible provisions compared to draft articles.

Secondly, as for the method of decision-making, the Commission used to consistently resort to voting, both in plenary and in Drafting Committees, until the end of the 1970s.[14] When the General Assembly started resorting to consensus in the 1980s, the International Law Commission also followed this pattern. In order to achieve a consensus, draft provisions proposed by the Special Rapporteurs become more and more obscure through repeated compromises made in the course of deliberations, the result of which may be considered more fitting for the forms other than draft articles.

Third, the change in the composition of the membership of the Commission may also have affected, albeit indirectly, the final forms of the Commission's products. In its early years, the members of the Commission were mostly academics. In recent years, in contrast, there have been more practitioners in the Commission. Academics tend to pursue preciseness of the provisions to be formulated according to their theoretical perspectives, while practitioners tend to place importance on compromise and accommodation of differing views, thus preferring more flexible forms than draft articles.

What are the legal effects of these non-binding instruments produced by the International Law Commission? Today, even the draft articles do not seem to enjoy the privilege of becoming binding treaties. Nevertheless, if certain draft articles are referred to in a convention, it certainly assures a strong legal status of the Commission's articles under international law. Thus, for example, in the case of the Guarani Aquifer Agreement of 2010, the preamble takes note of the International Law Commission's articles on the law of transboundary aquifers of 2008.[15]

Another channel for ascertaining the normativity of the Commission's draft articles is through their quotations in the judgments, opinions and decisions of the International Court of Justice and other international courts and tribunals, a point discussed by Danae Azaria in her presentation[16] and by other writers.[17] These judicial pronouncements referring to the Commission's articles,

14 For a discussion of voting in the International Law Commission, see the contribution of Danae Azaria in this Section.

15 Acuerdo sobre el Acuífero Guarani (adopted 2 August 2010, not yet in force) <https://www.internationalwaterlaw.org/documents/regionaldocs/Guarani_Aquifer_Agreement-Spanish.pdf>. The fourth preambular paragraph of the Agreement provides: "Taking into account, also, Resolution 63/124 of the United Nations General Assembly on the Law of Transboundary Aquifers."

16 See the contribution by Danae Azaria in this Section.

17 Giorgio Gaja, 'Interpreting Articles Adopted by the International Law Commission' (2016) 85 BYIL 10.

together with the commentaries thereto, may be taken as evidence of customary international law under Article 38, paragraph 1 (b) of the Statute of the International Court of Justice, or be assessed at least as subsidiary means for the determination of rules of law under article 38, paragraph 1 (d). It remains to be seen whether the Commission's products adopted in the forms of guidelines and conclusions will also be quoted by courts in the future.

II Other Issues Concerning Working Methods

A *Distinction between Codification and Progressive Development*

The International Law Commission has a long tradition not to identify whether a specific provision of its product belongs to "codification" (based on "established" rules of customary international law) or "progressive development" (based on its "emergent rules").[18] However, this distinction is crucial in dispute settlement, to determine whether or not a particular provision reflects existing customary international law.[19] It may be viewed as irresponsible for the producer (the International Law Commission) not to indicate to the consumers (States and dispute settlement bodies) the precise character of its products. Thus, the present writer, when he was the First Vice-Chair of the Commission in 2014, suggested to the Bureau informally to establish a working group within the Commission to discuss this distinction. However, some members of the Commission objected to this proposal, fearing that it might open "Pandora's Box".

It may not be proper, however, for the Commission to continue ignoring the distinction, since the statute of the Commission clearly distinguishes codification from progressive development, with different procedures for identification and selection of topics. It is hoped that the Commission will consider whether the distinction is possible and, if so, on what criteria, and whether it is desirable to identify its product either as codification or progressive development.

B *Decision-Making Procedure*

Another issue that needs to be addressed is the decision-making procedure in the Commission. The International Law Commission is a subsidiary organ of the General Assembly, and the Commission follows its rules of procedures,

18 Donald McRae, 'The Interrelationship of Codification and Progressive Development in the Work of the International Law Commission' (2013) 111 JILD 75.

19 E.g. *North Sea Continental Shelf, (Federal Republic of Germany/Denmark; Federal Republic of Germany/The Netherlands)* [1969] ICJ Rep 3, 4–54.

according to which, if there is a member requesting a vote, a vote should be taken. Voting has been unduly criticized.[20] I do not agree with the view that voting would be damaging to the collegiate solidarity among Commission members. The Commission has been voting since its creation up to the end of the 1970s both in plenary as well as in the Drafting Committees, but the solidarity among its members back then was much stronger than today. I believe that we should get more used to voting. Of course, voting should not be resorted to unless the discussion has been sufficiently exhausted. There is no reason, however, that the Commission should shy away from it.

I believe it was good that the Commission took votes in 2017 on draft article 7 of the topic "Immunity of State officials from foreign criminal jurisdiction". The votes were cast with overwhelming majority in favour of the exception of the immunity as proposed by the Special Rapporteur, and all the members of the Commission should respect the result of the vote, including those who proposed the vote and who lost the vote. The issue on draft article 7 should not be re-opened during the first reading. It is also hoped that the Sixth Committee would respect the result reached by the Commission, either by consensus or by vote.

The problem with the consensus rule is that "there is no consensus as to the meaning of consensus".[21] Consensus is not to give a "veto power" to a small number of members, but it is sometimes used to block the views of the majority (or the silent majority). Under the consensus rule, nobody in the Commission really takes responsibility for the decision that has been taken. By voting, in contrast, every member must decide which side he/she should take, and on what ground, which I believe is good for an expert body such as the International Law Commission. Besides, as mentioned earlier, voting will clarify the normative content of the provisions adopted in a precise manner, which should be considered desirable for the Commission's products.

(i) Study Groups

The format of study groups is still favoured by some members of the Commission.[22] The Commission's study groups have produced important conclusions on the fragmentation of international law, and also on the most-favoured-nation

20 See, with further references, see the contribution of Danae Azaria in this Section.

21 Dapo Akande, 'What is the Meaning of "Consensus" in International Decision Making?' (EJIL:Talk!, 8 April 2013) <www.ejiltalk.org/negotiations-on-arms-trade-treaty-fail-to-adopt-treaty-by-consensus-what-is-the-meaning-of-consensus-in-international-decision-making/>.

22 The topic on "Sea-level rise in relation to international law", included in the long-term programme of work in 2018, envisages a study group, if added to the active agenda of the Commission, see footnote 8 above.

clause. However, certain doubts have been expressed as to the desirability of setting up study groups in the International Law Commission, which is not an academic institution but an authoritative and normative organ. There are also some concrete problems about study groups.

First, the reports by the Chair of a study group are not translated into the other official languages of the United Nations, and are placed only on the website as "L-documents" for limited circulation, unlike the reports of Special Rapporteurs that are translated and issued for general circulation. Second, attendance at the meetings of the Study Groups is not mandatory for Commission members, and the meetings are held in the afternoon sometimes with a small number of members attending. Third, there is no drafting committee and no commentaries for the conclusions of the study group. Fourth, only a few pages are allocated in the annual report of the International Law Commission to summarize the discussion of the study group. So, why do the members want to bother with a study group? New topics should be proposed to follow the normal procedure of appointing Special Rapporteurs.[23]

As mentioned earlier, the International Law Commission is not an academic institution but is supposed to be a normative and authoritative organ charged with codification and progressive development of international law. Simply "clarifying" the contents of international law rules is not what is expected of the Commission. From such a point of view, it must be said that a study group has no place in the International Law Commission.

C *Special Rapporteurs' Reports and the Commission's Commentaries*

The Special Rapporteurs' reports are supposed to be submitted "six weeks" before the beginning of the session each year[24] (late March or early April), which is complied with by most Special Rapporteurs. The late submission in some past cases caused confusions for planning the plenary debate on the report, and resulted in delaying the conclusion of the debate to the following year.

The length of each report is supposed to be "50 pages" (some 25,000 words),[25] a rule that is often ignored by Special Rapporteurs, extending their reports two or three times as long as the agreed page limit. The lengthy reports are not sufficiently digested by members of the Commission to allow meaningful

23 According to the report of the Working Group on Working Methods of 2011,"[t]he possibility of replacing a Study Group by appointing a Special Rapporteur as the topic progresses should be considered, as appropriate." ILC, 'Report of the International Law Commission on the work of its seventieth session' (2018) UN Doc A/73/10, para 373.

24 Ibid para 372 (iii).

25 Ibid para 372 (ii).

debates. These extensive reports are difficult for members to understand fully over a short period of time, potentially affecting the quality of the debate within the Commission. Likewise, if the Special Rapporteur proposes more than four or five draft provisions, which are the maximum number for one session, its consideration is not likely be completed within that session. Discipline is required for these matters on the part of Special Rapporteurs.

The use of informal working groups for drafting commentaries may seem useful, but they are not without problems. It is often difficult to remember in detail after a few years what the issues were, how the Drafting Committee adopted a particular wording, etc. The Commission should discuss commentaries each year while the members' memory is fresh. The plenary should try to adopt draft conclusions together with commentaries before the end of each session. If the Commission allows prolonged adoption of draft provisions, it means that the Sixth Committee is deprived of the opportunity to comment on them for several years. Besides, there is a problem of transparency, since there is no record of these informal working groups. It may be difficult to trace the *travaux preparatoires* in the commentaries, since the members who spoke at the working group may not repeat their views in the plenary.

D *Input From Scientists*

Furthermore, I would like to address the question of external contact that the Commission occasionally needs to rely on for its work. Since traditional topics have largely been exhausted, the Commission has shifted its emphasis to new topics of "special regimes" of international law, such as human rights law, environmental law and economic law. We have witnessed rapid development of these special regimes, but it has been without any linkages or coordination with other regimes and with general international law. The Commission's members are usually experts on general international law, and not experts on special regimes. However, I believe that the International Law Commission can play an important role in treating these special regime topics from the viewpoint of general international law, which is necessary to avoid fragmentation.

It is obvious that, in dealing with these special regime topics, the Commission needs to have input from experts and specialists of these regimes. For instance, on environmental law topics that are often of "fact-intensive and science-heavy" character, we need input from competent scientists. This is what the Commission did for the topic on the "Law of transboundary aquifers" and what it has been doing for "Protection of the atmosphere".[26] The statute

26 Shinya Murase, 'Scientific Knowledge and Progressive Development of International Law: With Reference to the ILC Topic on the Protection of the Atmosphere' in James

authorizes the Commission in article 16 (e) to "consult with scientific institutions and individual experts" for the purpose of progressive development of international law.[27] I believe that the Commission should seek to have more contacts with outside experts to facilitate its work.

E *Support by the Secretariat*

Finally, I cannot agree more with Maurice Kamto about the great contribution of the members of the Secretariat, the Codification Division, to the work of the Commission.[28] The Division, serving as the secretariat of the Commission, renders substantive support to the Special Rapporteurs and members of the Commission. The staff members of the Codification Division, led by its most competent Director, are international lawyers of the first rank, to whom the Commission owes immensely in research and drafting of the texts of draft provisions and the commentaries thereto.

While the Secretary to the Commission has traditionally kept a modest stance in the Commission, Mr. Liang Yuen-li (from China), who served for the Commission's initial years as its Secretary, was exceptionally active in setting out the necessary standard of the work of the Commission. Reading summary records of the Commission of those days, one would find that Mr. Liang frequently spoke in the plenary and gave advice and suggestions to the Special Rapporteurs. With his authority of having participated in the 1930 Hague Codification Conference, he sounded as if he had been the most senior member of the Commission, and his leadership was without doubt indispensable during the Commission's formative years. Anticipating many difficulties in the work of codification and progressive development of international law, he nonetheless stressed the importance of having "juristic optimism" in order to overcome those difficulties.[29] Today, the International Law Commission is at a crossroads and its *raison d'être* is questioned in some quarters. At this time, the Secretariat, as the backbone of the Commission, is expected play a pivotal role, like Mr. Liang, in preserving this important institution.

Crawford, Abdul Koroma, Said Mahmoudi and Alain Pellet (eds), *The International Legal Order: Current Needs and Possible Responses: Essays in Honour of Djamchid Momtaz* (Brill 2017), 41.

27 ILC statute (n 2).

28 See the contribution by Maurice Kamto in this Section.

29 Liang Yuen-li, 'The Progressive Development of International Law and its Codification under the United Nations' (1947) 41 ASILPROC 24. See also UN Doc A/CN.10/5 (1947).

SECTION 5

The Function of the Commission: How Much Identifying Existing Law, How Much Proposing New Law?

Opening Remarks by Davinia Aziz

The International Law Commission* exists in organic symbiosis[1] with the General Assembly through its Sixth Committee. They are bound together in a chapter of Schachter's "invisible college"[2] spanning Lake Geneva and the East River. Together, the International Law Commission and the Sixth Committee are responsible for discharging the General Assembly's mandate relating to the "progressive development of international law and its codification", in furtherance of no less than the purposes and principles of the United Nations.

The records of the 1945 San Francisco Conference indicate that drawing the right balance for expressing the General Assembly's international law function was a challenge from the very beginning. The alternative formulations before the drafters of Article 13, paragraph 1(a), of the Charter of the United Nations were: "progressive development" of international law, or "revision" of international law.[3] The matter went to a vote. In the preparatory work, the following view is recorded just before the vote: " 'Progressive development' would establish a nice balance between stability and change, whereas 'revision' would lay too much emphasis on change."[4]

Readers familiar with the statute of the International Law Commission will be aware that the statute specifies different procedural steps for "progressive development" and for "codification". However, article 15 of the statute also contains the provision that the two different concepts are defined only "for

* This contribution is made in my personal capacity, and should not be attributed to the institutions with I am affiliated. I thank Kristi How (International Affairs Division, Attorney-General's Chambers, Singapore) and Marcus Teo (Centre for International Law, National University of Singapore) for allowing me to draw from their own work on the Commission in the course of preparing this contribution.

1 H.E. Ambassador Burhan Gafoor, Permanent Representative of Singapore to the United Nations in New York, "Statement of the Chairperson of the Sixth Committee at the Seventieth Anniversary of the ILC" (New York, 21 May 2018) ("[T]he relationship between the Sixth Committee and the ILC … is an organic and symbiotic relationship that is based on a common objective, which is to support the progressive development and codification of international law and to strengthen the multilateral rules-based system.")

2 Oscar Schachter, 'The Invisible College of International Lawyers' (1977) 72 Nw U L Rev 217.

3 'Summary report of the twenty-first meeting of Committee II/2', United Nations Conference on International Organization (7 June 1945) Document 848, II/2/46, 177–178.

4 Ibid.

convenience".[5] By 1996, the Commission had become explicit about the view that the distinction between the two concepts was "difficult if not impossible to draw in practice."[6] The Commission continued: "Flexibility is necessary in the range of cases and for a range of reasons."[7]

Despite these prior acknowledgements of the analytical limits, the conceptual difference between "progressive development" and "codification" continues to preoccupy the Commission's stakeholders across the legal departments of Member States, international courts and tribunals, as well as academia. Refashioned in the rubric of this panel, the Commission's happy medium is assumed to lie somewhere between "identifying existing law" and "proposing new law". In one sense, the preoccupation with the Commission's mandate is not surprising. As lawyers, our professional proclivity is to parse the texts that describe the Commission's mandate. But in another sense, the preoccupation seems to have little practical application in light of the Commission's own abandonment of the distinction between "progressive development" and "codification". Still, sitting in the Sixth Committee room, it is not uncommon to hear Member States asking for the Commission to clarify which elements of its output are "codification", and which elements amount to "progressive development of international law".

I have been asked to write this contribution setting out my reflections on the panel that I was privileged to chair at the Geneva commemorative event. What might we usefully draw from the rich discussions that took place, as the Commission moves into a future where the international order may take shape along lines we do not yet know? Given the practical assimilation of "progressive development" and "codification", why do stakeholders still ask the Commission to account for the difference?

I suggest that continuing conversations about the Commission's mandate of "progressive development", on one hand, and "codification", on the other, are undergirded by fundamental anxieties about the authorship of international law. These anxieties are not new to the codification movement. To some extent, the elements of the *travaux préparatoires* of the Charter and the statute outlined earlier in this contribution demonstrate this. Travelling yet further back in time, the slim outcome of the 1930 Hague Conference reminds us that

5 Statute of the ILC, UNGA Res 174(II) (21 November 1947) as amended by UNGA Res 485(V) (12 December 1950); UNGA Res 984(X) (3 December 1955); UNGA Res 985(X) (3 December 1955) and UNGA Res 36/39 (18 November 1981).

6 ILC, 'Report of the International Law Commission on the work of its forty-eighth session' [1996] II(2) ILC Ybk 1, 86 at para 156.

7 Ibid.

the codification of international law was not easy even when the delegates were few in number. I would like to draw three points from the panel discussions held in Geneva to illustrate why the debate on the right balance between stability and change in the Commission's mandate remains relevant in 2018 and beyond.

First, as an exercise in reconciling and accommodating different perspectives, "codification" – used now in the sense of transposing international law to writing – presents different challenges today. Some 50 States were represented at the dawn of the United Nations. With successive waves of decolonization and other political reconfigurations – some more or less traumatic than others – we now number 193 Member States of the United Nations. By numbers alone, this fourfold increase is exponential. More remarkable, however, and at the heart of the Commission's contemporary and future challenges, is the sheer diversity of cultures, values, and interests converging at the United Nations. Over seventy years after the San Francisco Conference, the United Nations remains the world's only universal international organization. It is thus a key site for making universal international law.

It is true that the Commission and the Sixth Committee have adapted to changing membership of the United Nations. The number of the members of the Commission has been enlarged three times, with the last and most significant membership reform taking place in 1981.[8] This was when the Commission's membership was stabilized at 34, with clear rules on geographical distribution, replacing the old "gentlemen's agreements" among regional groups.[9] Such membership reforms acknowledge the Commission's role as a "microcosm" of the United Nations, as a sort of proving ground for new texts. Seen in this light, the Commission's general preference for working by consensus – thus refraining from explicit disclosure of whether a codification project is more "identifying existing law" or more "proposing new law" – takes on a certain significance. In this image of the Commission as "microcosm", consensus in the Commission aims to facilitate consensus writ large among the United Nations membership. This image of the Commission may also explain why Member States notice when the Commission votes.

But there may be important reasons why Member States might ask the Commission to draw back the curtain on consensus. It is worth remembering that the majority of delegates at Bandung did not, or did not yet, represent Member States of the United Nations.[10] Bandung's Final Communiqué was

8 UNGA Res 36/39 (18 November 1981).

9 Ibid.

10 See the keynote speech by Abdulqawi A. Yusuf in Section 9 of this volume.

framed in the inherited Westphalian vernacular, but expressed the cultures, values, and interests of peoples acquiring agency in the international legal order for the first time. Moreover, speaking in the vernacular of international law does not resolve the inherent tensions underlying participation in an inherited system. A clear technical understanding of how the Commission has approached specific legal issues, especially where those issues are novel and touch on vital interests, can enhance Member States' ability to respond meaningfully to the work products of the Commission. In short, knowing how the Commission regards its own output is helpful to all Member States when they participate, with the Commission, in the collective endeavour of formulating international law.[11]

Second, beyond the United Nations, the Commission's operating environment has changed. Contemporary international law is characterized by a plurality of different actors. Information, including about the Commission and its work, flows freely through submarine fibre optic cables and via satellite to those who can access it. Today, the Commission's audience and interlocutors have expanded to include regional courts, investor-state arbitral tribunals, human rights treaty bodies, and academia, each with their own socio-legal cultures and respective legal standing under classical sources doctrine. Indeed, some of these actors may even overlap in membership with the private codification institutions of the late nineteenth century, which are still active today.

In this pluralist environment, the Commission's institutional role as the codification body of the sole universal international organization comes into sharper focus. Member States react to Commission output through General Assembly action. This reaction, in turn, informs how international lawyers assess the normative weight of the Commission's work. This direct connection to States is unique to the Commission. It is also firmly grounded in the Commission's original institutional design.

Third, the Commission's use of form in its work products has evolved alongside changes in the nature of multilateral treaty-making,[12] as well as

11 See Antony Anghie, 'Bandung and the Origins of Third World Sovereignty' in Luis Eslava, Michael Fakhri and Vasuki Nesiah (eds), *Bandung, Global History, and International Law: Critical Pasts and Pending Futures* (CUP 2017).

12 Representative examples include the new architecture of the international climate change regime pursuant to the Paris Agreement and the so-called "mega-regional" economic agreements. On the former, see e.g. Richard B Stewart, Michael Oppenheimer and Bryce Rudyk, 'Building Blocks: A Strategy for near-Term Action within the New Global Climate Framework' (2017) 144 Climatic Change 1; Daniel Bodansky, 'The Legal Character of the Paris Agreement' (2016) 25 RECIEL 142; Lavanya Rajamani, 'Ambition and Differentiation

broader developments relating to the sites and techniques of global governance.[13] It is true that the extent to which the Commission has evolved its formal output since the late 1990s can sometimes be overstated. The Commission's first projects did not all result in draft articles intended to form the basis for a diplomatic conference. Instead, they included the Nuremberg Principles, formulated at a time when, notwithstanding the judicial activity of the war crimes tribunals, international criminal law was still largely regarded as *de lege ferenda*, and the initial package of practical measures recommended as ways and means for making the evidence of customary international law more readily available. This early work on customary international law remains salient today.

However, calls for a considered approach when assessing the authority of the Commission's "non-legislative codifications" are valid.[14] Due attention to "the context and factors militating in favour of the authority of codification conventions and International Law Commission's draft articles, combined with an awareness of the role that these texts may play in the crystallization or formation of new rules"[15] ultimately leads to a more robust international law. This responsibility to appraise does not fall on the Commission alone. It applies to all members of the "invisible college" engaged in the "common intellectual enterprise" of applying and developing international law.[16]

In the old League of Nations Council Chamber inaugurated just three years after the outbreak of further war, there was a palpable sense among those present in the Chamber, surrounded by the striking murals of José Maria Sert, that the rules-based multilateral system, established in the late hours of that terrible conflict, stood at a crossroads. Ineta Ziemele's frank contribution highlighted the pluralist and technological realities of contemporary international law. Yifeng Chen's masterful study of the codification movement reminded us that the International Law Commission was not international law's first

in the 2015 Paris Agreement: Interpretative Possibilities and Underlying Politics' (2016) 65 ICLQ 493. On the latter, see e.g. scholarship under the auspices of the MegaReg Project based at the New York University School of Law <https://www.iilj.org/megareg/megareg-papers/>.

13 For an illustrative and succinct exposition of different governance techniques, see Benedict Kingsbury, 'Three Models of "Distributed Administration": Canopy, Baobab, and Symbiote' (2015) 13 IJCL 478.

14 Fernando Lusa Bordin, 'Reflections of Customary International Law: The Authority of Codification Conventions and the ILC Draft Articles in International Law' (2014) 63 ICLQ 535.

15 Ibid 566.

16 Schachter (n 2) 217.

codification institution, while the response by Sean D. Murphy reminded us how the Commission is unique among other codification institutions. The Commission faces complex times in an ambiguous world.[17] But the Commission's history has shown that it can respond and adapt. There is every reason to look forward to the Commission's continuing positive contribution, in partnership with Member States through the Sixth Committee, to better and inclusive international law.

17 Bilahari Kausikan, *Dealing with an Ambiguous World* (World Scientific Publishing Co Pte Ltd 2017).

Between Codification and Legislation: a Role for the International Law Commission as an Autonomous Law-Maker

Yifeng Chen

1 Introduction

The United Nations International Law Commission, an institution entrusted with the responsibility to codify and progressively develop international law,[1] continues to play a pivotal role in the international legal process. Challenges and doubts notwithstanding,[2] the Commission has proved itself as a pertinent contributor to the international law-making process over the course of the past seventy years.

The past decade has witnessed the reinvigoration of the International Law Commission, both institutionally and intellectually. In terms of its legislative functions, the Commission has been actively expanding its working territory. The Commission has not only continued to address traditional topics primarily in public international law, in accordance with paragraph 2 of article 1 of its statute,[3] such as customary international law, the law of treaties, and *jus cogens*, but also started considering more specialized fields of international law, as seen in the agenda items "Protection of atmosphere", "Protection of the environment in relation to armed conflicts", "Crimes against humanity" and others.[4] The International Law Commission is imbued with a renewed confidence to take up topics "that reflect new developments in international law and pressing concerns of the international community as a whole".[5]

The intellectual reinvigoration of the Commission has also led to the diversity in the forms of the final products of the Commission. The Commission

1 Statute of the Institute of International Law (adopted 10 September 1873) article 1.

2 Doubts were once raised about the continual relevance of the International Law Commission. See Christian Tomuschat, 'The International Law Commission – An Outdated Institution?' (2006) 49 GYIL 77–105.

3 Statute (n 1) article 1 (2).

4 See UN Doc A/CN.4/709/Rev.1 and UN Doc A/CN.4/723.

5 See ILC, 'Report of the International Law Commission on the work of its forty-ninth session' [1997] II(2) ILC Ybk 1, para 238.

has produced not only conventions and draft articles, but also declarations, model rules, draft codes, draft statutes, guiding principles, draft principles, conclusions, guides to practice and draft guidelines. The Commission has shown much flexibility in adopting different forms for its work. It is evident from those designations that some topics were not conceived as necessary or desirable for further development into conventions. This diversity in form raised the issue of practical usefulness and, theoretically, the legitimacy of this type of work.[6]

This brings to the forefront of debate the role of the Commission in international law-making. This article argues that both the notion of "codification" and the positivistic concept of international law, which have for long determined the Commission's working methods and self-identity, require critical re-examination. The contribution of the Commission to the development of international law should not be solely measured by reference to its ability to produce conventions. It is also desirable to investigate the multiple roles that the Commission has played in the broad international law-making process.

In light of the expanding reach of the Commission's work, the diversity of form in its work products, and its increasing impact, this article aims to critically assess the role the International Commission played in the development of international law over the past seven decades. While Part II traces the historical emergence of the Commission's mandate back to the second half of the 19th century, it argues that "codification of international law" has been constructed as a political project for international peace. In Part III, this concept of codification is examined from the point of view of a spectrum, where two approaches, "registering" and "legislative", are placed at its ends. The article asserts that competing conceptions of codification have not only been determinative of the work of the Committee of Experts for the Progressive Codification of International Law, but are also affecting the institutional role that the International Law Commission plays today. This amalgam of registering and legislative approaches, evident in the Commission's dual mandate for "promotion of the progressive development of international law and its codification", has provided room for flexibility for the Commission to adapt to the changing landscape of international law. In light of the historical analysis of the Commission's mandate, Part IV focuses on the practice of the Commission today, and critically assesses the Commission's work in respect to their diversity of

6 See Sean D Murphy, 'Codification, Progressive Development, or Scholarly Analysis? The Art of Packaging the ILC's Work Product' in Maurizio Ragazzi (ed), *The Responsibility of International Organizations: Essays in Memory of Sir Ian Brownlie* (Martinus Nijhoff 2013) 29–40.

form and sources of authority. The article concludes by a theoretical account of the future of the Commission, as an institution becoming an autonomous law-maker in international law.

II Situating the Codification Project Historically

The idea of codifying international law has its intellectual roots in the pioneer works of Jeremy Bentham, who not only coined the term international law, but also advocated for an international code. The codification project started to take its shape in the second half of the 19thcentury, first through personal engagement by individual international lawyers, including Johan Caspar Bluntschli and David Dudley Field, and later continued to develop through collective efforts of private associations of international lawyers.[7] While the Hague Conferences of 1899 and 1907 have often been characterized as being instrumental for the codification of international law,[8] conscious and sustained efforts of codification at inter-governmental level, however, only started in the 1920s under the auspices of the League of Nations.[9] A critical step towards institutionalized codification was the establishment of the International Law Commission, by General Assembly resolution 174(II) of 21 November 1947, a permanent institution of experts entrusted with a general competence to codify and progressively develop international law.

Several observations can be made on the evolution of codification as a historical project. First of all, codification of international law as a professional aspiration was deeply internalized in the international legal profession from its very beginning in the late 19th century. The Institute of International Law, established in 1873 by eminent European-American jurists, was preoccupied with the codification of international law. The statute of the Institute of International Law states expressly that "its purpose is to promote the progress of international law", among other means, "by lending its co-operation in any serious endeavour for the gradual and progressive codification of international law".[10] Indeed several distinguished members of the Institute served in the

---

7 For an overview of various private efforts at codification, see Ramaa P Dhokalia, *The Codification of Public International Law* (Manchester University Press 1970) 37–75.

8 See Arthur Watts, 'Codification and Progressive Development of International Law' *Max Planck Encyclopedia of Public International Law* (December 2006) <opil.ouplaw.com/home/EPIL>.

9 See Shabtai Rosenne, 'The International Law Commission 1949–1959' (1960) 36 BYIL 104, 107–109.

10 Statute of the Institute of International Law (adopted 10 September 1873) article 1.

League of Nations Committee of Experts on the Progressive Development of International Law, or later played an active role in the Codification Conference of 1930.[11] The Association for the Reform and Codification of the International Law (later renamed as the International Law Association) established in 1873, with its origin in the American peace movement, was equally committed to furthering the codification of international law alongside its project advocating the institutionalizing a world court.[12] Codification was a professional vision shared among elite European and American international lawyers, seen as an instrument for the progress of international law, and as a political project for international peace. The project of codification embodied the liberal ideas of progress, reason and humanity.[13] Codification is also a constitutive element of an international society in the sense that it "presupposes for the society concerned a sufficient basis of common experience and conviction to ground effective rules regulating the group's future social relationship".[14]

Secondly, the codification of international law was closely associated with the emergence of international courts and tribunals. The development and relative success of arbitration as of the late 18th century had prompted much hope for establishing a permanent judicial body to settle disputes among States. For instance, the peaceful settlement of the *Alabama* case through arbitration in 1872 was perceived as an encouraging development by international lawyers and pacifists. Establishment of a world court and codification of international law become twin projects advocated by the international peace movement of late 19th century. Codification of international law became more pressing with the world's growing faith in international dispute settlement mechanisms by the turning of the 20th century. In this regard, a code of international law was expected to help clarify the mutual rights and obligations of States: and avoid disputes. "Codification is plainly of the greatest value for assuring certainty and clearness in the law. These advantages ... are especially valuable in the

11 For example, Hjalmar Hammarskjöld, who contributed remarkably to the work of the Committee of Experts for the Progressive Codification of International Law as its chair, was a member and president (1928) of the Institute of International Law.

12 For the early codification project in the United States, see Mark Weston Janis, *The American Tradition of International Law: Great Expectations 1789–1914* (Clarendon Press 2004) 117–133.

13 See Martti Koskenniemi, 'International Legislation Today: Limits and Possibilities' (2005) 23 WILJ 61, 65–68.

14 Julius Stone, 'On the Vocation of the International Law Commission'(1957) 57 ColumLRev 16, 33. The constitutive role that codification plays in international society is also emphasized by Shabtai Rosenne, 'Codification Revisited after 50 Years' (1998) 2 MaxPlanckUNYB 1.

case of international law."[15] Especially with the establishment of the League of Nations and of the Permanent Court of International Justice, States possessed much optimism and enthusiasm for the codification of international law. It was felt that the gradual restatement of international law into more precise written form had "become still more necessary since the creation of the Permanent Court of International Justice".[16] To tie the codification of international law to international dispute settlement produced a profound effect on our understanding of international law as a body of rules for the peaceful resolution of disputes between States.

Thirdly, the codification of international law was conceived as an instrument for social reform and progress. In the absence of a centralized legislature at the international level, the exercise of codification was largely appreciated as a substitutive form of international legislation. In the words of the former American Sectary of State Elihu Root, "what is called for now and what we mean when we speak of codification of international law is the making of law."[17] A similar view was held by Robert Jennings that "codification properly conceived is itself a method for the progressive development of the law".[18]

The codification project in the early 20th century was a continuation of the peace conferences of 1899 and 1907 in the sense that the object of the project was to produce a systemized body of rules for international relations.[19] However, it was also well understood that codification would offer a novel way, different from that of a diplomatic conference, to advance international law and

---

15 Speech addressed by Mr. Hjalmar Hammarskjöld, Chair of the Committee of Experts for the Progressive Codification of International Law, in the first session of the Committee on 1 April 1925, see Shabtai Rosenne (ed), *League of Nations Committee of Experts for the Progressive Codification of International Law (1925–1928)* (Oceana 1975) Volume I (Minutes) 3.

16 Ibid 5.

17 Elihu Root, 'Codification of International Law' (1925) 19 AJIL 675, 681.

18 Robert Y Jennings, 'The Progressive Development of International Law and its Codification' (1947) 24 BYIL 301, 302.

19 In a memorandum entitled 'A Historical Survey of the Development of International Law and its Codification by International Conferences', submitted by the United Nations Secretariat to the Committee of Experts for the Progressive Codification of International Law, the codification of international law was traced back to international conferences of mid-19th century. It was noted that "the development of written international law through the restatement of principles of existing law or through the formulation of new law (these two methods being frequently undistinguishable), was pursued at over 100 international conferences or congresses held between 1864 and 1914, resulting in over 250 international instruments." United Nations Secretariat, 'A Historical Survey of the Development of International Law and its Codification by International Conferences' (29 April 1947) UN Doc A/AC.10/5, reprinted in (1947) 41 AJIL Supp 29, 32.

peace. Codification had been seen as a soft means of formulating international legislation. Compared to legislation in diplomatic conferences, the method of codification was welcomed as an exercise that was undertaken by experts and deeply rooted in reason and human conscience. It was also commended for its scientific nature. Of course, codification also indicated a gradual and limited diversion of powers from rulers of States to experts in international law. However, the tension between codification and legislation has never been properly settled. The uncertainty about the very nature of codification is in constant debate and still has an impact on the work of the International Law Commission today.

As the idea of codification emerged as a historical project of a specific time, the codification project carries with it a specific intellectual and ideological outlook on international law. First of all, the idea of codification is built upon a rule-based, formalistic notion of international law.[20] Rules are objective and their meanings ascertainable. It keeps a distance from both morality and politics. Secondly, it assumes a scientific approach to international law.[21] International law is perceived as a discipline of science, based on rationality, logic and structure, and amenable to systemization and organization. The justification of codification rests upon the scientific nature of the discipline of international law. Thirdly, it is developed by a faith in international law as an organic system, in subjecting the totality of international relations to the rule of law.[22] The idea of international law as an organic system implies the completeness of international law as well as its dynamics. It is a progressive and structured notion of international law. It is observed that the International Law Commission is pre-eminently guided by, among other general principles, "its faith in the potential of international law for achieving international peace, security and justice".[23] Fourthly, as with other projects of international law, the codification project embeds a State-centered, positivistic perspective to international law. Exactly because of its inherently legislative nature, any credible codification project would require sovereign endorsement in one way or another. The success of the International Law Commission is often attributed to its healthy

---

20 Martti Koskenniemi refers to "the culture of formalism", see Martti Koskenniemi, *The Gentle Civilizer of Nations: The Rise and Fall of International Law 1870–1960* (CUP 2001) 500–509.

21 For a critical examination on international law as a science, see Anne Orford, 'Scientific Reason and the Discipline of International Law' (2014) 25 EJIL 369.

22 For a seminal work in this regard, see Hersch Lauterpacht, *The Function of Law in the International Community* (Clarendon Press 1933).

23 Bertrand G Ramcharan, *The International Law Commission: its Approach to the Codification and Progressive Development of International Law* (Martinus Nijhoff 1977) 164.

interaction with governments, for example, through the Sixth Committee of the General Assembly.

III The Concept of Codification Revisited

While the notion of codification in international law borrows from domestic analogies, the very nature and boundary of codification is much disputed in international legal scholarship as well as in practice. The issue is not simply of a theoretical interest. Rather, as international practice has illustrated, the choice of an institutional philosophy for codification profoundly defines and constrains the actual work of that codification institution. This is because competing ideas of codification carry with them varying implications for their nature, working methods, and limitations.[24] At times, the tension between various notions of codification may even frustrate the work of the codification institution. The success or failure of the codification endeavors can hinge upon the ability of the codifier to develop an appropriate institutional approach to codification.[25]

1 *Competing Conceptions of Codification*

In international law scholarship and practice no single, generally accepted conception of codification exists. Many competing and even contradicting notions of codification can be found.[26] On the one end of the spectrum is a "registering approach" that refers to codification as a scientific registration of unwritten international law. Here, codification is more concerned with the

24 The observation by Yuen-Li Liang in 1947 is an illustrative example. "The very fact that codification always involves certain legislative processes, aside from the process of consolidation, has resulted in a paradox as to method. While the work of consolidation is generally admitted to be a scientific task which can best be done by professional lawyers, rather than by governmental representatives, the legislative processes require the consent of governments." See Yuen-Li Liang, 'The Progressive Development of International Law and its Codification under the United Nations' (1947) 41 ASILPROC 24, 33.

25 The failure of the Codification Conference during the League of Nations is attributable to, among others, the lack of a common understanding of codification to guide through its work. See Dhokalia (n 7) 129–131.

26 See, for example, Liang (n 24) 32; James Brierly, 'Codification of International Law' (1948) 47 MichLRev 2; also Alain Pellet, 'Responding to New Needs through Codification and Progressive Development' in Vera Gowlland-Debbas (ed), *Multilateral Treaty-Making: The Current Status of Challenges to and Reforms Needed in International Legislative Process* (Kluwer 2000) 13–23.

systemization of law, aiming at the systematic statement of the law in written form. Its application is retrospective, therefore one has to wait until a topic is ripe for codification. Under this approach, codification should mainly deal with the identification, consolidation and elaboration of existing laws. The ripeness of a topic is measured primarily by the abundance of agreed rules on the topic. Progressive development of law is discouraged in the codification process, if not completely avoided. While room for creativity in codification is acknowledged, it is often understood as an exception or unavoidability, and, in any case, marginal.[27] The output of such codification can take form of a code-like restatement and does not need to be sent for State ratification. The Declaration concerning the Laws of Naval War adopted by principal naval powers during that time on 26 February 1909 is an illustrative example.[28] The value and authority of the statement would depend on the merit of the work itself.[29] As the very idea of codification is to restate existing law, to present it in the form of a draft treaty and ask for State ratifications might only be detrimental to the codification exercise, as States may refuse to ratify, or make reservations to, treaties.[30] Under the registering approach, codification is a scientific exercise, which is better entrusted to a group of legal experts. If codification is essentially scientific in nature and the work is to be judged by its quality, private codifications by individuals or associations such as Institute of International Law are also of great importance.

At the other end of the spectrum, however, lies a "legislative approach" which perceives codification in terms of international legislation, a political exercise of legislative power pursued by States collectively, usually through diplomatic conferences. There, codification is not constrained by existing laws. It is seen as a technique for the progress of international law,[31] and encompasses

27 This is the understanding of codification usually among English lawyers, see Brierly (n 26) 2.

28 See United Nations Secretariat (n 19) 43–49.

29 See United Nations Secretariat, 'Methods for Encouraging the Progressive Development of International Law and its Eventual Codification', A/AC.10/7 (6 May 1947), reprinted in (1947) 41 AJIL Supp 111, 116. The same opinion was advocated by Professor James Brierly at the Committee on the Progressive Development of International Law and its Codification when drafting the statute of the International Law Commission, see 'Summary Record of the 2nd Meeting' (13 May 1947) A/AC.10/SR.2, 5.

30 For an account of the limits of using international treaties to codify customary international law, see Jennings (n 18).

31 The memorandum written by Hersch Lauterpacht actively advocated a liberal and progressive interpretation of codification, see ILC, 'Survey of International Law in Relation to the Work of Codification of the International Law Commission: Preparatory work within the purview of article 18, paragraph 1, of the of the International Law

law-making activities including both the restatement of existing laws and the development of new laws. It may revise old law when needed, and may also formulate new law in novel fields where few written rules exist. Codification is then a forward-looking exercise and should address the pressing needs of international society. The criterion for the selection of topics for codification is determined by the needs of international society and the boundaries of the work are marked by the political will of States. In other words, in deciding whether a topic is ripe for codification, ripeness is assessed not by reference to abundance/scarcity of existing rules on the topic, but by a careful evaluation of the acceptability of the proposed rules to States. From the perspective of the "legislative approach", codification is an unavoidable political exercise, and for this reason, should involve State representatives in the process. Therefore, draft conventions are considered to be the only proper form of codification. The codified texts are subject to further scrutiny and acceptance of States. The codification process is completed with the convocation of diplomatic conferences and the formal adoption of conventions. Under this legislative approach, the authority of the codified texts derives from the consent of States.

Although the two approaches at the end of the spectrum are in a way exaggerated and overly simplified, they are nevertheless useful to highlight the divergent views of codification in international law. A purely registering or legislative approach is only possible as a theoretical construction. In reality, when the task of codification is institutionalized, the codification institution often embarks on a middle road, as the examples of the League of Nations Committee of Experts for the Progressive Codification of International Law and the International Law Commission have shown.[32] Both of these bodies have exhibited a great extent of flexibility in absorbing elements of both approaches.

2 *Experience of the Committee of Experts for the Progressive Codification of International Law*

At the initiative of the Swedish Government, the League of Nations established the Committee of Experts for the Progressive Codification of International Law (hereafter "Committee") in 1924, with the mandate to identify the subjects of international law which were "desirable and realisable" for codification.[33] The

Commission – Memorandum submitted by the Secretary-General' (10 February 1949) UN Doc A/CN.4/1/Rev.1.

32 For an excellent exposition of the actual work of codification at the International Law Commission in its formative period of time, see Hersch Lauterpacht, 'Codification and Development of International Law' (1955) 49 AJIL 16.

33 League of Nations, 'Resolution adopted by the League of Nations Assembly on 22 September 1924' (1924) League of Nations Official Journal Spec Supp 21, 10.

Committee, consisting of 17 members representing "the main forms of civilisation and the principal legal systems of the world",[34] comprised judges from the Permanent Court of International Justice, governmental legal advisors, professors, diplomats and practitioners. From 1925 to 1928, the Committee convened for four sessions, where it deliberated on appropriate approaches and possible topics for codification. This was the first time that codification of international law had been officially undertaken under the auspices of an international organization. Although the actual outcomes of the codification efforts are often greeted with regret, the institutional experience gained during the League of Nations Committee remains highly relevant.

Central to the debates of the Committee, among other issues, were the notion of "codification" and its implications for the scope, methodology and procedures of the work of the Committee. Even before the Committee embarked upon its work, its chairperson, the Swedish member Mr. Hjalmar Hammarskjöld circulated an advance working paper and brought up the nature of codification. He asked: "Are we simply asked to give methodological form and arrangement of rules which already exist, at the most, to reduce to writing ideas on which there is universal agreement? Or are we to go further, and to consider how far innovations are desirable or possible and how far resolutions may be found for questions which are still subject to controversy?"[35] The Committee devoted its first five meetings elaborating the idea of codification in international law and its implications for the Committee's mandate.

During the debates, two different conceptions of codification emerged. The two positions were nicely summarized by the Chinese member Wang Chung-Hui, Deputy-Judge at the Permanent Court of International Justice at that time,[36] who stated that "[c]odification in a narrow sense might be taken

---

34 The members of the Committee of Experts were not elected by the Council or the Assembly on an individual basis, were approved as a whole by the Council at the recommendation of Sweden. The composition of the Committee is dominantly European. The Committee was composed by Hjalmar Hammarskjöld (Sweden) (Chairman), G. Diena (Italy) (Vice-Chairman), M. C. Botella (Spain), James Brierly (United Kingdom), M. Fromageot (France), J. Gustavo Guerrero (Salvador), Bernard Cornelis Johannes Loder (Netherlands), Barbosa De Magalhaes (Portugal), Adalbert Mastny (Czechoslovakia), M. M. Matsuda (Japan), Szymon Rundstein (Poland), Walther Schücking (Germany), José León Suarez (Argentine), Charles de Visscher (Belgium), Wang Chung-Hui (China), and George W. Wickersham (United States of America).

35 UN Doc C. P. D. I/2, 6 March 1925, in Rosenne (n 15) xxxvii.

36 Wang Chung-Hui [王宠惠] (1881–1958) was the first law graduate from a modern Chinese university (Beiyang University, Tianjin, 1900). Dr. Wang had a prominent political career in Republican China, holding important positions, for example, the Minister of Foreign Affairs and Prime Minister at the Peking Government and the Minister of Justice

to mean simply a restatement of existing law, a reduction to writing of what was already accepted and acted upon in practice" and that "codification in the broader sense involved proposals for the alteration of existing rules, either by modifications or additions".[37] The majority of the Committee, including its chairperson, was in favour of a progressive idea of codification. For Hammarskjöld, "the duty, therefore, of the Committee was not merely to codify in the strict or Anglo-Saxon sense of the word", he added that "it could make proposals with a view to codifying, amending and completing international law".[38] Similar ideas were expressed by other members who shared an optimistic outlook on codification.[39] These members were ambitious about codification projects and were keen to promote peace through international law. Codification was seen as a tool for social progress. In the view of Suarez, for example, "the task of the Committee was not merely passive and confined to codifying points on which the States seemed to be in agreement … The Committee had also an active mission in the sense of drawing attention to general principles and seeking general conclusions, and of steeling questions in regard to which the modern international community of interests made it necessary to secure legal uniformity."[40] While codification did not aim to produce a code of international law, it should respond to the legislative needs of international society.

To the contrary, some other members stick to a conservative approach to codification through a pragmatic reading of the Committee's mandate.[41] In the view of Professor de Visscher and Professor Brierly, the Committee was only instructed to "prepare a provisional list of the subjects of international law" capable of being developed into international agreements. Professor de Visscher stated that: "the Committee must aim at encouraging the conclusion of new conventions between States … The essential object was to discover, in a concrete and practical form, what was acceptable to the Governments."[42] For him, the theoretical debates on the difference between codification and legislation "would lead to no result".[43] In any case, the Committee should not enter into

and Minister of Foreign Affairs at the Nanjing Government. Internationally, he served as deputy judge and then judge at the Permanent Court of International Justice (1922–1936). Dr. Wang was also a member of the Chinese delegation to the United Nations Conference in San Francisco in 1945.

37 Rosenne (n 15) 21.

38 Ibid 11 (Hammarskjöld).

39 Ibid 6–7 (Suarez), 7–8 (Diena), 10 (Schücking), 12–13 (Rundstein), 20–21 (Wang).

40 Ibid 6 (Suarez).

41 See, for example, ibid 9–10, 24–25 (de Visscher), 15–16 (Brierly).

42 Ibid 24 (de Visscher).

43 Ibid 9 (de Visscher).

the sphere of international legislation, a reserved prerogative for sovereigns only. As emphasized by the French member Mr. Fromageot, State consent, "either registered by means of conventions or tacit [sic]", was as the only existing basis of international law.[44]

The lengthy debate in the Committee did not lead to any definitive or generally accepted concept of codification. No general agreement emerged in the Committee as to the very nature of codification. The tension between the "legislative" and "registering" conceptions was recognized by the Committee. As Professor de Visscher observed, "[q]uoting the terms of the Assembly resolution, it might be said that codification in the strict sense appeared to be the most realisable task, and in the broader sense the most desirable."[45] This foreran the debate on the criterion of ripeness for codification in the context of the International Law Commission. Meanwhile, the dynamic and mixed nature of codification was also appreciated by the Committee. As de Visscher stated, "codification, even in the strictest sense, always implied a certain legislative element".[46]

Having agreed on the disagreement, the Committee then proceeded with its work without settling on a concept of codification. The ongoing state of unsettlement left the Committee and its members with little guidance on the actual performance of their task. Some sub-committees concluded their reports with "draft conventions", "draft provisions" or "conclusions", and some not even conclusions.[47] The diversity of the reports produced by various sub-committees was in a way reflective of different interpretations among members on the nature of codification and the expected output from various sub-committees.

The vagueness associated with the term "codification" was also to a certain extent accountable for the failure of the eventual Codification Conference of 1930. States came with divergent expectations on the objectives of the conference, whether it be for registration or legislation.[48] A predominantly registering notion of codification underlying the preparation of the conference encountered a legislative experience in the actual codification exercise. The differences between States were often revealed only in the course of codification. This left the States with a negative perception that the conference was underprepared and disorganized.[49]

44 Ibid 16 (Fromageot).
45 Ibid 24 (de Visscher).
46 Rosenne (n 15) 24 (de Visscher).
47 Ibid lviii.
48 See United Nations Secretariat (n 19) 87–90.
49 Dhokalia (n 7) 126–133.

3 *The Statute of the International Law Commission: Distinguishing Codification from Progressive Development*

Article 13 of the Charter of the United Nations on the codification of international law had its origin in a proposal of the Chinese government to the Dumbarton Oaks Conference in its second phase, suggesting that "the General Assembly should be responsible for initiating studies and make recommendation with regard to the development and revision of rules and principles of international law".[50] China, who had experienced the injustice of unequal treaties and the impotence of the League of Nations, placed high hopes on international law and the future, which the United Nations could bring about for a just world order. At the Committee II/2 of the San Francesco Conference, lengthy discussion took place on the notions of "codification", "development" and "revision". "Revision" was eventually removed from the text, partly on the suggestions of some States that "development" could comprise "revision".[51] In the final formula, the General Assembly would encourage "the progressive development of international law and its codification".

The Committee on the Progressive Development of International Law and its Codification, which was entrusted with drafting the statute of the International Law Commission, again had heatedly debated on the concept of codification and the role of the Commission.[52] On the one hand, Professor James Brierly, the representative of the United Kingdom, proposed a scientific approach to codification. In his view, "[c]odification was a scientific and not a political task", and the work should be entrusted to "a small group of personal experts".[53] The codification institution should "not concern itself with the substance of international legislation", as "the task of selecting topics was for political representatives not for lawyers".[54] On the other hand, Professor Vladimir Koretsky from the then Union of Soviet Socialist Republics advocated for a political approach to codification. For him, an international convention was the only proper form of codification, as codification would necessarily involve

50 Chinese Proposal on the Dumbarton Oaks proposals: 'Dumbarton Oaks Proposals' Washington Conversations on International Peace and Security Organization (Washington DC 21 August – 7 October 1944) in *Documents of the United Nations Conference on International Organization*, Volume 3, Doc 1, G/1 (a) (1 May 1945) 25.

51 See Liang (n 24) 29–30; also Rosenne (n 9) 109–110.

52 For a useful summary of the discussion at the Committee, see Yuen-Li Liang, 'The General Assembly and the Progressive Development and Codification of International Law' (1948) 42 AJIL 66, 69–77.

53 For the opinions of Professor James Brierly, see 'Summary Record of the 2nd Meeting' (13 May 1947) UN Doc A/AC.10/SR.2, 5.

54 Ibid.

the creation of laws. He further considered that the United Nations "is an intergovernmental agency and not a superstate" and "could not oblige the states to accept norms". The task of codification was better entrusted to governmental representatives.[55] The form of international convention should apply to progressive development as well as the restatement of international law.

It was during the drafting process of the statute of the International Law Commission that the normative distinction between codification and progressive development was consolidated, in consequence of which the term codification started to receive a technical connotation. In a memorandum prepared by the Secretariat of the United Nations, a distinction was drawn as to the method of codification between international convention and restatement.[56] The United States also formally proposed a clear distinction between "progressive development" and "codification".[57] With codification being "the scientific restatement of existing rules and principles of international law",[58] progressive development meant, in the words of Professor Philip Jessup, "development of new law to meet the world's needs".[59] While both concepts should fall within the working scope of the International Law Commission, the methods and procedures for the two different types of work necessarily varied. The proposed distinction between codification and progressive development was well received among the members,[60] although it was also generally felt that an absolute distinction was impossible to retain in reality.[61]

---

55 For the opinions of Professor Vladimir Koretsky, see Committee on the Progressive Development of International Law and its Codification, 'Summary Record of the 4th Meeting' (15 May 1947) UN Doc A/AC.10/SR.4, 4–7; 'Summary Record of the 9th Meeting' (22 May 1947) UN Doc A/AC.10/SR.9, 13–15.

56 United Nations Secretariat (n 29) 111–116.

57 See 'Suggestions by the United States' (12 May 1947) UN Doc A/AC.10/14; also printed in United States Department of State Bulletin (1947) Vol 16, 1029–1030.

58 See ibid.

59 'Statement by the United States Representative on that Committee, Philip C. Jessup' in United States Department of State Bulletin (1947) Vol 16, 1026–1029.

60 During the discussion, this view is generally shared by members like Professor James L. Brierly (United Kingdom), Dr Alexander Eudzinski (Poland), Dr Enrique Ferrer Vieyra (Argentina), Dr J. G. de Beus (Netherlands), Professor Henri Donnedieu de Vabres (France). An opposite opinion was however held by Professor Vladimir Koretsky, see 'Summary Record of the 4th Meeting' (15 May 1947) UN Doc A/AC.10/SR.4, 5.

61 For example, the Chinese representative Dr Shuhsi Hsu (China) considered codification to be part of the development of international law, see 'Summary Record of the 3rd Meeting' (14 May 1947) UN Doc A/AC.10/SR.3, 5. Professor Milan Bartos (Yugoslavia) also stated that "development of international law and codification might be distinguished in abstracto, but it would be impossible to say where codification ends and development begins." in 'Summary Record of the 6th Meeting' (20 May 1947) UN Doc A/AC.10/SR.6, 7.

The distinction between codification and progressive development, however artificial and untenable in practice, was politically useful to channel the consensus of the Committee.[62] The distinction enabled both the scientific and the political approaches to find their expressions in the mandate of the future Commission, codification being scientific and progressive development political, and the work of the International Law Commission then should cover both aspects. The two terms "codification" and "progressive development" were then assigned clear-cut normative connotations in the final report of the Committee.[63] As the Committee stated:

> Some of the tasks might involve the drafting of a convention on a subject which has not yet been regulated by international law or in regard to which the law has not yet been highly developed or formulated in the practice of States. Other tasks might on the other hand involve the more precise formulation and systematization of the law in areas where there has been extensive State practice, precedent and doctrine. For convenience of reference, the Committee has referred to the first type of task as 'progressive development' and to the second type of task as 'codification' ...[64]

This formula was later incorporated into the statute of the International Law Commission.[65]

This dichotomy of codification/progressive development has a direct impact on the working methods and output of the International Law Commission, as embodied in its statute. For progressive development, the Commission

62 Dhokalia (n 7) 213.

63 In the same report, however, the Committee acknowledged that the line of distinction was bound to be a blurred one. As the Committee stated: "For the codification of international law, the Committee recognized that no clear-cut distinction between the formulation of the law as it is and the law as it ought to be could be rigidly maintained in practice. It was pointed out that in any work of codification, the codifier inevitably has to fill in gaps in and amend the law in the light of new developments." 'Report of the Committee on the Progressive Development of International Law and its Codification on the Methods for Encouraging the Progressive Development of International Law and its Eventual Codification' (18 July 1947) UN Doc A/331, para 10.

64 Ibid para 7.

65 During the debate the sub-committee set up by the Sixth Committee, the formula was taken without reopening the issue. It met the expectations of both those favoured codification by conventions and those favoured codification by scientific restatement. See 'Report of the Sixth Committee Subcommittee 2' (18 November 1947) UN Doc A/C.6/193, 8–10.

shall apply articles 16 and 17 of its statute, and the initiative is expected to come from the General Assembly, governments, intergovernmental organizations and others. In this case, a draft convention is the only appropriate form for the International Law Commission product. In contrast, the codification procedure applies in articles 18 to 24. Here, the Commission may, on its own motion, "survey the whole field of international law with a view to selecting topics for codification", subject to the approval of the topics by the General Assembly. This conceived difference of procedures did not prove to be sustainable, however. Very soon the Commission had to abandon the difference as a matter of practicality.[66]

By distinguishing yet including codification and progressive development in the mandate of the International Law Commission, the Commission was given a dual task, both as a codifier and a legislator. There were irreconcilable tensions between the two different roles and visions of the International Law Commission. Many of the confusions and difficulties faced by the Commission today could be understood in light of this structural division and the dichotomy inherent in its identity. The International Law Commission was a balanced project, i.e. it was designed to balance conservativism and progressivism. Its statute also reflects a compromise between political law-making and expert law-making, "a compromise between those who are in favour of government representatives and those who want personal experts to be charged with the task".[67]

4 *Dynamics of the International Law Commission*

While the International Law Commission is entrusted with the dual tasks of codification and progressive development, its early work contained more elements of codification, than that of progressive development.[68] Classic examples are the Commission's work on the law of the sea, diplomatic immunities, the law of treaties, and other topics in the 1950s and 1960s.[69] The development

66 See United Nations, *The Work of the International Law Commission*, Volume I (8th edn, United Nations 2012) 47.

67 'Summary Record of the 3rd Meeting' (14 May 1947) UN Doc A/AC.10/SR.3, 5.

68 A similar observation was made also by Vaughan Lowe, see United Nations, *The International Law Commission Fifty Years after: An Evaluation – Proceedings of the Seminar Held to Commemorate the Fiftieth Anniversary of the International Law Commission* (United Nations 2000) 172.

69 This led to the conclusion of the 1958 Convention on the Territorial Sea and the Contiguous Zone, the 1958 Convention on the High Seas, the 1958 Convention on Fishing and Conservation of the Living Resources of the High Seas, the 1958 Convention on the Continental Shelf, the 1961 Vienna Convention on Diplomatic Relations, the 1963 Vienna

of law was exercised with caution and restraint, and often only in connection with clarification of established rules. The underlying idea was to transform unwritten rules of international law into international *lex scriptum*. Therefore, the International Law Commission had worked carefully not to embark on topics that did not contain any rules of customary or general international law, unless requested by the General Assembly for the purposes of preparing draft conventions. The 1969 Vienna Convention on the Law of Treaties was considered the International Law Commission's "last real success",[70] by some. The validity of this judgment holds only if the work of the Commission was measured in terms of its ability to produce widely accepted conventions.

In the following decades, step by step, the International Law Commission started to engage with topics with law-making elements. Examples include law of treaties between States and international organizations or between international organizations, State succession, and non-navigational uses of international watercourses and international liability. An assessment done more than thirty years ago led to the conclusion that "the Commission at the present time is engaged primarily in progressive development, and the task of putting agreed customary practices and rules into treaty form is a small if not negligible part of that process".[71]

In recent years, the International Law Commission however engaged in the progressive development of international law more often and openly. The legislative elements of codification are more explicitly acknowledged by the Commission.[72] The International Law Commission no longer considers itself barred from selecting a topic simply for the sparsity of established rules of

Convention on Consular Relations, and the 1969 Vienna Convention on the Law of Treaties.

70 Donald M McRae, 'The International Law Commission: Codification and Progressive Development after Forty Years' (1987) 25 ACDI 355, 357.

71 Ibid 362.

72 For example, the International Law Commission recognizes the rules on the responsibility of international organizations may be less established. As the commentary states: "It may occur that a provision in the articles on State responsibility could be regarded as representing codification, while the corresponding provision on the responsibility of international organizations is more in the nature of progressive development. In other words, the provisions of the present draft articles do not necessarily yet have the same authority as the corresponding provisions on State responsibility." ILC, 'Draft articles on the responsibility of international organizations' [2011] II(2) ILC Ybk 40. Another example is the principles on the allocation of loss in the case of transboundary harm arising out of hazardous activities: ILC [2006] II(2) ILC Ybk 59. Its commentaries set out that "the draft principles are therefore intended to contribute to the process of development of international law in this field".

international law.[73] Instead, the Commission seems to profess progressive development in a strategic way to steer the development of the law.[74] By openly conceding the progressive nature of the work in question, the Commission is less bound by existing State practice and is capable of pushing further. This is what the Commission has done, for example, in its draft articles on the protection of persons in the event of disasters. The draft articles, "at the outset … highlight the fact that the draft articles contain elements of both progressive development and codification of international law".[75] In the case of draft guidelines on the protection of the atmosphere adopted on first reading in 2018, the International Law Commission highlights that it "seeks, through the progressive development of international law and its codification, to provide guidelines that may assist the international community as it addresses critical questions relating to transboundary and global protection of the atmosphere".[76] These drafts are elaborated to prepare, equip or guide States in managing certain situations. Novel elements in those drafts are accepted precisely because it has been openly conceded that they constitute progressive development of international law.

One observes that on certain subjects the International Law Commission increasingly acts in the role of a legislator rather than a registrar.[77] It can be said that "[t]he task is primarily of bringing the old principles upto date, of introducing the inevitable changes in the old rules, of reformulating them in

73 This is the case for the International Law Commission's draft articles on the expulsion of aliens. It is openly recognized by the International Law Commission in the commentaries that "the entire subject area does not have a foundation in customary international law or in the provisions of international conventions of a universal nature". "This is why the present draft articles involve both the codification and the progressive development of fundamental rules on the expulsion of aliens." See ILC, 'Draft articles on the expulsion of aliens' (2014) UN Doc A/69/10, 11.

74 The author once suggested certain constraints that might be placed on the work of the International Law Commission as a consequence of the dichotomy of codification and progressive development, see Chen Yifeng, 'Structural Limitations and Possible Future of the Work of the International Law Commission'(2010) 9 Chinese JIL 473.

75 ILC, 'Draft articles on the protection of persons in the event of disaster' (2016) UN Doc A/71/10, 13.

76 ILC, 'Draft guidelines on protection of atmosphere' (2018) UN Doc A/73/10, 161.

77 For contrary opinions, see Pellet (n 26) 16; Hisashi Owada, 'International Law Commission and the Process of Law-formation' in United Nations, *Making Better International Law: the International Law Commission at 50 – Proceedings of the United Nations Colloquium on Progressive Development and Codification of International Law*(United Nations 1998) 171; also Michael Wood, 'The United Nations International Law Commission and Customary International Law' (Gaetano Morelli Lecture 4th edn: Rethinking The Doctrine Of Customary International Law, Rome, 27 May 2017).

accordance with the new basic legal ideas, and of legislating in areas uncovered by traditional international law."[78] The move from registrar to legislator is made possible by a constant oscillation between codification and progressive development. The strategic use of the interplay of codification and progressive development, rather than its opposition, has enabled to the International Law Commission to act proactively to advance the development of international law on certain important subjects.

IV Products of the International Law Commission: Forms and Authority

1 *Diversity of Forms*

In recent years, the International Law Commission has shown flexibility and diversity in the final forms for its output.[79] The Commission produces not only draft conventions and draft articles, but also draft declarations,[80] model rules,[81] draft codes,[82] draft statutes,[83] guiding principles,[84] draft principles,[85] conclusions,[86] draft conclusions,[87] and guides to practice,[88] and draft guidelines.[89] It would seem that international conventions as the end result of the

78 See Subir Goswami, *Politics in Law Making: A Study of the International Law Commission of the UN* (Ashish Publishing House 1986) 59.

79 For a useful discussion, see Ramcharan (n 23) 73–78.

80 ILC, 'Draft declaration on rights and duties of states' [1949] I ILC Ybk 287.

81 ILC, 'Model rules on arbitral procedure' [1958] II ILC Ybk 83.

82 ILC, 'Draft code of offences against the peace and security of mankind' [1954] II ILC Ybk 134; ILC, 'Draft code of crimes against the peace and security of mankind' [1996] II(2) ILC Ybk 17.

83 ILC, 'Draft statute for an international criminal court' [1994] II(2) ILC Ybk 26.

84 ILC, 'Guiding principles applicable to unilateral declarations of States capable of creating legal obligations' [2006] II(2) ILC Ybk 160; ILC, 'Principles of international law recognized in the Charter of the Nuremberg Tribunal and in the judgment of the Tribunal' [1950] II ILC Ybk 374.

85 ILC, 'Draft principles on the allocation of loss in the case of transboundary harm arising out of hazardous activities' [2006] II(2) ILC Ybk 59.

86 ILC, 'Conclusions of the work of the Study Group on the fragmentation of international law: Difficulties arising from the diversification and expansion of international law' [2006] II(2) ILC Ybk 177 at para 251.

87 ILC, 'Draft conclusions on subsequent agreements and subsequent practice in relation to the interpretation of treaties' (2018) UN Doc A/73/10, 12; ILC, 'Draft conclusions on identification of customary international law' (2018) UN Doc A/73/10, 122.

88 ILC, 'Guide to practice on reservations to treaties' [2011] II(3) ILC Ybk 23.

89 ILC, 'Draft guidelines on the protection of the atmosphere' (2018) UN Doc A/73/10, 158.

International Law Commission codification work have become an exception rather than the rule. During the past three decades, only three international conventions resulted from the work of the International Law Commission.[90]

Of course, international conventions remain a highly pertinent form of the Commission's output. Taking a recent example, in 2016 the International Law Commission recommended the General Assembly to elaborate a convention on the basis of the draft articles on the protection of persons in the event of disasters. The draft articles on crimes against humanity, whose first reading was completed in 2017, are also conceived in the form of a draft convention. During the debates of the Sixth Committee, proposals emerged for concluding an international convention on State responsibility based on the articles adopted by the International Law Commission in 2001. The argument made here is rather that the Commission no longer sees the elaboration of draft conventions as the only necessary form of its work.

The declining production of conventions is attributable to a number of factors. First of all, the making and ratification of treaties are politically costly because they require the involvement of various domestic political constituencies. In recent years, States are seen to have less appetite for treaty making. Some treaties received a strikingly low number of ratifications, a phenomenon that must be rather discouraging and disturbing to the International Law Commission and its members. Nowadays the Special Rapporteurs, the International Law Commission and the Sixth Committee of the General Assembly are all less enthusiastic in pursuing the conclusion of multilateral conventions. Secondly, some recent topics of the Commission are by nature not suitable for treaty making. A typical example could be the report of the study group on "Fragmentation of international law: difficulties arising from the diversification and expansion of international law".[91] Thirdly, the final products of the International Law Commission are increasingly seen as possessing a certain autonomous normative quality. They are capable of generating a broad influence on their own over the international legal process, independent of formal acceptance by States. The Special Rapporteurs and the Commission seem increasingly willing to accept soft forms other than formal treaties as the

90 Convention on the Law of the Non-Navigational Uses of International Watercourses, adopted 21 May 1997, entered into force 17 August 2014, UNTS registration no 52106; Rome Statute of the International Criminal Court, adopted 17 July 1998, entered into force 1 July 2002, 2187 UNTS 38544; United Nations Convention on Jurisdictional Immunities of States and their Property, adopted on 2 December 2004, not yet in force, UN Doc A/59/508.

91 ILC, [2006] II(2) ILC Ybk 175.

second-best choice for the outcome of their work, when the chance of having an international convention seems slim.

This brings the issues of authority and legitimacy to the forefront. Some scholars consider the growing diversity of form as an encouraging phenomenon to propel the International Law Commission "a much more effective organ".[92] Some others are more concerned with the legitimacy and usefulness of the Commission's products in forms other than conventions.[93] Questions are asked such as whether these soft forms are at all desirable or appropriate, what the legal nature and legal impact of those documents would be, and whether the adoption by the General Assembly would add any normative force to the Commission's final products. In essence the new forms raise normative doubts in three aspects: first, the nature of the International Law Commission's unconventional output; second, constitutionality of the mandate and methodology of the Commission; and third, the proper role and function of the Commission in the international law-making process.

2 *Sources of Authority*

The authority of the work of the Commission increasingly comes from varying sources, which might have a profound transformative effect upon its work. The change in the form of the products of the ILC is no more than a natural projection of the evolving role of the International Law Commission in a dynamic international society.

The following four sources can be identified as the sources of the Commission's authority. The first rests upon the political authority vested on the Commission by States. This is what was originally conceived of the work of the International Law Commission. The International Law Commission was expected to seek the approval of States for its work products, for example through the conclusion of international conventions at diplomatic conferences. The Commission was further expected to be guided with a view to consider the acceptability of its work by States. The political authority from States can also often seen be from a procedural perspective. The participation of States in the debates of the Sixth Committee of the General Assembly and in their responses to questionnaires gives certain democratic procedural legitimacy to the work of the International Law Commission. Although the responses of the Special Rapporteurs to States' concerns are often selective, the procedure does flush out the elements of the work, which States would actively oppose.

---

92 McRae (n 70) 364.

93 For a detailed account on the forms and authority of work products of the International Commission, see Murphy (n 6) 29–40.

Outside the treaty-making context, States also quote the Commission's products in daily diplomacy and in dispute settlement procedures. Moreover, the International Law Commission's articles are also quoted by national courts. The political authority gained by States' endorsement is the authority traditionally associated with the Commission's work. This reflects the State-centered paradigm of international law. States remain central to the international law-making process.

The second source of authority flows from inter-institutional cross-fertilization. One should not overlook the fact that the reference and application of the work of the Commission by other institutions, including the International Court of Justice, has contributed to another level of authority through cross-reference and recognition. Notwithstanding the fact that the products of the International Law Commission are contained in soft forms or remain draft conventions, they are nevertheless often referred to by the International Court of Justice, other international tribunals, regional courts, and various international organizations as authoritative statements of international law. This gives weight to the authoritativeness of the work of the International Law Commission. It has been said that "[t]he court, for its part, has nevertheless not hesitated to invoke the work of the International Law Commission where it has seemed appropriate to do so, without concerning itself with the formal question of how that work might fall within Article 38 of the Statute of the International Court of Justice."[94] The International Law Commission's articles on responsibility of States for internationally wrongful acts are a well-known example in this regard. The articles have been quoted by the International Court of Justice, the World Trade Organization Appellate Body, the European Court of Human Rights, International arbitral tribunals and others in a number of cases and relevant rules have been treated as demonstrative of customary international law.[95]

The third source of authority derives from the intrinsic quality of the rules elaborated by the International Law Commission. This particularly applies to the work of the Commission in the realm of secondary rules, such as those topics concerning jurisdiction, the sources of international law, and international responsibility. In case of secondary rules, the practical influence of a topic often arises from the nature of the subject matter being part of the necessary normative infrastructure of international law. This may be further assisted by the fact that in the international legal order, there exists no rival work of

94 Watts (n 8).

95 See UNGA, 'Report of the Secretary-General', UN Doc A/62/62, UN Doc A/65/76, UN Doc A/68/72 and UN Doc A/71/80.

comparable systemization and equivalent weight as that of the International Law Commission. All these factors combined have consolidated the authority of the work of the Commission in those fields where the express acceptance of States in the form of treaties is often considered redundant.[96] On the contrary, the soft form of an outcome, such as draft articles, draft guidelines, or draft conclusions, does not by itself prevent States, or international organizations, from invoking and applying it. It is recognized that under certain circumstances codification in the form of a soft law instrument may prove as effective as a treaty.[97]

The fourth source of authority comes from the International Law Commission itself. The Commission is composed of experts of recognized competence and represents as a whole "the main forms of civilization" and "the principal legal systems of the world".[98] The work of the International Law Commission embodies the laborious efforts of its members as collective wisdom, and is adopted, with rare exceptions, through consensus. The work is well recognized among the teachings of the most highly qualified publicists of various nations, and constitutes "a subsidiary means for the determination of rules of international law".[99] Moreover, the Commission is increasingly seen by international society as endowed with an institutional authority of its own. This authority has been cultivated and accumulated on the basis of its outstanding performance during the past seven decades.[100] Therefore, authority of the work of the Commission, legal or political, may derive from the very fact that the work is produced by the Commission.

This list of the sources of authority is not exhaustive. Yet, it is illustrative of the diversified, blended sources from which the products of the Commission are capable of drawing their authority. The significance of this development is that it may produce some subtle but profound transformative effect

---

96 Even if it takes the form of a treaty, States may not accede to it simply because the States consider that the treaty rules are customary in nature.

97 See for example, Tomuschat (n 2) 104.

98 Statute of the ILC, UNGA Res 174 (II) (21 November 1947) as amended by UNGA Res 485(V) (12 December 1950) article 8.

99 Huang Huikang, 'The work of the International Law Commission and the Shaping of International law: in Commemoration of the Fiftieth Anniversary of the Commission' in United Nations (n 77) 314.

100 For an illustration of the achievements of the International Law Commission in a publication published more than twenty years ago, see 'Introduction: The Achievement of the International Law Commission' in United Nations, *International Law on the Eve of the Twenty-First Century: Views from the International Law Commission* (United Nations 1997) 1–18.

on the identity and the work of the Commission. The richness of the sources of authority further provides room for the Commission to act more autonomously in its codification work, more detached from the political influence of States, more engaged with other actors in a globalized world. In some cases, the International Law Commission has sought to address its work to other actors in the international community, not necessarily only to States. This is the case for the Commission's draft articles on the responsibility of international organizations.

This also partly explains why the products of the Commission have not been much hampered by their soft form. The authority of the Commission's products does not necessarily require the conclusion of an international convention by States. The expertise of the International Law Commission in matters of international law is highly regarded by international society as a whole, and this allows its work to stand on its own institutional reputation.

V The Future of the International Law Commission: towards Becoming an Autonomous Law-Maker

At a time of global social change, the Commission is increasingly called upon to work creatively and progressively. The Commission often has to advance the law rather than simply record the law. The recent work of the International Law Commission has shown an evolving notion of codification through restatement of existing law towards codification through formulating and legislating new law. This can be seen from the fact that the International Law Commission increasingly resorts to its mandate to promote the progressive development of international law when taking up new work. The International Law Commission more and more plays the role of an autonomous law-maker. This part offers a theoretical account on the law-making role of the International Law Commission.

1 *The Institutional Nature of the International Law Commission*

The institutional nature of the International Law Commission is an important yet often overlooked issue. Yet if one is to reconceive the Commission as an autonomous law-maker, a primary issue to be asked from the outset is whether the Commission is constitutionally authorized to engage in the making of international law?

There are three possible ways to approach the Commission as an institution. The first one is from the perspective of international institutional law. The Commission is established by the General Assembly as a subsidiary body of the Assembly. The United Nations is neither a super-State nor a world government.[101] If the General Assembly has only recommendatory power, the International Law Commission cannot have legislative power which its creator does not possess.[102] It follows that the products of the Commission do not have binding force unless they are formally accepted by States through the ratification of treaties. In cases where the draft conventions do bind States as reflective of customary international law, the authority of the products emanates from the substance of the rules, rather than their form.

The second approach is from the perspective of international relations. Under this view, the Commission may be interpreted as an agent of States, collectively. According to some, the Commission "has been empirically demonstrated to serve as a tool of States rather than as an independent body".[103] The formation and operation of the Commission in essence falls back on the sovereign wills of States. The work of the Commission is to accomplish the tasks that are entrusted to it by States through the General Assembly, namely the codification and development of international law. It follows that not only is it important for the Commission to seek the opinions of States when selecting topics, it is also essential that "the task of codification must be approached with the view of its eventual adoption within the framework of positive international law".[104] This interpretation of the nature of the Commission is a crude reduction of the multiple roles and great potentials of the Commission.

A third perspective is to conceive of the International Law Commission as a trustee for the advancement of the international rule of law.[105] It is true that the establishment of the Commission is based on the resolution of the General Assembly, and it is equally true that the effective operation of the Commission is only possible through constant interactions with and support from States. However, once created, the Commission is governed by its own statute solely. It is formally independent from States. Its mandate of codification stems from a long human history of pursuing international *lex scriptum* and, ultimately, the international rule of law. In this sense, the International Law Commission

---

101 See *Reparation for injuries suffered in the service of the United Nations* (Advisory Opinion) [1949] ICJ Rep 174, 179.

102 This is emphasized by Peter Tomka, 'Major Complexities Encountered in Contemporary International Law-making' in United Nations (n 77) 212.

103 Jeffrey S Morton, *The International Law Commission of the United Nations* (University of South Carolina Press 2000) 109.

104 Lauterpacht (n 28) 35.

105 For a useful construction of international courts and tribunals as trustees in relation to their creators, see Karen Alter, 'Agent or Trustee: International Courts in Their Political Context' (2008) 14 EurJIntlRel 33.

is different from other political bodies established under the United Nations. It has a transcendental mandate. The International Law Commission is not a political body. Instead, "it is an organ *sui generis*".[106] The International Law Commission is observed to have occupied "the *de facto* status of principal legal instrument of the United Nations".[107]

The International Law Commission should be studied as "an organ in the universal process of codification and development of international law".[108] As discussed below, the legislative role of the International Law Commission might receive social recognition in the constitutionalization process of international law.[109] In turn, the constitutional role of the Commission as a curtailed legislator also deserves more theoretical consideration.[110] This may provide a thin but sustainable justification to conceive the Commission as an autonomous law-maker.

2 *The Concept of International Law Reconsidered*

The transformation of the International Law Commission into an autonomous law-maker is also facilitated by the changing nature of international law. Traditional international law is a law that developed through adjudication. International law, by reference to article 38 of the Statute of the International Court of Justice, is tied to the philosophy and practical need of using law for adjudicating inter-State disputes. The formalism of international law is closely related to the need of settling disputes between States, which has also driven early efforts to codify international law. An international court, when asked to resolve a specific dispute, should be able to apply the rules of international law in order to determine the respective rights and obligations of the State parties.

More recently, however, such an adjudicative concept of law has met with some criticism. It is seen as an expression of parochial "judiciary-centrism".[111]

106 Lauterpacht (n 32) 37.

107 See Goswami (n 78) 199.

108 For a useful discussion of the different institutional role of the International Law Commission, see Ramcharan (n 23) 9–28.

109 For useful reflections on the idea of constitutionalization, see Jan Klabbers, Anne Peters, and Geir Ulfstein, *The Constitutionalization of International Law* (OUP 2009).

110 Alain Pellet suggests that the work of the International Law Commission is valuable as "they are part of the 'constitutional law' of the international society": Pellet (n 26) 22.

111 See, for example, an insightful critique on the "judiciary-centrism" by Onuma Yasuaki, 'A Transcivilizational Perspective on International Law: Questioning Prevalent Cognitive Frameworks in the Emerging Multi-Polar and Multi-Civilizational World of the Twenty-First Century' (2009) 342 RdC 77, 250–65.

The adjudicative function is but one of the several functions that international law operates through.[112] International law is a language of empowerment and legitimization for certain specific claims or actions. International law also has a communicative and normative power which conditions a specific understanding and offers possible solutions. Furthermore, international law provides a regulatory scheme for international administration and governance.

Outside the adjudicative setting, the normative threshold for a rule to be recognized as part of the corpus of international law is considerably more lenient than the rigour required by Article 38 of the Statute of the International Court of Justice. "It is thus evident", as one author writes, "that in most cases, forums where international law is referred to, invoked, discussed, applied, and realized or implemented are outside the International Court of Justice."[113] A large number of rules used in those non-judicial contexts do not belong to the traditional edifice of international law. It is now necessary to reconstruct the notion and corpus of international law in light of other functionalities of international law.

The concept of international law deserves a systemic reflection which requires a separate treatment and cannot be dealt with here. Yet, it is useful to highlight a few points about the process of building a new concept of international law. First, it is a move beyond formalism. A broad notion of international law could encompass informal forms such as guidelines, best practices, resolutions, programmes, guiding principles and such like.[114] Under the traditional paradigm, these are at best appreciated as soft law, practically relevant but short of legal normativity. The new concept of international law should deal with the abundance of normative materials with a more receptive attitude.[115] Secondly, in connection to informality, the new concept of international law should also go beyond positivism and the State-centered paradigm. Not only are new global laws emerging outside the sovereign domain,[116] but the increasing legislative role of international organizations and other global actors also

112 See ibid 195–199.

113 Ibid 258.

114 For some useful accounts on soft law, see Christine Chinkin, 'The Challenges of Soft Law: Development and Change in International Law' (1989) 38 ICLQ 850; Alan E Boyle, 'Some Reflections on the Relationship of Treaties and Soft Law' (1999) 48 ICLQ 901.

115 For example, the idea of graded normativity is suggested by Prosper Weil, 'Toward Relative Normativity in International Law' (1983) 77 AJIL 413.

116 See Gunther Teubner, *Constitutional Fragments: Societal Constitutionalism in the Globalization* (OUP 2012); also Gunther Teubner (ed), *Global Law without a State* (Aldershot 1997).

deserves full recognition. The work of the International Law Commission may fit well into this revised concept of international law.

3 *Types of Legislation*

Legislation may also be understood in different senses. Legislation in a narrow sense refers to a sovereign exercise of laying down rules for its subjects, and is performed through national parliaments in the modern day. This definition applies nicely to legislation in the domestic context: the making of law in accordance with a constitutional procedure. Legislation is thus an exclusive prerogative of the sovereign. In a broad sense, however, legislation could be understood as a normative exercise in the formulation of general rules, with the constitutional implications for distribution of wealth, power and justice in a given society. This concept of legislation measures law-making by looking into normative outcome and distributive consequence. In the international society where there is no global sovereign, the narrow definition of legislation finds no application. The best yet narrow analogy is to interpret the conclusion of international conventions as a joint exercise of sovereign powers. Instead, the broad definition of legislation may offer better insights into the law-making process at the international level.

Alongside this broad notion of legislation, I venture to suggest that the International Law Commission engages in the following four types of legislation: "legislation through conceptualization", "legislation through lex scriptum", "legislation through codification" and "legislation through convention". These different types of legislation may not be mutually exclusive. It is possible that the International Law Commission engages different types of legislative work in a single work. Yet the typology aims at allowing for ae nuanced examination of how and when the Commission has become a law-maker, and how autonomous from States the Commission is in different circumstances.

Firstly, the International Law Commission may perform a legislative function by formulating a certain conceptual and normative framework, or sanctioning a certain paradigmatic and epistemic framework. In the words of Kenneth Keith, "the Commission's work has played a structural role in the international legal process. It has strongly influenced the way in which we think about international law and has helped to establish the intellectual framework within which we address, solve and answer international legal problems."[117] The construction of State responsibility in terms of the failure of performance of international obligations and the exclusion of damage from the defining

117 See 'Presentation by Sir Kenneth Keith' in United Nations (n 77) 120.

elements is a noteworthy example.[118] The same holds true for the introduction of the concept of *jus cogens* in the 1969 Vienna Convention on the Law of Treaties.

Secondly, the International Law Commission may engage in international legislation by producing international *lex scriptum*. One should not underestimate the normative pull of the work of the Commission. The articles and guidelines are systemized and clearly stated, with credible authorities and preparatory work. They are readily available, easy to consult and apply. It may be noted that "[t]he change of source from custom to treaty may seem to be purely formal and adjectival, but it has inevitable repercussions on the substance."[119] As a result of the deliberations and of the approval of the Commission, "they will be of considerable potency in shaping scientific opinion and the practice of Governments".[120]

Moreover, the value of the work products of the Commission could also be appreciated in light of the revised concept of international law. In addition to their valuable role as evidence of customary international law, the products of the Commission could also be invoked and applied by States and actors in diplomatic discourse and other non-judicial contexts. Its work could play the functions of persuasion, legitimation and communication. The very existence of a systemized text carefully elaborated by the International Law Commission, whether legally binding or not, carries with it an inherent force of normativity that cannot be lightly denied or bypassed.

Thirdly, the International Law Commission may legislate in the course of codification.[121] The interpretation of codification as transformation of rules in formality (from unwritten into written rules) seems to be a profound misinterpretation or a simplistic reduction, as the presumed existence of agreement on unwritten rules is largely a convenient fiction. Often differences among States are latent or deliberately withheld. They only emerge because of codification efforts when States are forced to take or reveal their positions on concrete points. An essential role of the codifying body is to formulate agreeable rules and to conduce States to agree on the relevant rules.[122]

---

118 See Brigitte Stern, 'A Plea for "Reconstruction" of International Responsibility' in Maurizio Ragazzi (ed), *International Responsibility Today: Essays in Memory of Oscar Schachter* (Martinus Nijhoff Publishers 2005) 93–106.

119 Jennings (n 18) 305.

120 ILC (n 31) 16.

121 Hisashi Owada, based on a different definition of international legislation, divides legislation into three categories, namely, codification, progressive development, and legislation *de novo*. See Owada (n 77) 167–70.

122 See James L Brierly, 'The Future of Codification' (1931) 12 BYIL 1, 2–4; Lauterpacht (n 32) 18–22.

This has been confirmed by various accounts made by the members of the International Law Commission. In reflecting upon his personal experience as a member and a Special Rapporteur of the International Law Commission, Hersch Lauterpacht concluded that "unlike codification in other fields, codification of international law must be substantially legislative in nature".[123] It is noticeable that even for a topic such as the well-worn law of treaties, disagreements, uncertainties, and gaps existed practically for almost every aspect of the law. It is natural for the International Law Commission to select, reject, extend, reshape or revise the rules of international law with a view to conducing States for eventual approval. Another more recent account was offered by the former member Donald McRae on the work of the International Law Commission on transboundary aquifers, the effects of armed conflict on treaties, the reservations to treaties, and the responsibility of international organizations. His detailed examination reveals that the final outcomes are fraught with choices or innovations made on purpose by the special rapporteurs and the International Law Commission.[124]

In other cases, the Commission may anchor the corpus of its work on established principles and rules of international law, and the legislative element is often presented in the form of an elaboration, extension or transposition of existing rules or general principles. This is the case for the International Law Commission conclusions on subsequent agreements and subsequent practice in relation to the interpretation of treaties where the conclusions draw heavily from the articles 31 and 32 of the 1969 Vienna Convention on the Law of Treaties.[125] The same can be said about the International Law Commission draft articles on the protection of persons in the event of disaster where the reference to human rights and to the principles of humanity, neutrality, impartiality and non-discrimination have the same function.[126]

Fourthly, the International Law Commission may legislate by drafting conventions for States. This applies to, for example, the drafting of the Rome Statute of the International Criminal Court. The role of the Commission is more of an advisor, functionally equivalent to a parliamentary draftsperson in some national framework. In this case, the legislative role of the Commission is highly decentralized or removed from the locus of power. While the work of the International Law Commission is appreciated, the final say lies with States.

---

123 Lauterpacht (n 32) 29.

124 Donald McRae, 'The Work of the International Law Commission (2007–2011): Progress and Prospects' (2012) 106 AJIL 322, 324–331.

125 ILC, 'Draft conclusions on subsequent agreements and subsequent practice in relation to the interpretation of treaties' (2018) UN Doc A/73/10, 12.

126 ILC (n 75) 13.

4 *Limits on the Legislative Role of the International Law Commission*

One also must concede that the legislative role of the Commission is subject to a number of important limitations. First of all, the International Law Commission cannot legislate against concerted State interests. It is important for the International Law Commission to proceed with the political support of the States. The comparative advantages of the Commission largely reside in its proven ability of conceptual elaboration of general international law and of generating general consensus of international society through its constructive interaction with States and others. Any legislative proposal that meets strong opposition from powerful States may not get through easily. As a matter of reality, the final product of the International Law Commission would need to take into account the legitimate concerns of States. Secondly, the legislative exercise by the Commission proceeds as expert deliberations, leaving little room for political bargains and compromises.[127] Its work "is lawyers' law, not politicians' law."[128] The scientific and political division of codification is valid subject to important qualifications, as only a limited degree of political difference could be absorbed and translated into matters of technicality. The International Law Commission itself is not a suitable organ for legislation on highly politicized subjects. The General Assembly has constantly relegated the more politicized topics away from the Commission so as to allow States to have more direct and closer political engagement with the Commission. This can be seen from the cases of drafting the Rome Statute of the International Criminal Court and of the 1982 United Nations Convention on the Law of Sea, as both projects were taken back to States after the Commission had worked substantively on the subjects. Thirdly, the actual legislative effect of the International Law Commission depends to a considerable extent on the acceptance of the users of the work product of the Commission. In other words, the normative effect of the work of the International Law Commission cannot be forced by the Commission itself, but rather comes from the actual application by other actors, be it a State or international organization, an international tribunal or a domestic court.

VI Conclusions

International law today is undergoing profound structural changes, as are the codification projects and thus the role of the International Law Commission.

---

127 See Gerhard Hafner, 'The International Law Commission and the Future Codification of International Law' (1995–1996) 2 ILSA JICL 671, 673–74.

128 Pellet (n 26) 16.

The codification work of the Commission is inherently legislative in nature. The International Law Commission has increasingly resorted to progressive development as a tactic to develop new law, and to keep itself occupied and relevant. The Commission performs a dual role in the international law-making process – as a registrar and legislator. The International Law Commission is seen to be operating with a renewed institutional confidence as an autonomous law-maker. The growing diversity in the form of the its products reflects the move of the Commission towards the role of a more autonomous law-maker.

The legislative function of the International Law Commission could be appreciated in light of constitutionalization of international law, where the constitutional role of the Commission could possibly be construed as a trustee for the development of the international rule of law. The work of the Commission is also a proof of need for a renewed understanding of international law being beyond a body of adjudicative rules.

The International Law Commission may exercise legislative functions in different situations, with varying levels of legislative depth from case to case. The contribution of the Commission should no longer be measured solely in terms of its contribution to the drafting of international conventions, but should be assessed in light of its own merit. Whilst the Commission's legislative authority remains limited, subject to various institutional and functional constraints, it has become an indispensable building block of law-making in the international legal order.

The Functions of the International Law Commission: Identifying Existing Law or Proposing New Law?

Ineta Ziemele

1 Introduction*

The question in the title of this article was suggested by the organizers of the International Law Commission's seventieth anniversary seminar. Before addressing the question, that is looking at the codification and development of international law, it is necessary to reflect on a broader issue relating to the functions of the Commission at a time marked by the plurality of actors on the international stage, their growing interdependence and the fact that these processes called globalization "seem to be beyond the control of even the most economically and militarily powerful States".[1] International law-making is clearly no longer the exclusive competence of States,[2] but the Commission continues to emphasize the primary role of States. Furthermore, it must be recognized that State consent is not a single given act; it is part of a complex process of interactions. Placed within the new context of law-making, this view of State consent as a process accepts in some manner the plurality of actors and their influence on States.

The question of the content and purpose of the International Law Commission's functions, i.e., of the role of the Commission today, has to be reviewed within this new context of international law-making and the results of this review should consistently be taken into account.

---

* The author is grateful to Kristaps Tamužs and Gatis Bārdiņš of the Constitutional Court of Latvia for their research assistance in the preparation of this text.

1 James Crawford, 'Chance, Order, Change: The Course of International Law' (2013) 365 RdC 9, 109.

2 Conclusion 4. [..] 3. Conduct of other actors is not practice that contributes to the formation, or expression, of rules of customary international law, but may be relevant when assessing the practice referred to in paragraphs 1 and 2. Conclusion 5. [..] 2. Other conduct, including by non-State actors, does not constitute subsequent practice under articles 31 and 32. Such conduct may, however, be relevant when assessing the subsequent practice of parties to a treaty; see ILC, 'Draft conclusions on identification of customary international law' (2018) UN Doc A/73/10, 122.

 | DOI:10.1163/9789004434271_024

II The Changing Nature of the International Law Landscape

Among the relevant concepts that capture the changing nature of the international law landscape are accountability, democracy, civil society, transparency, the international rule of law and constitutionalization. There is by now a considerable amount of scholarship posing questions about the new or changing nature of the international legal system. Certainly, the density of this scholarship and the examples of international normative practices that feed into this debate have grown over the last decades. A fair characterization as to where we are today has been provided by James Crawford in his Hague Academy lectures:

> There are certainly subfields of international law that can be described more or less accurately as having been legalized by means of multilateral framework treaties [...]. The existence of these potentially constitutionalized sectoral regimes and the fact that there is no hierarchy that can determine the outcome of conflicts between them might suggest that the international system is characterized not by a single constitution for an international society, but by many – and therefore by none.[3]

Despite this negative conclusion, Crawford returns to this point later in acknowledging that the "notion of a constitutional order in which domestic, regional and sectoral orders coexist and complement each other is somewhat more plausible than the idea of a single instrument".[4]

There are indeed by now several treaty regimes that have entered a constitutionalization stage. They co-exist in a decentralized and horizontal relationship which is constantly evolving because international law remains a process of claim and counterclaim, assertion and reaction by the plurality of subjects and actors.[5] One can add that domestic constitutional orders have come to have an increasing role in this process through the direct application and interpretation of international rules by domestic courts and their use by the political branches of power. We are increasingly seeing that international law-making processes and domestic legal systems are parts of

---

3 James Crawford (n 1) 463.

4 Ibid 465–466.

5 Ibid 20. See also Jan Klabbers, 'Setting the Scene' in Jan Klabbers, Anne Peters, and Geir Ulfstein (eds), *The Constitutionalization of International Law* (OUP 2009) 1.

a single universal legal process, if not a system, even if at a rather rudimentary level.

The International Law Commission has also come to recognize this development. In the conclusions on subsequent agreements and subsequent practice in relation to interpretation of treaties under articles 31 and 32 of the Vienna Convention on the Law of Treaties,[6] "subsequent practice" refers to "any conduct of a party in the application of a treaty, whether in the exercise of its executive, legislative, judicial or other function".[7] Conclusion 6 describes the forms of State practice which "include, but are not limited to: diplomatic acts and correspondence; conduct in connection with resolutions adopted by an international organization or at an intergovernmental conference; conduct in connection with treaties; executive conduct, including operational conduct 'on the ground'; legislative and administrative acts; and decisions of national courts".[8]

These developments are further reflected in the debate on the sources of international law. Does the current list of sources of international law and Article 38 of the Statute of the International Court of Justice form the backbone of the international legal system when new sources have emerged which are not listed in Article 38? I believe that the debate on whether Article 38 is a kind of rule of recognition in international law, or whether the emergence of new sources of law challenges that view, is in fact a debate on whether the glass is half-full or half-empty.[9] There is no question that the primary sources of international law have been identified and are there to stay, but similar to the processes in democratic legal systems additional sources emerge over periods of time. I shall give an example.

In some domestic legal systems, it has become very clear that the caselaw of domestic courts and judge-made law constitute a source of law.[10] The debate on the legal nature of the caselaw of international courts has also been evolving. I have argued elsewhere that, for example, the caselaw of the European

6 Adopted 23 May 1969, entered into force 27 January 1980, 1155 UNTS 331.

7 See ILC, 'Draft conclusions on subsequent agreements and subsequent practice in relation to the interpretation of treaties' (2018) UN Doc A/73/10, conclusion 5.

8 See ILC, 'Draft conclusions on subsequent agreements and subsequent practice in relation to the interpretation of treaties' (2018) UN Doc A/73/10, conclusion 5.

9 Jan Klabbers, 'Law-making and Constitutionalism' in Jan Klabbers, Anne Peters, and Geir Ulfstein (eds), *The Constitutionalization of International Law* (OUP 2009) 87; Samantha Besson, 'Theorizing the Sources of International Law' in Samantha Besson and John Tasioulas (eds) *The Philosophy of International Law* (OUP 2010) 181–182.

10 Daiga Rezevska, 'Judikatūra kā tiesību avots: izpratne un pielietošana' (2010) 1 *Latvijas Republikas Augstākās tiesas Biļetens* 31.

Court of Human Rights has become more then *lex interpretata* – it is a source of European human rights law.[11]

To sum up, the international legal system is composed of a plurality of actors and sources of law and has multiple, sometimes competing, potentially constitutional regimes. If we agree that these are the features of the international law landscape today, then the functions of the International Law Commission, and, in particular, its methods of work, should be revised accordingly. I would argue that even after such a revision, taking into account the current features of the international legal landscape, there remains a choice to be made with regard to the kind of role the International Law Commission ought to play in this context. It is always possible to take either a broader or a narrower view on its role.

III Proposition for a Broader View on the International Law Commission's Functions

The International Law Commission continues to be an independent expert body which responds to the requests of the Sixth Committee of the General Assembly. It has been pointed out that these characteristics of the International Law Commission are a source of both its strength and its weakness. They have enabled it to provide a deliberative and often authoritative process for the codification and, to a modest degree, the progressive development of general international law.[12] On the fiftieth anniversary of the International Law Commission, the Study Group within the auspices of the British Institute of International and Comparative Law reviewed the work and the methods of the Commission. It is interesting to note that already then, the Study Group pointed to the changing landscape of international law. It came to the conclusion that the Commission should have a broader law-making role which would require a number of adjustments.[13] The Commission "could assume a more progressive role in a number of areas and that a re-conceived, more innovative Commission which co-operated more closely with other bodies while maintaining its unique strength of drawing on knowledge of the

11 Ineta Ziemele, 'Case Law of the European Court of Human Rights as s Source of Human Rights' (2020) 17 BaltYIL Online 143 (forthcoming).

12 Michael Anderson, Alan Boyle, Vaughan Lowe and Chanaka Wickremasinghe (eds), *The International Law Commission and the Future of International Law* (BIICL 1998) 22.

13 Ibid 49.

international legal system as a whole, has much to offer".[14] I share the conclusions of the Study Group and submit that the Commission should further build on them.

The new features of the international legal landscape have also given rise to such new debates as fragmentation, conflicts of rules and regimes. These debates are a reflection on the perceived weakness of the international legal system when confronted with a growing plurality of actors and density of legal regimes while maintaining a system of horizontal sources of law with a very limited hierarchy. Also, what could be called the downside of the changing nature of the international legal landscape, requires the continued evolution of the role of the International Law Commission. The new role of the Commission needs to be articulated conceptually and not only at the level of working methods and the types of output, which the Commission has already diversified to some extent.

I would thus like to situate the role of the International Law Commission within a pluralist vision of the world and the international normative process therein. Let me recall the constitutional pluralist discourse as regards the plurality of constitutional sites and the way to address it, i.e., "what is required in acknowledging and handling competing claims to authority coming from national and supranational constitutional sites is an ethic of political responsibility premised on mutual recognition and respect".[15] Competing claims to authority typically are channeled through the development of legal norms either within international, regional or domestic legal orders. One can mention a strong example of such a claim to authority which unless further explained may lead to the isolation of a particular legal regime. For example, the Court of Justice of the European Union, in deciding on measures to counter terrorism in the *Kadi* case, insisted that the European Community had high fair trial standards when compared to those used by the United Nations Security Council. The Court of Justice recalled that:

> In this connection it is to be borne in mind that the Community is based on the rule of law, inasmuch as neither its Member States nor its institutions can avoid review of the conformity of their acts with the basic constitutional charter, the EC Treaty, which established a complete system of

---

14 Ibid.

15 Jean L Cohen, 'Sovereignty in the Context of Globalization: A Constitutional Pluralist Perspective' in Samantha Besson and John Tasioulas (eds) *The Philosophy of International Law* (OUP 2010) 275; Klabbers (n 10) 29–30.

> legal remedies and procedures designed to enable the Court of Justice to review the legality of acts of the institutions.[16]

In view of the plurality of such legal orders and their oftentimes competing claims to authority, the key to harmonious development of a more universal legal order lies in mutual recognition and respect.

It is therefore clear that today the International Law Commission ought to have the capacity to survey the normative claims across the plurality of actors such as states, international and regional organizations, international and regional courts, supranational and national constitutional orders, and to have the methodology that can distinguish normative claims from other types of practice. The role of the Commission in fulfilling its functions of codification and development of law is to reach out to those actors whose actions may decisively impact the formation and application of legal rules at an international level. Pluralism works towards a certain democratic nature of the international normative landscape. Since the establishment of the United Nations an understanding emerged that for its decisions to have a "compliance pull",[17] the process of their adoption should take into account the views of as many States as possible around the world. Certainly, the composition of the International Law Commission tends to reflect all the major legal systems and cultures. Where one is able to capture the modern phenomenon of a growing plurality of actors, it contributes to the overall legitimacy of the exercise of power at an international level. There is no doubt that also the International Law Commission, in carrying out its functions of codification or development of international law, exercises power. It is therefore suggested that the Commission should reflect on the various aspects of legitimacy of its work, including input legitimacy and not only output legitimacy.[18]

The Study Group of the British Institute of International and Comparative Law had already proposed that the Commission should actively engage the co-operation of other inter-governmental actors and also the legal profession. It can only be reiterated that openness and accessibility of the Commission's working processes should be encouraged.[19]

A further democratization of the working methods of the Commission is necessary if it is to strengthen its legitimacy and maintain its role as the

---

16 C-402/05 P *Kadi* [2008] ECR I-06351, para 281; see also C-294/83 *Les Verts v Parliament* [1986] ECR 01339, para 23.

17 Thomas M Franck, *The Power of Legitimacy among Nations* (OUP 1990), 234.

18 For more on legitimacy, see Klabbers (n 9) 37–43.

19 Anderson, Boyle, Lowe and Wickremasinghe (n 12) 51.

principal body of legal expertise on general international law. States ought not to be the sole dialogue partners either through the Sixth Committee or other inter-governmental entities. A more organized and transparent network of non-State actors and scholars with interest and expertise in the work of the International Law Commission needs to be put in place. Some thought should go into democratizing the ways of receiving input for the work programme of the Commission. In this regard, regular meetings could be held with regional courts and *ad hoc* tribunals.

Given that constitutional courts have also formed joint forums of discussion, such platforms as the World Congress of Constitutional Courts as well as the European Conference of Constitutional Courts could be useful interlocutors. There are several reasons why the International Law Commission should not only follow the jurisprudence of the international and highest national courts but should also develop a dialogue with those courts for the purposes of its broader role in carrying out the functions of codifying and developing international law. These courts apply international law, follow the work of the International Law Commission and by now certainly engage in some law-making. Let me use the example of the European Court of Human Rights.

IV Engagement of the European Court of Human Rights with the Work of the International Law Commission

It is generally known that the European Court of Human Rights has consistently declared that it interprets the European Convention on Human Rights in accordance with the rules of interpretation of treaties as enshrined in the Vienna Convention on the Law of Treaties. In order to determine the meaning of the terms and phrases used in the European Convention on Human Rights, the Court is guided mainly by articles 31 to 33 of the Vienna Convention on the Law of Treaties.[20] However, the Court does not take a dogmatic approach to the wording of article 31 nor to the sequence in which this article lists the methods of interpretation. As evidenced by the language of *Demir and Baykara v Turkey*, the Court may not be too concerned as to whether the State has ratified the treaty or whether the common domestic practices emerge specifically in the application of the European Convention, as the wording of article

20 Adopted 23 May 1969, entered into force 27 January 1980, 1155 UNTS 331. See, for instance, *Golder v United Kingdom* (1975) Series A no 18, para 29; *Johnston and Others v Ireland* (1986) Series A no 112, para 51; *Witold Litwa v Poland* ECHR 2000-III 289, paras 57–59.

31, paragraph 3, would indicate.[21] The Court is interested in seeing the common developments and trends relevant to the scope of the European Convention without necessarily identifying the binding character of those developments and practices. In other words, while article 31 of the Vienna Convention on the Law of Treaties offers a frame of reference for the Court as such, the Court has followed the methods of interpretation with a certain flexibility.[22]

In view of the pending work of the International Law Commission with regard to the "Immunity of State officials from foreign criminal jurisdiction", I will refer to two cases of the European Court on Human Rights. In *Al-Adsani* and *Jones*, which concerned the jurisdictional immunity of states or state officials from civil claims concerning torture, the European Court of Human Rights was required to ascertain the contents of international law rules in this area and their interplay with the right to a fair trial provided for in article 6 of the European Convention, that is whether the relevant domestic courts, when restricting the applicants' right of access to a court, had pursued a legitimate aim which was "complying with international law to promote comity and good relations between States through the respect of another State's sovereignty".[23] In other words, the Court had to establish whether the domestic courts had correctly applied the rules of international law that existed at the time when they examined the case. If that was the case, then the "measures taken by a High Contracting Party which reflect generally recognised rules of public international law on State immunity cannot in principle be regarded as imposing a disproportionate restriction on the right of access to a court as embodied in Article 6 § 1".[24]

The obligation incumbent upon domestic courts in this regard can be said to be both procedural and substantive. The procedural obligation is to "fully engag[e] with all of the relevant arguments" concerning the state of international law at the relevant time.[25] The substantive obligation is to reach conclusions that are not "manifestly erroneous nor arbitrary, but [are] based on extensive references to international-law materials and consideration of the applicants' legal arguments".[26]

---

21 *Demir and Baykara v Turkey* App no 34503/97 (ECtHR, 12 November 2008).

22 See further, Ineta Ziemele 'European consensus and international law' in Anne van Aaken and Iulia Motoc (eds), *The European Convention on Human Rights and General International Law* (OUP 2018).

23 *Jones and others v United Kingdom* App nos 34356/06 and 40528/06 (ECtHR, 14 January 2014), para 188.

24 *Al-Adsani v United Kingdom* App no 35763/97 (ECtHR, 21 November 2001) para 56.

25 *Jones* (n 23) para 214.

26 Ibid.

The European Court of Human Rights is charged with the task of verifying whether domestic courts have complied with these obligations. In order to do so, the Court has to embark upon independent research to reach its own conclusions about what international law provides. This is because the Court does not apply the European Convention in a vacuum. However, the Court only has a mandate to interpret and apply the European Convention. So it has to rely on the interpretation of other relevant rules of international law provided for by those with the relevant competence. Clearly, one of the most important sources of information that enables the European Court of Human Rights to form its own opinion on what international law requires is the work of the International Law Commission. For the specific function of any court, it is important to clearly understand the view of the International Law Commission as to whether it has engaged in codification of existing rules or rather in their progressive development. The reason for the judicial interest in this distinction has to do with the fact that courts determine the responsibility of a State which can only arise in relation to existing law.

In the first of the two above-mentioned cases, *Al-Adsani v the United Kingdom,* the Grand Chamber of the European Court of Human Rights delivered its judgment on 21 November 2001. In the judgment, it made very little use of the work that had, at that stage, already been done by the International Law Commission in the field of sovereign immunity of States. The Court referred to the 1999 Report on Jurisdictional Immunities of States and their Property of the working group of the International Law Commission, but only to note "that national courts had in some cases shown sympathy for the argument that States are not entitled to plead immunity where there has been a violation of human rights norms with the character of *jus cogens*, although in most cases the plea of sovereign immunity had succeeded".[27] After conducting its own analysis of the rules of international law in force at the time, the European Court of Human Rights could not "find it established that there is yet acceptance in international law of the proposition that States are not entitled to immunity in respect of civil claims for damages for alleged torture committed outside the forum State".[28]

The second judgment, in the case *Jones and Others v the United Kingdom,* referred to and relied extensively upon the work of the International Law Commission. Delivered on 14 January 2014, the *Jones* judgment not only took into account the work that the International Law Commission had done in

27 *Al-Adsani* (n 24) para 23.
28 Ibid para 66.

the relevant field in the more than 13 years that had elapsed since the adoption of the *Al-Adsani* judgment, but also referred to the International Law Commission's draft articles on the jurisdictional immunities of States (which had been adopted in 1991 and hence well before the *Al-Adsani* case was decided).[29] Because the United Nations Convention on Jurisdictional Immunities of States and Their Property of 2004[30] was not in force at the time of the *Jones* judgment and is still not in force today (having been signed by 28 States and ratified by 22 out of the 30 required States),[31] the Court had to ascertain the contents of the rules of customary international law concerning sovereign immunities in cases where there are allegations of torture or breaches of other *jus cogens* norms. What is particularly interesting is that the European Court of Human Rights took into account the fact that the International Law Commission had been given an opportunity to revise the draft articles in order to incorporate an exception to sovereign immunity in cases where there had been torture but had not used this opportunity.[32] This failure of the working group of the International Law Commission to propose amendments to the draft articles was one of the factors which led the Court to conclude that international law was developing in the direction where the *jus cogens* exception to the sovereign immunity rule would eventually become an established rule of international law but that this stage of development had not yet been reached.[33]

The approach of the European Court of Human Rights towards the work of the International Law Commission can be best described as casuistic. While it is most likely that the outcome of *Al-Adsani* and *Jones* would have remained unaffected by the depth of the study of the International Law Commission's materials, these cases clearly demonstrate the utility of the International Law Commission's function of codifying customary international law for the decision-making in Strasbourg. The two discussed cases also indicate the European Court of Human Rights' own reluctance to take the next step towards progressive development of law, although such progressive development cannot be ruled out when taking into account the dissenting opinions of some of the judges.

---

29 *Jones* (n 23) para 74.

30 Adopted 2 December 2004, not yet in force, UN Doc A/59/508.

31 United Nations Treaty Collection, 'Status of Treaties Deposited with the Secretary-General' Ch 3, 13. <treaties.un.org/Pages/ViewDetails.aspx?src=TREATY&mtdsg_no=III-13&chapter=3&clang=_en> (as of 26 October 2018).

32 *Jones* (n 23) para 79.

33 *Jones* (n 23) para 209.

In view of the approach of the European Court of Human Rights towards the work of the International Law Commission, a few observations are warranted. Establishing a dialogue among these bodies is of great importance since both are involved in the development of international law broadly speaking through their respective competences. A better awareness of each other's work in the globalized world is necessary. Furthermore, courts such as the European Court of Human Rights are not necessarily composed of international lawyers. The trend that can be observed is that the domestication of international law has led to a reduction of the number of international lawyers in different fora which previously were composed of international lawyers to a significant degree. In view of the place of the European Court of Human Rights' judgments within the international legal system, the informal dialogue of the European Court of Human Rights and other courts and tribunals with the International Law Commission is a way to build mutual respect rather than confrontation. Secondly, one can already identify the issues that need to be discussed between these and other actors. These issues include the European Court of Human Rights' development of human rights law through a more flexible approach to the Vienna Convention on the Law of Treaties' interpretation criterion of subsequent State practice, which the Court sometimes simply calls a trend but which may nevertheless be sufficient to contribute to a judicial decision. In view of the International Law Commission's current work on custom and State practice and with a view to attributing more legitimacy to both the input and output of the Commission's work, such an exchange of views with courts would be very useful.

v Conclusions

There are generally known constraints of time and resources at the disposal of the Commission. That may lead to questioning the possibility of a more prominent or all-embracing role of the Commission in a globalized world. I do not doubt that the availability of resources will have an impact on the definition of the Commission's role; however, that should not be the main or the primary factor in rethinking the Commission's role.

Furthermore, in view of some of the work accomplished by the Commission in recent years, the difficulties of maintaining the line between codification and progressive development is apparent. A good example in this respect are the articles on responsibility of States for internationally wrongful acts. Those articles have not only captured the attention of the International Court of Justice while they were being drafted but also became a point of reference for the European Court of Human Rights and domestic constitutional courts very early onwards.[34] On the one hand, for courts in particular, it is important to know the view of the Commission as to whether it is engaged in codification or progressive development of law with regard to a particular topic. On the other hand, it ought to be also made clear that maintaining a conceptual distinction between the two may be a challenge, especially since the Commission works on a topic for several years and in the meantime international practice could already have been inspired by some of the views expressed by the Commission in its work. This reality of the world becoming smaller and faster, in my view, points even more to the importance of adapting the working methods of the Commission towards more openness, dialogue and communication which, on the one hand, is made easy in our digital époque and, on the other hand, may be more time-consuming in our pluralistic world. Such an adaptation of the working methods is necessary for the Commission to maintain its role, authority and legitimacy in international law-making. This line of reflection is particularly relevant with regards to the question of the Commission's competence to develop international law.

34 See the judgments of the Constitutional Court of the Republic of Latvia referring to the International Law Commission's draft articles on responsibility of States for internationally wrongful acts: Case no 2004-01-06 7 July 2004, 8 at para 3.2; Case no 2004-10-01 17 January 2005, 14.

Concluding Remarks by Sean D. Murphy

1 Introduction

My thanks to the organizers of this conference in celebration of the Commission's seventieth anniversary. The topic of this panel is an important one, as it goes to the heart of what the Commission has done in the past and will do in the future. Indeed, when I first joined the Commission in 2012, I often found myself asking, when a particular rule was under discussion, "are we trying to codify the law or progressively develop it?" I believed the answer to that question to be extremely important, as otherwise it was unclear on what terrain a discussion was taking place. There seemed little point in trying to persuade colleagues why a particular rule was not grounded in existing law if, in their view, that position was irrelevant to the task at hand.

Through their papers, Yifeng Chen and Ineta Ziemele have provided important insights into the Commission's mandate with respect to the progressive development and codification of international law, and its implementation of that mandate from its inception to the present. Yifeng Chen quite rightly reminds us of the aspirations for codification over the past century, the philosophy underlying the codification movement, and the distinction between codification and progressive development, all as a backdrop to asking important questions about the authority and legitimacy of the Commission.

Ineta Ziemele argues that the international law landscape has changed since the inception of the Commission, raising serious questions about what should be the function of the Commission as it pursues its twin mandates. The real impact of the Commission is brought alive in her discussion of the engagement of the European Court of Human Rights with the work of the Commission, but that impact arguably can only be maintained if the Commission pursues a more activist approach to our "globalized world", bringing into its thinking the views of disparate actors beyond just States.

In my brief role as discussant of those papers, I would like to address some of the themes advanced within them principally by considering, from an "insider's perspective", two questions: (1) what factors push the balance within the Commission either in the direction of "codification" of international law or in the direction of "progressive development?"; and (2) what factors push the balance with respect to any given draft article (or other provision) in the direction of transparency by the Commission as to what it thinks it is doing (codification or progressive development) or in the direction of obscuring what it thinks it is doing?

In considering the answers to those questions, it is important to understand two points. First, the original scheme envisaged in the Commission's statute drew a relatively bright line between the process of codification and the process of progressive development, which was never operationalized.[1] Rather, from the start, the Commission recognized that its projects inevitably contained elements of both codification and progressive development.

Second, precise definitions of "codification" and of "progressive development" of the law are allusive. The Commission's statute defines the two terms in a certain way,[2] but those definitions typically are not what most persons mean when they use the terms. In fact, and ironically, the contemporary understanding seems to be the opposite of what is said in the statute, in that many today regard the "draft articles" prepared by the Commission (ostensibly as possible articles for a treaty) as codifying international law, when the statute indicates that the preparation of draft conventions is done to progressively develop the law. Even so, I think the contemporary understanding of these two terms is relatively widespread, and centers on the idea of "codification" as an exercise in systematizing existing rules of international law, and on progressive development as an exercise in: (1) identifying a rule for which there is some but not widespread support in State practice; (2) filling gaps in the existing law; or, perhaps, (3) proposing entirely new law.[3]

1 See, for instance, Donald McRae, 'The Work of the International Law Commission, 2007–2011: Progress and Prospects' (2012) 106 AJIL 322, 324 ("the widely held view is that the Commission has never actually followed that distinction in practice"); Michael Wood, 'The United Nations International Law Commission and Customary International Law' (Gaetano Morelli Lecture 4th edn: Rethinking The Doctrine Of Customary International Law, Rome, 27 May 2017) para 27. <https://www.scienzegiuridiche.uniroma1.it/sites/default/files/varie/GML/2017/GML_2017-Wood.pdf >("it has long been accepted that the Commission does not and cannot follow the distinction made in its statute, at least as far as working methods are concerned").

2 Article 15 of the ILC statute provides: "In the following articles the expression "progressive development of international law" is used for convenience as meaning the preparation of draft conventions on subjects which have not yet been regulated by international law or in regard to which the law has not yet been sufficiently developed in the practice of States. Similarly, the expression "codification of international law" is used for convenience as meaning the more precise formulation and systematization of rules of international law in fields where there already has been extensive State practice, precedent and doctrine."

3 For a thoughtful discussion, see Donald McRae, 'The Interrelationship of Codification and Progressive Development in the Work of the International Law Commission' (2013) 111 JILD 75.

II Factors Influencing Codification versus Progressive Development

With that in mind, I turn to the first question: what factors push the balance within the Commission either in the direction of "codification" of international law or in the direction of "progressive development"? In my view, much of what the Commission does is progressive development of the law, even if it is commonly perceived by others as codification.[4]

One major factor pushing the Commission in the direction of codification is the desire for the rules contained in its work to be generally accepted by States and others, which is maximized if the work is based not on the preferences of the members of the Commission, but on a rigorous and systematic analysis of existing State practice and international jurisprudence.

A related factor is the desire by the Commission to have influence on the field of international law even if its work is not transformed into a treaty. The fact that the Commission's work in recent years has rarely resulted in a treaty instrument,[5] and that the Commission instead has moved toward other forms of "packaging" its work,[6] is well understood. Indeed, of the nine topics on the Commission's agenda in July 2018, only three are cast as "draft articles"[7] and, of those three, I would venture to say that only one is viewed as actually having the potential for transformation into a treaty.[8] The remaining topics cast as

4 McRae (n 1) 324 ("much of what the Commission does is progressive development, although not necessarily seen or characterized as such"); *see also* David Caron, 'The International Law Commission Articles on State Responsibility: The Paradoxical Relationship Between Form and Authority' (2002) 96 AJIL 857, 861 ("the fact that the International Law Commission study is written as though it were a treaty in many instances will not result in its being a document that changes and grows with the testing of particular cases, but one that is inappropriately and essentially accorded the authority of a formal source of law.").

5 See Michael Wood, 'The General Assembly and the International Law Commission: What Happens to the Commission's Work and Why?' in Isabelle Buffard et al (eds), *International Law between Universalism and Fragmentation, Festschrift in Honour of Gerhard Hafner* (Brill 2008) 373.

6 See Sean D Murphy, 'Codification, Progressive Development, or Scholarly Analysis? The Art of Packaging the International Law Commission's Work Product' in Maurizio Ragazzi (ed), *The Responsibility of International Organizations: Essays in Memory of Sir Ian Brownlie* (Martinus Nijhoff 2013) 29.

7 The topics of "Crimes against humanity," "Immunity of State officials from foreign criminal jurisdiction," and "Succession of States in respect of State responsibility".

8 The topic of "Crimes against humanity". See also ILC, 'Report of the International Law Commission on the work of its sixty-eighth session' (2016) UN Doc A/68/10, 140 at para 3.

"draft conclusions,"[9] "draft guide,"[10] "draft guidelines,"[11] or "draft principles,"[12] will not become treaty instruments. The closer the work adheres to codification, the more influence it will likely have, for it is validated by existing State practice and international jurisprudence (rather than through subsequent adoption and ratification by States).

A third factor is a recognition by many if not most members of the Commission that it was not established as a law-maker or legislator.[13] Rather, its mandate of "progressive development" was originally designed as a part of a process of treaty-making *by States*. Assuming a role of law-maker by advancing new rules in instruments that are not expected to become treaties is perilous, potentially threatening over the long-term the legitimacy of the Commission.

On the other side of the ledger, one factor pushing the Commission toward progressive development of the law is a desire to build a better world. Codification is sometimes seen as accepting and even "freezing" in place lacunae, faults, inadequacies, or inequities in existing law, whereas progressive development presents an opportunity to improve upon the law, to push States to do better. For some, the value of the Commission is not to just look backwards, but to look forward, extrapolating from where we are to where we might and should be.

A second factor pushing the Commission toward progressive development of the law is, quite frankly, that true codification is an extremely difficult and time-consuming task. To properly codify a rule, one must try to account for the practice of 193 different States, consider those practices in conjunction with *opinio juris*, and then analyze if such practice and acceptance of the practice is sufficiently widespread and representative. It becomes quite a daunting task, even when there are multilateral treaties, or resolutions of international organizations or intergovernmental conferences, that may assist in the analysis.

A third factor is that even assuming perfect knowledge with respect to the practice of States (and, if deemed relevant, thousands of international organizations), there will inevitably be some gaps in that practice, often making it difficult to say that a rule is definitively settled. As such, there is an impetus to

9 The topics of "Identification of customary international law," "Subsequent agreements and subsequent practice in the interpretation of treaties," and "peremptory norms of general international law (*jus cogens*)".

10 The topic "Provisional application of treaties".

11 The topic "Protection of the atmosphere".

12 The topic "Protection of the environment in relation to armed conflict".

13 Wood (n 1) at para 11 ("neither the General Assembly, nor its subsidiary organ, the Commission, has the power to make law").

see the practice as "good enough" for at least progressive development of the law, even if not for codification.

III Factors Influencing Transparency about What the Commission is Doing

Turning to the second question: what factors push the balance in the direction of transparency by the Commission as to what it is doing (codification or progressive development) or in the direction of obscuring what it thinks it is doing? Such disclosure normally would occur through what is said in the Commission's commentary, either at the outset in a "general commentary" of a project[14] or along the way in its commentary with respect to individual draft articles or other provisions. As it happens, the Commission typically does not disclose, as least expressly, whether it is engaged in codification or progressive development.[15]

One factor that pushes the Commission toward disclosure as to whether an entire project or a given provision is codifying or progressively developing international law is that helps it address the legitimacy concern noted above. If the Commission is convinced that it is codifying international law, it can say as much and then back up the claim with its evidence. If the Commission knows that a particular provision is progressively developing the law, and

14 A good example of this would be the inclusion in the Commission's general commentary to the articles on the responsibility of international organizations of a statement that the fact that several of the draft articles are based on limited practice 'moves the border between codification and progressive development in the direction of the latter [...] In other words, the provisions of the present draft articles do not necessarily yet have the same authority as the corresponding provisions on State responsibility'. ILC, 'Report of the International Law Commission on the work of its sixty-third session' [2011] II(2) ILC Ybk 40, 46.

15 By way of example, the beginning of the Commission's general commentary to the draft articles on responsibility of States for internationally wrongful acts essentially reiterates the mandate of the Commission when noting: "These articles seek to formulate, by way of codification and progressive development, the basic rules of international law concerning the responsibility of States for their internationally wrongful acts." Draft articles on responsibility of States for internationally wrongful acts, in ILC, 'Report of the International Law Commission on the work of its fifty-third session' [2001] II(2) ILC Ybk 26, 141 ("The present articles set out by way of codification and progressive development the general secondary rules of State responsibility"). At the same time, the commentary thereafter expressly identifies two situations where a rule constitutes progressive development of the law, ibid at 127, 114, which might imply that the Commission regards the other rules as codification.

further knows that its work will not be adopted as a treaty, then disclosing that the provision is progressive development helps insulate the Commission from charges that it is assuming the mantle of legislator. Instead, the Commission is offering a rule that it thinks appropriate, but is candidly acknowledging that the rule is a product of the Commission's own views, rather than a synthesis of settled law.

Another factor that pushes the Commission towards transparency is an understanding that relevant actors who may be relying on the Commission's work, in certain circumstances, need clarity as to what is *lex lata* and what is *lex desiderata*. A court for example, and especially a criminal court, typically must know the law as it is, not as it might be. Transparency by the Commission helps the court to understand, in any given instance, which of the Commission's twin mandates is in play.

A final factor is that, in some instances, such transparency can help members to reach consensus on the adoption of a provision. Some members may be resisting a proposed rule due to a belief that the rule is not well-settled. Identifying the rule as a form of progressive development is a means of addressing such a concern, allowing agreement to be reached on the rule by means of its characterization in the commentary.

Yet there are also factors that push the Commission away from transparency. Indeed, the dominant posture of the Commission is not to be transparent about what it is doing, at least in the sense of expressly identifying in the commentary whether a particular provision is codification or progressive development of the law. One factor pushing in the direction of non-disclosure picks up where the prior paragraph left off, which is to say that members often do not agree whether a particular provision is codification or progressive development. The easiest course to take, then, is for the Commission to say nothing at all, leaving members individually to characterize the rule as they wish.

A second factor is a sense among some members of the Commission that transparency already exists. Relevant actors already know that the Commission's mandate spans both codification and progressive development, so they are on notice at a general level as to what the Commission is doing. It is possible that the packaging of the project provides certain signaling; the title "conclusions" may signal codification, whereas "guidelines" or "principles" signal softer, more progressive thinking (since the Commission has nowhere indicated what these titles mean, however, it is hard to know exactly their significance). If a more granular understanding is needed for any given provision, then a close reading of the commentary helps guide the reader. Where the Commission has cited to copious State practice and jurisprudence backing up the asserted rule, then codification can be assumed; if not, then progressive development.[16]

A third factor is the desire not to "freeze" the law. Even if all members view a particular provision as progressive development, saying as much might inhibit the crystallization of the rule as law, since the Commission is on record doubting that it is yet well-settled. As the late David Caron noted, "the freezing effect of a code may be greater because the system lacks both a legislative body to amend the codes and an authoritative judiciary with jurisdiction over enough cases to adapt them to new circumstances and needs."[17]

Finally, no doubt some members view the concern with diminishment of the "legitimacy" of the Commission as misguided, given the Commission's relationship with States through the Sixth Committee of the United Nations General Assembly.[18] Even if the Commission's work is not transformed into a treaty, it is reviewed, debated, and sometimes expressly accepted or rejected by States through oral comments made in the Sixth Committee debate each fall, and through written comments submitted send to the United Nations. If the Commission goes out on a limb of progressive development that States do or do not like, they can react accordingly. Reading the Commission's work in conjunction with the reaction of States provides for assessing and even generating law, through State practice prompted by the Commission's work. On this account, there is no need for greater transparency by the Commission as to what it is doing, for the key ingredient is not what the Commission says but what States say about what the Commission says. A weakness, of course, in this line of argument is that the reaction of States to the Commission's work is serious and substantial, but far from thorough. At most, 40 to 50 States participate in the debate in the Sixth Committee, with interventions that are often vague, circumspect or ambiguous, and even fewer States submit written comments.

In conclusion, the perplexing phenomenon of codification versus progressive development is an enduring characteristic of the work of the International Law Commission, one that will no doubt be at issue in anniversary celebrations to come.

---

16 *See* McRae (n 1) 330 ("When no practice is available on which [to] base a draft article, the case for saying that it represents an existing principle of customary international law is weak.").

17 Caron (n 4) 861.

18 For discussion of that relationship, see Franklin D Berman, 'The International Law Commission within the United Nation's Legal Framework: Its Relationship with the Sixth Committee' [2006] 49 GYIL 107; see also Pemmaraju Sreenivasa Rao, 'International Law Commission' in Rüdiger Wolfrum (ed), *Max Planck Encyclopedia of Public International Law* (OUP 2012), para 14.

SECTION 6

The Changing Landscape of International Law

Opening Remarks by Elinor Hammarsjköld

The celebration of the seventieth anniversary of the International Law Commission has given us the opportunity to pay tribute to the achievements of the Commission in carrying out its mandate to promote the progressive development of international law and its codification. I join all those colleagues who have pointed to the importance and the success of the Commission in shouldering this responsibility, and who have already paid tribute to its members, current and previous.

This morning's topic encourages us to look ahead to future perspective for the International Law Commission and indeed to future challenges and developments facing international law. The Commission itself has taken the view over the years that it should not have to restrict itself to traditional topics, but that it could also consider issues that reflect new developments in international law. This is also an important aspect of the interaction between the Commission and governments.

Today's panel topic, "The Changing Landscape of International Law", begs the question, as a point of departure, to what extent and how that landscape is changing, and what the role of the Commission should be in responding or, indeed, driving change. We benefit of course from the excellent presentations and speeches that were given yesterday, which touched on some of these aspects. We heard from the President of the International Court of Justice and others speak both of the challenges facing international law today and the challenges and potential in the work of the Commission: changes in reality, changes in the actors in international law and developments within the Commission itself.

DOI:10.1163/9789004434271_026

Challenges of Codification for the International Law Commission in a Changing Landscape of International Law

Hajer Gueldich

1 Introduction

As is well-known, efforts to systematically codify and develop international law have a long tradition, starting with Jeremy Bentham in 1789,[1] and continued by numerous academic institutions, conferences and committees.[2] The founders of the United Nations, in 1945, mandated the General Assembly to "initiate studies and make recommendations for the purpose [...] of encouraging the progressive development of international law and its codification".[3] Two years later, the General Assembly delegated this task to a body of independent experts, the International Law Commission.[4] Today, this Commission can look back on – and continues to produce – an impressive body of work, covering most areas of international law.

It is only natural that the Commission's work would evolve with the legal system it operates in. Over the past 70 years, international law has undergone fundamental changes: it accommodated the tension of the Cold War, the emergence of newly independent States, and the establishment of a global economic order. Since the end of the 20th century, there has been an unprecedented expansion of international law, with a focus on international organizations, human rights, and the environment. The International Law Commission has adapted to these changes, for example by increasingly venturing into specialized areas of international law[5] and elaborating "soft" instruments rather than draft treaties.[6]

---

1 Jeremy Bentham, *The Works of Jeremy Bentham*, vol 2 (William Tait 1843) 537.

2 For an overview of the historic development of codification efforts see the contribution by Keun-Gwan Lee in this Section.

3 Article 13, paragraph 1 (a) of the Charter.

4 UNGA Res 174 (II) (21 November 1947). By the same resolution, the General assembly adopted the statute of the ILC, which has subsequently been amended by UNGA Res 485(V) (12 December 1950); UNGA Res 984(X) (3 December 1955); UNGA Res 985(X) (3 December 1955) and UNGA Res 36/39 (18 November 1981).

5 The topics "Protection of the environment in relation to armed conflicts" and "Protection of the atmosphere" are examples from the field of international environmental law.

6 Recent examples include the "draft conclusions" on subsequent agreements and subsequent practice in relation to the interpretation of treaties (UNGA Res 73/202 (10 December

DOI:10.1163/9789004434271_027

To maintain its authority, the International Law Commission must continue to review the impact of a constantly changing legal environment on its work. Such assessment first requires a brief overview of the contemporary landscape of international law: the new challenges which form the context of the Commission's future work (II). Based on these observations, important future topics for codification can be considered (III). In addition, these challenges have implications for the Commission's methods of work (IV). Finally, it is possible to venture some conclusions and recommendations for a successful future of the International Law Commission in a challenging landscape of international law (V).

II The Context: New Challenges Facing International Law

Codification may seem a technical operation, but in reality it has to mediate clashes of State interest, changing geopolitical conditions and a variety of legal traditions. As Charles de Visscher put it, codification is a progressive operation,[7] which requires balancing the continuity of international law with the need to change and innovate the rules and structures of the international legal system to respond to new challenges.[8]

The challenges facing the Commission in the twenty-first century may be symbolized by the events on 11 September 2001, which effectively marked the start of the new millennium. Since then, the international community has struggled with increasingly complex security challenges and an evolving interpretation on the prohibition on the use of force. A growing number of humanitarian crises and disasters require an effective global response. Meanwhile, States are confronted with other players in the international sphere: international relations are increasingly shaped by the acts of non-state actors, from non-governmental organizations and multinational corporations to private military companies and terrorist groups. Furthermore, advances in information technology, from big data to social media, require coordinated regulatory action to protect the world from novel threats such as cyber crime or even

2018)) and identification of customary international law (UNGA Res 73/203 (20 December 2018)).

7 Charles De Visscher, 'La codification du droit international' (1925) 6 RdC 325, 397.

8 See further Hajer Gueldich, 'La mission des Nations Unies quant à la codification et au développement progressif du droit international au niveau régional' (2015) 2 Journal of the African Union Commission on International Law 296.

cyber war. Perhaps less visible, though not less serious, are the growth of global inequalities between and within states and the waning enthusiasm for multilateral engagement.

It would be naive to assume that the Commission could turn the tide of global affairs by itself and fundamentally change the parameters of contemporary international relations. Nevertheless, the Commission cannot ignore the context in which its outcomes are received, interpreted and applied. By carefully selecting the topics on its programme of work, as well as by adapting its working methods to changing circumstances, the Commission may continue to provide the normative guidance it has offered in the past 70 years.

III The Substance: Current Trends and New Topics to Codify

Identifying topics suitable for codification by the International Law Commission remains a complex exercise. It is one of the central characteristics of the International Law Commission that its field of work comprises international law in its entirety, even extending to private international law.[9] Not without reason has the idea that the Commission could prepare a comprehensive code of international law been abandoned shortly after its inception.[10] In light of the expansion international law has experienced over the last decades, such an endeavour has certainly not become any more feasible. Taking stock of the Commission's work, it is nevertheless remarkable that few areas of international law have remained untouched. So far, the Commission contributed to such diverse fields as the law of the sea, diplomatic relations, the responsibility of States and international organizations, international criminal law, the protection of the atmosphere, extradition and many other topics.

This illustrative – and heterogenous – list raises the question which substantive criteria govern inclusion of a topic in the Commission's programme of work. The statute of the Commission offers only limited guidance in that regard. The General Assembly and certain other bodies may set subjective priorities through special requests for codification[11] or proposals for progressive

---

9 Article 1(2) of the ILC statute.

10 When the International Law Commission was established, a lively debate took place whether it should elaborate a comprehensive code of international law or work on individual topics. The latter approach prevailed. See Keun-Gwan Lee (n 2).

11 See article 18(3) of the ILC statute.

development of international law.[12] On its own initiative, the Commission may consider any topic it deems "necessary and desirable" for codification.[13]

Through its practice, the Commission has clarified the criteria for topics to be included in its programme of work:

(a) The topic should reflect the needs of States in respect of the progressive development and codification of international law;

(b) The topic should be sufficiently advanced in stage in terms of State practice to permit progressive development and codification;

(c) The topic is concrete and feasible for progressive development and codification.[14]

The Commission further emphasized that it "should not restrict itself to traditional topics, but could also consider those that reflect new developments in international law and pressing concerns of the international community as a whole."[15]

It is especially this latter aspect which the Commission should not disregard as it approaches its eighth decade. As outlined above, there are several "pressing concerns" which international law needs to address. In particular, the Commission may consider examining in the future the areas of international security and the use of force (A); humanitarian response to conflicts and disasters (B); non-State entities in international law (C); and new technologies, cyber war and cyber criminality (D).

These suggestions may perhaps seem not "feasible" or not "sufficiently advanced in stage in terms of State practice to permit progressive development and codification". Indeed, the topics proposed here are not elaborate enough to resemble a concrete proposal for the Commission's agenda.[16] Nevertheless, they certainly reflect "new developments in international law and pressing concerns of the international community as a whole" and would benefit greatly from the clarity and certainty that the Commission's work can provide. Naturally, the fields in which legal certainty is most necessary also tend to be

---

12 See articles 16(1), 17(1) and 18(3) of the ILC statute. For further discussion see below.

13 Ibid article 18(2).

14 ILC, 'Report of the International Law Commission on the work of its forty-ninth session' [1997] II(2) ILC Ybk 1, 72 at para 238.

15 Ibid.

16 When a topic is added to the Commission's long-term programme of work, a detailed proposal outlining the scope of the topic and plan of work is annexed to the Commission's annual report. See, for example, the proposals for the topics "Universal jurisdiction" and "Sea-level rise in relation to international law" annexed to the 'Report of the International Law Commission on the work of its seventieth session' (2018) UN Doc A/73/10, 307 and 326, respectively.

particularly controversial and politically sensitive. The Commission must strike a delicate balance between political realities and the aspirations of the broader international community,[17] but it should not shy away from making meaningful contributions in the most pressing areas of international law. Codification has never been understood as a static exercise. Echoing De Visscher's notion of a "progressive operation", Roberto Ago noted that "to codify the law has always meant modifying it partially, and sometimes even profoundly".[18] The fact that certain questions of international affairs remain unregulated does not mean they are not susceptible to the grasp of international law. After all, the process of codification and progressive development of international law focuses specifically on those issues "not yet been regulated by international law or in regard to which the law has not yet been sufficiently developed in the practice of States".[19] To paraphrase the International Court of Justice, "in situations in which political considerations are prominent it may be particularly necessary [...] to obtain [guidance on] the legal principles applicable".[20] The Commission's work may help to clarify the current state of the law and give a neutral impetus for necessary progressive development from a "technical" perspective.

A *International Security and Use of Force*

The general prohibition of the use of force is one of the cornerstones of the international legal order. However, the system of exceptions to this prohibition established by the Charter of the United Nations in 1945 has proven ill-equipped to deal with new challenges for international security. Following a traditional interpretation of the Charter, legitimate use of force is limited to inter-State self-defence[21] and Security Council authorization.[22] Given the well-known deadlock in the Security Council precipitated by the right to veto,

17 Sompong Sucharitkul, 'The role of the ILC in the decade of International Law' (1990) 3 LJIL15, 40.

18 See Roberto Ago, 'La codification du droit international et les problèmes de sa réalisation' in Maurice Batteli and others (eds), *Recueil d'études de droit international en hommage à Paul Guggenheim* (Imprimerie de la Tribune de Genève 1968) 94. Translation by the author.

19 Article 15 of the Commission's statue. See also A Mahiou, 'Le paradigme de la codification' in SFDI, *La codification en droit international* (Pedone 1999).

20 *Interpretation of the Agreement of 25 March 1951 between the WHO and Egypt* (Advisory Opinion) [1988] ICJ Rep 73, 87.

21 Article 51 of the Charter of the United Nations. See also *Military and Paramilitary Activities in and against Nicaragua (Nicaragua v United States)* (Merits) [1986] ICJ Rep 14, para 195; *Legal Consequences of the Construction of a Wall in the Occupied Palestinian Territory* (Advisory Opinion) [2004] ICJ Rep 136, para 139.

22 Article 42 of the Charter of the United Nations.

States have resorted to unilateral uses of force in legal grey areas to address the security challenges of today. Two issues stand out: invocation of the right of self-defence to combat international terrorism and humanitarian intervention to prevent atrocities during internal conflicts. While the motivation for both approaches is understandable, the absence of clear legal boundaries lends itself to politicization, double-standards and abuse, ultimately undermining the stability of international relations and the rule of law.

The International Law Commission may contribute to clarifying and developing the law in this respect. It may, on one hand, rein in excessive interpretations of the established exceptions to the prohibition of the use of force by restating their boundaries. On the other hand, the Commission may contribute to progressive development in this area by transcending the inter-State paradigm, emphasizing the protection of the individual as the ultimate objective of international law. To this end, the Commission could, for example, build on the work of the Evans/Sahnoun Commission of 2001[23] and elaborate a draft convention on the responsibility to protect.

B *Humanitarian Response to Conflicts and Disasters*

Somewhat interlinked with the "responsibility to protect" is the broader field of humanitarian responses to conflicts and disasters. The International Law Commission has recently made an important contribution in this area when it completed the draft articles on protection of persons in the event of disasters.[24] Building on this work, it may want to focus its attention on the pressing issue of internally displaced persons. Millions of persons remain displaced, yet apart from the Kampala Convention of 2009[25] – which is restricted to Africa – there is so far no international legal instrument addressing this topic. A universal convention prepared by the International Law Commission could thus be a significant step forward in this area.

C *Non-State Entities in International Law*

The increased presence of non-State actors in international relations touches on the very foundations of the international legal system. Prominent examples

23 Gareth Evans and others, *Report of the International Commission on Intervention and State Sovereignty* (International Development Research Centre 2001).

24 ILC, 'Draft articles on the protection of persons in the event of disasters' (2016) UN Doc A/71/10, 13.

25 African Union Convention for the Protection and Assistance of Internally Displaced Persons in Africa, adopted 23 October 2009, entry into force 6 December 2012, UNTS registration no 52375.

include non-governmental organizations influencing diplomatic processes and operating actively "on the ground", multinational corporations shaping economies and affecting the realization of human rights, and insurgents or private military companies fighting in armed conflicts. Recalling the resounding success of the International Law Commission's work on fundamental topics such as the law of treaties and State responsibility, it seems well-positioned to address the questions arising from these developments.

Some aspects still need time to develop before they are suitable for treatment by the International Law Commission. Integrating non-state actors into the framework of the law of treaties and international responsibility, for example, has received attention in academia,[26] but has yet to take hold in legal practice. These issues should nevertheless be part of a long-term vision for the Commission's work. It will not be too long before (after States and international organizations) a third generation of treaties, involving non-governmental organizations will catch the imagination of the international community. The fourth generation would soon also be in sight, covering treaty relations or international agreements where international or multinational enterprises are contracting parties. Such new conventions will also trigger questions over the international responsibility of non-state actors, which should be clarified.

Some concrete phenomena seem suitable for treatment by the Commission in the shorter term. One example may be the use of private military companies during or after armed conflicts, an issue that touches upon the law of State responsibility, humanitarian law and human rights law.[27] Here,

26 See Cedric Ryngaert, 'Non-State Actors in International Law: A Rejoinder to Professor Thirlway' (2017) 64 NILR 155; Edda Kristjansdottir, Andre Nollkaemper and Cedric Ryngaert, *International Law in Domestic Courts: Rule of Law Reform in Post-Conflict States* (Intersentia 2012); Nicolas Carrillo Santarelli, 'Non-State Actors Human Rights Obligations and Responsibilities under International Law' (2008) Revista Electronica De Estudios Internacionales 1; Janne Nijman, 'Non-State Actors and the International Rule of Law: Revisiting the "Realist Theory" of International Legal Personality' in Math Noortman and Cedric Ryngaert (eds), *Non-State Actor Dynamics in International Law: From Law-Takers to Law-Makers* (Ashgate 2010); Math Noortman, August Reinisch and Cedric Ryngaert (eds), *Non-State Actors in International Law* (Hart 2015); and Noemi Gal-Or, Cedric Ryngaert and Math Noortman (eds), *Responsibilities of the Non-State Actor in Armed Conflict and the Market Place* (Brill 2015).

27 See Peter Benicsák, 'Advantages and disadvantages of private military companies' (Univerzita Obrany V Brně, Economics and Management 2012); Erika Calazans, *Private military and security companies: The implications under international law of doing business in war* (Cambridge Scholars 2016); Lindsey Cameron and Vincent Chetail, *Privatizing War: Private Military and Security Companies under Public International Law* (CUP 2013); Lindsey Cameron, *The privatization of peacekeeping: Exploring limits and responsibility*

the Commission could clarify the obligations of States which employ such companies and develop a framework for responsibility of the companies themselves.

D *New Technologies, Cyber War and Cyber Criminality*

The digitalization of ever more parts of our lives has not left international relations untouched. The internet may be – and allegedly has been – used by States and non-State actors to attack infrastructure or spread misinformation and propaganda. "Cyber crime" or "cyber warfare" are further concerns whose global nature requires a global response. With intergovernmental negotiations on cyber-related legal issues currently stalling,[28] the International Law Commission could make a useful contribution by clarifying the applicability of established norms, such as the principle of non-intervention, in the digital realm. The technical complexity of this area should not dissuade the Commission from addressing it, as it may consult scientific experts to supplement its efforts.[29]

IV The Methods: New Approaches to Codification

Apart from adapting the substance of its work, the changing conditions of international affairs must also be reflected in the working methods of the Commission. Increased technical complexity of specialized fields of international law is one, but certainly not the only, challenge in this regard. To retain its relevance, the Commission must step out of its own circle of legal experts and engage with the international community – in the broadest sense of the term – to effectively fulfil its mandate.

---

under international law (CUP 2017); William Feldmann, *Privatizing war: A moral theory (war, conflict and ethics)* (Routledge 2016); Thierry Garcia, *Les entreprises militaires et de sécurité privées appréhendées par le droit* (Mare & Martin 2017); Robert Mandel, *Armies without States: The privatization of security* (Lynne Reinner 2002); Hannah Tokin, *State control over private military and security companies in armed conflict* (CUP 2011); Nikolaos Tzifakis, *Contracting out to private military and security companies* (Centre for European Studies 2012); Al Venter, *War Dog: Fighting Other People's Wars: The Modern Mercenary in Combat* (Casemate 2005); and Peter W Singer, *Corporate Warriors: The Rise of the Private Military Industry* (Cornell UP 2003).

28 See e.g. Adam Segal, 'The Development of Cyber Norms at the United Nations Ends in Deadlock. Now What?' (Council on Foreign Relations, 29 June 2017) <https://www.cfr.org/blog/development-cyber-norms-united-nations-ends-deadlock-now-what>.

29 See article 16(e) of the ILC statute.

A *Selection of Topics*

This increased engagement must start at the beginning of the Commission's work, the selection of topics. According to the Commission's statute, proposals for progressive development of international law may be made by the General Assembly, Members of the United Nations, other principal organs of the United Nations, specialized agencies, or official bodies established by intergovernmental agreement to encourage the progressive development of international law and its codification.[30] While it seems that there are plenty of avenues to entrust the Commission with tasks, assignments by the General Assembly – let alone proposals from other entities – have been the exception throughout the work of the International Law Commission.[31] Encouraging stronger participation of other United Nations entities in the selection of topics should be a priority for the Commission to increase the relevance of its work. Although not envisaged by its statute, the Commission may even wish to consider including the suggestions of non-governmental organizations in the topic-selection process.

B *Dissemination of International Law*

It is important to increase dissemination of international law including through teaching, research, publication and translation of instruments. The Commission already actively contributes to this mission through lending its participation to the International Law Seminar, which takes place annually during the Commission's session in Geneva. Participants in the Seminar attend public meetings of the Commission, as well as lectures and briefings delivered by its members and representatives of other organizations based in Geneva.[32]

In addition, the Codification Division of the United Nations Office of Legal Affairs, which serves as the secretariat of the Commission, facilitates regular training courses in international law at the regional and international level through the Programme of Assistance in the Teaching, Study, Dissemination and Wider Appreciation of International Law.[33]

In terms of research, publication and translation of instruments, the Commission's Yearbook offers an authoritative account of its meetings and their outcomes. The Yearbook is published in all official United Nations languages, even though sometimes with a little delay. Moreover, the website of the

30 Ibid articles 16(1) and 17(1).

31 United Nations, *The Work of the International Law Commission*, vol I (9th edn, United Nations 2017) 34–47.

32 See <https://ilsgeneva.ch/>.

33 See <http://legal.un.org/poa/index.html>.

Commission offers a comprehensive Analytical Guide, with links to all publicly available documents relating to the Commission's work.

Nevertheless, there is always a need for more national, regional, and international workshops on the implementation of international law, in order to pursue legal developments in the general interest and for the common benefit of mankind.

C *Increased Engagement with Developing States*

To combat the increasing global inequalities in political power and legal expertise, the Commission should increase its engagement with developing States. Increasing awareness of international law in developing countries and allowing them to contribute to its formation would counter impressions of international law as a one-sided system serving only the interests of a particular set of powerful States. Such cooperation would require developing countries to actively promote international law in academic curricula and judicial practice, and to provide opportunities for lawyers to participate globally in research and the practice of international law.

D *Cooperation with Other Institutions and Academics*

The Commission's statute allows formal consultations with organs of the United Nations, official or non-official international or national organizations, and with scientific institutions and individual experts.[34] Article 26, paragraph 4, of the Commission's statute highlights the importance of consultation with "intergovernmental organizations whose task is the codification of international law".

The International Law Commission already cooperates with a number of regional institutions promoting international law, namely the African Union Commission on International Law, the Asian-African Legal Consultative Organization, the Inter-American Juridical Committee and the Council of Europe's Committee on Legal Cooperation and Committee of Legal Advisers on Public International Law.[35] Intensifying these relationships has been endorsed by the Commission for a long time.[36] Considering the growing importance of regional arrangements in international law, this endeavour can only be welcomed. An alternative to a largely formalized exchange of views between representatives of these bodies would be to hold joint sessions and collaborate on certain

---

34 See articles 16(e), 25(1) and 26(1) of the ILC statute.

35 United Nations (n 31) 84–85.

36 See ILC, 'Report of the International Law Commission on the work of its forty-eighth session' [1996] II(2) ILC Ybk 97 at para 239–240.

topics.[37] Such close cooperation may provide mutual inspiration and help avoid redundancies.

In addition, a stronger relationship with academia and civil society may prove beneficial for the International Law Commission. While events such as the commemoration of the Commission's anniversaries provide an opportunity for organized academic exchange,[38] a more sustained exchange of views may help the Commission staying abreast of new trends and developments.

V Conclusion

Throughout these 70 years, the International Law Commission has stood the test of time. It has done much to clarify the rules of international law on topics which are of the greatest importance in a very wide range of areas. As indicated above, the codification and progressive development of international law is a continuous and progressive process, not a static one. Since its establishment, the Commission has been the main driver of and point of reference for this process. As has been observed by a former member of the Commission, "[l]ike most other things associated with human imperfections, the work of the Commission is not infallible, nor beyond improvement. On the contrary, the law itself is not static. It is changing with a dynamic force. And so must be the Commission ..."[39]

Several concrete recommendations have been made for the Commission to retain its relevance in challenging time. Two general lessons can be drawn. First, to effectively deal with the "pressing concerns of the international community as a whole", the Commission must diversify – not only the topics on its programme of work, but also the dissemination of its outcomes, the way it brings in external expertise and viewpoints from developing States, and its interaction with other bodies, from regional organizations to academia (not to speak of diversity in the composition of its membership, a very valid point made by others in this publication).

---

37 Ibid, suggesting the possibility of joint studies on particular legal topics.

38 See United Nations (ed), *Making Better International Law: The International Law Commission at 50, Proceedings of the United Nations Colloquium on Progressive Development and Codification of International Law* (United Nations 1998) and United Nations, *The International Law Commission Fifty Years After: An Evaluation* (United Nations 2000).

39 Sucharitkul (n 17) 37.

Second, the Commission should not shy away from dealing with some of the most complicated dilemmas in international relations today. Questions over the use of force, self-defence, humanitarian action, the role of non-State actors and cyber threats clearly have a political character, but there is always a legal angle to be found. The lack of leadership on these issues by prominent political bodies, in particular the Security Council, compels other institutions to step in. As a subsidiary body of the General Assembly, composed of eminent academics and practitioners in international law, the International Law Commission can lend its expertise, if not to solve current challenges, then at least to promote a common language – the language of international law – in which to constructively debate how to deal with them. This is a significant responsibility, but one that the Commission in the past 70 years has demonstrated to be able to bear. By reducing the gap between the legal and the political, the Commission can make a practical contribution to a world that is more secure, more peaceful, and more just.

Recalibrating the Conception of Codification in the Changing Landscape of International Law

Keun-Gwan Lee

1 Introduction

In a book that looks back on the first 50 years of the International Law Commission, a general evaluation was given as follows:

> The extent to which, at the end of the twentieth century, international law is a more mature system of law and its practitioners can regard their subject with self-confidence in its worth is very largely due to the contribution made over the first fifty years of its existence by the International Law Commission.[1]

A decade earlier, a no less enthusiastic assessment ("the most remarkable achievements yet known in the field of the progressive development and codification of international law") was made by another eminent authority.[2] On the seventieth anniversary of the establishment of the International Law Commission, one can readily agree to these opinions. Having said this, it is also true that one hears of "a deep-seated uncertainty about the contemporary role of the Commission".[3] About a decade ago, a former member of the Commission wrote an article entitled "The International Law Commission – An Outdated Institution?".[4]

In this contribution, written on the occasion of the seventieth anniversary of the Commission, I will try to address some questions concerning the proper role and status of the Commission and venture a few suggestions.

---

1 Arthur Watts, *The International Law Commission 1949–1998*, vol 1 (OUP 1999) 20.

2 José Sette-Camara, 'The International Law Commission: Discourse on Method' in *International Law at the Time of its Codification: Essays in Honour of Roberto Ago*, vol 1 (Giuffrè 1987) 467.

3 David McRae, 'The Interrelationship of Codification and Progressive Development in the Work of the International Law Commission' (2013) 111 JILD 75, 76.

4 Christian Tomuschat, 'The International Law Commission – An Outdated Institution?' (2006) 49 GYIL 77.

The main function of the International Law Commission, which is composed of individual experts, is "the promotion of progressive development of international law and its codification".[5] Since the idea of codification of international law is a concept with a long historical pedigree, I will start by retracing the evolution of the concept from the late 18th century until the end of the Second World War (II). This is not done only for historical interest; the overview will show that some common themes have shaped conceptions of codification of international law for more than two centuries.

I will go on to briefly analyze the debate which took place at the first meetings of the inaugural session of the International Law Commission (III). This will demonstrate that there existed much divergence among the members of the Commission on the conception of codification and how to approach it. In the next section, I will introduce a taxonomy of the codification of international law as discussed and conducted by the Commission (IV). In addition to an explanatory function, the taxonomy will be instrumental in venturing some suggestions for the future role and function of the Commission, which I will attempt at the next section (V). A few concluding remarks will follow (VI).

II Codification of International Law: an Idea with a Long Pedigree

In this section, I will discuss how the idea of codification of international law has evolved since the late 18th century. As a concept that has been around for more than two centuries, it is not surprising that it would experience a certain evolution. At the same time, we can find some themes undergirding most conceptions of codification of international law.

Jeremy Bentham is generally regarded as having initiated the idea of codification of international law.[6] In his *Principles of International Law,* he started his discussion by raising the following hypothetical question: "If a citizen of the world had to prepare an universal international code, what would he propose to himself as his object?"[7] In the same essay, he offered a list of seven

5 Article 1(1) of the statute of the ILC, UNGA Res 174(II) (21 November 1947) as amended by UNGA Res 485(V) (12 December 1950); UNGA Res 984(X) (3 December 1955); UNGA Res 985(X) (3 December 1955) and UNGA Res 36/39 (18 November 1981).

6 For a detailed discussion of Bentham's idea on the codification of international law, see Ernest Nys, 'The Codification of International Law' (1911) 5 AJIL 871, 876.

7 Jeremy Bentham, *The Works of Jeremy Bentham,* vol 2 (William Tait 1843) 537. The manuscripts of *Principles of International Law* bear dates from 1786 to 1789. In Essay 1 entitled

"causes of offences *de bonne foi* [among sovereigns], and of wars" and went to propose "Means of Prevention" as follows:

1. Homologation of unwritten laws which are considered as established by custom.
2. New conventions – new international laws to be made upon all points which remain unascertained; that is to say, upon the greater number of points in which the interests of two states are capable of collision.[8]

What is important for our purposes is the fact that Bentham, who has been called "the arch-priest of codification",[9] put forth the distinction between the "homologation" of existing custom and the regulation of "unascertained" questions by treaty-making.[10] This distinction bears striking similarities to that introduced by article 15 of the Commission's statute, that is, the distinction between codification and progressive development of international law.[11]

"Objects of International Law", Bentham provided an answer based on his utilitarian thinking: "the greatest happiness of all nations taken together" or "the most extended welfare of all the nations on the earth". Ibid 538.

8 Ibid 540. Bentham adds the third means of prevention as follows: "Perfecting the style of the laws of all kinds, whether internal or international. How many wars have there been, which have had for their principal, or even their only cause, no more noble origin than the negligence or inability of a lawyer or a geometrician!".

9 This was the expression used by the "Sub-Committee upon the History and Status of Codification" formed under the "Committee of the American Society of International Law on the Codification of the Principles of Justice in Times of Peace between Nations, appointed under the Resolution of the Society of April 24, 1909". See the Committee's preliminary report (1910) 4 ASILPROC at Its Annual Meeting (1907–1917) 197, 208.

10 For Bentham's later writings on codification of international law, see Jeremy Bentham, *Traités de Legislation Civile et Pénale,* vol 3 (3rd edn, Rey et Garavier 1830). The first edition of this book was published in 1802. The three chapters mentioned in volume 3 of the book are included in the part dealing with "Vue Générale d'un Corps Complet de Législation". See also Bentham's unpublished letters addressed to Jabez Henry from July 1827 and January 1830; for a succinct discussion of these letters, see Ernst Nys, 'Notes inédites de Bentham sur le droit international' (1885) 1(2) LQR 225.

11 Article 15 of the Commission's statute provides as follows: "In the following articles, the expression 'progressive development of international law' is used for convenience as meaning the preparation of draft conventions on subjects which have not yet been regulated by international law or in regard to which the law has not yet been sufficiently developed in the practice of States. Similarly, the expression 'codification of international law' is used for convenience as meaning the more precise formulation and systematization of rules of international law in fields where there already has been extensive State practice, precedent and doctrine."

Bentham did not regard the codification as a purely academic or utopian exercise.[12] He suggested "l'idée de la redaction d'un corps de droit international par un congrès qui serait composé d'un délégué par Etat civilisé".[13] He proposed a confederation of States which "has for its objects, or say ends, in view the preservation, not only of peace (in the sense in which by peace is meant absence of war), but of mutual good-will and consequent mutual good offices between all the several members of this confederation".[14] He envisaged this confederation to be equipped "with the Code of International Law approved, adopted and sanctioned by it".[15] Thus, Bentham was well aware of the dual nature of codification of international law both as the work of "a world citizen [called on] to prepare an universal code of international law" and as requiring sovereign approval to be granted on this work to achieve normative effectiveness. This dual nature mirrors the tension between, on the one hand, the International Law Commission as a body of independent experts, and, on the other, States concerned about their "legislative monopoly" in international law. To borrow the expression employed by an international lawyer well versed with the work of the International Law Commission, Bentham was keenly cognizant of the "diplomatic character" inherent in the codification of international law.[16]

12 In his 1924 article, Baker observed that "Jeremy Bentham first proposed the codification of international law. The conception of his fertile, logical, but not wholly practical mind, was not that of a code of the existing law of nations, but of a new Utopian code which would create a legal foundation for eternal peace." PJ Baker, 'The Codification of International Law' (1924) 5 BYIL 38. That Bentham was far from being a utopian daydreamer is shown by, among others, the following argument of his: "Under a system of international law the imperative could not be exercised by any authority: not even by the international congress. The admission of the faculty of issuing imperative decrees with power for giving execution and effect to them, would have the effect of an attempt to establish an Universal Republic, inconsistent with the Sovereignty of the several Sovereigns within their respective dominations." As quoted in Nys (n 6) 879. See also Nys (n 10) 229.

13 Nys (n 10) 227–228.

14 Article 6 of Bentham's proposed code, as quoted in Nys (n 10) 227–228. One can also find the text of the code as an appendix to the preliminary report of the Committee of the American Society of International Law on the Codification of the Principles of Justice in Times of Peace between Nations (n 9) 223–224.

15 Ibid.

16 Carl-August Fleischhauer, 'The United Nations and the Progressive Development and Codification of International Law' (1985) 25 IJIL 1, 2. For a detailed discussion of the political character of the Commission's work, see BG Ramcharan, *The International Law Commission: Its Approach to the Codification and Progressive Development of International Law* (Martinus Nijhoff 1977) ch 5.

This short analysis shows that the key problems often discussed in connection with the International Law Commission are already found in Bentham's ideas on the codification of international law, if not exactly in the same shape or form. This observation attests to the tremendous fecundity of Bentham's mind. At the same time, the afore-mentioned dual nature of codification of international law is inevitable given that the codification of international law is ultimately geared towards the practical goal of attaining peace in international relations.

As is well known, Bentham's idea was further developed by a series of efforts at what is often termed "private codification"[17] or "private attempts at codification".[18] These attempts were made by academic lawyers, working both individually and in learned societies such as the *Institut de Droit international* or the International Law Association, which was originally called "the International Association for the Reform and Codification of the Law of Nations". In connection with the private attempts at codification, one often encounters names such as Abbé Grégoire,[19] Alfons von Domin-Petruschévecz,[20] Francis Lieber, Johann Caspar Bluntschli, David Dudley Field,[21] Pasquale Fiore,[22] E. Duplessix[23] and Jerome Internoscia.[24]

---

17 In French, this is also known as "la codificadftion privée ou scientique". See, for instance, Georges Abi-Saab, 'La Commission du Droit International, la Codification et le Processus de Formation du Droit International' in United Nations (ed), *Making Better International Law: The International Law Commission at 50, Proceedings of the United Nations Colloquium on Progressive Development and Codification of International Law* (United Nations 1998) 188.

18 For a detailed discussion of various private attempts at codification, see RP Dhokalia, *The Codification of Public International Law* (Manchester University Press 1970) 37–75. See also United Nations, 'Note on the Private Codification of Public International Law' (1947) 41(4) AJIL (Supplement: Official Documents) 138–147; Hersch Lauterpacht, *International Law: Collected Papers, Volume 1 (The General Works)* (CUP 1970) 98–100.

19 The text of his "Declaration of the Law of Nations" appears as an appendix to the preliminary report of the Committee of the American Society of International Law on the Codification of the Principles of Justice in Times of Peace between Nations (n 9) 226–227.

20 *Précis d'un Code du Droit International* (Brockhaus 1861).

21 *Draft Outlines of a Code of International Law* (Diossy & Company 1872). For a detailed discussion of Field's work on the codification of international law, see Herbert W Briggs, 'David Dudley Field and the Codification of International Law' in *Institut de Droit international* (ed), *Livre du Centenaire, 1873–1973: Évolution et Perspectives du Droit International* (S. Karger 1973) 67–73.

22 *Il Diritto Internazionale Codificato e la Sua Sanzione Giuridica* (Unione Tipografico-Editrice 1890). For the English translation from the fifth edition of this book, see Edwin M Borchard, *International Law Codified and its Legal Sanction* (Baker, Voorhis and Company 1918).

23 *La Loi des Nations ; Projet d'Institution d'une Autorité Nationale, Législative, Administrative, Judiciaire. Projet de Code de Droit International Public* (L. Larose & L. Tenin 1906).

24 *New Code of International Law* (The International Code Company of New York 1910).

According to an assessment by Professor Rosenne, these private efforts undertaken during the 19th century "made little impression on Governments".[25] Nevertheless, scholars persisted. One of the best-known attempts at the codification of international law, that is, Bluntschli's *Das moderne Völkerrecht der civilisirten Staten als Rechtsbuch dargestellt* (1868) was written on stimulus provided by the resounding success of the codification of the law of war on land by Lieber. In 1863, Lieber's *Instructions for the Government of the Armies of the United States in the Field*, revised by a board of officers and approved by the President of the United States, was published by the United States War Department as General Order No. 100. Bluntschli welcomed this document as "a first codification of the law of wars on land".[26] He was acutely aware of the difference between private and official codification. He stated that "[s]ince the academic codes (*Rechtsbücher*) are the product of private individuals, whereas the legal codes (*Gesetzbücher*) are promulgated by State authority, the former cannot claim the binding authority that secures the duty of obedience to the statutes."[27]

Some attempts at private codification were undertaken with the aim of ultimate approval by official authorities (and the resultant acquisition of binding legal authority). The *Institut de Droit international* unanimously adopted the Oxford Manual on the Laws of War on Land on 9 September 1880.[28] In its preamble, the *Institut* tried to reassure "military men", who were the immediate addressees of the norms contained in the Manual, by emphasizing that the document was an exercise in "consolidating codification".[29] It also made clear that it did not propose an international treaty, but "a 'Manual' suitable as the basis for national legislation in each State".[30] After the adoption of this Manual, Bluntschli sent a copy of it to Marshal Moltke of Germany, asking for the recognition, or endorsement, of it.[31] In this way, Bluntschli wanted to replicate the success of the Lieber Code in Europe.[32]

---

25 Shabtai Rosenne, 'The International Law Commission, 1949 – 1959' (1960) 36 BYIL 104, 106.

26 Johann Caspar Bluntschli, *Das moderne Völkerrecht der civilisirten Staten als Rechtsbuch dargestellt* (C.H. Beck 1868) 5 (translation by the author).

27 Ibid 7 (translation by the author).

28 IDI, 'Les lois de la guerre sur terre. Manuel publié par l'Institut de droit international.' (Oxford 1881–1882) 5 AnnIDI 157.

29 "The Institute has not sought innovations in drawing up the 'Manual'; it has contented itself with stating clearly and codifying the accepted ideas of our ages so far as this has appeared allowable and practicable." Ibid preamble.

30 Ibid (translation by author).

31 Johann Caspar Bluntschli, *Denkwürdiges aus Meinem Leben*, vol III (C.H. Beck 1884) 471. According to Moltke, Bluntschli "wünsch[te] [s]eine Anerkennung desselben".

32 In the Introduction to his 1868 *Rechtsbuch*, Bluntschli urged the European States "not to lag behind the example of the American States any longer" in respect of the laws of

The project of codification no longer remained in the private and academic sphere as it was taken up by the governments. A long list of conferences, usually starting with the 1815 Congress of Vienna through the 1856 Congress of Paris leading up to the 1899 and 1907 Hague Peace Conferences, is often presented as exemplifying "official efforts at codification"[33] of international law. Whether the instruments adopted at these conferences can be regarded as the result of "conscious and sustained" attempts at official codification or represent "to a large extent a secondary development, accepted universally, of a contractual arrangement originally destined to remove serious sources of international friction"[34] is open to debate.[35]

---

war on land, (n 26) 6. The correspondence between Bluntschli and Moltke is introduced in the following books. Jules Guelle, *La Guerre Continentale et les Personnes* (Librairie Militaire de J. Dumaine 1881) v-vii ; Martti Koskenniemi, *The Gentle Civilizer of Nations* (CUP 2010) 84–85.

Another champion of the codification of international law, David Dudley Field, is a case in point. In the preface to *Draft Outlines of an International Code*, he stated in no uncertain terms that "[his] scheme embraced not only a codification of existing rules of international law, but the suggestion of such modifications and improvements as the more matured civilizations of the present age should seem to require." Also, the very first article of his International Code is titled "adopting clause", according to which "[t]he following rules are established and declared by the nations assenting hereto, as an International Code ..." Field (n 21) 1.

33 This expression is used in chapter 3 of Dhokalia's book (n 18).

34 Rosenne (n 25) 107.

35 For the latter view, see Rosenne (n 25) 107. In this connection, he referred to the 1815 Vienna Regulation and the 1856 Declaration of Paris. One can raise the question of whether Rosenne's assessment applies to other instruments, in particular those adopted at the 1899 and 1907 Hague Conferences. The 1899 Conference was "unusually for the 19th century, whose end [it] marked, ... called not for the great European powers to resolve a specific war or conflict or to divide territory or other spoils of war." Betsy Baker, 'Hague Peace Conferences (1899 and 1907)' *Max Planck Encyclopedia of Public International Law* (November 2009) <opil.ouplaw.com/home/EPIL>, para 1. In a 1904 telegram concerning the convocation of the Second Hague Conference, John Hay, the then Secretary of State of the United States of America, stated that in the First Hague Conference the subjects such as "the rights and duties of neutrals, the inviolability of private property in naval warfare, and the bombardment of ports, towns, and villages by a naval force" had been relegated to a future conference. James Brown Scott (ed), *The Conventions and Declarations of 1899 and 1907* (OUP 1915) xxii. It is true that the adoption of some instruments was prompted by specific incidents or disputes. The 1907 Convention Relative to the Opening of Hostilities, the conclusion of which was precipitated by the concern raised about Japan's surprise attack on a Russian ship at Port Arthur in early 1904, is a prime example. However, this does not detract from the codificatory character of the Hague Conferences. For a discussion of "the juridicalization of the world in the 19th century" (*die Verrechtlichung der Welt im 19. Jahrhundert*), see Marcus M. Payk, *Frieden durch Recht? Der Aufstieg des modernen Völkerrechts und der Friedensschluss nach dem Ersten Weltkrieg* (De Gruyter 2018) 29–45.

What is beyond doubt is that international relations were progressively "juridicalized" since the second half of the 19th century and that this trend was strengthened with the establishment of the League of Nations. In its preamble, the Covenant of the League of Nations declared the commitment of the High Contracting Parties to, among others, "the firm establishment of understandings of international law as the actual rule of conduct among Governments" and "the maintenance of justice and a scrupulous respect for all treaty obligations in the dealings of organized peoples with one another".[36] It is not surprising that many commentators believed that the launch of the League of Nations had brought about "a remarkably rapid growth of the International Law of Peace".[37] They also pinned much hope on the prospect of "preparation of the conventions through a permanent international organization representing the whole society of States".[38]

In the specific context of codification of international law, it was the first resolution of the Advisory Committee of Jurists ("assembled at the Hague, to prepare the constituent Statute of a Permanent Court of International Justice")[39] which gave an impetus to the 1930 Hague Codification Conference. At the close of the proceedings that extended from 16 June to 24 July 1920, the Committee recommended the calling of a new inter-state conference "to carry on the work of the two first Conferences at the Hague".[40] The objectives of this "successor conference" as proposed by the Committee clearly carried the dual character of the codificatory endeavour.[41] The Committee also recommended that "the new Conference should be called the Conference for the advancement of international law".[42]

---

36 Adopted 28 April 1919, entered into force 10 January 1920.

37 Baker (n 12) 59. See also Manley O Hudson, *International Legislation*, vol 1 (Carnegie Endowment for International Peace 1931) xxxvii ("The future of international legislation will probably be very much influenced by the Assembly of the League of Nations"). He regarded the Assembly as "the nearest approach made to date to an international legislature". Ibid. Judge Guerrero opined in a similar vein that "[n]ous voici parvenus enfin à la troisième période, celle où la S.D.N. pregnant la Codification sous son égide, va lui ouvrir des voies nouvelles et lui imprimer son veritable caractère." J Gustave Guerrero, *La Codification du Droit International* (A. Pedone 1930) 15.

38 Baker, n 12, 61.

39 Preamble of the First Resolution. Permanent Court of International Justice, Advisory Committee of Jurists, *Procès-Verbaux of the Proceedings of the Committee, June 16th – July 24th 1920, with Annexes* (1920) 747.

40 Ibid.

41 The objectives were, among others, "[r]e-establishing the existing rules of the Law of Nations, ..." and "[f]ormulating and approving the modifications and additions rendered necessary or advisable by the War, and by the changes in the conditions of international life following upon this great struggle". Ibid.

42 Ibid 748.

It was four years after the adoption of this resolution that the League of Nations took up the issue by appointing the Committee of Experts for the Progressive Codification of International Law.[43] When the League of Nations Conference for the Codification of International Law was finally convened at The Hague in March 1930, the fluidity and indeterminacy of the concept of codification and the concomitant question, that is, the diplomatic and political character involved in the process, proved to be points of substantial controversy. The Preparatory Committee composed of five experts (formed in 1927 and chaired by Basdevant from France) prepared, in addition to the "Bases of Discussion", the Draft Rules for the Conference. Article 25 of the Draft Rules provided that "Declarations by which the signatory Governments will *recognise certain principles as being sanctioned by existing international law may* also be signed as acts of the Conference …"[44] This provision, which reflected the conception of codification held by the Preparatory Committee, was agreed to be deleted at the fifth plenary meeting.[45] As a result, only conventions were supposed to be produced at the Conference.[46] This episode illustrates the persistence of the controversy around the meaning of codification.

It is also to be noted that a heated debate ensued over the question of whether the conventions adopted according to article 20 of the Rules of Procedure would, as "codified law", be "binding on all States, even on those which do not accede to [them]".[47] This question was put to rest by the powerful intervention of Rolin (Belgium) who, after pointing out the difficulty of maintaining the distinction "between pure codification and the adoption of new rules", affirmed that "in so far as any such instrument would go beyond existing international

---

43 League of Nations, 'Resolution adopted by the League of Nations Assembly on 22 September 1924' (1924) League of Nations Official Journal Spec Supp 21, 10.

44 League of Nations, *Acts of the Conference for the Codification of International Law: Vol. I, Plenary Meetings* (1930) 65 (emphasis added).

45 Ibid 29. A historical survey prepared by the United Nations Division of Development and Codification of International Law called the debate on whether to retain article 25 of the draft rules "the first and perhaps the most important question" among the questions of procedure. United Nations, 'Historical Survey of Development of International Law and its Codification by International Conferences' (1947) 41(4) AJIL (Supp: Official Documents) 81.

46 According to the memorandum prepared by the United Nations Secretariat entitled "Progressive Development of International Law and Codification" (A/122, 17 October 1947) 5, "sentiment at the Conference rapidly developed against making any such distinction [between 'conventions' and 'declarations'], and even the idea of having any declarations at all was opposed." The deletion of article 25 of the draft rules of procedure reflected such a sentiment.

47 Guerrero (Salvador) answered in the positive to this question. League of Nations (n 44) 33.

law, it would … only bind the States acceding to it."[48] Nevertheless, a high degree of uncertainty persisted about the meaning and normative impact of codification at this Codification Conference.[49]

In the light of such divergence of opinions on some of the basic questions of the Conference, it is not surprising that the 1930 Codification Conference produced a disappointing result,[50] even though some commentators tried to put it in a positive light.[51] In a 1946 speech before the Grotius Society, a well-known authority suggested that the "mixing-up" of codification as "ascertaining and declaring the existing rules of international law" and codification as "amending law as well as defining it, so that the provisions in the code shall state the rules of international law as they ought to be" was the main cause of failure of the 1930 Conference.[52] He went on to argue that the job of clarifying and defining the broad principles of international law could not be undertaken by governments.[53] For the tackling of these persistent questions, international society had to wait for another fifteen years.

This historical overview on the evolution of the codification of international law since the late 18th century until the end of the Second World War highlights some of the core questions surrounding the idea of codification in international relations, in particular the distinction between "consolidating codification" and codification of a legislative character. It also shows that the identity and capacity of codifiers remained an important question throughout the evolution of the idea of codification of international law. In

48 Ibid 33–34.

49 A historical survey prepared by the United Nations points out some difficulty the Conference encountered "in drawing a distinction between codifying existing and drawing up new rules of international law". United Nations (n 45) 85.

50 Judge Ago observed that "la Conférence de La Haye de 1930 dut enregistrer *un échec presque complet*." Roberto Ago, 'La Codification du Droit International et les Problèmes de sa Réalisation' in *Recueil d'Études en Droit International en Hommage à Paul Guggenheim* (La Tribune de Genève, 1968) 101. The 1947 historical survey discusses "Reasons for Failure of the [Hauge] Conference". United Nations (n 45) 84–86.

51 For instance, Manley O Hudson, "The First Conference for the Codification of International Law" (1930) 24 AJIL 447, 465–466; Green H Hackworth, 'Responsibility for States for Damages caused in their Territory to the Person or Property of Foreigners: The Hague Conference for the Codification of International Law' (1930) 24 AJIL 500, 515.

52 Cecil Hurst, 'A Plea for the Codification of International Law along New Lines' (1946) 32 Transactions of the Grotius Society 135, 146.

53 Ibid., p. 148. For a view critical of Hurst's position, see Hersch Lauterpacht, 'Codification and Development of International Law' (1955) 49 AJIL 16, 34 ("so-called private codification must assume its proper place as a desirable aid and stimulus to official activity in this field").

the following, I will look into how these questions played out in the United Nations era when the codification of international law was provided with a "statutory basis".

III Diverging Conceptions of Codification within the Inaugural International Law Commission

The codification of international law in the post-1945 period was founded on Article 13(1)(a) of the Charter of the United Nations. In stark contrast to the Covenant of the League of Nations, the Dumbarton Oaks proposals of 1944, which constituted the basis for the Charter, were characterized by the absence of recognition of the role of law in the international community.[54] At the San Francisco Conference, some governments tried to fill this gap, if insufficiently, by adopting Article 13(1)(a) of the Charter which reads: "The General Assembly shall initiate studies and make recommendations for the purpose of: (a) … encouraging the progressive development of international law and its codification."[55]

The implementation of Article 13(1)(a) was undertaken in the second part of the first session, leading to the appointment of the Committee for the Progressive Development of International Law and its Codification (also known as the "Committee of Seventeen") on 11 December 1946.[56] The Committee held its

---

54 At the San Francisco Conference, this deficiency of the Dumbarton Oaks proposals was pointed out by several governments, in particular, by the Egyptian Government which stated that "the draft Agreement does not mention the principles of International Law as being the basis of the new Organization." It also suggested that "the new Organization should ndeavor to further and develop International Law either *by the channel of some special agency depending on the General Assembly*, or through the existing Economic and Social Council." (emphasis added) *Documents of the United Nations Conference on International Organization, San Francisco 1945*, vol III 447, 448; Herbert W Briggs, *The International Law Commission* (Cornell University Press 1965) 3.

55 For a detailed discussion of the "legislative history" of this provision, see Yuen-Li Liang, 'The General Assembly and the Progressive Development and Codification of International Law' (1948) 42 AJIL 66, 66–68. See also Rosenne (n 25) 109–122; Briggs (n 54) pt 1. According to Rosenne, the very idea of providing for the progressive development and codification of international law in the constituent instrument of the United Nations Charter was "revolutionary". Rosenne (n 25) 111. Jennings saw "nothing novel" in Article (13)(a) of the UN Charter. According to him, this provision stands in "a continuous history extending over rather more than a century". RY Jennings, 'The Progressive Development of International Law and its Codification' (1947) 24 BYIL 301.

56 UNGA Res 94(I) (11 December 1946).

first meeting on 12 May 1947, adopting the report of the Rapporteur (J.L. Brierly of the United Kingdom) on 13 June 1947.[57]

In the course of the Committee's discussions, the distinction between progressive development and codification of international law appeared as one of the core problems. Brierly and Jessup (United States of America) supported the distinction between the two. According to Brierly, codification was a scientific task to be carried out by "a small committee of personal experts",[58] while the adoption of conventions necessarily brought in political factors.[59] In contrast, Koretsky (Soviet Union) supported "only one of the methods, namely, that of international conventions [the other being 'the method of scientific restatements']."[60] In the end, the Committee adopted the final report in which a distinction between progressive development and codification of international law was drawn merely "for convenience".[61]

In the report, the Committee recommended the General Assembly to establish the International Law Commission for the purpose of carrying out the progressive development of international law and its eventual codification. After presentation of the Committee's report to the General Assembly, the Second Sub-Committee of the Sixth Committee was tasked with the drafting of the statute of the International Law Commission. The General Assembly adopted the statute on 21 November 1947, although it decided to postpone the election of the inaugural Commission until 1948.[62]

In discussing various conceptions of codification of international law, it is worthwhile to revisit the discussions which took place at the inaugural session of the International Law Commission (1949). At the first meeting of the first session, Mr. Kerno, Assistant Secretary-General made opening remarks. Even though the dark clouds of what would be subsequently known as the "Cold War" loomed menacingly large, it is not surprising, given the nature of

57 Liang (n 55) 69–70. During the period between the constitution of the Committee and the first meeting, the Division of Development and Codification of International Law of the Secretariat carried out preliminary studies, producing a series of documents, including a historical survey of the development of international law and its codification by international conferences (n 45).

58 UN Doc A/AC.10/SR.2 (13 May 1947) 5.

59 Liang (n 55) 74.

60 UN Doc A/AC.10/SR.9 (24 May 1947) 13; Liang (n 55) 75; Rosenne (n 25) 116.

61 United Nations, 'Report of the Committee of the Progressive Development of International Law and its Codification on the Methods for Encouraging the Progressive Development of International Law and its Eventual Codification' UN Doc A/AC.10/51 (17 June 1947) 41(3) AJIL (Supplement: Official Documents) 20.

62 UNGA Res 174(II) (21 November 1947) and 175(II) (21 November 1947).

the occasion, to see him utter optimistic remarks on the role of international law. He likened international law to "a great and ancient edifice the doors of which were being opened so that it could be put in order, as it had to serve as *a shelter to mankind*."[63] With regard to codification as provided for in Article 13 of the Charter of the United Nations, he opined that "codification should be looked upon as forming part of a comprehensive, long-range plan for *the eventual codification of international law as a whole*."[64]

Mr. Kerno's high hopes pinned on the newly established International Law Commission appear to be reflective of similar sentiments expressed in the memorandum submitted by the Secretary-General titled "Survey of International Law in Relation to the Work of Codification of the International Law Commission".[65] In the memorandum, the ultimate object of the Commission was presented as "*the eventual codification of the entirety of international law*."[66] One is struck by the fact that the author of the memorandum believed that the object of the Commission could be achieved in a relatively short period of time ("in two decades or so"[67] or "over a period which may cover a generation").[68] Through its work of codification, the Commission would, among others, enhance the authority of international law through "the introduction of certainty, precision and uniformity in matters of detail."[69] The Commission was afforded "the opportunity, long awaited, of removing a grave defect in international law and of enhancing its usefulness and authority as a true system of law".[70]

While acutely aware of the differences between the mandate of the League of Nations' Committee of Experts and the International Law Commission,[71] the Secretary-General's memorandum proceeded from the premise of strong continuity between the two. We have already seen that the roots of the Commission's mandate of progressive development and codification of international law can be traced down to the 19th century, when scholarly efforts at

63 [1949] ILC Ybk 9 at para 2 (emphasis added).
64 Ibid 9 at para 4 (emphasis added).
65 ILC, 'Survey of International Law in Relation to the Work of Codification of the International Law Commission: Preparatory work within the purview of article 18, paragraph 1, of the of the International Law Commission – Memorandum submitted by the Secretary-General' (10 February 1949) UN Doc A/CN.4/1/Rev.1.
66 Ibid 14 at para 19 (emphasis added).
67 Ibid 17 at para 22.
68 Ibid 62 at para 103.
69 Ibid 8 at para 12.
70 Ibid 70 para 119.
71 Ibid 60 para 101.

codification of international law were undertaken in a systematic way. To draw up a new "Benthamite code" of international law was often put forth as the right course to get rid of war.[72] This idea was firmly anchored in the desirability and practicability of articulating a uniform and universal code of international law.

At the inaugural session of the International Law Commission, one can easily find some members of the Commission adhering to this traditional idea of codification of international law. Mr. Spiropoulos observed that the Commission could make a strong impression on the General Assembly by announcing that the Commission's ultimate aim was "to give to the world *a complete code of international law*."[73] His position was echoed by some Commission members from Latin America, who had substantial experience in the codification of international law, as exemplified by the activities of the "International Commission of American Jurists for the Codification of International Law, Public and Private", which was held in Rio de Janeiro, 19 April – 20 May 1927. For instance, Mr. Alfaro (Panama) pointed out that the International Law Commission's task was "to draft a work that might be entitled: 'The Law of Nations Codified'."[74] It is evident that such positions and observations aligned with the traditional movement for the codification of international law.

Other members of the Commission voiced opinions which were sceptical or critical of the traditional conception of codification of international law. First, questions were raised concerning the practicality of preparing "a general code of rules of international law."[75] Mr. François (Netherlands), who was deeply involved in the codification efforts within the framework of the League of Nations, warned against the overly ambitious approach supported by some members of the Commission. According to him, it was "better to obtain positive results on one or two less important questions than to draw up a general systematic plan which would subsequently prove impracticable."[76] He went so far as to recommend the method used at the Conference on International

72 Norman Bierman, 'Codification of International Law – A Basis of World Government' (1930) 15 Washington University Law Review 151, 155.

73 [1949] ILC Ybk 54–55 at para 80 (emphasis added).

74 Ibid 11 at para 25.

75 Ibid 34 at para 30. Concerning the approach to be taken by the Commission in its future work, Mr. Spiropoulos observed as follows: "the Commission should decide whether it proposed simply to codify certain subjects of international law, or whether it intended drafting a code of international law." His answer to the question was that the Commission's task would seem rather to be "the preparation of a general code of rules of international law." Ibid.

76 Ibid 17 at para 20.

Private Law at The Hague as a model for the International Law Commission.[77] The fact that Mr. François' suggestion is premised on the heterogeneity and diversity of international society (as is implied by the Anglo-American term "conflict of laws" denoting the subject of private international law) reflected his belief in the absence of "unity of spirit" in the area of public international law.[78] Mr. Scelle, despite being an ardent proponent of the idea of solidarity in international society and jurisdictional activism of the International Law Commission in its relations with the General Assembly,[79] went along with Mr. François. Affirming the impossibility of drawing up a general plan of codification, he opined that "the only possible solution was to choose a limited number of topics."[80]

Mr. Koretsky (Soviet Union) was highly critical of the traditional idea of codification of international law. According to him, a radical transformation took place in international relations since the first efforts of the League of Nations to codify international law. This profound change in international relations impelled many topics for codification that seemed essential at that time (such as the control of territorial waters and that of nationality) to

> give place to other questions which had become of primary importance from the point of view of the maintenance of peace in an international community based on the equality of all States, absolute respect for their sovereignty and the exclusion of any intervention in affairs which fell within their domestic jurisdiction.[81]

He went to observe that "[t]he question of codification must therefore be *completely reconsidered*, for it could be solved only by the peaceful co-operation of all forms of civilization, without distinction as to colour, and of all political systems of whatever shade of opinion."[82]

Under such understanding, codification of international law should be geared toward articulation of "progressive" principles of international law that would contribute to the peaceful co-existence of nations (or blocs) with widely differing political systems and ideologies. This understanding diverges

---

77 Ibid 17 at para 22.

78 Ibid 17 at para 20.

79 According to Scelle, in the selection of suitable topics for codification, the Commission was "a body with complete freedom, the equal of the International Court of Justice." Ibid 19 at para 45.

80 Ibid 34 at para 36.

81 Ibid 29 at para 50.

82 Ibid 29 at para 51 (emphasis added).

radically from the traditional idea of codification of international law premised on the homogeneity of international society.

This short analysis of the first meetings of the Commission shows that the members of the inaugural Commission harboured widely diverging views of the term "codification." The traditional idea of codification of international law was founded on the basic homogeneity of international society. This led some members of the Commission to propose a wholesale codification of international law ("Law of Nations Codified"). Other members, while not discarding the thesis of homogeneity of international society, proposed a more practical approach of selecting a limited number of international law topics for codification. In contrast, Mr. Koretsky, keenly aware of the profound transformation which took place in international relations since the 1920s, put forth a radically different concept of codification (and a very different list of topics to be "codified"). Shabtai Rosenne has argued that the success of the International Law Commission in the first 25 years of its codification efforts was paradoxically attributable to the international tension brought on by the Cold War. According to him, the instruments adopted by the Commission during that period supplied "a basic agreed code for their mutual contacts in periods of high tension and suspicion."[83] This is assessed as "legal diplomacy at its best."[84]

Now one needs to investigate how the divergence on the conception of codification of international law as demonstrated by the discussions at the inaugural session of the International Law Commission was subsequently addressed by the Commission.

IV The Evolution of the Concept of Codification within the United Nations and a Taxonomy of Codification Carried out by the International Law Commission

In the post-1949 period, the question of distinguishing between progressive development and codification of international law and the tension between the academic and diplomatic character of the Commission's work appear to have all but lost their poignancy. The rather abstract mandate for the General Assembly as stipulated in Article 13, paragraph 1 (a) of the Charter of the United Nations has been concretized and clarified by the subsequent practice relating to the provision.

83 Shabtai Rosenne, 'Codification Revisited After 50 Years' (1998) 2 MaxPlanckYrbkUNL 1, 11.
84 Ibid 13.

The substantive and procedural elaboration of the provision by the Committee for the Progressive Development of International Law and its Codification was discussed above. The distinction between progressive development and codification of international law, as provided for in the statute of the International Law Commission "for convenience", was acutely taken cognizance of by the Commission in its early years. For instance, the first report submitted by the inaugural Special Rapporteur on the law of treaties, J.L. Brierly, started with the question of "whether to confine his attention strictly to the law as it may be generally acknowledged to be, or to suggest what are in his view improvements in the existing law."[85] In handling one of the first tasks entrusted by the General Assembly, the draft declaration on rights and duties of States,[86] the Commission asked under which of its two principal duties, i.e. progressive development or codification of international law, the assigned task fell. The Commission concluded that it fell under neither of them, but constituted a special assignment from the Assembly.[87]

In the final report presenting the draft articles on the law of the sea,[88] the Commission admitted as follows:

> In preparing its rules on the law of the sea, the Commission has become convinced that, in this domain at any rate, the distinction established in the statute between [progressive development and codification of international law] can hardly be maintained. ... Although it tried at first to specify which articles fell into one and which into the other category, the Commission has had to abandon the attempt, as several do not wholly belong to either.[89]

85 [1950] II ILC Ybk 224 at para 2. He also enumerated the principal existing drafts on the law of treaties. Ibid 225–226 at paras 11–12.

86 [1949] ILC Ybk 287.

87 Ibid 290 at para 53.

88 [1956] II ILC Ybk 256.

89 Ibid 255–256 at para 26. Although the Commission initially worked on the regime of the high seas and that of territorial waters separately, in 1956 it produced a single set of draft articles dealing with the "problems relating to the high seas, territorial waters, contiguous zones, the continental shelf and the superjacent waters" that "were closely linked together juridically as well as physically". UNGA Res 899(IX) (14 December 1954). At the first United Nations Conference on the Law of the Sea, it was decided to divide the Commission's draft into four conventions. Among the conventions, the Convention on the High Seas (adopted 29 April 1958, entered into force 30 September 1962, 40 UNTS 11) affirms in its preamble that "[the Conference] adopted the following provisions as generally declaratory of established principles of international law." It also stated that the States Parties to the Convention desired to "*codify* the rules of international law relating to the high seas"

Concerning the subject of "diplomatic intercourse and immunities" where "la plupart des règles qui existent ont été formé par la coutume et la tradition",[90] it was no wonder that some Commission members regarded their task as ascertaining existing principles and rules,[91] this field of law being "one of the subjects least open to innovation".[92]

If one fast-forwards to the recent work of the International Law Commission, one hardly comes across the distinction between the two categories of activities. Despite all the efforts made for the distinction between the two, in particular, the different working methods elaborately stipulated in articles 16 to 24 of the Commission's statute,[93] the practice of the Commission evolved towards a merger of the two distinct procedures into one consolidated and practical method.[94] According to Judge Sette-Camara, this development represents "the Commission's wisdom in departing from the original perception of its mandate as comprising two watertight compartments and, without the need for any amendment of its statute, evolving towards a consolidated method of work which proved to be fruitful and effective".[95]

That the International Law Commission by now operates without being burdened by the distinction between the two types of function is well illustrated by the Commission's work on "Fragmentation of international law: difficulties arising from the diversification and expansion of international law". First of all, questions were raised at the initial stage of the work whether the topic was

(emphasis added). As far as the law of the high seas is concerned, the "confession" of the "codifiers" to the impossibility of the distinction between progressive development and codification of international law was overridden by the 1958 Conference.

90 A.E.F. Sandström, 'Diplomatic intercourse and immunities. Rapport presente par M. A. E. F. Sandström, rapporteur special' [1955] II ILC Ybk 9, 14 at para 14.

91 This was the view of Yokota; [1957] I ILC Ybk 3 at para 12.

92 Garcia Amador; ibid 3 at para 21.

93 Chapter 2 of the statute ("Functions of the International Law Commission") is composed of Section A, providing for the procedures to be followed in progressive development of international law, and Section B, providing for the procedures for codification of international law. The two procedures are very different from each other. For instance, Section B does not mention the appointment of a Special Rapporteur.

94 Sette-Camara (n 2) 483. Lauterpacht welcomed the merger of the two methods through the practice of the Commission. Lauterpacht (n 53) 30. A former member of the Commission goes so far as to state that "a transition from codification *stricto sensu* to progressive development of international law currently takes place." Gerhard Hafner, 'Codification and Progressive Development of International Law' in Franz Cede and Lilly Sucharipa-Behrmann (eds), *The United Nations: Law and Practice* (Martinus Nijhoff 2001) 152.

95 Sette-Camara (n 2) 487.

suitable for study by the International Law Commission. The Commission itself recognized "the unique nature of the topic".[96] The substantive uniqueness of the subject was later "tamed" by the decision "to set aside the institutional implications of fragmentation" and to "focus work on the Vienna Convention [on the Law of Treaties]".[97]

Procedurally, the Commission took a highly innovative approach. For the first time in its history, the Commission formed a "Study Group" to carry out the work, which fell under neither progressive development nor codification. In a significant departure from the well-established practice of the Commission, no Special Rapporteur was appointed.[98] The outlines and studies produced in the process leading to the finalization of the work (the final product was composed of (i) a relatively large analytical study on the question of fragmentation and (ii) a single collective document containing a set of conclusions)[99] have not been published officially.[100] The Commission, rather than adopting, took note of the forty-two conclusions and commended them to the attention of the General Assembly.[101]

It is evident from this example that the International Law Commission now enjoys a substantial degree of discretion in choosing its subjects, methods of work and the forms of the final outcome (admittedly, subject to interaction and cooperation with the General Assembly). As far as the Commission is concerned, the centuries-old debate over various meanings of codification, in particular the distinction between progressive development and codification of international law, has been all but resolved, without the official amendment of the statute of the International Law Commission, through the subsequent

96 ILC, 'Report of the International Law Commission on the work of its fifty-fourth session' [2002] II(2) ILC Ybk 1, 97 at para 496.

97 ILC, 'Report of the International Law Commission on the work of its fifty-sixth session' [2004] II(2) ILC Ybk 1, 111 at para 302. As a result, the Commission's work on fragmentation of international law can be regarded as falling largely under the category of "annotative codification", a concept which will be elaborated later.

98 Arnold Pronto and Michael Wood, *The International Law Commission 1999–2009, Volume IV: Treaties, Final Draft Articles, and Other Materials* (OUP 2010) 609.

99 ILC, 'Report of the International Law Commission on the work of its fifty-eighth session' [2006] II(2) ILC Ybk 175 at para 235. This unique composition of the final outcome of the Study Group's work gave rise to a discussion as to what measures should be taken on the two components of the report. See [2006] I ILC Ybk 240 at para 6.

100 Pronto and Wood (n 98) 611.

101 ILC report 2006 (n 99) para 239; Pronto and Wood (n 98) 611. On December 2006, the General Assembly took note both of the 42 conclusions and the "analytical study on which they were based". UNGA Res 61/34 (4 December 2006).

practice relating to the work of the Commission.[102] Reflecting such an evolution within the International Law Commission, I will subsume both activities of the Commission as stipulated in its statute under the nomenclature of codification in the following discussion.

Given the large number of topics the Commission has dealt with and the enormous amount of materials it has produced, it is beyond my ability to offer an assessment of the Commission's work over the past seven decades. A large number of proposals for the improvement of the Commission's work, in particular, the proper role of the Commission (such as "the role of an International Law Research Center"[103] or "the role of an advisory body along the lines of the Commission of Jurists of the League of Nations"),[104] its working methods,[105] the selection of topics,[106] the Commission's relationship with other relevant bodies,[107] have been made. In this paper, I will not walk again this well-trodden path. Instead, I will venture a taxonomy of various conceptions of codification discussed and conducted within the Commission. As will be made clear soon,

---

102 The distinction between progressive development and codification of international law is still relied on by States within the Sixth Committee, in particular when they find the Commission's proposal or work to be *de lege ferenda*. For instance, the United Kingdom delegation observed concerning the topic of responsibility of international organizations that "limited availability of pertinent practice moved several of the draft articles in the direction of progressive development, rather than codification." UN Doc A/C.6/66/SR.19, 3 at para 9. For a suggestion that the distinction be maintained within the ILC, see Franklin Berman, 'The ILC within the UN's Legal Framework: Its Relationship with the Sixth Committee' (2006) 49 GYIL 107, 127.

103 Julius Stone, 'The Vocation of the International Law Commission' (1957) 57 ColumLRev 16, 49–51.

104 Hisashi Owada, 'The International Law Commission and the Process of Law-Formation' in *Making Better International Law: The International Law Commission at 50, Proceedings of the United Nations Colloquium on Progressive Development and Codification of International Law* (United Nations 1998) 180. For a critical view on this suggestion, Christian Tomuschat, 'L'Exemple de la Commission du Droit International' in Société Française pour le Droit International (ed), *Colloque d'Aix-en-Provence : La Codification du Droit International* (Pedone 1999) 190.

105 Christopher Pinto, 'The International Law Commission: Methods of Work and Selection of Topics' in *Making Better International Law: The International Law Commission at 50, Proceedings of the United Nations Colloquium on Progressive Development and Codification of International Law* (United Nations 1998) 233–255.

106 For instance, Franz Cede, 'Das künftige Arbeitsprogramm der ILC' in *Völkerrecht zwischen normativem Anspruch und politischer Realität: Festschrift für Karl Zemanek zum 65. Geburtstag* (Duncker & Humblot 1994) 25–43; Tomuschat (n 105) 179–182; Karl Zemanek, 'Codification of International Law: Salvation or Dead End?' in *International Law at the Time of its Codification: Essays in Honour of Roberto Ago*, vol 1 (Giuffrè 1987) 590–596.

107 For instance, Berman (n 102).

this taxonomy is not offered only for descriptive purposes; it will serve some prescriptive purposes as well.

First, we have seen above that in the 19th century, the term codification was largely understood as articulation of a complete code of international law or production of a single-volume code of the entire law of nations. This conception of codification was, among others, influenced by what a leading Japanese commentator perceptively termed "domestic model centrism" in international law. Domestic model centrism means our habit of conceptualizing and evaluating international law based on the (idealized) model of domestic law. When engaging in international law discourse, people "– mostly unconsciously – tend to assume the domestic law of the (modern) state as a frame of reference."[108] Codification in this vein can be called "total codification" or "mega-codification" which, despite the strong support expressed by Spiropoulos and Alfaro at the inaugural session of the Commission, appears not so "realizable" (to use the term employed by the League of Nations). Due to its impracticality, the Commission did not pursue this conception of codification.

Second, now left with the only option of choosing a limited number of topics for codification, the Commission sometimes took up subjects that constitute the very foundation or architecture of international law as a system of law. The Commission's work on the law of treaties, diplomatic relations, State responsibility, and the law of the sea could be adduced as appropriate examples. It would be fair to say that the impact and contribution of the International Law Commission is most strongly felt through its codification efforts in these areas of international law. The 1969 Vienna Convention on the Law of Treaties[109] is accepted by almost all States as "a working statement of the applicable rules by which they can in practice be guided in their international dealings".[110] The International Court of Justice in many contexts treated the provisions of the Vienna Convention as representing a codification of customary international law.[111] The 2001 articles on responsibility of States for internationally wrongful acts,[112] although not adopted as a convention, made a substantial contribution

108 Onuma Yasuaki, *International Law in a Transcivilizational World* (OUP 2017) 2.

109 Adopted 23 May 1969, entered into force 27 January 1980, 1155 UNTS 331.

110 Arthur Watts, *The International Law Commission 1949–1998*, vol 2 (OUP 1999) 613.

111 Ibid. For a list of recent cases of the International Court of Justice where the Court declared certain provisions of the Vienna Convention on the Law of Treaties reflective of customary international law, see Stefan Talmon, 'Determining Customary International Law: The ICJ's Methodology between Induction, Deduction and Assertion' (2015) 26(2) EJIL 417, 437 at footnote 145.

112 UNGA Res 56/83 (12 December 2001), annex.

to the exposition not only of the law of State responsibility itself, but also of fundamental questions relating to the normative structure of international society through their tackling of, among others, serious breaches of obligations arising under peremptory norms of general international law and obligations *erga omnes*. These articles are frequently utilized and invoked by States and other actors of international law. For instance, the International Court of Justice found the provisions of the articles as reflecting customary international law.[113] The 1961 Vienna Convention on Diplomatic Relations[114] is regarded as "a cornerstone of the modern international legal order" by the author of a leading textbook on the subject.[115] In these examples, the Commission can be said to have engaged in "foundational or architectural codification".[116]

Third, the Commission also chose topics that fall under the "special part" of international law. Various topics relating to State succession, jurisdictional immunities of States and their property, nationality including statelessness, protection of persons in the event of disasters, various topics relating to international criminal law, protection of the atmosphere, internationally protected persons and most favoured nation clauses can be adduced as examples. These exercises could be called "thematic codification".

The Commission made a great contribution to the clarification and systematization of international law in these diverse fields, although it has to be admitted that the Commission's work on some topics, for instance, arbitral procedure and most-favoured nations clause, could not be judged to be successful. Some of these topics were selected based on the discussion of the 1949 survey of international law by the Secretary-General,[117] thus constituting rather traditional subjects of international law. Others were selected based on the needs felt by the international community. The Commission's work leading to the adoption of the Convention on the Prevention and Punishment of Crimes

113 For instance, in *Gabčíkovo-Nagymaros Project (Hungary/Slovakia)* [1997] ICJ Rep 7, the International Court of Justice placed reliance on article 33 of the draft articles on the responsibility of States which the Commission adopted on first reading. An extensive overview of recent references by international courts and tribunals to the articles on State responsibility can be found in United Nations, Materials on the Responsibility of States for Internationally Wrongful Acts (United Nations Legislative Series 2012); and United Nations, 'Responsibility of States for internationally wrongful acts. Compilation of decisions of international courts, tribunals and other bodies' (2016) UN Doc A/71/80.

114 Adopted 18 April 1961, entered into force 24 April 1964, 500 UNTS 95.

115 Eileen Denza, *Diplomatic Law: Commentary on the Vienna Convention on Diplomatic Relations* (4th edn, OUP 2016) 1.

116 I acquired the hint for the expression "architectural codification" from the book of Professor Watts. Watts (n 1) 6.

117 ILC (n 65).

against Internationally Protected Persons including Diplomatic Agents[118] is an apt example of the latter type. On the request made by the General Assembly in December 1971, the Commission submitted its draft articles in July 1972.[119] The General Assembly adopted the Convention in December 1973. This showed that the Commission could deal rapidly and successfully with "matters to which the General Assembly ... attached real political urgency".[120]

Fourth, not a small amount of the Commission's work has been devoted to what one could call "complementary or annotative codification". The Commission expanded the scope of application of the 1969 Vienna Convention on the Law of Treaties by producing the draft articles that led to the adoption of the 1986 Vienna Convention on the Law of Treaties between States and International Organizations or between International Organizations,[121] although it is true that the latter Convention contained a number of provisions that reflected the peculiarities of international organizations.[122] The same could be said concerning the 2001 articles on responsibility of States for internationally wrongful acts and the 2011 articles on the responsibility of international organizations, although the latter contain provisions dealing with matters specific to international organizations (for example, articles 61 and 62).[123] The articles on State responsibility, on the one hand, and the two international liability projects ("Prevention of transboundary damage from hazardous activities"[124] and "International liability in case of loss from transboundary harm arising out of hazardous activities"),[125] on the other, can be characterized in a similar way.

118 Adopted 14 December 1973, entered into force 20 February 1977, 1035 UNTS 167.

119 ILC, 'Draft articles on the prevention and punishment of crimes against diplomatic agents and other internationally protected persons' [1972] II ILC Ybk 312.

120 Watts (n 1) 11, 415–417.

121 Adopted 21 March 1986, not yet in force, A/CONF.129/15. See Watts (n 1) 614 ("No work on the law of treaties could be regarded as complete if it did not also deal with treaties to which international organizations were parties.")

122 Professor Rosenne made a rather harsh assessment of this Convention. Rosenne (n 83) 15 ("Much of this is unchanged repetition of provisions already included in the major Vienna Convention on the Law of Treaties of 1969").

123 The complementary character of part five of the 2011 articles on the responsibility of international organizations is indicated in the Commission's commentary. ILC, 'Draft articles on the responsibility of international organizations' [2011] II(2) ILC Ybk 40, 96 (general commentary to part five, para 1: "In accordance with article 1, paragraph 2, the present draft articles are intended to *fill a gap that was deliberately left* in the articles on responsibility of States for internationally wrongful acts.") (emphasis added).

124 ILC, 'Draft articles on prevention of transboundary harm from hazardous activities' [2001] II(2) ILC Ybk 146.

125 ILC, 'Draft principles on the allocation of loss in the case of transboundary harm arising out of hazardous activities' [2006] II(2) ILC Ybk 58.

The Commission engages in what one could term "annotative codification" when it expands on, or further clarifies, some of the provisions or issues that are already regulated by foundational or thematic codifications. When one looks at the analytical guide to the work of the International Law Commission,[126] one is struck by the preponderance of the Commission's work falling under this category. In particular, the "annotative codification" in the law of treaties has been and is quite conspicuous. Reservations to treaties (in addition to the work of the Commission on "reservations to multilateral conventions" which was in the nature of "special assignment" by the General Assembly), subsequent agreements and subsequent practice in relation to interpretation of treaties, provisional application of treaties and peremptory norms of general international law (*jus cogens*) can be adduced. As was pointed out above, "fragmentation of international law: difficulties arising from the diversification and expansion of international law", despite its unique character and format, can be regarded as falling under this category.

Outside the law of treaties, the diplomatic courier and the diplomatic bag not accompanied by diplomatic courier falls within this category. This topic expands on the relevant provisions of the 1961 Vienna Convention on Diplomatic Relations and the 1963 Vienna Convention on Consular Relations.[127] The necessity of the Commission's work on this topic was justified based on the increasing number of violations of the relevant part of the diplomatic and consular law.[128] The Commission's work, based on the recognition that "the rules on [the status of the diplomatic courier and the diplomatic bag] contained in the four codification conventions needed to be further elaborated"[129](thus

126 Available at <http://legal.un.org/ilc/guide/gfra.shtml>.

127 Adopted 24 April 1963, entered into force 19 March 1967, 596 UNTS 261. The primary purpose of the draft articles prepared by the Commission was to "establish a coherent and, in so far as possible, uniform régime governing the status of all kinds of couriers and bags, on the basis of the 1961 Vienna Convention on Diplomatic Relations, the 1963 Vienna Convention on Consular Relations, the 1969 Convention on Special Missions and the 1975 Vienna Convention on the Representation of States in their Relations with International Organizations of a Universal Character". ILC, 'Report of the International Law Commission on the work of its forty-first session' [1989] II(2) ILC Ybk 1, 9 at para 31. While the Special Rapporteur had originally proposed a "global concept of 'official courier and official bag' " (ibid 10 at para 37), the Commission decided to "confine the scope of the articles to diplomatic and consular and courier bags as well as couriers and bags of permanent missions and delegations". ILC, 'Draft articles on the status of the diplomatic courier and the diplomatic bag not accompanied by diplomatic courier and draft Optional Protocols thereto' [1989] II(2) ILC Ybk 14 (commentary to article 1, para 3).

128 [1980] II(1) ILC Ybk 245.

129 ILC report 1989 (n 127) 12 at para 58. Rosenne wondered aloud when he said "But did this [the subject of diplomatic courier and the unaccompanied diplomatic bag] require

confirming the "annotative" nature of the work), was criticized during the debates in the Sixth Committee and in the written observations by some States for the lack of consideration in terms of priority and urgency.[130]

V Lessons to Be Drawn From the Taxonomy of Codification

As mentioned above, the taxonomy of the Commission's codification, which no doubt runs the risk of over-simplification that is compounded by overlap among the different categories, was for "prescriptive" purposes, that is, to help the Commission take stock of its codification efforts extending over 70 years and reaffirm and recalibrate its main function, "the promotion of the progressive development of international law and its codification".

A lesson to be drawn from the taxonomy of the Commission's codification is that it would be desirable to have a proper balance between the different kinds of codification. From the analytical guide to the work of the International Law Commission, one might get the impression that the overall balance is skewed in favour of the annotative codification, in particular, in the law of treaties.

It is often said that the days of codification in the proper (and the grand) sense of the word are over.[131] According to Professor Watts, "the large architectural subjects having been mostly dealt with, the Commission is now inevitably left with more compact items – none the less important for that, although less eye-catching."[132] When one turns one's eyes to the field of "thematic codification", the Commission faces various challenges. Some topics have already been handled by other learned bodies, notably, the *Institut de Droit international* and the International Law Association.

More serious challenges are posed for the Commission in those areas of "thematic codification" where concern is raised over the possible conflict with the ongoing negotiations between States. For instance, when the Commission proposed the topic of protection of the atmosphere, some States (including all

a draft convention running to 32 articles together with two protocols, adopted by the Commission in 1989, only to be buried by the General Assembly [in] 1995?" Rosenne (n 83) 16. For a similar critical view of the draft articles, see Denza (n 115) 204–207.

130 ILC report 1989 (n 127) 9–10 at para 33.

131 McRae (n 3) 87.

132 Watts (n 1) 6. A keen observer of the Commission and a former insider, Mr. Tomuschat, observed in an even darker tone: "Since the structural needs of codification have been largely satisfied after many decades of intense work, the ILC will probably more often have to face up to actual urgencies as legal counsel of the GA." Tomuschat (n 4) 104–105.

permanent members of the Security Council) advised the Commission "not to attempt to codify rules in that area at present".[133] Such a position seems to be based on the view that it is preferable to entrust newly emerging issues of international law to "policy decision at the political level" rather than to legal regulation.[134] The Commission upended such reservations, *inter alia*, by assuring that its work on the topic would not interfere with related political negotiations and that the final outcome of the work on the topic would be a set of draft guidelines.[135] Concern along similar lines was expressed on the topic of crimes against humanity with particular reference to the regulation of the crime by the Rome Statute.[136]

Under the circumstances, it is not surprising that the Commission's substantial workload has been and is devoted to the complementary or annotative codification expanding on its own former "foundational" or "architectural" codification work. Take, for example, the 1969 Vienna Convention on the Law of Treaties. Considering the obvious utility of the work involved (given the primordial importance of treaties in the construction and management of international relations)[137] and the concomitant political, or diplomatic, acceptability, coupled with the firmly established authority of the 1969 Convention, the law of treaties can be said to constitute a kind of "comfort zone" (as far as the selection of topics is concerned) for the Commission.[138]

---

133 Shinya Murase, 'First report on the protection of the atmosphere' (2014) UN Doc A/CN.4/667, 4 at para 3.

134 Judge Owada proposed the concept of "international legislation *de novo*" in addition to codification and progressive development of international law. He is of the opinion that the former is not suitable for consideration by the International Law Commission. Owada (n 104) 174–175.

135 ILC, 'Report of the International Law Commission on the work of its sixty-eight session' (2016) UN Doc A/68/10, 115 at para 168; Murase (n 133) 4 at para 5.

136 Rome Statute of the International Criminal Court, adopted 17 July 1998, entered into force 1 July 2002, 2187 UNTS 3.

137 For instance, the discussion on the topic of reservation to treaties within the Sixth Committee in 1997 and 1998 proves this point. Many delegations pointed out that the 1969 Vienna Convention had some "lacunae" or ambiguities as regards reservations. Thailand (UN Doc A/C.6/52/SR.17, para 36), Germany (ibid para 46), Bahrain (ibid para 50), Australia (ibid para 52), South Africa (ibid para 56), Korea (UN Doc A/C.6/52/SR.22, para 4), Ghana (ibid para 12), Chile (ibid para 36), Russia (ibid para 76), Portugal (UN Doc A/C.6/52/SR.24, para 55), Hungary (UN Doc A/C.6/53/SR.19, para 23), Greece (UN Doc A/C.6/53/SR.22, para 44). The practical usefulness of the topic was also stressed. Indonesia (UN Doc A/C.6/52/SR.17, para 44), United Kingdom (UN Doc A/C.6/53/SR.14 para. 15), Sweden (UN Doc A/C.6/53/SR.17, para 4), Portugal (UN Doc A/C.6/53/SR.20, para 35).

138 Other topics falling within the realm of the law of treaties were approved without much reservation on the part of the General Assembly. Concerning the topic of provisional

Regarding the selection of the Commission's topics, the current snapshot does not seem to be very encouraging. It is often said that the Commission ran out of topics for foundational, structural or architectural codification. In the field of thematic codification lying beyond the complimentary or annotative codification, the Commission has been (and is) constantly warned not to interfere with or derogate from the pre-existing treaties or agreements or overstep into the "legislative" activities which constitutes a jealously guarded realm for the sovereign States. As a result, in this arena of codification, even after a certain topic has been approved for inclusion into the Commission work programme, the room for manoeuvre for the Commission is substantially circumscribed, particularly, in terms of the form or normative density of its final outcome. It is against such a background that the Commission's work tends to be derivative of its former glories (i.e., the architectural codifications) or runs the risk of handling "actual urgencies as legal counsel of the [General Assembly]".[139]

One should hasten to add that this sketchy diagnosis does not intend to underestimate in any way the practical importance and utility of the International Law Commission's work and the acute intellectual and diplomatic challenge this work poses for the Commission. This diagnosis was conducted in order to help devise ways for strengthening the *raison d'être* of a body charged with the function of no less than "promoting the progressive development of international law and its codification". It is difficult to say that Article 13, paragraph 1 (a) was founded on the very idea of "peace through law", but the provision was

application of treaties, there was some skepticism on the merits of the project. For instance, France (UN Doc A/C.6/SR.20, para 48). However, the topic garnered general support from delegations. Czech Republic (UN Doc A/C.6/SR.18, para 69); Austria (UN Doc A/C.6/SR.19, para 4); United Kingdom (ibid para. 7: the consideration of the topic, while valuable, "should not result in a set of draft articles, but rather in a study of the implementation of article 25" of the 1969 Vienna Convention); USA (ibid para 16); Singapore (UN Doc A/C.6/SR.21, para 80). As regards the topics of subsequent agreements and subsequent practice in relation to the interpretation of treaties, aside from the reservation expressed by the USA (UN Doc A/C.6/62/SR.20, para 24:the United States delegate was "not aware of any pressing real-world issues that necessitated consideration of the topic at the present juncture") and the support from Finland (UN Doc A/C.6/62/SR.18, para 40) and Germany (UN Doc A/C.6/62/SR.19, para 28), the delegations refrained from expressing their opinion on the advisability of adopting the topic. This reticence on the part of the delegations stands in contrast to their approach to the other topics suggested for the Commission's future work, such as expulsion of aliens, most-favoured-nations clause and fair and equitable treatment. This reticence can be interpreted as reflective of the largely uncontroversial and increasingly acceptable character of the topics related to the law of treaties.

139 Tomuschat (n 4) 104–105.

adopted in the belief and hope that progressive development and codification of international would contribute to the attainment of the main purpose of the United Nations, i.e. the maintenance of international peace and security.

In connection with (at least, some of) its work, the Commission was keenly aware of the peace-promoting function of international law. For instance, when the Special Rapporteur on State responsibility, Arangio-Ruiz, submitted his seventh report, a member of the Commission thanked him for "his courage in placing the strengthening of the rule of law in international relations before the cold, calculating and selfish realism of the individual interests of States".[140] In debates within the Commission about what finally became article 54 of the articles on State responsibility, the view was expressed that the International Law Commission was engaged in "constructing a system of multilateral public order", going beyond its proper function of codifying the law of State responsibility.[141] I will not conduct a detailed discussion of the thorny question of to what extent (and in what way) the Commission's work is (or should be) geared toward the promotion of peace in international relations.[142] It is beyond doubt that the Commission's work in the nature of complementary or annotative codification will strengthen the fabric of international law by further clarifying or filling the *lacunae* of architectural or foundational treaties. It is also true that as a body whose core function is progressive development and codification of international law (an idea with a long pedigree which had the preservation and promotion of international peace as its point of departure), the Commission can be said to carry out its function in a satisfactory manner when it remains active and effective beyond the realm of complementary or annotative codification, in particular, in the field of foundational or architectural codification.

Given the preponderant view that "the field open for new initiatives has considerably shrunk",[143] how can one come up with ideas for revitalizing the Commission's role in architectural or foundational codification? One way

---

140 [1995] I ILC Ybk 116 at para 47.

141 ILC, 'Report of the International Law Commission on the work of its fifty-second session' [2000] II(2) ILC Ybk 1, 60 at para 365.

142 For a detailed discussion of the connection between the Commission's work (particularly on State responsibility, the law of treaties and the international law of shared natural resources) and the promotion of peace, see Georg Nolte (ed), *Peace through International Law: The Role of the International Law Commission* (Springer 2009). The link between the codification of international law and peace was keenly heeded by an American proponent of the codification of international law. Elihu Root, 'The Codification of International Law' (1925) 19 AJIL 675, 681.

143 Tomuschat (n 4) 78.

would be to call into question this preponderant view. Since the establishment of the International Law Commission 70 years ago, the international community has gone through significant transformations.[144] Even a cursory look at the 1949 survey of international law (and the 1971 survey of international law prepared by the Secretary-General)[145] reminds one of the structural and substantive changes international law has undergone. As examples, the erosion of ontological centrality (even monopoly) of States within the system, the transfiguration in the discourse of sources of international law (e.g., *jus cogens*, "soft law"), the (at least, partial) multilateralization of the law of State responsibility (obligations *erga omnes* as elaborated by article 48 of the 2001 articles on State responsibility) and the emergence of new subject-matters (various environmental questions including global warming, cyber space) can be adduced.

More recent changes that are likely to have an impact on the configuration of international law include, among others, the growing role of non-State actors in the international sphere, the increasing confluence of public and private international law,[146] and the normative pressure exerted by the "global" on a normative system constructed based on the "inter-State". No less importantly, the challenge posed by the "rise" of new powers could lead to the increasing multiplicity of the international legal order,[147] as symbolized by the constructively oxymoronic expression "comparative international law".[148] These transformations carry structural or architectural implications that urge responses

144 In the early 1980's, the United Nations Institute for Training and Research submitted a report making proposals for the improvement of the International Law Commission. It started by pointing out "a change in the environment" as represented by the emergence of new States, advances in science and technology, the urgent need for economic and social development, and the demands of the Third World for greater participation in the management of the system. Mohammed El Baradei, Thomas M Franck and Robert Trachtenberg, *The International Law Commission: The Need for a New Direction* (United Nations Institute for Training and Research 1981) 3–4.

145 [1971] II(2) ILC Ybk 1.

146 For a detailed discussion of these questions, see Alex Mills, *The Confluence of Public and Private International Law* (CUP 2009).

147 Henry Kissinger, *On China* (Penguin Press 2011); Henry Kissinger, *World Order* (Penguin Press 2014) 225. ("But [the Chinese] expect – and sooner or later will act on this expectation – the international order to evolve in a way that enables China to become centrally involved in further international rule making, even to the point of revising some of the rules that prevail.")

148 Anthea Roberts, *Is International Law International?* (OUP 2017); Anthea Roberts, Paul B Stephen, Pierre-Hugues Verdiera and Mila Versteeg (eds), *Comparative International Law* (OUP 2018).

from the body tasked with the progressive development and codification of international law.

If, under the circumstances surveyed above, it is difficult for the Commission to undertake another foundational or architectural codification as it did in the 1950's and 1960's, it would be still possible and desirable for the Commission to "turn foundational or architectural" in the field of thematic, complementary and annotative codification. Actually, the Commission has been doing that in respect of certain topics. The conspicuous "architectural gaze" of the Commission on the topic of State responsibility was mentioned above. Another example are the articles on diplomatic protection.[149] Within the Sixth Committee, many governments heavily criticized the Commission's work on this topic for its tendency to "de-centre" the primordial subject of international law (that is, States). They strongly argued that the conception of the right of diplomatic protection as consecrated by the *Mavrommatis Palestine Concessions* case should remain intact (despite all the changes in international law that took place over the past century),[150] attempting to place the topic of diplomatic protection and that of human rights "in clinical isolation" from each other.[151] The Commission did not blindly incorporate these comments of governments. If it had done so, it would have engaged in a mummification, not codification, of international law. The final outcome of the Commission tries to strike a delicate (even precarious) balance between the traditional, State-centric conception of diplomatic protection and a newly emergent one influenced by the law of human rights.[152] Similar examples can be provided without much difficulty.

The question can be raised whether the Commission as an institution is equipped to handle such evolution. The statute of the Commission has been said to be characterized by "deliberate elasticity".[153] The Commission's responses to a number of challenges for the past seventy years represent an

149 ILC, 'Draft articles on diplomatic protection' [2006] II(2) ILC Ybk 24.

150 For instance, United Kingdom (UN Doc A/C.6/53/SR.14, para 8); Japan (ibid para 20); France (ibid para 32); China (UN Doc A/C.6/53/SR.15, para 52); Italy (ibid para 73); Mexico (UN Doc A/C.6/53/SR.16, para 17); Uruguay (UN Doc A/C.6/53/SR.16, para 96); Spain (UN Doc A/C.6/53/SR.18, para 45); Cuba (ibid para 52); Slovakia (UN Doc A/C.6/53/SR.22, para 32).

151 Mexico (UN Doc A/C.6/53/SR.16, para 18); Uruguay (UN Doc A/C.6/53/SR.16, para 97); Spain (UN Doc A/C.6/53/SR.18, para 46); Slovakia (UN Doc A/C.6/53/SR.22, para 32). For a view that stresses the close connection between diplomatic protection and human rights, see Chile (UN Doc A/C.6/53/SR.14, para 29).

152 ILC, 'Draft articles on diplomatic protection' (n 149) 27 (commentary to article 1, paras 3–4).

153 ILC, 'Survey of International Law in Relation to the Work of Codification of the International Law Commission' (n 65) 15 at para 20.

apt example of evolutionary interpretation of an international document "of continuing duration". One knows well that the Commission of 2018 operates within a substantially changed landscape as compared to the Commission of 1948. The international community, composed of almost 200 States and over seven billion human beings, is destined to undergo a constant change and evolution that inevitably affects the contours and (even) structures of international law. The International Law Commission, whose statute has remained almost unchanged, has no alternative but to resort to an evolutionary interpretation of its constituent instrument, including articulating its understanding of the Commission's core function and role in an evolutionary manner. In so doing, the Commission should make every effort to bring itself up to the honourable task of meeting the normative expectations of the international community as the body for the progressive development and codification of international law.

VI Concluding Remarks

In this contribution, I conducted an overview of the historical evolution of the concept of codification of international law, beginning with Bentham's proposals, leading up to the adoption of the Commission's statute. The overview drew our attention to, among others, the two questions that maintained their relevance throughout the subsequent discussions of codification of international law, i.e. the distinction between codification and legislation (or development) of international law and the diplomatic, or political, character of the work involved. Ideas or concepts having a long pedigree such as codification of international law inevitably end up being composed of different layers of meanings. This was shown by the short analysis of the discussion at the inaugural session of the International Law Commission where members held widely diverging conceptions of codification of international law. The murky state of affairs in 1949, in particular the distinction between progressive development and codification of international law, did not disappear for some time. But the question was addressed by the subsequent practice of the Commission; the two methods have been largely merged into one. This was achieved without amending the relevant provisions of the statute.

In this paper, I ventured a taxonomy of codification discussed or carried out by the Commission. This taxonomy, composed of (i) mega- or total codification, (ii) foundational or architectural codification, (iii) thematic codification, and (iv) complementary or annotative codification, was conducted for prescriptive as well as descriptive purposes. Based on that taxonomy, I hazarded a few suggestions for the strengthening of the role and status of the International Law Commission. The main suggestion is to redress the balance between various categories of codification, particularly in favour of what I termed foundational or architectural codification.

On its seventieth anniversary, the Commission is fully entitled to look back on the past seven decades with a sense of pride. At the same time, this anniversary should provide an opportunity to take stock of its activities up to now and devise some ways to live up to its task mandated by the international community. Such an exercise is necessary in light of some concerns raised on the future role and relevance of the Commission.[154]

In so doing, the Commission may want to remind itself that, despite the inherently diplomatic and political character of codification of international law, the Commission is composed of "persons of recognized competence in international law" serving in individual capacities (even though the individual capacities are not expressly provided for in the statute). In charting the choppy waters through which it has to navigate in the coming decades, the Commission can draw some inspiration and courage from the document that constituted the basis of discussion at the inaugural session of the International Law Commission. In discussing the value of drafts to be produced by the Commission, the author of the document stated as follows:

> They would exercise influence partly as statements of the existing law and partly as pronouncements of what is a rational and desirable development of the law on the subject. They would be at least in the category of writings of the most qualified publicists, referred to in Article 38 of the Statute of the International Court of Justice as a subsidiary source of law to be applied by the Court. Most probably their authority would be considerably higher. For they will be the product not only of scholarly research, individual and collective, aided by the active co-operation of Governments, of national and international scientific bodies, and the resources of the United Nations. They will be the result of the deliberation and of the approval of the International Law Commission. Outside the

154 It was not that long ago that a former member of the Commission mentioned "often-expressed concerns about the relevance of the ILC as an institution for the progressive development of international law and its codification". McRae (n 3) 76. For an exceptionally candid discussion of the same question by a current member of the Commission, see the statement by Professor Murase speaking as a member of the Japanese delegation. UN Doc A/C.6/66/SR.18, para 58 ("In recent years some critics, particularly in academic circles, had been saying that the Commission was useless and should be disbanded.")

sphere of international judicial settlement they will be of considerable potency in shaping scientific opinion and the practice of Governments.[155]

---

155 ILC, 'Survey of International Law in Relation to the Work of Codification of the International Law Commission' (n 65) 16 at para 20. The author is understood to have been Hersch Lauterpacht, who himself became a member of the Commission in 1952, until his election to the International Court of Justice in 1954.

Concluding Remarks by Claudio Grossman Guiloff

In comparing the thought-provoking papers by professors Keun-Gwan Lee and Hajer Gueldich, we see recurrent themes, such as the strengths of the Commission that have kept it relevant for 70 years. Both offer suggestions for how the Commission can modernize its approach to remain effective in light of the evolving landscape of international relations and the transformative effects of globalization. Their reflections on the Commission's work and their suggestions for the future are very informative. At the same time, the fact that these authors chose to focus on separate, although related, aspects of the Commission forced me to think creatively in responding to their concerns. In performing my own analysis of the Commission after 70 years, I considered many of the issues raised by the professors in their papers, but I also considered some issues that have not, in my opinion, been adequately addressed so far. With due appreciation for the issues highlighted by the professors, I believe it would be great to have their learned opinions about three additional topics: the lack of gender balance on the Commission; the current geopolitical environment amidst declining primacy of the rule of law in international relations and the rise of nationalism; and finally, the "human factor" of international law. We would benefit greatly from receiving the perspectives of these professors on the impact these additional developments have on the work of the Commission.

Both contributors discuss the strengths of the Commission that have allowed it to remain relevant and effective within the field of international law. In my opinion, these strengths can be summarized as follows: (1) the Commission's ability to adapt to meet the changing demands of the international community; (2) the diversity of the Commission; and (3) the Commission's independence. Together, these strengths might prove even more valuable in times of dramatic change, such as now.

The first strength I will address is the Commission's adaptability. In his paper,[1] Professor Lee quotes Sir Arthur Watt's evaluation of the Commission after 50 years, writing:

> The extent to which, at the end of the twentieth century, international law is a more mature system of law and its practitioners can regard their

1 Keun-Gwan Lee, 'Recalibrating the Conception of Codification in the Changing Landscape of International Law' in this Section.

© THE UNITED NATIONS, 2021 | DOI:10.1163/9789004434271_029

> subject with self-confidence in its worth is very largely due to the contribution made over the first fifty years of its existence by the International Law Commission.[2]

I believe by quoting this statement, Keun-Gwan Lee is implying a question: Has the Commission been as influential over the past 20 years as it was in its first 50? I believe the answer is "yes." While I believe the Commission's approach has changed, I believe its impact continues to be just as influential. Changes in the way the Commission approaches its work does not mean the value of its work to the international community is any less apparent. As the Spanish poet Jorge Manrique famously said, "todo tiempo pasado fue mejor," or, "all the past time was better." It is important to consider to what extent our reflections on the past work of the Commission are influenced by nostalgia. Given the tense Cold War environment in which many of the Commission's past achievements were realized, I do not believe the international community saw these achievements the same way we do now.[3] It seems that only with hindsight these times appear to have been so golden. The Commission's approach has adapted to fit the needs of its clients – States. The international landscape of today is different than it was 50, or even 20 years ago, and the Commission's approach to its role within that landscape has changed accordingly. While both contributors agree that the historical work of the Commission has tremendously impacted the development of international law and helped stabilize international relations, they also recognize how the Commission's adaptability has enabled it to continue to produce results. In my opinion, when projecting as to the Commission's future, it is important to consider the context within which the Commission's past successes have been achieved, the way the Commission has responded to past challenges, and how the Commission's past experiences have prepared it to face future challenges. We should be careful to view the past successes of the Commission objectively, and in light of their contexts, just as we should be careful not to underestimate the Commission's ability to continue to respond to change.

---

2 Arthur Watts (ed), *The International Law Commission 1949–1998*, vol 2 (OUP 2000) 20.

3 See e.g. the 'Articles Concerning the Law of the Sea' [1956] II ILC Ybk 254, adopted by the Commission in 1956 and eventually becoming the 1982 United Nations Convention on the Law of the Sea (adopted 10 December 1982, entered into force 16 November 1994, 1833 UNTS 3); the 'Draft articles on consular relations' [1961] II ILC Ybk 92, adopted by the Commission in 1961 and becoming the Vienna Convention on Consular Relations (adopted 24 April 1963, entered into force 19 March 1967, 596 UNTS 261); and the 'Draft articles on the law of treaties' [1966] II ILC Ybk 177, adopted by the Commission in 1966 and converted into the Vienna Convention on the Law of Treaties (adopted 23 May 1969, entered into force 17 January 1980, 1155 UNTS 331).

In their papers, the contributors detail the emergence of increasingly global concerns that have traditionally been seen as outside the purview of general public international law, including climate change and the growing influence of non-State actors.[4] Due to these changes, the contributors take note of existing concerns within parts of the international community regarding the Commission's role in developing solutions to these new problems. In his contribution, Keun-Gwan Lee refers to an account of the Commission written by former Commissioner, Donald McRae, which mentioned "a deep-seated uncertainty about the contemporary role of the Commission."[5] While it is important that we continue to evaluate the relevance of all institutions against their designated purpose and their current realities, it is also important to recognize that the existence of challenges or geopolitical tensions in the international community does not necessarily impede the effectiveness of the Commission. In fact, both contributors note the successes of the Commission, even amidst challenges and times of serious tension.[6] As both professors acknowledge, it is undeniable the Commission contributed to the creation of many foundational building blocks of international law, such as the Vienna Convention on the Law of Treaties, the United Nations' Convention on the Law of the Sea, the Vienna Convention on Diplomatic Relations, the articles on responsibility of states for internationally wrongful acts,[7] and the Rome Statute of the International Criminal Court.[8] This body of work is even more noteworthy considering many of these achievements took place during the challenging political times of the Cold War. As Keun-Gwan Lee notes in his paper, the tensions of the Cold War may have, in some respects, contributed to these successes.[9] He refers to an article by Shabtai Rosenne, which explains how the conventions adopted during the Cold War period based on drafts by the Commission entered into force very quickly,[10] whereas later instruments, established as the level of tension began to subside, were more slowly adopted by States.[11] In his paper, Keun-Gwan Lee finds value in the ability of the Commission to find alternative ways to respond to international challenges

4 Hajer Gueldich, 'Challenges of Codification for the International Law Commission in a Changing Landscape of International Law', 289 in this volume, and Lee (n 1) 328.

5 Donald McRae, 'The Interrelationship of Codification and Progressive Development in the Work of the International Law Commission' (2013) 111 JILD 75, 76.

6 Lee (n 1) 331, and Gueldich (n 4) 288.

7 UNGA Res 56/83 (12 December 2001), annex.

8 Adopted 17 July 1998, entered into force 1 July 2002, 2187 UNTS 3.

9 Lee (n 1) 315.

10 Shabtai Rosenne, 'Codification Revisited After 50 Years' (1998) 2 MaxPlanckYrbkUNL 10.

11 Ibid.

when traditional diplomacy is at a stalemate.[12] Quoting the same article by Rosenne, Keun-Gwan Lee suggests the Commission's ability to open new diplomatic channels is "legal diplomacy at its best."[13] The Commission's diplomatic successes during the Cold War may be instructive as the international community evaluates the role of the Commission in today's political climate, and indeed, as the Commission itself works to draw a balance for the future.

The Commission's ability to adapt is also reflected in its approach to codification. Gueldich and Lee addressed the enduring tension concerning the concept of codification and the balance between rigidity and flexibility the Commission has attempted to strike throughout its 70-year history.[14] In his paper, Keun-Gwan Lee vividly lays out the tensions within the concept, which have been present within the Commission since its earliest days. He explains how, at the Commission's first meeting, some members saw the goal of codification as creating a code for all of humankind, while others viewed codification as a more modest exercise requiring a topic-oriented approach.[15] Still, for others, the goal of codification was to promote principles of peaceful coexistence among States with different social and economic systems.

Although "the eventual codification of the entirety of international law" was the goal of many major legal minds at the time of the formation of the Commission, both papers demonstrate the experience of codification within the Commission has diverged from this idea, especially in recent years.[16] As both contributors noted in their papers, much of the later work products of the Commission, beginning with the articles on responsibility of States for internationally wrongful acts, has come from blending the roles of codification and progressive development to construct normative frameworks of law that States can use to navigate international relations, rather than from stipulating strict rules that leave little or no flexibility for tackling new and varied issues.[17] Indeed, it is precisely this dual approach taken by the Commission, enabling it to produce soft law instruments addressing specific topics of concern to the international community, which has proved practically useful to States.

12 Lee (n 1) 315.

13 Rosenne (n 10) 13.

14 Lee (n 1) 315, and Gueldich (n 4) 298.

15 Lee (n 1) 313.

16 The Commission's change in focus is demonstrated by comparing its early work, such as the articles concerning the law of the sea, the draft articles on consular relations, and the draft articles on the law of treaties, with its later work, such as the articles on responsibility of states for internationally wrongful acts, and its current work topics, only one of which, crimes against humanity, is taking the form of an international convention.

17 Lee (n 1) 322, and Gueldich (n 4) 298.

The Commission's ability to transition its focus from hard law instruments to soft law instruments is further explained in an article written by former member of the Commission Christian Tomuschat, which Keun-Gwan Lee refers to in his paper.[18] The article is entitled "The International Law Commission – an Outdated Institution?".[19] Although its title suggests the Commission may have already served its purpose in the progressive development and codification of international law, it is evident, at least in my opinion, that Tomuschat's intention was to show the enduring relevance of the Commission, despite changes in the landscape of international law and international relations since its inception.[20] While Tomuschat's article does not take for granted that the Commission will always have a place in the international legal system, it demonstrates the Commission is capable of adapting its approaches to meet the current demands of the international community. Tomuschat points to the standalone success of the articles on responsibility of States for internationally wrongful acts as an example of the Commission's intentional move away from focusing primarily on developing conventions to creating soft law instruments.[21] He explains the value of the Commission's capacity for adaptation and the power of soft law in international relations, writing:

> It would be erroneous to believe that norm setting by framing "principles" or "guidelines" should be valued as only second-rate. Sometimes, codification in the form of a soft-law instrument may prove as effective or even more effective than a treaty which after its launching receives only a hesitant response from the international community.[22]

This example shows the Commission's ability to reform its approach while remaining true to the heart of its purpose, clarifying and balancing international standards. As both papers suggest, international law is not a fixed normative body, it is constantly developing, and we are currently in a moment of transformation. Indeed, due to the Commission's adaptability, we should be cautious in heeding the criticism by some that the Commission does not have a role to play in the current situation of international relations. Perhaps the experience

18 Lee (n 1) 324.

19 Christian Tomuschat, 'The International Law Commission – An Outdated Institution?' (2006) 49 GYIL 95.

20 Ibid 95–98.

21 Ibid.

22 Ibid 104.

of the Commission shows us we should not so quickly dismiss the relevance of an institution in challenging times.

The second strength of the Commission referred to by both contributors is its diversity. In their papers, both of them refer to the new challenges facing the Commission, the opportunities and added complexities unmasked by globalization, and the increasing heterogeneity within the international community, all of which are transforming and diversifying the landscape of international law. As Gueldich writes in her paper, "[i]t is only natural that the Commission's work would evolve with the legal system it operates in".[23] She goes on to note that the current international landscape is much different than that in which much of international law developed. On a similar note, Lee refers to recent changes in the structure of the international community and the rise of China, which is making it necessary to consider how such a powerful country with different ideas about the use and structure of the international system will impact the international legal order, and by extension, the work of the Commission.[24] While the first few hundred years of international law were dominated by a few powerful States with common interests, the international community of today is represented by States with a variety of interests, legal cultures and ideologies. For international law to continue to be relevant, useful and respected by States, it must reflect the changing composition of the international community and the expansion of the community of States. As the contributors imply in their papers, these developments create opportunities for the Commission to take advantage of its diversity in tackling global issues. In fact, the Commission's diversity has been, and likely will remain, critical to its ability to establish widely-accepted and workable frameworks for addressing the current issues of international law. As Christian Tomuschat wrote in the article mentioned previously:

> The great advantage of the ILC is that it constitutes a body whose composition establishes a fair balance between all of the different regions of the world, and whose members have learned to cooperate with one another in a peaceful and constructive manner. Thus, together with the ICJ, the ILC guarantees that international law remains an effective instrument determining the conduct of all relevant actors in the international field.[25]

23 Gueldich (n 4) 288.
24 Lee (n 1) 328.
25 Tomuschat (n 19) 105.

Social science calls the practice of bringing together different ideas to create more innovative solutions the "edge effect." The term was co-opted from ecologists who discovered the boundaries between different ecosystems boost higher levels of biodiversity because they share qualities of both neighboring systems.[26] These "edges" often contain species not found in the individual systems.[27] In the social science realm, scientists have similarly found that a diversity of viewpoints breeds more creative solutions.[28] The diversity of the Commission can also be viewed as creating a sort of edge effect, where the bringing together of legal experts from diverse legal traditions can lead to more creative, collective solutions to global problems. Additionally, as Hajer Gueldich points out, this type of cooperative approach is necessary because the problems facing the global community today cannot be solved by States acting in isolation.[29] However, the diversity of the Commission could be even stronger, namely in respect to gender equality. I will address this concern later in my remarks.

The final common strength referred to by the contributors is the Commission's independence. The Commission's diversity and adaptability reinforce its crucial role as an independent body during times, such as now, where the political environment shows dramatic change. The Commission has demonstrated a capacity that is not immediately vulnerable to changing and challenging political climates. The Commission's independence does not mean it is disconnected from political realities. Rather, its independence allows it to see past short-sighted political expediency to find enduring, equitable solutions to international issues. In his paper, Keun-Gwan Lee acknowledges that the Commission's position as a subsidiary organ of the General Assembly links it to the political realities of States without handicapping its ability to find solutions.[30] From this point of view, we can see the Commission represents the legal interests of the larger international community, and has, due to the nature of its mandate regarding codification and progressive development of international law, created a space for autonomy and independent action in its quest to promote the role of international law in international relations.

In times like the present, it might be the case that the value of the Commission's independence is especially noticeable. That being said, the competence

26 National Public Radio, 'The Edge Effect' (Hidden Brain 2018) <https://www.npr.org/2018/07/02/625426015/the-edge-effect>.

27 Ibid.

28 Ibid.

29 Gueldich (n 4) 298.

30 Lee (n 1) 329.

for international law is vested with States as the primary subjects of international law. Therefore, for the Commission's work to be effective, it cannot ignore this basic reality and must remain attuned to the political climate in which it operates. It does not advance the position or utility of international law to exaggerate its role in international relations, which are also subject to political, military, and economic concerns. However, international law is critical to harmonizing States' interests, including safeguarding the stability and security of individual States, ensuring peace among States, stabilizing international relations, and channeling demands for adaptation and change.

Considering the current times of change, both papers also refer to the need for the Commission to modernize both its topic selection process and its working methods. While acknowledging existing criticism, by some, of the Commission's choice to study more divisive topics, both papers also acknowledge the importance of the Commission's attention to these issues. The idea that the Commission should not focus on divisive issues has been discussed throughout the Commission's existence. In the papers discussing the Commission's fiftieth anniversary, similar criticisms to those we hear today were lodged in response to the Commission's consideration of topics related to protection of the environment, human rights, and self-determination.[31]

While I believe the Commission must stay apprised of the political realities of the world it operates in, so its work can be useful to States, I also believe the Commission would be neglecting its role in the progressive development and codification of international law if it ignored any topic that might be perceived as problematic. Most issues facing the international community today are in some way controversial. As Hajer Gueldich notes in her paper, globalization is shaping the international order and raising new global issues that cannot be tackled by individual States.[32] Similarly, Keun-Gwan Lee suggests the Commission transition its focus from inter-State topics to global and transnational ones that have more relevance to States today.[33] I agree with these suggestions; part of the Commission's endeavour to remain relevant should involve modernizing its selection of topics. I also believe the Commission should not ignore the role it can play by employing the powerful tradition of international law to contribute to the development of normative concepts acceptable to the international community. The Commission should not shy away from

31 Vaughan Lowe, 'Presentation by Mr. Vaughan Lowe' in United Nations (ed), *The International Law Commission Fifty Years Later: an Evaluation* (United Nations 2000) 134–135.

32 Gueldich (n 4) 289.

33 Lee (n 1) 330.

topics that have a tremendous impact on States and the international community as a whole, such as rights and protections for refugees and internally displaced persons; peace, security, and lawful uses of force; protection of the environment; data security and privacy; and general principles relevant to the conduct of international economic relations. Many of these topic suggestions were also noted in the papers presented by the professors. I believe the writings of the preeminent international jurist, Rosalyn Higgins, regarding the political aspects of law, correctly illustrate the tension the Commission faces in deciding whether to take on controversial, but critically important topics. As Judge Higgins explains, for some, the judicial process is neutral; it is a process of applying objective norms.[34] For others, the judicial process involves values and political consequences.[35] Even if one accepts the non-positive approach to international law, it must be acknowledged that the lines between law and politics are both blurred and interconnected. Politics create a domain in which law can develop. In my opinion, the Commission is strategically positioned to operate within that domain.

In addition to suggesting ways the Commission can modernize its topic selection, both contributors also suggest ways the Commission can modernize its working methods to include new perspectives and ideas. They suggest the Commission work more closely with other international actors and institutions. Keun-Gwan Lee suggests prioritizing the Commission's work and taking into account codification efforts done by other actors – even if they may not have the same legitimacy as the Commission – to ensure the efficient use of the Commission's resources.[36] On the other hand, Hajer Gueldich notes trends in international law towards granting rights and imposing obligations on non-State actors, and therefore advocates for increased cooperation with civil society, NGOs, and technical experts.[37] I very much agree with these suggestions, and believe that by considering the work done by others, we can "open the windows" of the Commission. The role of non-State actors in international law is growing – whether the issue be economic rights, environmental protection, or armed conflict. While States remain the primary subjects and creators of international law, the political, social, and economic realities of the world require enriching the work of the Commission by considering the concerns and opinions of other international actors. In my opinion, both

34 Rosalyn Higgins, *Problems and Process: International Law and How We Use It* (OUP 1994) 2–6.

35 Ibid.

36 Lee (n 1) 324–330.

37 Gueldich (n 4) 295–296 and 298.

papers also suggest that by considering the full spectrum of international actors, the Commission would not in any way be questioning the relevance of States. Instead, considering the opinions and actions of these other actors, and taking into account current political realities, should be seen as a way to enrich the decision making process, and accordingly, the outcomes of the Commission's work.

I will move now to some additional concerns I feel have been unfortunately left out of our discussion so far: the lack of gender balance on the Commission; the decline in support for multilateralism coupled with the rise of nationalism; and the significance of the "human factor" within international law and the Commission's work.

As many here know, in the past 70 years, there have only been seven women elected to the Commission. This figure is extremely concerning, and lags far behind the advancements in gender equality achieved in other areas of international law, international relations, and politics generally. In fact, women represent only 3 per cent of the Commission's membership over its entire 70-year history. If the Commission is going to represent "the main forms of civilization and ... the principal legal systems of the world," as mandated in article 8 of its statute,[38] and truly reflect the international community of States and citizens it serves, States from all regions of the world will need to nominate more women to the Commission and the General Assembly will need to elect more women to the Commission. This likely also means States will need to increase opportunities for women within international law. Judging from the attendance of the panel discussion in Geneva, it is obvious that there is no lack of interest or ability among women in this field. Achieving a more balanced and diverse Commission will help ensure that the Commission's work remains relevant and pertinent to the international community. Gender equality on the Commission should be viewed as equally important to other forms of diversity within the Commission. Gender diversity would contribute to the "catalyst of reason,"[39] created by the joining of diverse perspectives, just as the Commission's diversity of legal cultures and legal backgrounds does. As almost every speaker at our commemoration in New York expressed, we must do more to achieve gender equality on the Commission, and I believe this concern would have deserved more attention from the speakers at our commemoration events in Geneva.

38 Statute of the ILC, UNGA Res 174(II) (21 November 1947) as amended by UNGA Res 485(V) (12 December 1950); UNGA Res 984(X) (3 December 1955); UNGA Res 985(X) (3 December 1955) and UNGA Res 36/39 (18 November 1981).

39 Tomuschat (n 19) 81.

Turning now to my second concern. A few years ago, it seemed the trends of globalization would strengthen international law; however, it is now necessary to revise our optimism. As the President of the International Court of Justice, Abdulqawi Yusuf, stated in his keynote address, the Commission must play a role in responding to threats to the integrity of the multilateral system and continue to promote multilateralism and inclusivity.[40] Responding to these threats is especially important when the role of law itself is at stake. Accordingly, I believe the Commission must pay attention to the current rule of law crisis facing the international community. In recent years, some States have questioned the core institutions and norms at the centre of the international community, as well as the importance of a rule-based order to international relations, including some States that were instrumental in the construction of these institutions and norms. Some States have instead turned to different forms of populism and nationalism, seeking to free themselves as much as possible from the normal constraints on the use of power in international relations. The rise of populism and nationalism, the erosion of settled law prohibiting the use of force in resolving disputes, and the general decline in the appreciation and observance of international law, cannot be ignored. Just as when the Commission was established 70 years ago, our world is facing challenges no State can address or solve alone. International cooperation on these issues is imperative. Political bodies, such as the Security Council, have failed to act in even the most appalling humanitarian circumstances, both historically, as in the cases of Kosovo and Rwanda, and currently, as in the cases of Syria and Myanmar. Similarly, the European Union has so far failed to adequately address the threats of populism and judicial corruption in certain member States, and these ideologies continue to spread, both in Europe and in other parts of the world, including the United States. Political scientist Joseph Nye has explained the Trump administration's approach to international affairs saying, in effect, that the administration has replaced the nation's former soft power, cooperative approach, with a hard power approach, focused on coercion and military might.[41] Hopefully, the international community can find ways to utilize legal institutions, like the Commission, to address these issues through international law and avoid the devastating catalytic events that have historically been required to motivate united action.

---

40 See the keynote address by Abdulqawi Yusuf in Section 9 of this volume.

41 Joseph S Nye, 'Donald Trump and the Decline of US Soft Power' *Project Syndicate* (6 February 2018) < https://www.project-syndicate.org/commentary/trump-american-soft-power-decline-by-joseph-s--nye-2018-02>.

Needless to say, these are concerning political trends that could have serious impacts on the international community, and on the concept of international law itself, which purports to establish agreed norms applicable to all. Even while we have seen some major players in the multilateral system retreat from their historically prominent positions, we have seen increases in activism by other States as well as citizen and local level engagement across many areas. We have seen movements around the globe mobilizing for change. For example, the Women's Marches around the World in 2017 and 2018,[42] and United States' corporations, states, and cities pledging to do their part to meet greenhouse gas emission reduction commitments under the Paris Agreement,[43] despite the Trump administration initiating a United States exit from the agreement.[44] We have seen local and city governments, businesses, and citizens innovating new solutions to local and global issues. While these developments cannot be exaggerated, they also cannot be ignored, as they have the ability to impact international relations. The Italians have an expression "chiaroscuro" – clear and dark at the same time – and current times, with all their complexity, show us the validity of this apparently contradictory concept. The Commission has a role to play in preserving and advancing the international commitment to a rule-based order that ensures and protects the rights of all States and individuals equally.

As both contributors suggest, these international developments leave a space for the Commission, as a body of independent experts, in touch with political realities, but not locked into specific and narrow political options, to objectively promote the development of international law for the benefit of humankind. While reading the papers, I thought of the value of the process, and the value of the effort itself. To quote the famous author, Miguel de Cervantes, in the crucial work of Spanish literature, *Don Quixote*, "mejor el camino

42 The 2017 Women's Marches in the US were likely the largest single day demonstration in US history, with as many as 5.2 million people participating in the US and over 300,000 people participating in at least 261 marches abroad. See Erica Chenoweth and Jeremy Pressman, "This is What we Learned by Counting the Women's Marches" *The Washington Post* (Washington, 7 February 2017) < https://www.washingtonpost.com/news/monkey-cage/wp/2017/02/07/this-is-what-we-learned-by-counting-the-womens-marches/?noredirect=on&utm_term=.1a4551ef0971>.

43 Adopted 12 December 2015, entered into force 4 November 2016, UNTS registration no 54113.

44 See e.g. the "We Are Still In" coalition is an organization made up of over 1,000 United States' CEOs, governors, and mayors pledging commitment to the Paris Agreement on climate change. See Mythili Sampathkumar, 'US Cities and Companies Declare "We Are Still in" Paris Agreement Despite Trump' *The Independent* (London, 10 November 2017) <https://www.independent.co.uk/news/paris-agreement-trump-us-cities-still-in-defiance-coalition-a8047086.html>.

que la posada" or "better the road than the inn." There is value in the process of preserving a way of thinking, a methodology. There is value in keeping and developing a space for legal reasoning, a space for discussion based on the common language of international law. We need to talk about these serious issues. We need to create space and keep space for strengthening the validity of the rule of law. In my opinion, the Commission has a major role to play in maintaining and developing the rule-based order of international relations, and that role is critically important in the current political environment.

This common narrative of international law has expanded due to interdependence, and as both professors have written, we cannot solve problems facing humankind solely through actions by individual States. As stated by Judge Álvarez in his dissenting opinion in the International Court of Justice advisory opinion on the *Effect of Awards of Compensation made by the United Nations Administrative Tribunal*:

> The *social* character of the international law of today is a result of the new *regime of inter-dependence* which has emerged and which tends to replace the traditional *individualistic* regime. Having regard to this social character, what may be called the new international law is particularly concerned with the maintenance of peace and the development of confidence and cooperation between States; it assigns an important place to the general interest and condemns *abus du droit*; it also has a new aim: the well-being of the individual and of society.[45]

Finally, I believe one other important topic has been absent here: the "human factor." Much of what happens in the world depends on human behavior, on leadership, on how things happen. When he was asked what we should expect in the 21st-century, Nobel Prize winning author, Gabriel Garcia Marquez, said we should not expect anything just because we are entering a new century. The most relevant things that have happened to us are the result of individuals imagining them before they became reality. This was, for example, the case with Beethoven's ninth symphony and heart transplants. These achievements began in the minds of their creators; they were imagined before they happened.

As we face the conditions of our time, we should remember that we are not mere spectators, but rather subjects in these events; and, in order to promote the change we wish to see, we need to imagine our contribution to the development of international law and translate what we imagine into action.

45 [1954] ICJ Rep 47, 70.

SECTION 7

The Authority and the Membership of the Commission

Opening Remarks by Djamchid Momtaz

During the final panel organized as part of the ceremonies to commemorate the seventieth anniversary of the International Law Commission, held on the theme "The authority and the membership of the Commission in the future", the remarks made and the debates inspired by the organizers' questions mainly addressed two matters: the criteria States should apply when choosing the candidates submitted to the General Assembly for election to the Commission's members and the respect for those criteria shown by voting States; and the improvement of the Commission's working methods to strengthen its efficiency in order to ensure that its efforts in the codification and progressive development of international law receive the broadest possible support of Member States. These matters are closely related inasmuch as the competence and mastery in international law of the members of the Commission are the best measure of its success.

1 The Composition of the International Law Commission

Pursuant to article 2 its statute, the members of the Commission shall be of "recognized competence in international law", the curricula vitae of the nominated candidates that States send to the Secretary-General of the United Nations constituting the irrefutable proof that that condition has been fully met. As required by the statute, when voting in the General Assembly States shall bear in mind that the persons to be elected to the Commission should individually possess the qualifications required and that in the Commission as a whole representation of the main forms of civilization and of the principal legal systems of the world should be assured. It has been rightly argued that the eminently political nature of the General Assembly has sometimes subjected the choice of candidates to political considerations at the expense of those criteria and at the risk of undermining the harmonious functioning of the Commission.

Due note was also made of certain factors that should be taken into account when applying those criteria to guarantee the efficiency of the Commission. Mention was made of the need to ensure that there was an adequate balance between men and women among the members of the Commission, a better generational representation of jurists and an improved balance among legal practitioners and those from an academic background. There was no doubt as

 | DOI:10.1163/9789004434271_030

to the relevance and usefulness of these observations regarding areas in which there were widely diverging rates of achievement.

II The Working Methods of the International Law Commission

One of the questions the organizers asked the panel participants that was not, unfortunately, debated was related to the means of avoiding the pitfalls for the Commission in the decade to come. Adding unsuitable topics would undoubtedly be one of the obstacles the Commission should avoid. It has always been aware of the importance of the issue. That was demonstrated by the cumulative criteria to be fulfilled, established by the Commission in 1997 and that remain valid, in the choice of new topics: the topic chosen should reflect the needs of States, be at a sufficiently advanced stage in terms of State practice to permit progressive development and codification, and be a feasible subject for consideration by the Commission.[1] Failure to comply with any of the criteria, as past experience has shown, could lead the Commission to abandon a topic on its programme of work or to work on draft articles that were stillborn and buried by States. Respecting the criteria obviously should not prevent the Commission, as it had stated at the time, from considering adding to its programme of work topics reflecting new trends and concerns of the international community as a whole, which are the Commission's lifeblood.

The role of the General Assembly in the selection of topics was addressed by the Commission. It depends, however, on continuous and constructive dialogue between the General Assembly and the Commission, a recurrent issue that has yet to find a satisfactory solution. Despite this failure, the Commission's work is, on the whole, seen in a positive light by both States and international bodies. At the international level, successive compilations by the Secretary-General of the United Nations of the decisions of international courts and other international organizations show that the Commission's articles on responsibility of States for internationally wrongful acts,[2] adopted by the Commission in 2001,[3] at least those articles codifying customary international law, frequently serve as references. In such conditions, nothing would prevent the Commission from continuing to be of use in the interest of the international community of States as a whole in the years to come.

1 ILC, 'Report of the Commission to the General Assembly on the work of its forty-ninth session' [1997] II(2) ILC Ybk 72 at para 238.

2 See UNGA, 'Report of the Secretary-General', UN Doc A/62/62, UN Doc A/65/76, UN Doc A/68/72 and UN Doc A/71/80.

3 ILC, 'Draft articles on responsibility of States for internationally wrongful acts' [2001] II(2) ILC Ybk 26.

The International Law Commission and the International Law Codification Market

Zuzana Trávníčková

I Introduction

There must be hundreds of university teachers of international law around the world, and I am one of them. I am teaching students at the University of Economics in Prague. Some of them head into national or international business or media, some become diplomats, others start their career at a ministry of foreign affairs or in international institutions. My aim is to introduce them to international law, visualize and explain the mechanisms of creation and application of international rules and principles, as well as of peaceful settlement of disputes, and also to provide them with some orientation among the many institutions in the "international law universe". My students, on the other hand, bring into our discussions in lectures and seminars their fresh, young look at different international legal topics and confront me with their knowledge from other courses. Compared to students pursuing a law degree, our students have a blurrier awareness of how legislation and the law work. In their deliberations about current international events, they are not restricted by such knowledge and that is why their arguments and views may be sometimes naïve and sometimes inspiring. I was thinking about my students often when I was preparing this presentation and I am very grateful for all the opinions and ideas about international law that they were willing to "trade" with me and that ultimately led me to the idea of the international law codification market.

Let me introduce this market, identify trends concerning it and formulate a few predictions. Further, this contribution will touch on other questions (e.g. the composition of the International Law Commission) discussed during the celebration of the Commission's seventieth anniversary event in Geneva in July 2018.

II Economics and International Law

Building bridges between economics and international law is not a new idea. However, economic issues seem to be more attractive for international lawyers than international law as a subject of study for economists. Whereas

DOI:10.1163/9789004434271_031

international economic law represents a developed and established field of public international law, there are only few attempts to apply economic perspectives to international law. Alan O. Sykes,[1] Andrew Guzman[2] and Eric A. Posner[3] can be mentioned as leading authors providing economic analysis of international law. Jeffrey L. Dunoff and Joel P. Trachtman present an analogy between the market of international relations and the traditional markets for goods.[4] The aim of the following text is to contribute to this discussion by applying simplified market theory to the codification of international law.

III The International Law Codification Market

Markets may be differentiated by many criteria: by geographic extension of the market, intensity of speculation, legality of exchange, volatility of the market or by products or factors sold. Codification of international law is not a good, but it could be understood as a service. It is a very special service, it demands deeply specialized knowledge and it has a very special clientele. Clients are paying not with money, but with recognition of the International Law Commission's legitimacy and respect. There is no free and fully competitive market of international law codification, but it is some kind of market, because there is an international law codification demand and – on the other side – the international law codification supply. The following text focuses on three characteristics of the market: on the codification of international law as the service offered, on the International Law Commission as the leading supplier and on States as demanders.

IV Codification as a Service on the Market

In this contribution, codification is discussed as a service and understood in a simplified way as the preparation of draft conventions. There is one fundamental question that must discussed before we approach the virtual codification

1 Alan O Sykes, 'The Economics of Public International Law' (2004) John M. Olin Program in Law and Economics Working Paper No. 216 <https://pdfs.semanticscholar.org/d48b/dff047413c0485d876a5f6e67cb522760d67.pdf>.

2 Andrew Guzman and Alan O Sykes, 'Economics of International Law' in Francesco Parisi (ed), *The Oxford Handbook of Law and Economics* (OUP 2017).

3 Eric A Posner (ed), *Economics of Public International Law* (Elgar 2010).

4 Jeffrey L Dunoff and Joel P Trachtman, 'Economic Analysis of International Law' (2004) 24(1) YaleJIntlL 1.

market where draft articles for possible future conventions are offered. Is the codification of international law a type of service that can be "sold and bought" or is it a service comparable to a public good? Pure public goods are not traded in markets, because they are supplied to the community as a whole and without direct charge being paid for the good. This is why the (profit-oriented) private sector is not willing to produce and supply them. The production and allocation of public goods is not determined by the market but by the political process.[5] Public goods create market failures because they cannot be allocated by the market mechanism. If codification is a public good, then it is useless to construct any market for it.

There are different ways to distinguish between private and public goods, mainly by testing the excludability/non-excludability and rivalry/non-rivalry of consumers and the possibility of consumers to reject/avoid the good.[6] Pure public goods are non-excludable and non-rivalrous, and their consumption is non-rejectable.[7] Regular examples of public goods include lighthouses, street lighting, flood control system or national defence. Academic literature has made different efforts to classify law,[8] natural law,[9] international law,[10] the international law "liability" system,[11] enforcement of international environmental agreements,[12] and law enforcement in the penal system[13] or in general[14] as

5 Vicky Allsopp, *Understanding Economics* (Routledge 2006) 129.

6 Ibid. See also Yew-Kwang Ng, *Welfare Economics: Towards a More Complete Analysis* (Palgrave Macmillan 2004) 165.

7 Finn R Førsund, 'Allocation in Space and Environmental Pollution' (1972) The Swedish Journal of Economics 19; Clara S Haignere, 'Closing the Ecological Gap: the Public/Private Dilemma' (1999) 4(14) Health Education Research 507; Stephen J Bailey, *Public Sector Economics: Theory, Policy and Practice* (Macmillan International Higher Education 1995) 30.

8 Tyler Cowen, 'Law as a Public Good: The Economics of Anarchy' (1992) 8(2) Economics and Philosophy 249; David D Friedman, 'Law as a Private Good: A Response to Tyler Cowen on the Economics of Anarchy' (1994) 10(2) Economics and Philosophy 319.

9 Peter Wivel, 'The State and The Citizen Natural Law as a Public Good' in Erik A Andersen and Birgit Lindsnaes (eds), *Towards New Global Strategies: Public Goods and Human Rights* (Martinus Nijhoff 2007) 3.

10 Thomas Gammeltoft-Hansen, 'Does International Refugee Law Still Matter?' (2016) Migration and Citizenship: "Newsletter of the American Political Science Association: Organized Section on Migration and Citizenship <connect.apsanet.org/s43/wp-content/uploads/sites/13/2017/06/APSACitizenshipMigrationNewsletter_42_final.pdf>.

11 Dunoff and Trachtman (n 24) 26.

12 Tseming Yang, 'International Treaty Enforcement as a Public Good: Institutional Deterrent Sanctions in International Environmental Agreements' (2006) 27 MichJIntlL 1131.

13 Randall Kennedy, 'The State, Criminal Law, and Racial Discrimination: A Comment' (1993) 107 HarvLRev 1255.

14 Mark Gradstein, 'Governance and growth' (2004) 73(2) JDevEcon 505, 518.

a public or a common good; however, the overall conclusions are ambiguous. But even if we had conclusive knowledge of the public/private nature of the law as a good, we could not apply it to codification of law as such.

When we look at the codification of international law as a service offered to States, we can test its characteristics in the light of excludability, rivalry and rejectability. As was said already, the drafting of conventions is a very special service. For purposes of this contribution, codification is understood in the wider sense of the term and covers both activities defined in article 16 of the statute of the International Law Commission,[15] i.e. not only the "more precise formulation and systematization of rules of international law"[16] but also as their progressive development.

The international community's efforts to codify international rules started in the 19th century[17] and are today embodied in Article 13, paragraph 1, of the Charter of the United Nations. The provision entrusts the General Assembly with initiating studies and making recommendations for the purpose of "promoting international co-operation in the political field and encouraging the progressive development of international law and its codification". Since the codification of international law is geared towards international co-operation, it fulfils the economic condition of non-excludability. Codification as a service is non-excludable by its very nature. With regard to the second condition of a public good, the non-rivalry of States in relation to codification drafts is obvious, States are regularly invited and called upon to sign, ratify or accede to multilateral international treaties (especially during the Treaty Events organized by the Secretary-General of the United Nations since 2001), regardless of whether their representatives participated in the preparation of the draft articles for those treaties.

Nevertheless, testing the third characteristic of public goods – non-rejectability – leads to the conclusion that the codification of international law is not a pure public good, because States – as consumers – may reject/avoid the offered product. In practice, we typically do not witness the direct or open rejection of the International Law Commission's outcomes; however States express their different views regarding the draft articles produced by the Commission in the Sixth Committee of the General Assembly. Moreover,

---

15 Statute of the ILC, UNGA Res 174(II) (21 November 1947) as amended by UNGA Res 485(V) (12 December 1950); UNGA Res 984(X) (3 December 1955); UNGA Res 985(X) (3 December 1955) and UNGA Res 36/39 (18 November 1981).

16 Ibid article 15.

17 On the history of the codification movement, see keynote address by Nico Schrijver in Section 8 of this volume.

States may adopt the draft articles in the form of a treaty, they may sign and ratify or accede to the treaty, or they may choose to do none of the above. Due to their sovereignty, States cannot be forced and are not obliged to accept draft articles prepared by the International Law Commission or other institutions. The Vienna Convention on the Representation of States in their Relations with International Organizations of a Universal Character,[18] which was adopted in 1975 and is still not in force, may be mentioned as an example of avoiding the outcome of the Commission's codification effort. Codification of international law as a service is non-excludable and not-rivalrous, but it can be rejected; then it can be concluded, that as a non-public good, the codification can be studied as a service supplied and demanded on the market.

Looking more closely at the market, several forms of output of the codification service may be identified. The most visible ones are drafts of multilateral conventions prepared by the International Law Commission (article 20 of its statute). Ideally, these drafts are accepted by the General Assembly and/or States, adopted in the form of a treaty which is widely ratified by States. The Commission may also complete its work on a topic (e.g. State responsibility for internationally wrongful acts in 2001,[19] or status of the diplomatic courier and the diplomatic bag not accompanied by the diplomatic courier in 1989)[20] and submit it to the General Assembly, without the adoption of a binding treaty. Other forms of outcomes include declarations, resolutions and model laws.[21] In addition, final or interim reports elaborated by a Special Rapporteur, a working or a study group represent an important outcome of the Commission, although it must be added that those products are not mainly used by States (as the leading demanders) but by international judicial institutions and scholars.

Since 2000 (exactly, when the topic "Fragmentation of international law: difficulties arising from the diversification and expansion of international law" was included in the Commission's long-term programme of work)[22] an inside-driven development in the methods of work at the Commission can be

---

18 Adopted 14 March 1975, not yet in force, UN Doc A/CONF.67/16.

19 ILC, 'Draft articles on responsibility of States for internationally wrongful acts' [2001] II(2) ILC Ybk 26.

20 ILC, 'Draft articles on the status of the diplomatic courier and the diplomatic bag not accompanied by diplomatic courier and draft optional protocols thereto' [1989] II(2) ILC Ybk14.

21 Pemmaraju Sreenivasa Rao, 'International Law Commission (ILC)' *Max Planck Encyclopedia of Public International Law* (March 2017) <opil.ouplaw.com/home/EPIL>, para 27.

22 ILC, 'Report of the International Law Commission on the work of its fifty-second session' [2000] II(2) ILC Ybk 1, 131 at para 729.

observed.[23] A new approach[24] emerged to topics that are of significant theoretical or practical importance – but not suitable for codification in international conventions, such as "Fragmentation of international law", "Peremptory norms of general international law (*jus cogens*)" or "Identification of customary international law". These topics go beyond the narrow mandate of preparing a draft treaty. These topics may be difficult for States to handle because their representatives tend to be more practical and problem-oriented. Lawyers working at ministries of foreign affairs would probably not have the time to study the historical background and theoretical aspects of the problem and might also be constrained by the foreign policy of their government. By preparing outcomes other than a draft treaty, the International Law Commission has thus found a new and innovative product to offer.

V The International Law Commission as the Supplier of Codification

The International Law Commission can be perceived as one of the main and the leading suppliers of international law codification. It is difficult to imagine what international law would look like without the International Law Commission. Of course, States have a lot of negotiating capacity and could have devoted it to the law of treaties, to diplomatic and consular law, to the succession of states and other topics, but would they have done so? Shortly after the International Law Commission was established in the late 1940s, the air in the international community was filled with political and ideological tensions. In the 1950s, political and economic relations between the two blocs of power were frozen or openly hostile. But still, there was a demand for treaties, expressed by States especially since the end of the First World War and not fully satisfied by the League of Nations and the Committee of Experts for the Progressive Codification of International Law. The Commission as a supplier was very active, worked hard on crucial legal topics and prepared several drafts of very successful (measured by the number of State parties) treaties in the

---

23 For a discussion of the Commission's methods of work, see the contributions in Section 4 of this volume.

24 The report of the International Law Commission in 2000 mentions only two previous Commission efforts (reservations to multilateral treaties in 1950 and participation of new States in certain general multilateral treaties in 1962, concluded under the auspices of the League of Nations), when the ILC was working on a topic with a plan to present a study, without an ambition to present draft articles as a basis for a future international convention. ILC (n 22) 149.

1950s and 1960s. The Vienna Conventions on Diplomatic Relations of 1961,[25] on Consular Relations of 1963[26] and on the Law of Treaties, adopted by States in 1969,[27] are the brightest examples.

Later, when relations in the international community became more constructive, the ability of States to co-operate did not replace the need for a professional and specialized codification body. Besides, the International Law Commission had demonstrated that codification through a specialized legal organ is not only possible, but also effective. The failure of the League of Nations codification efforts had been overcome. The International Law Commission's position in the market became firm, undisputable, and also unique.

Why is the International Law Commission unique? The first answer is its authority. First of all, the Commission has formal authority based on the way it was created and the Commission's position in the United Nations system. The members of the International Law Commission are elected by the General Assembly, the Commission's reports are regularly discussed in the Sixth (Legal) Committee of the General Assembly, and in Switzerland, members of the Commission enjoy the privileges and immunities to which the judges of the International Court of Justice and the heads of missions accredited to international organizations in Geneva are entitled.[28] But besides this formal authority, there is also another form of authority that may be called "professional authority" and that is not bestowed but must be earned. Although not every draft prepared by the International Law Commission is subsequently transformed into a treaty, the list of conventions based on the International Law Commission drafts is still very impressive.

The second answer is the composition of the International Law Commission. Article 2 of the Commission's statute requires that the members of the Commission are persons of recognized competence in international law and that they must be nationals of different States. According to article 8, the composition of the Commission as an organ should represent the main forms of civilization and of the principal legal systems of the world, and a defined number of seats is assigned to each of the regional groups.[29] When my students look at the picture of Commission members on the Commission's website, the first thing they notice is the disproportion between the number of women and

25 Adopted 18 April 1961, entered into force 24 April 1964, 500 UNTS 95.
26 Adopted 24 April 1963, entered into force 19 March 1967, 596 UNTS 261.
27 Adopted 23 May 1969, entered into force 27 January 1980, 1155 UNTS 331.
28 ILC, 'Report of the Commission to the General Assembly on the work of its thirty-first Session' [1979] II(2) ILC Ybk 1, 8 at para 12.
29 UNGA Res 36/39 (18 November 1981), para 3.

men. They express their disapproval and say that "it is not fair" to have more male than female members. We then read articles 2, 8 and 9 of the Commission's statute together and discuss the election process for members of the Commission. We discuss who is "responsible" for the small number of women in the International Law Commission. It is neither the Commission itself nor is it the statute. Candidates are nominated by States and elected by the General Assembly (except for cases of casual vacancies under article 11 of the statute). Our partial conclusion usually is that amending the statute to introduce a quota for women would not be helpful. And there is a question hidden behind this reasoning. Is it wrong, or is it a real problem, that there are less women than men? It would be wrong if women were excluded from membership. It would be a problem, when the feminine attitude to international law would be something else than the masculine one and as a result, the small number of women would influence the quality of commission outcomes. However, my students and I are not able to answer those hidden questions. So we usually conclude that knowledge of and attitude towards international law are a matter of expertise and experience and not a matter of gender, and that the natural development in this question does not require any formal interference.

There is one more argument supporting the strength of the International Law Commission in the codification process: the Commission's capacity to deal with international affairs comprehensively, to provide a wide range of services. The agenda of the Commission since its inception has been very colourful, and its members enjoy quite interesting (of course not unlimited) freedom to propose new topics. The Commission may not only provide different forms of outcomes (drafts of multilateral treaties, reports, studies), but also, from the material point of view, it may focus on any topic that relates to public (and theoretically private) international law.

Does that mean that there is no competition in the market of codification of international law and that the International Law Commission has the monopoly? Definitively not. As Sir Arthur Watts stated, the International Law Commission "is not the exclusive vehicle for the codification and progressive development of international law".[30] Watts further gives a list of other codification endeavours that includes the General Assembly, conferences convened by the United Nations, the United Nations Commission on International Trade Law (UNCITRAL), the Human Rights Committee, the International Committee of the Red Cross, the Organization for Economic Co-operation and Development

---

30 Arthur Watts, 'Codification and Progressive Development of International Law', *Max Planck Encyclopedia of Public International Law* (December 2006) <opil.ouplaw.com/home/EPIL>, para 23.

(OECD), the Hague Conference on Private International Law and academic institutions such as the International Law Association or Institute for the Unification of Private Law (UNIDROIT).[31] The codification of international law is thus carried out by many institutions, which can be classified by their scope of operation (their specialization on public or private international law, international trade law, international economic law or human rights), on the one hand, and by their "distance" from States, on the other hand.

Although this codification environment looks very competitive, in fact the general or specialized focus of every supplier ensures sufficient space for operation for all of them. In the advisory opinion on *Reparation for Injuries Suffered in the Service of the United Nations*, the International Court of Justice argued that "[t]he subjects of law in any legal system are not necessarily identical in their nature or in the extent of their rights, and their nature depends upon the needs of the community".[32] The establishment of the International Law Commission, the United Nations Commission on International Trade Law and other intergovernmental codification institutions was in every case motivated by the concrete and topical need of the international community to cover a smaller or bigger part of the codification demand. On the one hand, the finding that States as demanders (at least partially) determine the group of suppliers is definitely contrary to the rules of the free market and challenges the argument made in this contribution; on the other hand, it confirms that there is no natural competition between actors participating in the codification of international law.

In a model market, several variables influence suppliers: the price of a good/ service, input prices, technology, expectations and the number of sellers. The number of suppliers and input prices play no role for sellers on the international law codification market. Assessment of the influence of technology on the Commission's activity is beyond the focus of this contribution. The price of a service is not expressed in money, but in the legitimacy of the International Law Commission. In the short-term, the price – legitimacy – does not matter. But in the long-term, the Commission must be sure to obtain and retain enough legitimacy for its existence and activities. Measuring the legitimacy of political institutions and international institutions is an attractive challenge for scholars in political studies;[33] however, this contribution does not

---

31 Ibid paras 23–26.

32 *Reparation for Injuries Suffered in the Service of the United Nations* (Advisory Opinion) [1949] ICJ Rep 174, 178.

33 Tetsuo Sato, 'Legitimacy of International Organizations and their Decisions: Challenges that International Organizations Face in the 21st Century' (2009) 37 *Hitotsubashi Journal of Law and Politics* 11; Mark C Suchman, 'Managing Legitimacy: Strategic and Institutional

apply any of the proposed models (based mainly on comparative qualitative-quantitative analysis) and approaches legitimacy more generally.

Legitimacy as a belief in the International Law Commission can be understood as depending on the workload of the Commission. Whether the International Law Commission identifies topics for codification by itself (and obtains the General Assembly's approval), or it receives special assignments by the General Assembly, which should be given priority according to article 18, paragraph 3, of the Commission's statute, in both situations the demand confirms the legitimacy of the Commission. The legitimacy is closely linked to expectations (on the side of supply as well as on the side of demand). Suppliers' expectations are expressed by the reports of the Commission's Planning Group, and States voice their expectations by accepting the Commission's programme of work.

VI States as the Main Demanders of Codification

Codification in the wider sense covers both aims contained in article 15 of the Commission's statute, "the preparation of draft conventions on subjects which have not yet been regulated by international law or in regard to which the law has not yet been sufficiently developed in the practice of States" as well as "the more precise formulation and systematization of rules of international law in fields where there already has been extensive State practice, precedent and doctrine". The terms "conventions", "States" and "State practice" used in the quotations above illustrate the crucial role of States in the creation of international law. Other provisions of the statute support the position of States as influential demanders; e.g. article 21, paragraph 2 grants them possibility to comment on International Law Commission's drafts and article 23 enables the General Assembly (an organ composed of States representatives) to refer drafts back to the Commission for reconsideration or redrafting.

There are also other actors interested in products of the codification of international law, namely international courts and tribunals, domestic courts, other codification bodies, legal advisers of international organizations, and the academy. However, their buying power and demand seems to be quite weak in comparison to States and it is more accurate to speak of them as consumers rather than demanders.

Approaches' (1995) 20(3) Academy of Management Review 571; Ian Hurd, 'Legitimacy and Authority in International Politics' (1999) 53(2) *International Organization Journal* 379.

The International Law Commission, as a subsidiary organ of the General Assembly, presents its work to the General Assembly, which means to all Member States of the United Nations. According to article 23, paragraph 1, of its statute, the Commission may recommend to the General Assembly to take note of or adopt the Commission's report by resolution, recommend a draft for adoption as a convention, or suggest the convening of a diplomatic conference for that purpose.[34] However, the verb "recommend" used in the introductory sentence of article 23 expresses clearly the position of the International Law Commission in relation to the General Assembly and Member States of the United Nations. By submitting the final draft with commentaries (according to article 22 of the Commission's statute), the work of the International Law Commission is completed and the future of the draft lies in the hands of General Assembly and Member States.

The International Law Commission studies topics and prepares draft articles, States adopt them as or use them as a basis to negotiate treaties. States obtain and use draft articles as the final product of the Commission's work. The fact that States do not act unilaterally, but use a multilateral channel – the General Assembly and its Sixth Committee – does not weaken the importance of States as actors in international legislation. It is sovereign States that nominate candidates, elect the members of the International Law Commission, may influence, through their comments and observations, the contents of the Commission's reports and decide the fate of the Commission's outcomes. The relationship between the International Law Commission and States respects the universal logic of international law as a set of rules created by States as the only holders of normative power. Of course, the influence of other actors should not be omitted, but in the field of general international law, it is not as visible as in human rights, humanitarian law or environmental protection.

Demanders on the ideal market make their decisions under the influence of many factors. They consider the price of goods/services, their income, prices of related goods/services, tastes, expectations and the overall number of buyers.[35] The international law codification market is not a market of that kind. Prices and income do not matter here, and the number of buyers is not important, because they are not competing for codification as a scarce service – draft articles are available for every State. "Tastes" and "expectations" are the main factors determining the demand for the codification of international law. Tastes and expectations may play such an important role because of the

34 It may, however, also recommend "[t]o take no action, the report having already been published".

35 See e.g. Hugh Stretton, *Economics: A New Introduction* (Pluto Press 2000) 259–263.

sovereignty of States. Codification takes some time and during that time the tastes and expectations of consumers may change. The law of special missions might serve as an example, especially when we compare this topic with diplomatic relations. In 1960, the General Assembly agreed to codify the law of *ad hoc* missions together with the law of permanent diplomatic missions at a diplomatic conference in Vienna.[36] This idea was later rejected, and the Vienna Convention on Diplomatic Relations was adopted in 1961 and entered into force in 1964.[37] The work on special missions was completed by the International Law Commission in 1966.[38] In 1969, the General Assembly adopted the Convention on Special Missions[39] and in June 1985, more than 15 years later, the Convention entered into force.[40] The fact that tastes and expectation of States regarding the codification of the law of *ad hoc* missions changed in time, is illustrated not only by the number of years between adoption and entry into force of both treaties, but also by the number of State parties (191 States had joined the Vienna Convention on Diplomatic Relations, 39 States ratified or acceded to the Convention on Special Missions by September 2018).

On the Commission's website, an overview called "Periods during which topics were on the agenda of the International Law Commission" can be found.[41] It presents not only the wide scope of topics covered from 1949, but also illustrates the dynamics of the Commission's work. Through this table, the changes and perhaps also difficulties on the market can be identified. A shift can be observed from "big topics" crowned by "big conventions" to more specialized particular issues, on the one hand, and to theoretical problems and general questions, on the other hand. Moreover, the average time devoted to a topic has increased. Excluding the very special topic of "State responsibility for internationally wrongful acts" and limiting the attention to completed topics only, the Commission has worked for an average of 4.9 years on topics opened between 1949 to 1959 and for 8.5 years on topics opened between 1996 and 2006.

The topic of State responsibility appeared on the agenda six times and took 41 years (1954, 1956–1961, 1963, 1967 and 1969–2001) to complete. From a

36 UNGA Res 1504 (XV) (12 December 1960).

37 Adopted 18 April 1961, entered into force 24 April 1964, 500 UNTS 95.

38 ILC, 'Draft articles on special missions, with commentaries' [1967] II ILC Ybk 347.

39 UNGA Res 2530 (XXIV) (8 December 1969).

40 Convention on Special Missions, adopted 8 December 1969, entered into force 21 June 1985, 1400 UNTS 231.

41 ILC, 'Periods during which topics were on the Agenda of the Commission' <http://legal.un.org/ilc/guide/annex1.shtml>.

marketing perspective, it was very difficult to introduce the product, that is the articles on responsibility of States for internationally wrongful acts of 2001.[42] The product concept was changed substantially over time, several responsible "product managers" (i.e. Special Rapporteurs) were in charge, and the demand and the tastes and expectations of demanders were not easy to identify and understand. In 1988, Philip Allott opened his article on "Unmaking of International Law" with the following statement:

> The Commission's work [on State responsibility] raises fundamental questions not only about the state of contemporary international law but also about the existence and functioning of the Commission itself. There is reason to believe that the Commission's long and laborious work on state responsibility is doing serious long-term damage to international law and international society.[43]

A profit-oriented business would probably give up such a project after a few years and devote its attention to a product with better prospects. The International Law Commission has the possibility to discontinue a topic (as it happened to privileges and immunities of international organizations in 1992),[44] but it decided to complete the challenging task. In the model market, the failure of the product endangers the reputation of the producer. Sometimes, buyers are tolerant and forgive a failure, but in the long-term they repudiate those who do not fulfil their expectations. In the international codification market, dropping a topic is perceived as failure.

In 2001, the articles on responsibility of States for internationally wrongful acts were launched on the market. It is not easy to find an appropriate adjective to characterize the reaction of the demand side to this launch. Maybe the word "half-hearted" describes most accurately the fact that the General Assembly "welcomed the conclusion of the work of the International Law Commission on responsibility of States for internationally wrongful acts and its adoption of the draft articles and a detailed commentary on the subject"[45] and decided to revisit it on a triennial basis.

---

42 ILC (n 19).

43 Philip Allott, 'State Responsibility and the Unmaking of International Law' (1988) 29 HarvIntlLJ 1.

44 ILC, 'Report of the International Law Commission on the work of its forty-fourth session' [1992] II(2) ILC Ybk 1, 53 at para 362.

45 UNGA Res 56/83 (12 December 2001), para 1.

VII The International Law Codification Market in the Future

As indicated above, the international law codification market is far from a perfect market, because suppliers and demanders are not two independent groups of actors, and States on the demanding side may influence and govern the activity of suppliers or create new suppliers. During the manufacturing of the product, they may carry out continuous control, from beginning to end. The application of the model market to the codification of international law is also deficient in many other aspects. Nevertheless, the market and marketing optics is useful to explain important processes surrounding the International Law Commission. Particularly in situations when States obtain draft articles as a product of the Commission's work and consider the further procedure (buying and using or rejecting), they act like demanders on a market. They weigh their expectations and tastes before they react.

What are the possibilities and the pitfalls for the Commission in the decade to come? From the economic perspective, we should consider ongoing and predictable changes on the side of demand, on the side of supply and in the market environment. The behaviour of demanders changes slowly but steadily, while the aggregate demand for codification weakens. States as clients examine each of the Commission's products carefully before they accept it and they can express their disapproval. They also can satisfy their demand on their own and conclude treaties at summits and other meetings. On the side of suppliers, the International Law Commission still holds a unique position; other suppliers currently offer, and will in the close future presumably remain limited to, highly specialized products on human rights, humanitarian law and international trade law. Regarding the market environment, other actors on the market – regional and national courts – should be considered. However, their role is ambiguous: they do not sell and buy, but they use the final outcomes of the International Law Commission and, at the same time, they influence the content of products of the International Law Commission.

Regarding the future production of the International Law Commission, the term "international law" as it is contained in the name of the Commission may be the key challenge. The statute of the Commission states in article 1, paragraph 2: "The Commission shall concern itself primarily with public international law, but is not precluded from entering the field of private international law." The drafters of the document were probably thinking about public international law as a set of rules governing the relations between States and also some aspects of relations with intergovernmental organizations and they also had a clear vision of what constitutes private international law. Their vision of international law is captured in contemporary literature[46] and also in the list of topics suggested for codification in 1949.[47]

However, human society and the international community have changed since 1947. Processes like globalization, humanization, constitutionalization, democratization and regionalization influence society and influence the law. They blur the boundaries between public and private international law, regional law and national law. They introduce terms like global law or transnational law to the discussion. Finding out what are fashionable terms and what are real trends in the international community and thinking about international interstate law in the context of other binding normative systems may be one of the future market possibilities for the International Law Commission.

46 International law definitions were discussed e.g. by Alfred von Verdross, 'On the Concept of International Law' (1949) 43(3) AJIL 435.

47 ILC, 'Survey of International Law in Relation to the Work of Codification of the International Law Commission: Preparatory work within the purview of article 18, paragraph 1, of the of the International Law Commission – Memorandum submitted by the Secretary-General' (10 February 1949) UN Doc A/CN.4/1/Rev.1.

The Authority and the Membership of the Commission in the Future

Mónica Pinto

I Introduction

The legal and political world order established after the Second World War envisaged a multilateral arena where States could have more interaction than in the past. International law aspired to deal with a larger field of objects in the relations among States. It also saw the end of the colonial world and, thus, an increase in the number of States. Soon after this new order's implementation, the question of the new subjects and their international legal capacity became an issue.

The enlargement of the field of the objects of international law and the increasing number of States led to the conclusion that there was a need for precise and universal rules, acceptable to all States, existing or yet to be created.

The Charter of the United Nations acknowledged that feature of the emerging international community and in Article 13, paragraph 1 (a), provided that the only plenary body of the United Nations – the General Assembly – should "initiate studies and make recommendations for the purpose of promoting international co-operation in the political field and encouraging the progressive development of international law and its codification". Consequently, in its resolution 174(II), the General Assembly established the International Law Commission to give effect to this Charter provision, and it also offered a description of what constitutes progressive development and codification, respectively.[1] Other colleagues have already addressed this issue in detail and with merit.[2] What I would like to stress here is that, shortly after commencing its work, the International Law Commission realized that making the distinction between progressive development and codification was not easy, and as early as in 1956, the Commission gave up any pretence to be strict in that differentiation.[3]

In fact, as it was emphasized by Secretary-General Dag Hammarskjöld, "[t]he reluctance of Governments to submit their controversies to judicial

1 UNGA Res 174 (II) (21 November 1947).
2 See the contributions in Section 5 of this volume.
3 José Alvarez, *International Organizations as Law-Makers* (OUP 2006) 308.

DOI:10.1163/9789004434271_032

settlement stems in part from the fragmentary and uncertain character of much of international law as it now exists".[4] It was then necessary to make rules of international law more certain and evident.[5]

The International Law Commission was the engineer in the establishment of the "essential building blocks in the development of the post-war international legal system",[6] producing a series of draft conventions in the 1950s and 1960s that were almost universally endorsed. But in the 1970s and 1980s its impact seemed to be decreasing, mainly because of the relatively low number of ratifications of the conventions in the field of succession of States (the convention dealing with succession in respect of treaties currently has only 22 States parties,[7] while that in respect of State property, archives and debt[8] has so far obtained only 7 of the 15 ratifications it needs to enter into force).

Legal scholars referred to the crisis of the International Law Commission and, in a study of the United Nations Institute for Training and Research (UNITAR), Thomas Franck, Mohamed ElBaradei and Robert Trachtenberg called for a new direction. The critique emphasized that the International Law Commission remained in its comfort zone and avoided addressing the changing priorities of the international community.[9]

The 1990s brought about some changes. On the one hand, in a couple of years, the International Law Commission succeeded in forwarding to the General Assembly a draft convention for the establishment of an international criminal court.[10] In the same year, on the other hand, the International Law Commission produced another set of draft articles which were later adopted as a convention,[11] the Convention on the Law of Non-Navigational Uses of

4 'Annual Report of the Secretary-General on the Work of the Organization, 1 July 1954 – 15 June 1955' (1955) UN Doc A/2911.

5 Luke T Lee, 'The International Law Commission Re-Examined' (1965) 59 AJIL 545, 546.

6 Thomas Franck and Mohamed ElBaradei, 'The Codification and Progressive Development of International Law: A UNITAR Study of the Role and Use of the International Law Commission' (1982) 76 AJIL 630, 631.

7 Vienna Convention on Succession of States in respect of Treaties, adopted 23 August 1978, entered into force 6 November 1996, 1946 UNTS 3.

8 Vienna Convention on Succession in respect of State Property, Archives and Debts (adopted in Vienna on 8 April 1983, not yet in force) (1983) 22 ILM 306.

9 Mohammed ElBaradei, Thomas M. Frank, Robert Trachtenberg, *The International Law Commission: The Need for a New Direction* (UNITAR 1981).

10 ILC, 'Draft Statute for an International Criminal Court, with commentaries' [1994] II(2) ILC Ybk 26; 'Draft code of crimes against the peace and security of mankind' [1996] II(2) ILC Ybk 15.

11 ILC, 'Draft articles on the law of the non-navigational uses of international watercourses' [1994] II(2) ILC Ybk 89.

International Watercourses, but this convention would take until 2014 to enter into force (ratified by only 36 States as of today).[12]

The Rome Statute of the International Criminal Court was adopted on 17 July 1998 and entered into force on 1 July 2002, being binding today for 123 States.[13] It is the constitutional text of one of the major developments of post-war international law. It established a full-fledged court that has worked on 28 cases[14] with a view to ending impunity and delivering justice.

Not all the products of the International Law Commission are intended to become treaties or are endorsed by States in the form of treaties. In the past, that was the case for the summary conclusions on the most-favoured nation clause,[15] the status of diplomatic courier and the bag of international organizations of a universal character,[16] State responsibility for internationally wrongful acts,[17] prevention of transboundary damage from hazardous activities,[18] diplomatic protection,[19] expulsion of aliens,[20] the protection of persons in the event of disasters,[21] or the draft conclusions on subsequent agreements and subsequent practice in relation to interpretation of treaties.[22] The International Law Commission also adopted draft guidelines on reservations to treaties and produced a guide to practice on reservations to treaties with a view to assisting practitioners.[23] These products of the Commission, which deserve the same attention as others that became treaties, have played an important role in international law.

12 Convention on the Law of Non-Navigational Uses of International Watercourses, adopted 21 May 1997, entered into force on 17 August 2014, UNTS registration no 52106 (number of ratifications as of 26 December 2018).

13 Adopted 17 July 1998, entered into force 1 July 2002, 2187 UNTS 3 (number of ratifications as of 26 December 2018).

14 An overview is available at <www.icc-cpi.int/cases> (as of 26 December 2018).

15 ILC, 'Summary Conclusions on the Most-Favoured-Nation Clause' (2015) UN Doc A/70/10, 19 at para 42.

16 ILC, 'Draft optional protocol two on the status of the courier and the bag of international organizations of a universal character' [1989] II(2) ILC Ybk 48.

17 ILC, 'Draft articles on responsibility of States for internationally wrongful acts' [2001] II(2) ILC Ybk 26.

18 ILC, 'Draft articles on prevention of transboundary harm from hazardous activities' [2001] II(2) ILC Ybk 146.

19 ILC, 'Draft articles on diplomatic protection' [2006] II(2) ILC Ybk 24.

20 ILC, 'Draft articles on the expulsion of aliens' (2014) UN Doc A/69/10, 11.

21 ILC, 'Draft articles on the protection of persons in the event of disasters' (2016) UN Doc A/71/10, 13.

22 ILC, 'Report of the International Law Commission on the work of its seventieth session' (2018) UN Doc A/73/10, 12 at para 49.

23 ILC, 'Guide to practice on reservation to treaties' [2011] II(3) ILC Ybk 23.

At present, the International Law Commission has 34 members, all of whom serve in their personal capacity. According to article 8 of the statute of the International law Commission, they should – globally – represent the main forms of civilization and the principal legal systems of the world.

The purpose of this paper is to critically assess and offer insights regarding the membership and authority of the International Law Commission in the future.

II The Composition of the International Law Commission

The main professions represented in the International Law Commission are diplomacy and legal services; to a lesser extent also academia. It has been stressed that when legal advisors and judges or members of the ministries of justice sit on the Commission, it may be difficult for them to avoid approaching their work from a semi-official perspective.[24] Be that as it may, it seems that litigants, i.e. those involved mainly in international judicial activities, are not given a reasonable place on the Commission. Some of the International Law Commission's members, at present and in the recent past, have worked as legal counsels in more than one case before the International Court of Justice, for instance, but right now there are not more than three or four members of the Commission that have represented States before the Court.[25] Since litigation is an activity frequently conducted jointly with the performance of academic roles, the risk that litigants may tend to tailor rules in a way that is favorable to their cases is ultimately curtailed by the prestige each of them earns throughout their careers.

The International Law Commission's members have been and are mostly men. At present, the Commission has four women among its members – Concepción Escobar Hernández, Patrícia Galvão Teles, Marja Lehto, and Nilüfer Oral – which amounts to 11.75 per cent. Women have only been elected to the Commission since the turn of the century. From 2002 to 2010, only two women, that is 5.88 per cent, worked in the International Law Commission with their male colleagues, Paula Escarameia of Portugal and Hanqin Xue of China, who became the first female Chair of the Commission. They were joined by Marie Jacobsson, so from 2007 until 2011 there were three female members of the Commission. Yet again, between 2011 and 2016 there were only two female members, Marie Jacobsson and Concepción Escobar Hernández.

24 Lee (n 5) 550.
25 See the Concluding Remarks to this Section by Dire Tladi.

In light of this imbalance of gender representation, there are convincing bases to improve this situation. Gender studies provide at least two sets of arguments to that end, those relying on the special contribution women make to international law, and those rooted in considerations of equity and fairness. Thus, it is possible to submit that they, or we, have to be more adequately represented because of our special position as women. But there are surely other arguments in favour of gender parity based on the principle of fairness, which implies that the increase in the number of women scholars[26] in international law should be reciprocated in the composition of the Commission.[27] I support the latter argument. States should be encouraged to nominate and elect women to be members of the Commission. The International Law Commission itself may adopt some policy on this matter just encouraging States to reach parity when proposing candidates.

Another feature that is to be considered is the lack of new generations in the International Law Commission's composition. The average age of the members is around 55 years, with individual ages ranging from 35 to 82 years. This means that almost all members obtained their law degrees by the late 1980s and consequently might not have the necessary knowledge with regard to new technologies or of some of the new developments in the big picture of international law during their studies. Their "co-habitation" with new generations, those in their mid-forties, could provide the International Law Commission with even more intellectual capacity to progressively develop and codify international law.

The allocation of the Commission's membership among the regional groups (the African Group and Western European and Others Group with 8 members each, the Latin American and Caribbean Group and Asia-Pacific Group with 7 members each and Eastern Europe with 4 members)[28] roughly corresponds to the distribution of population around the world, but it is not translated to the level of the appointment of Special Rapporteurs of the Commission. In fact, of the 61 Special Rapporteurs listed on the International Law Commission's

26 Elizabeth Olson, 'Women Make Up Majority of U.S. Law Students for First Time', *The New York Times*, 16 December 2016; Staci Zaretsky, 'There Are Now More Women In Law School Than Ever Before', *Above The Law*, 7 March 2018. Another example is provided by the University of Buenos Aires Law School, where the 60 per cent of students are women: see Universidad de Buenos Aires, 'Resultados de Finales' (2011), available at <http://www.uba.ar/institucional/censos/Estudiantes2011/estudiantes2011.pdf>.

27 Kate Malleson, 'Justifying Gender Equality on the Bench: Why Difference Won't Do' (2003) 11 FemLS 1.

28 UNGA Res 36/39 (18 November 1981), para 3.

webpage,[29] 31 belong to the Western European and Others Group, 9 to Eastern Europe, 9 to the Latin American and Caribbean Group, 7 to the African Group and 5 to the Asia Pacific Group.

Fifty per cent of the Special Rapporteurs of the Western European and Others Group come from the common law system. However, at present, only 5 members of the International Law Commission belong to countries with a common law tradition. Africa's representation among the International Law Commission's Special Rapporteurs is mainly francophone and from Maghreb countries. The Commission's imbalance is illustrated by its work on the law of treaties, custom and State responsibility where Special Rapporteurs have all been white and male, generally from common law countries, nearly always from North America and Europe. It may therefore be questioned whether the work of the Commission reflects "the main forms of civilization and of the principal legal systems of the world", as stipulated in article 8 of its statute.

As the international community has become increasingly multicultural and diverse, efforts should be made to incorporate those trends into the work of the Commission by nominating candidates from other systems of law. Those systems are generally in a minority position and survive in contexts in which one of the more widely spread legal systems prevail. Due to their difficult standing, those legal systems are used to legal syncretism. Their views should be valuable in enriching the Commission's work.

III The Authority of the International Law Commission in the Future

The authority of the International Law Commission in paving the way for the written, more certain, rules of post-war international law is undisputed. However, when the Commission was close to reaching its forties, it experienced a crisis, mainly because its products seemed of less interest to the community of States. Comments by Sixth Committee delegates were not favorable at all. Delegations pointed out that the Commission preferred its needlepoint in safe domains as diplomatic courier and bag, instead of focusing on the challenging issues of the evolving international law. It was also noted that the role of the Commission as a diverse mediator between the interests of established and recently independent States was, in part, challenged by its formalistic approach to international law.[30]

29 ILC, 'Membership: Special Rapporteurs of the International Law Commission (1949–2016)', available at <http://legal.un.org/ilc/guide/annex3.shtml>.

30 Mathias Forteau, 'Comparative International Law Within, Not Against, International Law: Lessons from the International Law Commission' (2015) 109 AJIL 498, 502–503.

That critique was the perception of a unique moment in the international community, that of the first years of the "new States". As time passed, these States became actors in different contexts and demonstrated their respective differences. Their reactions to the International Law Commission's work have also been heterogeneous.

The trend towards "hard law" in the classic work of the International Law Commission stands in contrast to the success of those products of the Commission which have not yet or were never intended to become a binding treaty. This so-called "soft" approach[31] proved to be effective as they are invoked by the parties in different litigation and by the tribunals. In fact, for instance, the International Court of Justice relied on the articles on State responsibility for internationally wrongful acts – the drafting of which was begun by Francisco García Amador, continued by Roberto Ago, Gaetano Arangio Ruiz, William Riphagen and was finalized by James Crawford – more than once in its judgments.[32] Moreover, as early as 1997, the International Court of Justice considered that a number of provisions in the then draft articles on State responsibility reflect *lex lata*.[33]

Other articles have also assisted adjudicators and litigants. Before the International Court of Justice, for instance, Nicaragua relied on the articles on prevention of transboundary harm from hazardous activities;[34] Uruguay did the same in the case with Argentina relating to the Pulp Mills.[35]

31 Alvarez (n 3) 310, 312. Daugirdas pointed out that the International Law Commission "reinvented itself", see Kristina Daugirdas 'The International Law Commission Reinvents Itself' (2014) 108 AJIL Unbound 7.

32 *Inter alia, Obligations concerning Negotiations relating to Cessation of the Nuclear Arms Race and to Nuclear Disarmament* (*Marshall Islands v India*) (Jurisdiction and Admissibility) [2016] ICJ Rep 255, para 42; *Ahmadou Sadio Diallo* (*Republic of Guinea v Democratic Republic of the Congo*) (Compensation) [2012] ICJ Rep 324, para 49; *Request for Interpretation of the Judgment of 31 March 2004 in the Case concerning Avena and Other Mexican Nationals* (*Mexico v United States of America*) [2009] ICJ Rep 3, para 64; *Application of the Convention on the Prevention and Punishment of the Crime of Genocide* (*Bosnia and Herzegovina v Serbia and Montenegro*) (Merits) [2007] ICJ Rep 43, para 17; *Armed Activities on the Territory of the Congo* (*Democratic Republic of the Congo v Uganda*) (Merits) [2005] ICJ Rep 168, paras 160, 293; *Legal Consequences of the Construction of a Wall in the Occupied Palestinian Territory* (Advisory Opinion) [2004] ICJ Rep 136, para 140.

33 *Gabcikovo-Nagymaros Project* (*Hungary/Slovakia*) (Merits) [1997] ICJ Rep 7, para 47.

34 *Certain Activities Carried Out by Nicaragua in the Border Area* (*Costa Rica v Nicaragua*) and *Construction of a Road in Costa Rica along the San Juan River* (*Nicaragua v Costa Rica*) (Merits) [2015] ICJ Rep 665, para 190.

35 *Pulp Mills on the River Uruguay* (*Argentina v Uruguay*) (Merits) [2010] ICJ Rep 14, paras 152, 203, 215.

Arbitral tribunals have relied on many pieces produced by the International Law Commission. Perhaps because, as José Alvarez pointed out, quoting David Caron,

> courts and arbitral panels, such as those charged with resolving investor-state disputes arising under bilateral investment treaties (BIT s), will turn to whatever is available and the ILC's Articles, soft or not, provide a handy recourse for those who need to fill a legal vacuum or who simply desire ostensibly "neutral" authoritative distillation of what would otherwise be an arduous search through innumerable digests of state practice to find applicable rules of custom.[36]

Many arbitral awards illustrate Caron's views.[37]

As a hybrid product, between articles and conventions, there is the Commission's guide to practice on reservations to treaties,[38] which is meant to provide assistance to practitioners based on and with the authority of an existing treaty, namely the Vienna Convention on the Law of Treaties.[39]

IV Conclusions

All these comments lead to some conclusions. One of them is that, at this point in the evolution of the international community and of international law, there seems to be no urgent need for new treaties. The International Law Commission adapted to this trend and produced other forms of outcomes. However, this way of working on the codification and progressive development of international law places States in the margins of the game. States are not invited to have a say with regard to the processes and the final product of the work of the Commission, and neither are other actors, which are generally outside the International Law Commission's scope of action and consultation. It may

36 See Alvarez (n 3) 312.

37 ICSID Case No ARB/15/21, 24 dealing with the draft articles on most-favoured-nation clauses; ICSID Case No ARB/14/8, 22 quoting the articles on diplomatic protection; ICSID Case No ARB/13/33, para 87 referring to the draft articles on most-favoured-nation clauses; ICSID Case No ARB/06/2, 178 referring to the articles on State responsibility for internationally wrongful acts; ICSID Case No ARB/14/3, para 191 dealing with the articles on State responsibility; ICSID Case No ARB/12/35, 291, dealing with the articles on diplomatic protection.

38 ILC, 'Guide to practice on reservations to treaties' [2011] II(3) ILC Ybk 23.

39 Adopted 23 May 1969, entered into force 27 January 1980, 1155 UNTS 331.

be that the interaction with the Sixth Committee replaces the lack of States' participation, but this cannot be said with certainty.

If the International Law Commission is going to further develop products other than draft articles, it may wish to consider consulting a broader field of stakeholders. In areas like environmental law, non-State actors are crucial as others whose opinions at least should be heard by the International Law Commission. This is illustrated by the work of the Commission on the topic "Protection of the environment" in which the Commission has regularly consulted with experts in the field.[40] If the International Law Commission's legitimacy is epistemic or technical, because of its methods or because of the expertise of its members, not many reasons would speak against more open and participatory procedures. Academia, litigants, non-governmental organizations and others may offer some important views with regard to the International Law Commission's work.

Some approaches chosen for the new ways of "packaging" the outcome of the Commission's work,[41] such as those on the identification of customary international law subsequent agreements and subsequent practice in relation to the interpretation of treaties, are especially useful for litigation in all fields.

At the end of the day, as Tom Franck and Mohamed ElBaradei put it, the International Law Commission is "[t]he only drafting body with versatile jurisdiction over *any* subject in the field of international law".[42]

The International Law Commission is a high-quality brand that could adapt to contextual changes in the past. It will find the ways to raise its profile and to further enhance the level of its brand in the future.

40 ILC, 'Fifth report by the Special Rapporteur on Protection of the Atmosphere' (2018) UN Doc A/CN.4/711, para 2.

41 See Sean Murphy, 'Codification, Progressive Development or Scholarly Analysis? The Art of Packaging the ILC's Work Product' in Maurizio Ragazzi (ed), *The Responsibility of International Organizations: Essays in Memory of Sir Ian Brownlie* (Martinus Nijhoff 2013).

42 Emphasis in original. See Franck and ElBaradei (n 6) 631 (emphasis in the original).

Concluding Remarks by Dire Tladi

The Authoriy and the Membership of the Commission in the Future—Art, Science and Economics: a Comment on Trávnička and Pinto

1 Introduction

It is appropriate to enquire into the authority and membership of the International Law Commission as the Commission enters its seventh decade of existence. While the authority of the Commission has been a given for most of its existence, the passage of the golden years and the emergence of a new era when treaties developed by the Commission are becoming fewer, have led some to ponder whether the Commission still commands the respect and authority of yesteryear. Similarly, this new era, dominated as it is by notions of equity and equality, rightly forces us to confront the question of the composition or membership of the Commission.

These two themes, the "authority" and "membership" of the Commission, as well as the interaction between the two themes, are addressed in two different, but equally fascinating ways, in the papers by Mónica Pinto and Zuzana Trávníčková. In addressing the two themes of "authority" and "membership", both papers arrive at interesting conclusions about representation on the Commission. Particularly interesting observations were made about gender and geographic representation, generational distribution and professional representation. The two papers, presented during a panel chaired by former member of the Commission, Professor Momtaz, approached the subject of "The authority and membership of the Commission in the future", in quite distinct ways and arrived at very different conclusions. The written papers, submitted subsequently, provide further detail explanation on the themes and conclusions advanced by the Professors Pinto and Trávníčková.

In this short comment, I do not intend to respond to everything raised in these very interesting papers. I intend only to offer observations on the overarching themes and conclusions presented by the papers. In particular, while the papers cover a wide array of issues, I wish to focus only on those issues that directly touch on the two themes – authority and membership – and in particular their interaction. In the next section, the themes in the papers are explored, before some concluding remarks are made. In these concluding remarks I try to illustrate how these papers are an advert – an inadvertent campaign – for

© THE UNITED NATIONS, 2021 | DOI:10.1163/9789004434271_033

diversity of approaches and views. The conclusion also suggests that these two very divergent papers, that come to very divergent views about the authority and membership of the Commission, perhaps teach us that the truth is, as is often the case, somewhere in the middle.

2 Comment on the Papers

I begin by a description of Zuzana Trávníčková's paper. She introduces her paper with a pedagogic slant – the presentation during the panel itself was centred around this pedagogic approach, illustrating how the Commission, and in particular this relationship, can provide a pair of binoculars through which to survey international law and its evolution for students. The presentation, and introduction of the written paper, has a literary feel to it. In her final written paper, Zuzana Trávníčková does not present us with the images of "beautiful temples somewhere in the mountains" and stories, stars, some not so bright, in the international law sky. While the paper begins with the pedagogic descriptions, with an artistic feel, it employs the metaphor of the market to describe the Commission's authority and membership and the interaction of these two themes. Zuzana Trávníčková considers the length of time it took to complete the articles on the responsibility of States for internationally wrongful acts,[1] and observes, in very market, business-like language, that in any other business enterprise the State responsibility project would have been shelved as not being worth the investment.[2]

In her metaphor, Zuzana Trávníčková presents codification, in the broad sense including also progressive development, as a service on the market. Legitimacy and respect are the consideration given for the service. In this metaphor, the International Law Commission is a supplier of the service of codification and States are the consumers – Zuzana Trávníčková refers to these as demanders. She is at pains to point out that the International Law Commission is not the only provider of the service of the codification. In this sense, the codification of international law is subject to competition and the Commission is not "the monopoly".[3] Other entities, such as the General Assembly itself, conferences convened under the auspices of the United Nations and the United

1 ILC, 'Articles on Responsibility of States for Internationally Wrongful Acts' UNGA Res 56/83 (12 December 2001), annex.

2 Zuzana Trávníčková, 'The International Law Commission and the International Law Codification Market', 363, in this Section.

3 Ibid 358.

Nations Commission on International Trade Law are but examples of other forums where international law is codified – not listed, but certainly one of the more prestigious is the *Institut de Droit international*.[4] These other forums are alternative service providers. But for the most part, with the notable exceptions of the General Assembly, these other service providers "can be classified by their scope of operation (their specialization ...), on one hand, and by their 'distance' from States, on the other hand".[5]

The International Law Commission is different from these. If I were inclined towards the market metaphor employed by Zuzana Trávníčková – and I am not – I would describe the Commission as the dominant, luxury brand of the market. It would occupy the dominant positions of German car-brands like BMW or Mercedes Benz, or technology giants like Apple or Microsoft. Zuzana Trávníčková is much more conservative, describing the Commission's place on the market only as "firm, undisputable and also unique".[6] What is more important is not so much how Zuzana Trávníčková describes the Commission's place in the market, but why it has this "firm, undisputable and [..] unique" position on the market – what I would refer to as a dominant position. She provides three reasons (answers), for the unique position. And it is these three reasons that lead Zuzana Trávníčková to address the representational issues which potentially affect the authority of the Commission and its place in the market of codification. The first reason for the uniqueness of the Commission as a service provider in the codification market is the authority that it commands.[7] The second is its composition.[8] The final reason for the uniqueness of the Commission in the market is the capacity of the Commission to address a variety of topics in different ways.[9]

The overall picture painted by Zuzana Trávníčková is a positive one. The main challenge for the Commission, according to the analysis, is the identification of public international law topics in the future. Yet, given the number of topics being proposed by the Commission, and the number of topics being placed on the long-term programme of work, identifying new topics for the Commission is unlikely to be a challenge.[10]

4 See the keynote address by Nico Schrijver in Section 8 of this volume.

5 Trávníčková (n 2) 359.

6 Ibid 357.

7 Ibid.

8 Ibid.

9 Ibid 358.

10 In the last nine years, the Commission has placed twelve topics on the long-term programme of work. These are, the "Protection of the atmosphere", "Formation and evidence

On the authority of the Commission, the paper endorses both the formal and professional authority. The formal authority is established on the basis of the Commission's creation as an organ of the General Assembly and its consequent relationship with the United Nations. Here, Zuzana Trávníčková refers to, for example, the fact that General Assembly discusses the work of the Commission and the fact that its members enjoy, in Switzerland at least, the same privileges and immunities as judges of the International Court of Justice and heads of Missions.[11] None of the other service providers in the market of codification enjoy quite the same formal recognition. As to the second form of authority, the professional authority, the paper recalls that this type of authority, unlike the formal authority based on the establishment, "is not bestowed but must be earned."[12] This type of authority speaks to the pedigree and quality of the Commission's work over the years, which Zuzana Trávníčková describes as "still very impressive".[13] I pause here to note that the phrase "still very impressive" suggests somewhat of a dip in the professional authority, but since Zuzana Trávníčková does not make much of this, neither will I.

The second reason for the uniqueness of the Commission is its composition. Here, I dare say, Zuzana Trávníčková is somewhat defensive of the Commission's track record. She notes, with approval, that formally the Commission has lived up to the requirements for regional representation and the representation of the main forms of civilizations and of the principal legal systems of the world. And then she turns to the question of gender representation, which has been a topical one during the seventieth session of the Commission and the associated celebration. Here, she returns to the pedagogic and artistic approach, momentarily leaving the market. When her students look at the picture of the Commission on its website, she reports, they notice the gender disparity in the composition of the Commission.[14] It is interesting that this particular issue is introduced and discussed in this paper, not through numbers as is often the

of customary international law" (which was subsequently renamed to "Identification of customary international law"), "The Fair and equitable treatment standard in international investments law", "Protection of the environment in relation to armed conflict"; "Provisional application of treaties"; "Settlement of disputes involving international organizations"; "Crimes against humanity"; *"Jus Cogens";* "Succession of States in respect of State responsibility"; "General principles of law"; "Universal jurisdiction"; "Evidence before International Court and Tribunals"; and "Sea-level rise". In addition, several other topics, were considered (and some still are being considered) by the Commission.

11 Trávníčková (n 2) 357.

12 Ibid.

13 Ibid.

14 Ibid.

case,[15] but through imagery. At any rate, her students, at seeing this image remark, as would expected, that it is not fair that women are so underrepresented.[16] There are two things that the paper does that I find interesting. The first, which I wholeheartedly agree with, is that the paper absolves the Commission from this travesty – it is I and not Zuzana Trávníčková, that describes the underrepresentation as a travesty. It is after all, not the Commission that elects members,[17] nor is it the Commission that nominates members for election. It is the States. Thus, ultimately States are responsible for the travesty. The conclusion she arrives at with the students– we are unfortunately not told how this conclusion is arrived at, although I agree with it too – is that it is probably would not be helpful to amend the statute to introduce quotas for women.[18]

But, and this is the part of the paper that really gets me excited, Zuzana Trávníčková states that there is probably a hidden question behind this image of underrepresentation of women. That hidden question is: "Is it wrong or is it real problem that there are less women than men?"[19] Her answer is interesting – and one that I do not agree with, but more on that in the conclusion. In her view "[i]t would be wrong if women were excluded [perhaps 'prohibited' is this better word] from membership. It would be wrong if the feminine attitude to international law would be something else than the masculine one …"[20] She and her students conclude that "international law knowledge of and attitude towards international law are a matter of expertise and experience, not a matter of gender and that the natural development in this question does not require any formal interference".[21] In her view (and it appears that this is normally the conclusion arrived at with the class) probably the outcomes of the Commission would not have been affected had there been more women. Although the final proposal is cautious in that she suggests that "this question does not require any *formal* interference"[22] – suggesting that an informal

15 I myself have adopted the slogan introduced by the four women currently on the Commission – Concepción Escobar Hernández Patrícia Galvão Teles, Marja Lehto and Nilüfer Oral – seven in seventy, to describe the poor record of the Commission in this area.

16 Trávníčková (n 2) 358.

17 The exception is in cases of a casual vacancy, see article 11 of the statute of the ILC, UNGA Res 174(II) (21 November 1947) as amended by UNGA Res 485(V) (12 December 1950); UNGA Res. 984(X) (3 December 1955); UNGA Res 985(X) (3 December 1955) and UNGA Res 36/39 (18 November 1981).

18 Trávníčková (n 2) 258.

19 Ibid.

20 Ibid.

21 Ibid.

22 Ibid (emphasis added).

interference may be warranted – it is telling that on the whole the suggestion seems to be that it is not a *real* problem. But I return to this issue in the conclusion.

Finally, a third reason for the Commission's uniqueness in the market of codification – and admittedly this reads a little bit like an afterthought – is that the Commission addresses a wide variety of topics and does so in diverse ways. The paper notes that the agenda of the Commission "since its inception has been very colourful". This statement is probably true and it is clear that in the future the Commission's choice of topic will become even more colourful. The inclusion of the topic "Sea-level rise in relation to international law" in the long-term programme of work and its likely inclusion in the agenda is testament to this fact. Of this potential, and rounding off the market analogy, Zuzana Trávníčková concludes her paper by encouraging the Commission to find out "what are fashionable terms and what are real trends" in order to enhance "future market possibilities" of the Commission.[23]

I turn now to the very different, but equally fascinating paper of Mónica Pinto.[24] This paper adopts a completely different, systematic and technical analysis of the themes under consideration – authority and members. Her paper presents numbers and statistics, not images of beautiful temples or bright or dim star. The paper does not evoke the pedagogic image of students with enquiring minds exploring, together with their Professor, the ins and outs of international law. The approach is based on hard facts and data to assess the authority of the Commission, its membership and the interaction between these two themes. It is not at all surprising that Mónica Pinto's paper comes to very different conclusions. It should also be noted that these conclusions are less sympathetic towards the Commission than those of Zuzana Trávníčková. The less sympathetic tone – and I have deliberately chosen less sympathetic instead of unsympathetic to indicate that I did not read Mónica Pinto's piece to be hostile to the Commission – is set out in the early part of the paper where low ratification of the conventions dealing with State succession prepared by the Commission is highlighted.[25] Already at this stage of the paper, it is clear that the authority of the Commission ought not to be assumed. The paper reminds us that legal scholars have criticized the Commission because it has "remained in its comfort zone and avoided the changing priorities of the

23 Ibid 365.

24 Mónica Pinto, 'The Authority and Membership of the Commission in the Future' in this Section.

25 Ibid 367.

international community".[26] Although the paper immediately adopts a positive note that the "1990s brought about some changes" with the work of the Commission on the elaboration of a draft statute for the International Criminal Court, this is subjected to a caveat since we are immediately referred to the less successful Convention on the Law of Non-Navigational Uses of International Watercourses.[27]

The paper begins by an assessment of the Commission and its composition and it paints a rather gloomy picture. First, it laments, or so it seems, the representation of different professions on the Commission.[28] It notes that the main field of activity for members of the Commission is "diplomacy and legal services",[29] in other words, government lawyers. There is a criticism, certainly not explicit, but veiled (perhaps implicit is the better word) that the large number of government lawyers on the Commission creates the risk that "the semi-official view"[30] of members of the Commission will influence the work of the Commission. But the main observation that I draw from reading this part of the paper is the lament that "litigants, i.e. those involved mainly in international judicial activities"[31] are underrepresented. She laments that currently there are no more than three or four of such litigants.[32] One point about this part of the paper is that it is different from the other parts in which the composition is considered since it does not rely on hard statistics. We are given a rough, almost thumb-suck, "three or four" as the test. Second, unlike in other sections, this "three or four", only refers to present composition whereas in the other sections, we are also given statistics about previous compositions to enable us also to draw conclusions about trends. Third, while the lament is for the lack of representation of those involved in international judicial activities, the numbers themselves only refer, it seems, to those who have served as counsel before the International Court of Justice. It seems those that may have served as counsel before arbitral tribunals or international criminal tribunals are, inexplicably, excluded. At any rate, the paper does not provide insights about how this affects the authority of the Commission or why having more litigants is a good thing, or even why "three or four" is not sufficient representation.

26 Ibid 267.
27 Ibid.
28 Ibid 369.
29 Ibid.
30 Ibid.
31 Ibid.
32 Ibid.

As with Zuzana Trávníčková's paper, the part that most intrigues me about Mónica Pinto's paper is the consideration of the gender representation. Having stated the obvious, that the members of the Commission "have been and are mostly men" the paper presents us with the stark statistical illustration of how underrepresented women are (and have been) in the Commission.[33] Unlike Zuzana Trávníčková, Mónica Pinto's conclusion is unequivocal. This state of affairs is, to borrow from Trávníčková, "wrong" and is "a real problem."[34] Although she too does not suggest an amendment of the statute, she proposes that States should be encouraged to nominate women.[35] Time and space do not permit me to address another of Mónica Pinto's criticism – the generational distribution.[36]

While Zuzana Trávníčková positively described the regional representation, Mónica Pinto digs into the numbers, to find that even here the Commission can do better. While the paper acknowledges that the regional representation on the Commission is generally acceptable, she notes that this does not translate into the appointment of Special Rapporteurs.[37] The figures are incredible, if unsurprising. Out of a total of 61 Special Rapporteurs between 1949 and 2016, more than half come from Western Europe and Others, 9 from Eastern Europe, 9 from Latin America and the Caribbean, 7 from Africa and 5 from Asia.[38] The paper drills further into the numbers of Special Rapporteurs, but the big take away is that there is a disproportionate imbalance in favour of "white males, generally from common law countries, nearly always from North America and Europe".[39] This, she warns, needs to change to reflect an international community "that has become increasingly multicultural and diverse."[40]

These two wonderful papers address many more issues, including choice of topics and products. I however, have limited this discussion to those issues that directly impact on *both* themes – membership and authority.

I turn now to offer a few concluding remarks.

---

33 Ibid. For the current Commission, women represent a measly 11.75 per cent while between 2002 and 2010, only two women, Paula Escarameia and Hanqin Xue, served on the Commission, signifying an underwhelming 5.88 per cent representation.

34 Trávníčková (n 2) 358.

35 Pinto (n 25) 370.

36 Here, she notes that "the average age of the members is around 55 years old, with individual ages ranging from 35 years to 82 years." Ibid.

37 Ibid.

38 Ibid 370–371.

39 Ibid 371.

40 Ibid.

3 Concluding Remarks

The fact that these two papers look at the same institution, looking at the same materials, in such different ways, and manage to come to such starkly different conclusions tells us so much. First, and I think for me most important, is that there is strength in diversity and diverse approaches. A cursory survey of the profiles of members of the Commission reveals that substantively and geographically, this is the case with the composition of the Commission – I return to gender momentarily. This diversity is borne out also by a study of the summary records of the Commission, where members of the Commission often display fundamental differences to their approach to international law and its codification and progressive development.[41]

The second point I wish to make is that while the papers use different analytical techniques and come to vastly different conclusions, there is a complementarity between them. To illustrate this point, I focus on gender representation since it is here that the two authors arrive at the most divergent conclusions. To take the Zuzana Trávníčková's paper, while I like the search for beauty implicit in a literary approach (and I wish it had been more dominant than the market analogy in the rest of the written paper), the truth is that beauty is in the eye of the beholder. So, while we can never have the answer to the hidden question of whether a more equitable representation would have affected the outcomes of the work of the Commission, surely there is value in diversity itself. Moreover, having experienced two versions of the Commission, I can attest that the presence of women has had an impact. I have served with five out of the seven women that have been on the Commission. All of them are nationals of States belonging to the Western European and Others Group. It is interesting that all five, including Marie Jacobsson who is no longer on the Commission, have supported exceptions to immunity while only one male counterpart from the Western European and Others Group has supported such exceptions – leaving the vast majority of its male representatives opposing exceptions to immunity.[42] I could apply this test to the question of "fundamental values" as characteristic of norms of *jus cogens* and come to the same conclusion. I should not be misunderstood. I do not suggest that they hold this position because they are women. I only wish to point to the risks in suggesting that having more women on the Commission would have had

41 If I can express a slight concern, it is that sometimes, some members express adopt the approach their view is not only the best approach, but the only approach, illustrated by the description of the views of others as "wrong".

42 The one male counterpart is August Reinisch.

no impact on the substance of the Commission's work. Similarly, on Mónica Pinto's paper, it is the case that statistics tell us a lot, but they also hide a lot, do they not? On gender distribution it is definitely true that women are inadequately represented – I would say unacceptably so – on the Commission. But if one looked at the statistics in a different way, one might see that there is a gradual improvement. Before 2002, there had been zero women. Now we have had seven. Between 2002 and 2010, women made up only 5.88 per cent of the Commission. They currently make up just over 11 per cent. While this number remains indecent, it is hard not to observe an improvement. Again, this should not be seen as a pat on the collective back of States for getting the number to the underwhelming 11 per cent, but simply a recognition of the empirical fact of change (I had wanted to say progress but that might be going too far).

In sum, like the Commission, I think these papers remind us that diversity in approaches, perspectives and views should be embraced.

PART 3

Celebratory Contributions on the Occasion of the Seventieth Anniversary of the Commission

SECTION 8

Commemorative Speeches Delivered in New York

Discurso de Eduardo Valencia-Ospina

Presidente de la Comisión de Derecho Internacional en su septuagésimo período de sesiones

(*Spanish original*)

Me honra, en nombre de la Comisión de Derecho Internacional, dar la bienvenida a todos Ustedes a este solemne acto con el que se da inicio a la conmemoración de su 70 aniversario. Permítanme expresar nuestro agradecimiento a los dignatarios que aceptaron la invitación para hacer uso de la palabra en esta oportunidad: el S.E. Miroslav Lajčák, Presidente de la Asamblea General; el Sr. Miguel de Serpa Soares, Asesor Jurídico de Naciones Unidas; S.E. Burhan Gafoor, Representante Permanente de Singapur y Presidente de la Sexta Comisión; los representantes de los países anfitriones de la Comisión tanto en su propia Sede en Ginebra, S.E. Jürg Lauber, Representante Permanente de Suiza, como en la Sede de la Organización, la Sra. Jennifer Newstead, Asesora Jurídica del Departamento de Estado de los Estados Unidos; y el Profesor Nico Schrijver, Presidente del Instituto de Derecho Internacional.

Extiendo nuestro reconocimiento a la concurrencia que nos distingue con su presencia: Representantes Permanentes y otros miembros de Misiones Permanentes; Asesores Jurídicos de Cancillerías y de Misiones Permanentes; altos funcionarios de la Secretaría y representantes de agencias especializadas y otras organizaciones internacionales; profesores y alumnos en Facultades de Derecho y otras instituciones académicas; y antiguos miembros de la Comisión y su Secretaría.

Excepcionalmente, la Comisión de Derecho Internacional celebra en la Sede de la Organización la primera parte de uno de sus períodos regulares de sesiones, el de 2018, por marcar éste al tiempo 70 años de vida de la institución. Por decisión expresa de la Asamblea General, su órgano creador, la Comisión sesiona por cinco semanas aquí en Nueva York donde, en Lake Success, tuviera su primera session en 1949.[1] De esta forma se concretiza el anhelo frecuentemente expresado en la Sexta Comisión, del cual se ha hecho eco la Comisión de Derecho Internacional, como medio conducente a fortalecer la ya estrecha relación entre los dos órganos.

1 Asamblea General de las Naciones Unidas, Resolución 72/116 (de 7 de diciembre de 2017), para. 14.

© THE UNITED NATIONS, 2021 | DOI:10.1163/9789004434271_034

Dicha relación se manifiesta sobre todo en las resoluciones periódicamente adoptadas por la Asamblea General, resultado de la consideración que en cada una de sus sesiones ordinarias le da la Sexta Comisión a los informes sometidos anualmente a ella por la Comisión de Derecho Internacional. En tales informes, setenta de ellos hasta el momento, se encuentra plasmada la fundamental contribución hecha por la Comisión a lo largo de su existencia al desarrollo progresivo y la codificación del Derecho Internacional. Esos setenta informes son la major prueba de la manera constructiva y eficaz como la Comisión ha sabido desempeñar la función que le encomendara la Asamblea, en cumplimiento del mandato a ella impuesto por el Artículo 13, 1 (a) de la Carta.

La inserción de dicha disposición en el instrumento constitutivo de las Naciones Unidas no fué el resultado de una iniciativa aislada en la Conferencia de San Francisco. Por el contrario, representó un decisivo paso adelante dentro del llamado "Movimiento de Codificación", que traza sus orígenes a las postrimerías del Siglo XVIII. El "Movimiento" había recibido fuerte impulso con la fundación, en 1873, del Instituto de Derecho Internacional y la Asociación de Derecho Internacional, instituciones que, doblando en edad a la Comisión, continúan canalizando los esfuerzos privados en pro del objetivo que les es común a una y otras. Por ello adquiere especial significado que para realzar el 70 aniversario de la Comisión, haya sido el Presidente del Instituto el escogido para dictar la Conferencia Magistral con la que concluirá esta solemne jornada.

Los múltiples e influyentes resultados sustantivos a que ha llegado la Comisión de Derecho Internacional en su larga e ingente labor sobre diversos temas no requieren recapitulación en esta corta intervención. Baste con destacar que la Comisión se ha ocupado, entre otros trascendentales temas, de las tres fuentes principales del Derecho Internacional mencionadas en el Artículo 38, párrafo 1 del Estatuto de la Corte Internacional de Justicia. De ello dan fé su proyecto definitivo sobre el Derecho de los Tratados, que sirvió de base para la elaboración de la Convención de Viena de 1969.[2] Este fundacional instrumento, refrendado por la casi unanimidad de los Estados Miembros, ha servido de fecunda fuente de inspiración a la Comisión de Derecho Internacional para emprender su estudio autónomo acerca de una docena de temas derivados de la Convención o estrechamente relacionados con ella. Asimismo el proyecto definitivo, a ser adoptado en el presente período de sesiones, de Conclusiones sobre la Identificación del Derecho Internacional Consuetudinario, la segunda de las Fuentes principales. Y la tercera de éstas, los Principios generales del Derecho, fué materia inscrita el año pasado en el Programa de Trabajo a Largo Plazo de la Comisión.

---

2 Convención de Viena sobre el Derecho de los Tratados (adoptada el 23 de mayo de 1969, entrada en vigor el 27 de enero de 1980) 1155 Serie de Tratados de Naciones Unidas 331.

Es también apropiado resaltar aquí cuál ha sido el rendimiento de la Comisión en relación con los temas incluidos en su Programa a Largo Plazo. Desde su primer período de sesiones en 1949 la Comisión configuró un Programa de catorce temas, seleccionados de la lista de veinticinco posibles enumerados en el célebre "Memorando Lauterpacht".[3] A más del de los escogidos en 1949, se ha emprendido en el curso de los años el estudio de otros 38 temas, algunos divididos en sub-temas autónomos, de los cuales están siendo considerados activamente los nueve que constituyen su agenda corriente. Exceptuando estos últimos, la Comisión ha presentado informes definitivos sobre todos los temas, salvo tres, que fueran incluidos en la lista inicial o agregados a ella. Al término de sus labores de este año, la Comisión someterá informes definitivos sobre otros dos temas, y proyectos aprobados en primera lectura en dos más. Dados los avances logrados en los demás temas de que se ocupa actualmente, la Comisión hubiera podido encontrarse al término del mandato quinquenal de sus actuales miembros en 2021, cerca de agotar su agenda corriente tal como ésta se presenta hoy en día.

Sin embargo, la Comisión continuará entretanto, desde este mismo período de sesiones, en su tarea permanente de seleccionar su temario para el futuro. En ese proceso, no deberá limitarse a temas tradicionales, como preponderamente lo ha hecho en el pasado, sino que deberá considerar también aquellos que reflejen las nuevas cuestiones surgidas en el ámbito del Derecho Internacional y las preocupaciones urgentes de la comunidad internacional en su conjunto, conforme al cuarto de los criterios adoptados en 1998 para la selección de temas. Al respecto es altamente significativo que, de conformidad con el Articulo 17 de su Estatuto, y en respuesta al llamado que hiciera en su informe del año pasado, la Comisión ha recibido de un Estado Miembro la petición formal de inscribir en su Programa de Trabajo un novedoso tema, que responde a una necesidad especialmente apremiante para el importante sector de la comunidad internacional a que ese Estado pertenece.

De lo expuesto anteriormente se deduce que la Comisión de Derecho Internacional ha cumplido con creces la noble misión que le asignara la comunidad de naciones, fielmente representada en la Asamblea General. De esa forma, su contribución ha sido fundamental para el afianzamiento del imperio del derecho en las relaciones internacionales, permitiendo su evolución después de la Segunda Guerra Mundial de un esquema de confrontación a un esquema

3 Naciones Unidas, 'Examen del derecho internacional en relación con la labor de codificación de la Comisión de Derecho Internacional: Trabajo preparatorio en el ámbito del artículo 18, párrafo 1, del Estatuto de la Comisión de Derecho Internacional' (1949) Documento de Naciones Unidas No. A/CN.4/1/Rev.1.

de cooperación. Ha sido éste un laborioso pero constructivo proceso de multilaterización el que, sin embargo, se ve amenazado hoy en día por la invocación unilateral de parte de influyentes actores en el concierto mundial, de una desmesurada noción de "interés nacional" en el ejercicio de la soberanía.

El deber de cooperar, que explícita o implícitamente ocupa un sitio céntrico en la arquitectura de los trabajos e informes definitivos de la Comisión, es un principio bien establecido en Derecho Internacional, anclado en la Carta y en la Declaración de 1970 sobre los Principios referentes a las Relaciones de Amistad y a la Cooperación entre los Estados,[4] y reflejado en multitud de otros instrumentos internacionales. Representa la concretización práctica del principio de Solidaridad el cual, como lo ha enfatizado un antiguo Secretario-General, "tiene sus raíces en los principios éticos de la Carta".[5] Es en la Solidaridad donde el mandato de la Comisión encuentra "*telos*", el fin último, como una expresión de una herencia común en un contexto global. La Solidaridad, como principio ético/jurídico internacional, da origen a un sistema de cooperación, en apoyo de la noción de que sirven mejor a la justicia y el bien común las políticas que benefician a todas las naciones.

No debe entenderse que la cooperación disminuya las prerrogativas de un Estado soberano dentro de los límites del Derecho Internacional. Por el contrario, el principio subraya el respeto de la soberanía de los Estados y su corolario, la no intervención y la función primordial de las autoridades del Estado en la adopción de medidas de toda índole que son las expresiones del "derecho de todo Estado soberano a conducir sus asuntos sin injerencias externas", como definió dicho principio la Corte Internacional en su fallo de 1986 en el caso relativo a las Actividades Militares y Paramilitares en y contra Nicaragua.[6] Los principios correlativos de la soberanía y la no intervención presuponen una determinada esfera nacional o un "*domain reservé*", en el que un Estado puede ejercer su autoridad exclusiva. Esa autoridad soberana es un atributo esencial de la condición de Estado, pero no es absoluta en modo alguno. Como lo enfatizara el Juez Alejandro Alvarez en su Opinión disidente en el caso del Canal de Corfú, "la Soberanía confiere derechos a los Estados y les impone obligaciones".[7] Y como sostuviera en un reciente artículo el antiguo miembro de

---

4 Asamblea General de las Naciones Unidas, Resolución 2625 (XXV) (de 24 de octubre de 1970).

5 Informe del Secretario General, 'Nuevo orden humanitario internacional: Asistencia humanitaria a la victimas de desastres naturales y situaciones de emergencia similares' (1990) Documento de Naciones Unidas No. A/45/587 para. 5 (traducción por el autor).

6 *Military and Paramilitary Activities in and against Nicaragua* (*Nicaragua v United States*) (sentencia de fondo) [1986] Reportes de la CIJ 14, 106 (traducción por el autor).

7 *Corfu Channel Case* (*United Kingdom v Albania*) (opinión separada del Juez Álvarez) [1949] Reportes de la CIJ 39, 43 (traducción por el autor).

la Comisión Martti Koskenniemi: "one is most Sovereign when one is mostly intensively engaged with the international world".[8]

La Organización de las Naciones Unidas es ejemplo, el más perfeccionado, de cooperación internacional institucionalizada a nivel universal. Y lo es también en sí misma la Comisión de Derecho Internacional, órgano subsidiario de la Asamblea General. Dada su competencia, que abarca la amplia gama de ramas del Derecho Internacional, lo es por su composición y la forma como se procede por la Asamblea a la elección de sus miembros, que garantiza dentro de una distribución regional equitativa el cumplimiento de los criterios enunciados en el Artículo 8 del Estatuto. En este contexto es de destacar el hecho de que, a pesar de encontrarse todavía muy lejos de realización en la Comisión de Derecho Internacional el perentorio objetivo de la paridad de género en los organismos internacionales, la Comisión cuenta en el presente quinquenio con el mayor número de mujeres miembro en su historia. Y es la Comisión asimismo ejemplo de cooperación gracias a sus métodos de trabajo, diseñados para facilitar la búsqueda de bases jurídicas comunes para sus proyectos.

La Comisión ha desempeñado un papel preponderante en la construcción del edificio sobre el cual se asienta y funciona la comunidad internacional de la post-guerra. Dadas las preocupantes tendencias aislacionistas que han hecho reciente irrupción en el panorama internacional, hoy más que nunca se hace necesaria la continuada realización de su vocación en pro del afianzamiento del derecho internacional. Sigue siendo éste el baluarte más firme para asegurar la supervivencia de una sociedad internacional que todas las naciones han ayudado a construir y de la cual todas se han beneficiado.

8 Martti Koskenniemi, 'The many faces of sovereignty. Introduction to critical legal thinking' (2007) 4(2) KustafinULRev 290.

Statement by Eduardo Valencia-Ospina

Chair of the International Law Commission at Its Seventieth Session

(*Translation from the Spanish Original*)

It is an honour for me, on behalf of the International Law Commission, to welcome you all to this solemn meeting to mark the beginning of the Commission's seventieth anniversary commemoration. Allow me to thank the dignitaries who have accepted the invitation to speak on this occasion: H.E. Miroslav Lajčák, the President of the General Assembly; Miguel Ferreira de Serpa Soares, the Legal Counsel of the United Nations; H.E. Burhan Gafoor, the Permanent Representative of Singapore and Chair of the Sixth Committee; the representatives of the host countries of the Commission at its seat in Geneva and at the United Nations Headquarters, H.E. Jürg Lauber, the Permanent Representative of Switzerland, and Jennifer Newstead, the Legal Adviser at the Department of State of the United States of America; and Professor Nico Schrijver, the President of the *Institut de Droit international*.

I would like to express appreciation to all those who have graced us with their presence today: permanent representatives and other members of permanent missions; legal advisers of foreign ministries and permanent missions; senior officials of the Secretariat and representatives of specialized agencies and other international organizations; teachers and students from law faculties and other academic institutions; and former members of the Commission and its secretariat.

Exceptionally, the Commission is holding the first part of its session for 2018 at United Nations Headquarters to mark its seventieth anniversary. By an express decision of the General Assembly – the Commission's founding body – the Commission is meeting for five weeks in New York, not far from Lake Success, where it held its first session in 1949.[1] Thus, the oft-expressed desire of the Sixth Committee, echoed by the Commission, has been made reality, serving to strengthen the already close relationship between the two bodies.

That relationship finds expression, above all, in the resolutions periodically adopted by the General Assembly, which result from the consideration given at each of its regular sessions by the Sixth Committee to the reports submitted to it every year by the Commission. Those reports, 70 to date all told, embody the crucial contribution made by the Commission in the course of its existence to the

1 UNGA Res 72/116 (7 December 2017), para 14.

progressive development and codification of international law. They provide the clearest evidence of the constructive and effective manner in which the Commission has fulfilled the functions entrusted to it by the Assembly, in accordance with its mandate under Article 13 (1) (a) of the Charter of the United Nations.

The inclusion of that provision in the constituent instrument of the United Nations at the San Francisco Conference was by no means a one-off initiative. On the contrary, it represented a decisive step forward within the "codification movement", the origins of which date back to the late eighteenth century. The movement was given a significant boost with the establishment, in 1873, of the *Institut de Droit international* and the International Law Association. Those institutions, at twice the age of the Commission, continue to work privately for their shared goal. It is, therefore, all the more significant that, on this seventieth anniversary of the Commission, the President of the *Institut* has been chosen to deliver the keynote address that will conclude today's solemn meeting.

There is no need here to enumerate the many influential substantive achievements of the Commission on various subjects in the course of its prodigious work down the years. Suffice it to underline that the Commission has addressed, among other crucial issues, the three main sources of international law mentioned in Article 38, paragraph 1, of the Statute of the International Court of Justice. Testimony to that is its final text on the law of treaties, which served as the basis for the Vienna Convention of 1969.[2] That foundational instrument, which received near-universal endorsement from Member States, has been a rich source of inspiration for the Commission in its own study of a dozen topics arising from the Convention or closely related to it. Likewise, the final text of the draft conclusions on the identification of customary international law, the second of the main sources, which is to be adopted at the current session. The third source, general principles of law, was added as a topic to the Commission's long-term programme of work last year.

It is appropriate mentioning here the accomplishments of the Commission with regard to the topics included in its long-term programme of work. Already at its first session in 1949, the Commission drew up a programme of work comprising 14 topics selected from a list of 25 options contained in the famous Lauterpacht memorandum.[3] Since 1949, a further 38 topics, some of them divided into separate sub-topics, have been selected for examination. The nine that make up the

2 Vienna Convention on the Law of Treaties, adopted 23 May 1969, entered into force 27 January 1980, 1155 UNTS 331.

3 United Nations, 'Survey of International Law in Relation to the Work of Codification of the International Law Commission: Preparatory work within the purview of article 18, paragraph 1, of the of the International Law Commission' (1949) UN Doc A/CN.4/1/Rev.1.

Commission's current programme of work are under active consideration. Those aside, the Commission has submitted final reports on all but three of the topics that were on the initial list or added subsequently. Upon concluding its work this year, the Committee will submit final reports on two more topics and will complete drafts, adopted on first reading, on another two. Given the progress made on the remaining topics, the Commission may find itself close to completing its current programme of work by the end of the present quinquennium in 2021.

The Commission will, however, from this session onwards continue the ongoing task of selecting topics for future consideration. It should not, as it has largely done in the past, limit itself to traditional topics. Rather, it should consider topics that reflect new developments in international law and the pressing concerns of the international community as a whole, in line with the fourth of the criteria agreed upon in 1998 for the selection of topics. In that regard, it is highly significant that, in accordance with article 17 of its statute and in response to the call in its report of last year, the Commission has received a formal request from a Member State for the inclusion of a new topic responding to a particularly pressing need of a large sector of the international community, to which that State belongs.

It may thus be concluded that the International Law Commission has fully accomplished the noble mission entrusted to it by the community of nations, duly represented by the General Assembly. Its contribution has been fundamental in terms of strengthening the rule of law in international relations, enabling them to evolve since the Second World War from a framework of confrontation to one of cooperation. Today, however, this painstaking yet constructive process towards the achievement of multilateralism is being threatened by the unilateral actions of some major players on the world stage and the outsized role that "national interest" is playing in their exercise of sovereignty.

The duty to cooperate, which lies, explicitly or implicitly, at the heart of the Commission's final outputs and reports, is a well-established principle of international law enshrined in the Charter and the 1970 Declaration on Principles of International Law concerning Friendly Relations and Cooperation among States in accordance with the Charter of the United Nations[4] and reflected in many other international instruments. It represents the practical expression of the principle of solidarity that, as one former Secretary-General emphasized, "has its roots in the ethical principles of the Charter".[5] Solidarity provides the

4 UNGA Res 2625 (XXV) (24 October 1970).

5 Report of the Secretary-General, 'New International Humanitarian Order: Humanitarian Assistance to Victims of Natural Disasters and Similar Emergency Situations' (1990) UN Doc A/45/587 para 5.

Commission's mandate with its *telos*, or ultimate purpose, as an expression of a common global legacy. As an international ethical and legal principle, solidarity gives rise to a system of cooperation underpinning the notion that justice and the common good are best served by policies that benefit all nations.

Cooperation should not be interpreted as diminishing the prerogatives of a sovereign State within the limits of international law. On the contrary, the principle emphasizes respect for the sovereignty of States and its corollary, non-intervention and the primary role of State authorities in the adoption of measures of any kind that are expressions of the "right of every sovereign State to conduct its affairs without outside interference", as the International Court of Justice put it in its judgment of 1986 in the case concerning *Military and Paramilitary Activities in and against Nicaragua*.[6] The correlating principles of sovereignty and non-intervention presuppose a given domestic sphere, or a *domaine réservé*, over which a State may exercise its exclusive authority. This sovereign authority remains central to the concept of statehood, but it is by no means absolute. As Judge Alejandro Álvarez made clear in his individual opinion in the *Corfu Channel case*, "sovereignty confers rights upon States and imposes obligations on them".[7] And Martti Koskenniemi, a former member of the Commission, maintained in a recent article that one is most sovereign when one is most intensively engaged with the international world.[8]

The United Nations is the supreme example of a global institution that embodies international cooperation. The Commission itself, a subsidiary body of the General Assembly, is another example, given its mandate covering a broad range of topics of international law, its membership and the way in which its members are elected by the Assembly, which ensures, within the framework of equitable regional representation, compliance with the criteria set forth in article 8 of its statute. Although the Commission is still a long way from achieving gender parity – an imperative goal for international organizations – in the current quinquennium it has the largest number of women members in its history. The Commission also sets an example of cooperation through its working methods, which are designed to facilitate the search for common legal ground on which to build its drafts.

---

6 *Military and Paramilitary Activities in and against Nicaragua* (*Nicaragua v United States*) (Merits) [1986] ICJ Rep 14, 106.

7 *Corfu Channel Case* (*United Kingdom v Albania*) (Separate Opinion Judge Alvarez) [1949] ICJ Rep 39, 43.

8 Martti Koskenniemi, 'The many faces of sovereignty. Introduction to critical legal thinking' (2007) 4(2) KustafinULRev 290.

The Commission has played a crucial role in laying the foundations for the proper functioning of the international community in the post-war era. Given the worrying isolationist tendencies that have recently surfaced on the world stage, there is a need, today more than ever, for it to continue its work of consolidating international law, which remains the sturdiest bulwark for ensuring the survival of an international society that all nations have helped to build and from which all have benefited.

Statement by Miroslav Lajčák

President of the General Assembly of the United Nations at Its Seventy-Second Session

Let me start by congratulating the International Law Commission on this landmark anniversary.

Over these past 70 years, 229 experts have given service of the highest quality. Each has contributed to making the Commission the unique success it has been. "Persons of recognized competence in international law";[1] experts from various legal systems and all geographic regions; professionals with different skills – lawyers, diplomats, academics, and jurists of the highest calibre. All working together despite differences. All working to achieve a common goal: the codification and progressive development of international law. I must, however, lament the limited number of women. It took 54 years before the first woman was elected. And even now only four of the 34 members are women. We must do better.

The Commission has contributed significantly to monumental pieces of work on many topics. The body of international law has become more robust. This is to the benefit of the people of the world. As we celebrate this occasion, I want to use the opportunity to make three points:

First, we must recognize the interface between the legal and the political. They are not at odds but complement each other. Both are essential for the success of the progressive development and codification of international law. In doing so we fulfil the mandate provided in the Charter.

The International Law Commission has helped to create many key international instruments. It is through the interaction between the legal and the political that the United Nations has made achievements in the international legal system. Debates in the Sixth Committee provide a way to foster this interaction. I welcome the efforts to streamline the dialogue between Committee and the Commission.

Further, the Commission's statute envisions an active role for States. Governments are invited to submit written comments to the Commission. We should make more use of this provision. It is important that such substantive input comes from all regions, groups and legal traditions.

Second, the ultimate beneficiaries are people. The United Nations exists for people. So too does the law. International law must continue to work both for

1 See article 2 of the ILC statute, UNGA Res 174(II) (21 November 1947) as amended by UNGA Res 485(V) (12 December 1950); UNGA Res. 984(X) (3 December 1955); UNGA Res 985(X) (3 December 1955) and UNGA Res 36/39 (18 November 1981).

 | DOI:10.1163/9789004434271_036

States and for people. For example, there has been significant progress with respect to the development of international criminal law. We have avenues for the prevention, prosecution and punishment of most serious crimes. The Rome Statute[2] and the International Criminal Court are the testimony of this achievement. The Commission was at the genesis of this process.[3]

I recently visited the Genocide Memorial in Rwanda. There I had the honour to make a $10,000 contribution on behalf of the General Assembly. But what stood out was the lasting impact of that horrific period. The law failed to prevent; it failed to protect. People suffered and died. We said "never again" and we must live up to that promise.

It is encouraging to see the Commission's focus on crimes against humanity. In 1946, these crimes were prosecuted at Nuremberg. Today our focus must be on prevention. I encourage the Commission to maintain its momentum in this area. Atrocity crimes shock our collective conscience. Accountability, and strong rule of law, are key to preventing them.

My final point is on multilateralism. Here again, the Commission plays an indispensable role. The rule of law is the bedrock on which multilateralism is built. However, we must acknowledge the current context: multilateralism is under pressure. We need to strengthen it. Developing the law is crucial to doing so. This is what many of us as Member States depend on: a rules-based international order.

We have elaborated dozens of legal instruments over the past decades. Many have brought order and accountability. Many of them have prevented conflict. Others have supported development. As we identify new and emerging challenges, it is our duty to develop appropriate legal responses.

The International Law Commission is not a static body. Rather, it has made a mark both with codification *and* progressive development. It has contributed to 22 multilateral conventions and protocols and this work continues as one looks at uncharted territory. I encourage the Commission to forge ahead with developing international law. In doing so, the Commission helps to reinforce multilateralism.

The seventieth anniversary is good to reflect on the past, but it also offers a fitting opportunity to look to the decades ahead. I wish the Commission every success in its crucial work for years to come. On behalf of all "the peoples of these United Nations", I thank you.

2 Adopted 17 July 1998, entered into force 1 July 2002, 2187 UNTS 3.

3 See ILC, 'Draft Statute for an International Criminal Court, with commentaries' [1994] II(2) ILC Ybk 26.

Statement by Miguel de Serpa Soares

Under-Secretary-General for Legal Affairs and United Nations Legal Counsel

On behalf of the Secretary-General, I am delighted to welcome you to New York today, as we have come together to mark the seventieth anniversary of the International Law Commission. Established in 1947, the Commission held its first session at the temporary headquarters of the United Nations at Lake Success in 1949, and it is only appropriate to celebrate its seventieth session close to where it all began.

It has been said that anniversaries are similar to birthdays: occasions to celebrate and to look ahead, among friends with whom one shares a past and a future. However, anniversaries are better than birthdays: anniversaries do not come with the regret of increasing age but are associated with the joys of achievement.

When I look around this room today, I see friends and companions of the International Law Commission. Like myself, as the former Legal Adviser of Portugal and now United Nations Legal Counsel, many of you have worked with the Commission in different capacities. Being among friends of the Commission, I would like to use this opportunity to look at its past achievements, current work and future challenges.

To recognize the great achievements of the International Law Commission, it is important to see it as part of the broader movement towards the codification of international law. As early as 1873, international lawyers founded two private associations: the *Institut de Droit international* and the Association for the Reform and Codification of the Law of Nations (now known as the International Law Association (ILA)). Both continue to promote the progress of international law in their own way. In fact, I am delighted that we have the President of the *Institut de Droit international law*, Professor Nico Schrijver, with us today.

Those private codification efforts were followed by the establishment of a major Codification Conference under the auspices of the League of Nations in The Hague in 1930. At the time, however, delegates found that they had too little time to cover the many complex issues on the agenda. As it turned out, codification involved more than mechanically transcribing customary law into written agreements; it also required the progressive development of new rules, to fill gaps and resolve conflicts – a political as much as a legal exercise. Although the Conference produced only a few notable results, it did make general recommendations to improve the codification process, which informed the drafting of the Statute of the International Law Commission.

The impetus for the creation of an International Law Commission arose out of the horrors of the Second World War. At the San Francisco Conference in 1945, the 50 States negotiating the Charter of the United Nations were anxious to revitalize and strengthen international law. Accordingly, Article 13, paragraph 1(a), of the Charter instructs the General Assembly to "initiate studies and make recommendations for the purpose of [...] encouraging the progressive development of international law and its codification." To make more precise recommendations on how to discharge this mandate, the first session of the General Assembly established a "Committee on the Progressive Development of International Law and its Codification", consisting of 17 government representatives, who recommended the creation of an International Law Commission.[1] The General Assembly endorsed that recommendation and approved the statute of the International Law Commission in 1947.[2]

Today and during the commemorative events in Geneva in July, we will contemplate the many accomplishments of the Commission in progressively developing and codifying international law over the past seven decades. It is hard to imagine contemporary international relations without the 1961 Convention on Diplomatic Relations,[3] the 1969 Vienna Convention on the Law of Treaties,[4] the Rome Statute of the International Criminal Court[5] or the articles on responsibility of States for internationally wrongful acts.[6] But what is the secret of the Commission's success? The answer to this question is manifold.

First, unlike private codification bodies such as the International Law Association or the *Institut de Droit international*, the Commission has an intergovernmental mandate. Members serve as independent legal experts, but the Commission consults with governments throughout the drafting process and submits the outcome of its work to the General Assembly, a political body. This afternoon, we will discuss the relationship between the Commission and the Sixth Committee, which prepares the draft resolutions on the Commission's work for adoption by the General Assembly. The Sixth Committee called its first session to order in 1946. In this and many other ways, the Commission and the Committee thus share a common journey and a common fate.

1 UNGA Res 94(I) (11 December 1946).
2 Statute of the ILC, UNGA Res 174(II) (21 November 1947).
3 Adopted 18 April 1961, entered into force 24 April 1964, 500 UNTS 95.
4 Adopted 23 May 1969, entered into force 27 January 1980, 1155 UNTS 331.
5 Adopted 17 July 1998, entered into force 1 July 2002, 2187 UNTS 3.
6 UNGA Res 56/83 (12 December 2001), annex.

Related to its intergovernmental nature is a second reason for the Commission's success: its unique composition. As a subsidiary organ of the General Assembly, the membership of the Commission is based on the five regional groups of the United Nations. As such, it is a melting pot of legal traditions and regional perspectives. Moreover, candidates for membership are drawn from the various segments of the international legal community, such as academia, the diplomatic corps, government ministries and international organizations. As the members typically serve in other international law-related professions, the Commission remains in close touch with the realities of international relations.

Third, the Commission's sophisticated working methods have contributed to the success of its codification efforts. As a permanent entity, the Commission is not subject to time-constraints associated with diplomatic conferences such as that in The Hague in 1930. It functions more like a legislative drafting body that develops draft provisions for international conventions in different readings. While typically appointing Special Rapporteurs to lead a drafting project, other Commission members participate actively in the drafting process in the Drafting Committee before the Commission as a whole adopts the draft provisions.

Last but not least, the Commission's success is contributed to by its Secretariat, the Codification Division of the Office of Legal Affairs. As I noted in my speech before the Commission earlier this month, the Codification Division has assisted the Commission from its very inception in progressively developing and codifying international law in important ways. Through Secretariat studies, memoranda and *ad hoc* research tasks, it has provided substantive input to the work of the Commission. The survey of international law that the Secretariat prepared in 1948 served as the basis for the 14 topics that the Commission selected for progressive development and codification at its first session in 1949. The Secretariat has continued to propose topics for codification, such as the recently adopted articles on protection of persons in the event of disasters. The most recent survey of international law carried out by the Codification Division in 2016 has made a notable contribution to the Commission's current consideration of possible topics for its programme of work.

The Codification Division also served as the secretariat of numerous diplomatic conferences, transforming the texts so carefully crafted by the Commission into international conventions. As the Codification Division has serviced quite a number of United Nations bodies, most notably the Sixth Committee, its expertise and long-standing experience have made a significant contribution to the progressive development and codification of international law in its different stages. This leads me back to the first reason I gave for the

Commission's success: the Commission's intergovernmental mandate. The Codification Division, as the Secretariat of the Commission, is part of the Office of Legal Affairs and the United Nations. As such, it has benefitted from the immense institutional support of the Organization.

After reflecting on the past successes of the Commission, allow me to briefly strike a balance for the future. After all, this is also what anniversaries are for. Times have changed since the International Law Commission was first established in 1947. As evidenced by the changing outcomes of the Commission's work, the needs of the international community are different today. While the Commission still produces draft articles, it also adopts draft guidelines and draft conclusions. The Commission has remained true to general international law topics such as the law of treaties and the law of international responsibility. But it has also taken up the challenge of addressing more specialized, technical topics, such as the protection of the atmosphere or the protection of persons in the event of disasters.

The Commission also faces important challenges with regard to its composition. As I have observed on previous occasions, the Commission suffers from a lack of equitable gender representation. Over the past 70 years, the Commission has only had seven women among its members. I am pleased that the number of women on the Commission was doubled to four in last year's election. And I remain hopeful that Member States, the General Assembly and the Commission will work together in achieving gender parity in the foreseeable future.

In light of its achievements over the past 70 years, I am confident that the Commission will live up to these current and upcoming challenges.

In closing, I would like to reiterate that the progressive development and codification of international law are fundamental to maintaining peaceful international relations. The International Law Commission has been a central contributor to making "peace through law" – to borrow a well-known phrase coined at the end of the Second World War. I can assure you that my office will continue to assist the Commission in discharging its indispensable mandate with professionalism, substantive expertise and enthusiasm.

Statement by Burhan Gafoor

Chair of the Sixth Committee of the General Assembly at Its Seventy-Second Session

We are meeting here on this very special occasion to pay tribute to the International Law Commission. It is not often that an international body celebrates seventy years of continued existence. The International Law Commission has not only existed for 70 years, it has made a significant contribution to progressive development and codification of international law, as well as to the work of the United Nations.

I am honoured to speak today in my capacity as Chair of the Sixth Committee of the seventy-second session of the General Assembly. The commemoration of the International Law Commission is also in many ways a commemoration of the work of the Sixth Committee. The International Law Commission and Sixth Committee are partners in the promotion of international law. We have worked very closely, as envisaged in General Assembly resolutions as well as the statute of the Commission. This working relationship and partnership is on full display each year at what has come to be known as "International Law Week", during which the Sixth Committee debates and considers the annual report of the International Law Commission to the General Assembly. This is an important avenue for members of the Sixth Committee to provide guidance and substantive inputs to the Commission, which in turn helps to develop and progress the work of the Commission. Equally important are the informal interactions that occur between the Committee and the Commission during this time of the General Assembly. Such interactions help to foster a deeper understanding between the two bodies that is so crucial for this partnership to work. In this regard, I am particularly pleased with the many opportunities for interaction over the past weeks, as evidenced by the numerous side events held at the sidelines of the Commission's meetings.

It is worth recalling that the establishment of the International Law Commission came from a recommendation of the Sixth Committee at its second session in 1947, with elections of members of the Commission taking place in 1948. Indeed, the Commission helps the General Assembly to discharge its Charter responsibility to initiate studies and make recommendations to encourage the progressive development of international law and its codification.

The Commission's annual meetings since 1949, and its work over the years, have led to the adoption of many substantive texts. The areas covered have ranged from the law of the sea to contemporary challenges like protection of

 | DOI:10.1163/9789004434271_038

the atmosphere and the responsibility of international organizations, as well as the immunity of State officials from foreign criminal jurisdiction. The wide areas of coverage, together with the large number of instruments eventually adopted, is impressive. Over the years, 17 multilateral conventions have been concluded under the auspices of the United Nations based on drafts prepared by the Commission. Equally impressive is the intellectual rigour and scholarship that have informed these outcomes, thanks to the contribution and hard work of members of the Commission.

There is no doubt that the International Law Commission has made an indispensable contribution to the progressive development and codification of international law. After 70 years, the role of the Commission remains as important as ever, especially at a time when multilateralism is being challenged. At this time, it is important for members of the United Nations to defend the multilateral rules-based system and the principles of international law. At the same time, the United Nations has a responsibility to continue to develop new norms and rules and codify State practice in the field of international law. The work of the International Law Commission has therefore become critical as a vehicle to reinforce the multilateral rules-based system. The strength of the Commission is that it is an independent body of experts who represent the principal legal systems of the world. Therefore, the work of the Commission can help to build understanding, bridge differences and lay the groundwork for political decisions to be made by Member States in the General Assembly.

As we look beyond, there is one particular area that deserves mention on an occasion like this. In the last seven decades, only seven women jurists have served on the International Law Commission, namely Paula Escarameia, Hanqin Xue, Concepción Escobar Hernández, Marie Jacobsson, Marja Lehto, Patrícia Galvão Teles, and Nilüfer Oral. At this rate, it will take more than 100 years to achieve gender parity. This is certainly not acceptable and clearly an area for improvement, for both the General Assembly and the Commission. All members of the United Nations have a responsibility to nominate women candidates to the Commission. It is my hope that we can all work together to bring gender parity to the Commission and hopefully we can achieve this when we celebrate the 80th anniversary of the Commission.

Let me conclude by saying that the relationship between the Sixth Committee and the International Law Commission is a special and long-standing one. On the one hand, the Commission looks at issues from an independent, technical and academic perspective. On the other hand, the Sixth Committee attempts to build political consensus on legal issues, so that legal instruments can be adopted by the United Nations. It is an organic and symbiotic relationship that is based on a common objective, which is to support the progressive development and codification of international law and to strengthen the multilateral rules-based system. On behalf of all members of the Sixth Committee, I can say with confidence that we are proud of the work done by the International Law Commission in the last 70 years. I take this opportunity to acknowledge the work done by each member of the Commission and the Chair of the Commission. You have our support and our appreciation. The Committee looks forward to continuing its engagement and partnership with the Commission in the service of international law and the United Nations.

Déclaration de Jürg Lauber

Représentant permanent de la Suisse auprès des Nations Unies

(*French original*)

J'ai l'honneur, en tant que représentant de l'État hôte des réunions de la Commission du droit international, de prononcer quelques mots pour célébrer cette occasion si spéciale qu'est le soixante-dixième anniversaire de la Commission du droit international.

L'importance de cette journée relève tout d'abord d'un simple constat: le droit international public est un élément central des relations entre les États et constitue la base d'un ordre international stable, juste et pacifique. Pour cette raison, le renforcement du droit international public est un élément fondamental de la Charte des Nations Unies et de la politique étrangère de la Suisse. Si ce constat valait il y a 70 ans déjà, force est de constater qu'il conserve toute sa pertinence de nos jours, particulièrement dans un monde en mutation.

La Commission du droit international a été créée dans le but de promouvoir le développement progressif du droit international et sa codification. Depuis 70 ans, la Commission s'est penchée sur des thèmes très variés tels que les réserves aux traités, les effets des conflits armés sur les traités, la succession d'États et de gouvernements, les immunités juridictionnelles des États et de leurs biens, la responsabilité des États, pour ne citer que quelques exemples. Le traitement de ces thèmes et de bien d'autres sujets d'actualité pour le droit international a permis à la Commission de contribuer activement au développement et à la codification du droit international public. Nous attendons déjà avec grand intérêt le résultat des travaux de la Commission sur les thèmes actuellement à l'agenda comme les normes impératives du droit international, les crimes contre l'humanité, la protection de l'environnement en rapport avec les conflits armés et l'immunité de juridiction pénale étrangère des représentants de l'État.

La Commission choisit des thèmes qui répondent à des critères tels que les besoins des États en matière de codification du droit international, les tendances nouvelles et les préoccupations pressantes des États. En faisant ceci, elle s'assure que le fruit de ses travaux est d'une grande utilité pour la communauté internationale. Ces critères conservent toute leur pertinence de nos jours.

Pour ces raisons, la Suisse est fière d'accueillir les réunions de la Commission du droit international à Genève et de pouvoir, par ce biais, contribuer à son activité.

 | DOI:10.1163/9789004434271_039

Tout en saluant tout effort visant à renforcer le dialogue entre la Sixième Commission de l'Assemblée générale et la Commission du droit international, le choix de Genève comme siège des réunions de la Commission du droit international permet notamment de garantir la complète indépendance de son activité par rapport à la Sixième Commission, qui siège à New York et dont le travail est également hautement apprécié. Nous estimons que la diversité des cultures juridiques propres à ces deux organes constitue un atout pour le développement du droit international. Par ailleurs, une présence à Genève offre des synergies avec plus de 30 organisations internationales actives dans les domaines qui influencent le quotidien de chacun.

Il nous paraît également important de rappeler dans ce contexte, et aussi dans une optique de valorisation de la langue française, qu'il est indispensable que le droit international et son développement soient promus non seulement depuis le siège de New York, mais également depuis celui de Genève. À cet égard, on rappellera le Séminaire du droit international qui se tient chaque année à Genève et permet à ses participants – étudiants, professeurs, fonctionnaires – de se familiariser avec les travaux de la Commission du droit international, notamment en assistant aux séances publiques et aux conférences animées par ses membres.

La Suisse se réjouit de participer aux événements organisés ici à New York et à Genève les 5 et 6 juillet pour célébrer la création si importante de la Commission du droit international il y a 70 ans.

Statement by Jürg Lauber

Permanent Representative of Switzerland to the United Nations

(*Translation from the French original*)

I have the honour, in my capacity as representative of the host State of the meetings of the International Law Commission, to say a few words to mark this special occasion, the seventieth anniversary of the International Law Commission.

The significance of this day stems, first and foremost, from a simple observation: public international law is central to relations between States and forms the foundation for a stable, just and peaceful international order. As such, the strengthening of public international law is a fundamental element of the Charter of the United Nations and the foreign policy of Switzerland. While this observation held true 70 years ago, it must be acknowledged that it remains highly relevant today, especially in a changing world.

The International Law Commission was established to encourage the progressive development of international law and its codification. Over the past 70 years, the Commission has addressed a wide range of topics such as reservations to treaties, the effects of armed conflict on treaties, the succession of States and governments, jurisdictional immunities of States and their property, and State responsibility, to name just a few. The treatment of these topics and many other topical issues of international law has allowed the Commission to contribute actively to the development and codification of public international law. We await with great interest the outcome of the Commission's work on the topics currently on the agenda, including peremptory norms of international law, crimes against humanity, the protection of the environment in relation to armed conflicts and the immunity of State officials from foreign criminal jurisdiction.

The Committee selects themes that meet criteria such as the needs of States with respect to codification of international law, new trends and pressing concerns of States. In so doing, it ensures that the results of its work are of great value to the international community. These criteria remain fully relevant today.

Switzerland is therefore proud to host the meetings of the International Law Commission in Geneva and, thereby, contribute to its work.

While all efforts to strengthen dialogue between the Sixth Committee of the General Assembly and the International Law Commission are welcome, the

© THE UNITED NATIONS, 2021 | DOI:10.1163/9789004434271_040

choice to hold the meetings of the International Law Commission in Geneva ensures notably the complete independence of its work from the Sixth Committee, which is based in New York and whose work is also highly appreciated. We believe that the difference in the legal cultures specific to these two bodies is an asset for the development of international law. In addition, a presence in Geneva enables synergies with over 30 international organizations active in areas that affect everyone's daily lives.

In this connection, and with a view to enhancing the status of the French language, we also consider it important to mention that international law and its development must be promoted not only from United Nations Headquarters in New York, but also from the United Nations Office at Geneva. It will be recalled that the International Law Seminar is held annually in Geneva and allows participants – students, faculty and officials – to learn about the work of the International Law Commission, including through public sessions and lectures given by its members.

Switzerland is pleased to participate in the commemorative events held here in New York, and in Geneva on 5 and 6 July, to mark the vital creation of the International Law Commission, 70 years ago.

Statement by Jennifer Newstead

Legal Adviser of the Department of State of the United States of America

It is an honor to be here with this distinguished group of speakers. First, I would like to congratulate Eduardo Valencia-Ospina upon his election this session as Chair of the Commission. In addition, I would like to congratulate Mr. Evgeny Zagaynov, the Legal Adviser of the Ministry of Foreign Affairs of the Russian Federation, upon his very recent election this session as a member of the Commission.

I would also like to recognize Miguel de Serpa Soares, whom I had the pleasure to meet in Washington this past March. The United States is delighted this May to be serving as the host country for the Commission during the first half of its seventieth session. Holding this event at the headquarters of the United Nations is a perfect reminder of our collective efforts to address today's global challenges and the vital role that international law plays in those efforts.

Since the inception of the Commission, the United States has closely followed the Commission's valuable work on the codification and development of international law. In its 70 years of work, the Commission has addressed a broad range of international law issues, and has produced comprehensive analyses that provide valuable insights to government lawyers, private practitioners, judges, and academics. The Commission's work at times has formed the basis for multilateral treaties that have become foundational elements of international law, such as the Vienna Convention on Diplomatic Relations.[1] The Commission's work also serves as a valuable resource for navigating the increasingly complex world of international law.

While the United States has not always agreed with proposed topics or particular conclusions, the United States recognizes the unique role the Commission plays in advancing the rule of law in the international arena. As it has in the past, the United States will continue to support the work of the Commission by engaging with the full range of the topics on the Commission's agenda, commenting in the Sixth Committee on the Commission's work, and nominating highly-qualified candidates for election to the Commission.

In this respect, the United States is very pleased there is currently a United States national on the Commission, Professor Sean Murphy, a distinguished international lawyer for more than 25 years with experience as both a

1 Adopted 18 April 1961, entered into force 24 April 1964, 500 UNTS 95.

 | DOI:10.1163/9789004434271_041

government practitioner and professor of law. Sean, who is the 11th American to have served on the Commission, is also serving as Special Rapporteur on the topic of "Crimes against humanity".

As you all know, the statute of the International Law Commission calls for the Commission membership as a whole to represent the main forms of civilization and the principal legal systems of the world. The Commission's diverse membership reflects this aspiration. Its members are elected in a manner that ensures all the world's major regions are represented. These members hail from 34 different nations and come from a wide range of professional backgrounds in government service, academia, and private practice.

In this context, I was pleased to see that in 2016 three women, Patríca Galvão Teles of Portugal, Marja Lehto of Finland, and Nilüfer Oral of Turkey were newly elected to the Commission. They are joining Concepción Escobar Hernández of Spain who was re-elected. In its 70-year history, I believe this is the largest number of women we have had on the Commission at one time. Still, with only 4 women out of 34 total members, I hope that last year's election is merely a step in a long-term development and that membership of women in the Commission will continue to grow.

Again, I appreciate the opportunity to be here today to celebrate the Commission's seventieth anniversary. On behalf of the United States, I extend my thanks to the members of the Commission for their dedication to the promotion of international law. The Commission is currently addressing a number of topics of great interest and importance. I wish the Commission a successful outcome for this year's session, both here in New York and in Geneva.

Keynote Address by Nico Schrijver

President of the Institut de Droit international *and Professor of Public International Law, Leiden University*

1 Introduction*

Mr. Chair, I greatly appreciate your invitation to participate in this debate and I thank you for the welcome that you have kindly extended to me. As President of the *Institut de Droit international* and professor of international law at Leiden University, it is an honour for me to have been invited by the International Law Commission to give the keynote address during the solemn part of the celebrations of seventy years of the International Law Commission. This meeting provides a welcome opportunity to reflect upon the role of the Commission and its members and the important work that you have been pursuing for the promotion of the progressive development of international law and its codification.

The theme for this celebration, "Drawing a balance for the future", is therefore very appropriate. As the afternoon programme will elaborate on the future challenges, I shall focus this morning on the progressive development of international law and its codification from a historical perspective up until today. I shall do this by making a comparison between the contributions made by the International Law Commission and the *Institut de Droit international*, two of the main institutions that have been working on these matters for many years.

As the *Institut* is almost 75 years older than the International Law Commission and stretches into three centuries, kindly allow me first to discuss our efforts for the progressive development of international law and its codification in the period before the creation of the International Law Commission. Subsequently, I will discuss some similarities and differences between the two institutions, followed by various examples where both institutions have contributed to the progressive development of international law.[1] I shall finish by giving reflections for the future, thus bridging you to the afternoon session on this.

---

* The author gratefully acknowledges the very valuable research assistance he received from Iris van der Heijden (LLM) of the *Institut de Droit international* (IDI) in preparing this contribution.

1 The references to the works of the International Law Commission and the *Institut de Droit international* that follow below can all be found on their respective websites: <http://legal.un.org/ilc/> and <http://www.idi-iil.org/>.

II Establishment of the *Institut*

The story of the *Institut* starts in 1873, a few years after the Franco-German War when it was realized that war is a nearly unavoidable element of the human condition. Nevertheless, the hope was expressed to succeed in making wars an exception, limiting them in number and diminishing their horrors by means of progressive development of international law.[2]

One of the founders of the *Institut*, Mr. Rolin-Jaequemyns, wrote an article in 1873 in which he acknowledged the progress made by diplomatic action and individual scientific efforts to progressively develop the law of nations (*jus gentium*), but he considered it to be insufficient. He identified as one of the main obstacles to diplomacy the apparent conflicts between political interests of a particular people and the general common interests of the nations together, especially in the absence of a sufficiently powerful authority. To overcome the insufficiency of diplomatic action and individual scientific efforts, he proposed collective scientific action.[3] Similar thoughts were expressed by other eminent lawyers, which led in 1873 to the establishment of the *Institut*[4] as well as the International Law Association, as non-political private associations for the promotion of progress of international law.

Indeed, since its inception the *Institut* has prepared several codes and proposals that facilitated the work of various diplomatic conferences. To mention some early examples, the draft regulations for international arbitral procedures adopted by the *Institut* in 1875[5] and its Oxford Manual on the laws of war on land adopted in 1880[6] served as a source of inspiration for the 1899 and 1907 Hague Peace Conferences.[7] Until then, such studies had been undertaken by the *Institut* and other scientific societies only, but in the Final

2 Albéric Rolin, *Les origines de l'Institut de Droit international 1873–1923 – Souvenirs d'un témoin par le Baron Albéric Rolin* (Vromant 1923), 7–8.

3 Gustave Rolin-Jaequemyns, 'La nécessité d'organiser une Institution scientifique permanente pour favoriser l'étude et les progrès du Droit International' (1873) RDILC 463, 463–465.

4 See 'Conférence juridique internationale de Gand. Fondation de l'Institut de droit international' ibid 529; 'Communications et documents relatifs à l'Institut de droit international' ibid 667.

5 IDI, 'Projet de règlement pour la procédure arbitrale internationale' (1877) 1 AnnIDI 126.

6 IDI, 'Les lois de la guerre sur terre. Manuel publié par l'Institut de droit international' (Oxford 1881–1882) 5 AnnIDI 157.

7 IDI, 'Séance solennelle d'ouverture de la session. Jeudi 6 septembre 1900 (2 h. après midi)' (Neuchâtel 1900) 18 AnnIDI 121, 138.

Act of the 1907 Hague Conference it was proposed that governments should charge a committee to prepare the work, including determining the topics that would be fit for regulation, and to be discussed for the next Hague Conference, originally envisaged for 1914.[8] It is interesting to note how this indicated a shift from individual scientific associations towards intergovernmental initiative for codification. However, the outbreak of the First World War prevented the convening of this third Hague Peace Conference scheduled for 1915. The war also led inevitably to a certain loss of faith in the strength of international law to maintain peace and observe the laws of war.[9] In order to achieve the objectives set after the First World War – permanent status of peace, restoration of confidence amongst populations and the establishment of close cooperation between nations – three organisms were created by the Treaty of Versailles: the League of Nations, the Permanent Court of International Justice and the International Labour Organization.[10] It was also decided to undertake the codification of international law (*jus gentium*) with the idea that this would foster the achievement of the aforementioned objectives.[11]

III Interaction between the *Institut* and the League of Nations

This attempt to undertake codification took shape in the context of the preparations for the League of Nations Codification Conference, held in 1930. In 1924, the League of Nations adopted a resolution on the creation of a standing organ that would be charged, after possible consultation of the most authorized institutions dedicated to the study of international law, to draft a provisional

8 'Final Act of the Second Peace Conference' (The Hague 15 June – 18 October 1907), reproduced in Shabtai Rosenne, *The Hague Peace Conferences of 1899 and 1907 and International Arbitration. Reports and Documents* (T.M.C. Asser Press 2001) 412.

9 The *Institut* held an extraordinary session in Paris in 1919 "que le Bureau a jugé utile de tenir pour marquer comme l'a bien dit un de nos membres 'l'intention de vivre'. C'est par cet acte de viabilité que répond l'*Institut* à quelques pessimistes – même quelques membres – qui avaient perdu leur foi dans l'avenir du droit international et dans la possibilité pour l'*Institut* de regalvaniser des doctrines dont la guerre avait plutôt montré l'inefficacité" 27 AnnIDI 295.

10 Treaty of Versailles, in particular the preamble, Part I, article 14 (PCIJ) and article 23(a) (ILO). Three IDI members were involved in the Paris Peace Conference as representatives of the following High Contracting Parties: the Cuban Republic represented by Antonio Sánchez de Bustamante, Greece (the Hellenes) by Nicolas Politis, and the Serbs, the Croats and the Slovenes by Milenko Vesnitch.

11 IDI, 'Travaux préparatoires de la Session de New-York' (New York 1929) 35-I AnnIDI 3.

list of topics of international law on which international agreement would seem the most desirable and achievable with a view to prepare a codification conference.[12] The "Committee of Experts for the Progressive Codification of International Law" was composed of 17 members, 6 of them members of the *Institut* at the time of its creation, including the President of the Committee, Mr. Hammerskjöld, and the Vice-President, Mr. Diéna.[13]

The League of Nations reached out to the *Institut* in 1925, requesting advice on topics of international law for which international agreement would be possible, and communicated a list of subjects adopted by the League's Committee of Experts for the *Institut* to study.[14] Following this, the *Institut* established a commission during its 1925 session in The Hague to study the topics adopted by the Committee of Experts and reported on it at the next session in 1927.[15]

After having received the views of States on the subject matters proposed to them,[16] the Assembly of the League of Nations ultimately identified three questions of international law (nationality, territorial waters and responsibility of States) to be discussed at the Codification Conference of the League of Nations in The Hague in 1930.[17]

In the meantime, the *Institut* had adopted resolutions on all three subject matters before the Codification Conference: in 1927 on the responsibility of

12 League of Nations, 'Resolution adopted by the League of Nations Assembly on 22 September 1924' League of Nations Official Journal Spec Supp 21, 10.

13 Members of the *Institut* at the time of creation: Hjalmar Hammerskjöld (President), Giulio Diéna (Vice-President), Henri Fromageot, Bernhard C.J. Loder, Walter Schücking and Charles de Visscher; members of the Committee who became members of the *Institut* after its creation: James Brierly (1929), Gustavo Guerrero (1947) and Barboza de Magalhaes (1932); other members of the Committee: Christobal Botella, Adalbert Mastny, Michikazu Matsuda, Raymon Rundstein, José Léon Suarez, Wang-Chung-Hui and George W. Wickersham.

14 Joost A van Hamel, 'Lettres du Directeur de la Section juridique de la Société des Nations' (The Hague 1925) 32 AnnIDI 406.

15 IDI, 'Résolution IV' ibid 542, 542–543.

16 Subjects proposed were: nationality, territorial waters, diplomatic privileges and immunities, responsibility of states in respect to injury caused in their territory to persons or property of foreigners, procedure of international conferences and procedure for the conclusion and drafting of treaties, piracy, and the exploitation of the products of the sea.

17 See 'Report of the Council of the League of Nations' (13 June 1927) and 'Resolution adopted by Assembly of the League of Nations' (27 September 1927). It also provided for a preparatory committee composed of five persons, of which Professor Basdevant (France), Professor François (Netherlands) and Sir Cecil Hurst (Great Britain) were also members of the *Institut*. The other two members were Counsellor Carlos Castro Ruiz (Chile) and Mr. Massimo Pilotti (Italy).

States[18] and in 1928 on nationality and territorial waters.[19] In 1928 it also created a commission for the codification of international peace law.[20] Hence, the preparatory work for the Codification Conference was to a large extent inspired by the resolutions of the *Institut*.[21] Furthermore, the plenary of the *Institut* adopted unanimously a Codification Declaration in 1928 in which it spelled out some modalities for codification and also emphasized the pertinence of having the study of codification carried out by independent scientific organisations. Ninety years later this declaration still provides interesting reading.[22]

The League of Nations Codification Conference took place in 1930. However, for various reasons[23] it proved not to be a great success; from the three subject matters that were put on the agenda only one, on nationality, led to the adoption of a treaty.[24] No further codification efforts were made until after the Second World War.

---

18 IDI, 'Responsabilité internationale des Etats à raison des dommages causés sur leur territoire à la personne et aux biens des étrangers' (Lausanne 1927) 33-III AnnIDI 330.

19 See 'La nationalité' (Stockholm 1928) 34 AnnIDI 760; and 'Projet de règlement relatif à la mer territoriale en temps de paix' ibid 755.

20 Rapporteurs: Lord Phillimore and Mr. Alvarez. Members: Mr. Cavaglieri, Mr. Diéna, Sir Cecil Hurst, Mr. de Lapradelle, Mr. Mercier, Mr. Nippold, Mr. Schücking, Count de Itostworowski, Mr. De Visscher, Mr. Wehberg.

21 IDI, 'La Codification du Droit International de la Paix. Séance du mercredi 16 octobre 1929' (New York 1929) 35-II AnnIDI 272, 281–282. During the League of Nations Codification Conference, Basdevant was appointed Chairman of the committee on responsibility of States and another member of the *Institut*, Nicolas Politis, was appointed Chair of the committee on Nationality. Also, J.P.A. François was appointed Rapporteur on territorial waters.

22 IDI, 'Déclaration relative à la Codification du droit international' (New York 1929) 35-II AnnIDI 312. In the Declaration the *Institut* declared that: a) codification shall not be limited to stating the prevailing *ius gentium* as it is but shall also develop the law as it should be; b) codification can only be achieved if the determination of the rules is undertaken first of all by independent scientific organisms, grouping jurists of different nationalities, which allows for the adoption of resolutions by majority instead of by unanimity as the practice of diplomatic conferences; c) the study of codification has to be preceded by independent scientific preparation, which should be based on observation, jurisprudence and doctrine; and d) the determination of the rules shall be completed by taking into account all parts of the law, without being guided by political interest but by the legal maturity of such rules following the progress of the doctrine and jurisprudence and inspired by the general principles of law.

23 See for example Shabtai Rosenne, 'Codification Revisited After 50 Years' (1998) 2 MaxPlanckYrbkUNL 3.

24 Convention on certain questions relating to the conflict of nationality laws (adopted 12 April 1930, entered into force 1 July 1937) 4137 LNTS 89. Nevertheless, a resolution was adopted by the Assembly establishing a procedure for the future on codification, enabling States to propose subjects for codification for the consideration of the Assembly to decide

IV Post-1945: the United Nations era

The *Institut* reconvened for the first time after the Second World War in Lausanne in 1947, where it focused on the most fundamental and contemporary issues at that time, in particular fundamental human rights and the codification of public international law. The report by Rapporteur Alvarez (Chile) revolved around the methods of codification of public international law.[25] The point of departure: on the one hand, the immense crisis that international law found itself in after the Second World War, and, on the other, the unanimous public opinion as also expressed in the Charter of the United Nations (Article 13) to return to international law its importance and prestige by progressively developing and codifying it.[26] Rapporteur Alvarez explained that different views existed among public international lawyers on how to address the crisis: some underlined the importance of reaffirming the principles of international law still in force (the Anglo-Saxon approach); others considered that the only means to render prestige to international law was to proceed rapidly to its codification.

In its 1947 resolution on codification, the *Institut* underlined the dangers of the method used in 1930 for the League of Nations Codification Conference, to the extent that the binding force of the rules codified depended on the express acceptance of States. This carried the risk that each government had the possibility to question it, or even to refuse to accept rules of law that the doctrine and jurisprudence considered as established. The resolution indicated that such an approach could likely result in the weakening of the rules which were meant to be detailed and consolidated through codification. Emphasis was therefore placed on the research of a scientific character to discover the current state of international law, which could then serve as a basis for both doctrinal and official efforts to fill the gaps in international law.[27]

In the proceedings one can nicely read how theory and practice can sometimes meet each other in our *Institut*.[28] During the deliberations, one of the members of the *Institut*, Mr. Donnedieu de Vabres from France, took the floor.

---

whether the subjects proposed appear at first glance suitable for codification. League of Nations, 'Resolution adopted by the Assembly of the League of Nations, 25 September 1931' League of Nations Official Journal Spec Supp 92, 9.

25 Alejandro Alvarez, 'Méthodes de la codification du droit international public' (Lausanne 1947) 41 AnnIDI 38.

26 Ibid 40.

27 IDI, 'La Codification du Droit international' (Lausanne 1947) ibid 261.

28 See 41 AnnIDI (Lausanne 1947) 38–71 (for the preparatory work) and 218–254 (for the deliberations).

He was also member of the Committee on the Progressive Development of International Law and its Codification, also known as the "Committee of Seventeen", established by the United Nations General Assembly to make recommendations for the setting up of the International Law Commission. Mr. Donnedieu de Vabres explained to the members of the *Institut* what the United Nations Committee was considering in its report.[29]

He stated that what the Rapporteur, Mr. Alvarez, proposed, namely first having the scientific societies preparing a draft before submitting it to States, would risk divergence between the universal conscience and the harsh international reality. This could well create a danger of not reaching any agreement at all. This is why the Committee insisted on a constant collaboration of all interested parties, including governments, in order to achieve conciliation of theory and practice. Furthermore, he informed the *Institut* of the discussions on the distinction between codification and progressive development of international law. He also explained the procedure foreseen and elaborated on the question of the form of the drafts: doctrinal or draft conventions. The influence of government representatives led the Committee to decide on a modality of conventions, either between two States or between multiple States.

The idea was that such an international law commission could be seized by the General Assembly, but also by other organs of the United Nations. The specialized agencies of the United Nations could also submit proposals and draft multilateral conventions.

The General Assembly, following the report of the Committee, adopted a resolution establishing the International Law Commission and approved its statute,[30] in which indeed a considerable role is given to States while also providing for the possibility of consultation with scientific institutions and individual experts.[31] The International Law Commission held its first session in 1949 and of the 15 members of the Commission at the first session, 10 also were, or subsequently became, members of the *Institut*.[32]

---

29 Ibid 224–227.

30 Statute of the ILC, UNGA Res 174 (II) (21 November 1947), subsequently amended by UNGA Res 485(V) (12 December 1950); UNGA Res 984(X) (3 December 1955); UNGA Res 985(X) (3 December 1955) and UNGA Res 36/39 (18 November 1981).

31 See article 26(1) of the ILC statute (n 31).

32 Mr. Ricardo J. Alfaro (Panama, 1954); Mr. James Leslie Brierly (United Kingdom, 1929); Mr. J.P.A. François (Netherlands, 1937); Mr. Manley O. Hudson (United States of America, 1936); Mr. Vladimir M. Koretsky (Union of Soviet Socialist Republics, 1965); Mr. A.E.F. Sandström (Sweden, 1950); Mr. Georges Scelle (France, 1929); Mr. Jean Spiropoulos (Greece, 1950); Mr. Jesús M. Yepes (Colombia, 1952); Mr. Jaroslav Zourek (Czechoslovakia, 1961). The year indicates the year of election to the *Institut*.

V The Commission and *Institut*: Similarities and Differences

Having both our institutions working toward a common goal, it is interesting to take a look at their similarities and differences, to better understand how this shared objective is achieved. Both institutions promote the progressive development of international law and its codification. The *Institut,* in its statutes, outlines six ways in which it aims to achieve this, namely: a) formulating general principles; b) working on gradual and progressive codification of international law; c) seeking official endorsement of the principles; d) contributing to the maintenance of peace, or to the observance of the laws of war; e) studying the difficulties in the interpretation or application of the law; and f) facilitating co-operation in the teaching and dissemination of international law.[33]

The statute of the International Law Commission states that "the International Law Commission shall have for its object the promotion of progressive development of international law and its codification". The two concepts are succinctly described in article 15: progressive development is to be understood as the preparation of draft conventions on subjects which have not yet been regulated by international law or in which law has not yet been sufficiently developed in the practice of States, while codification means the more precise formulation and systematization of rules of international law in fields where there has already been extensive State practice, precedent and doctrine.

As regards the scope of the work, the Commission "shall concern itself primarily with public international law, but is not precluded from entering the field of private international law", which differs from the scope of the work of the *Institut* in that it covers both fields of international law (public and private) equally.[34]

---

33 In a full quote: "a) by striving to formulate the general principles of the subject, in such a way as to correspond to the legal conscience of the civilized world; b) by lending its co-operation in any serious endeavour for the gradual and progressive codification of international law; c) by seeking official endorsement of the principles recognized as in harmony with the needs of modern societies; d) by contributing, within the limits of its competence, either to the maintenance of peace, or to the observance of the laws of war; e) by studying the difficulties which may arise in the interpretation or application of the law, and where necessary issuing reasoned legal opinions in doubtful or controversial cases; f) by affording its co-operation, through publications, public teaching and all other means, in ensuring that those principles of justice and humanity which should govern the mutual relations of peoples shall prevail." See 'Statutes of the Institute of International Law' (adopted 10 September 1873, English translation) <www.idi-iil.org/app/uploads/2017/06/Statutes-of-the-Institute-of-International-Law.pdf>.

34 Article 1(2) of the ILC statute; Article 9(5) of the IDI rules.

As already mentioned, the *Institut* is an exclusively learned society without any official nature. The total number of members under the age of 80 shall not exceed 132 and there can be more than one national from the same State.[35] In fact, in case of three or more members of the same nationality, national groups can be formed.[36] Currently, we have 21 of such national groups. The plenary assembly elects associate members from a list of candidates proposed by the national groups and the Bureau. After having attended three sessions of the *Institut,* associate members qualify to become full members. In principle, membership can be for life.

In contrast, the International Law Commission is a subsidiary organ of the United Nations General Assembly, reporting to the plenary meeting of States and hence with a close link to its Sixth Committee, as we will discuss this afternoon. Over the years, the membership of the International Law Commission has increased to a total number of 34 and there cannot be two members with the nationality of the same State.[37] Members are elected by the General Assembly from a list of candidates nominated by States.[38] They are elected for a period of five years with possibility of re-election. Even though the statute of the Commission does not explicitly bar it,[39] no judges of the International Court of Justice are simultaneously members of the International Law Commission, while currently out of the 15 judges 8 are a member of the *Institut.*[40]

Members of the International Law Commission can be members of the *Institut* at the same time. In fact, from the 229 persons that have been members of the Commission, 83 have been or are members of the *Institut*, either concurrently or at an earlier or later point in time.[41] Thirty-seven of them have served as Special Rapporteur for the Commission and 16 of them as Rapporteur of a commission

35 Article 3 of the IDI statute.
36 Article 9 of the IDI rules.
37 Article 2 of the ILC statute.
38 Article 3 of the ILC statute.
39 Article 10 of the ILC statute.
40 Mr Yusuf (President), Mrs Xue (Vice-President), Messrs Tomka (former President), Bennouna, Cançado Trindade, Crawford, Gaja, Owada (succeeded by Mr Iwasawa on 22 June 2018 who is also a member of the *Institut*).
41 Roberto Ago, Ricardo J. Alfaro, Gaetano Arangio-Ruiz, Milan Bartoš, Mohamed Bedjaoui, Mohamed Bennouna, Boutros Boutros-Ghali, Derek William Bowett, James Leslie Brierly, Herbert W. Briggs, Sir Ian Brownlie, Lucius Caflisch, Jorge Castañeda, Erik Castrén, James Richard Crawford, C. John R. Dugard, Abdullah El-Erian, Taslim Olawale Elias, Nihat Erim, Constantin Th. Eustathiades, Jens Evensen, Luigi Ferrari Bravo, Sir Gerald Fitzmaurice, J.P.A. François, Giorgio Gaja, André Gros, Gerhard Hafner, Edvard Hambro, Manley O. Hudson, Eduardo Jimenez de Arechaga, Maurice Kamto, James Lutabanzibwa Kateka, Roman Anatolyevich Kolodkin, Vladimir M. Koretsky, Abdul G. Koroma, Martti

of the *Institut*. Both institutions aim for a representation of the principal legal systems and the candidates should have the necessary qualifications. We have a number of fantastic female members. Unfortunately, women are still underrepresented in both bodies.

Neither the International Law Commission nor the *Institut* is a full-time body. The *Institut* has one session every two years of some seven days, whereas the Commission convenes on an annual basis for 11 to 12 weeks. The methods of work of the *Institut* are fairly settled and quite similar to those of the International Law Commission. Commissions are led by a Rapporteur and work on a subject of international law that has been put on the agenda by the Plenary, on proposal of the Programme Committee.[42] The Plenary Assembly examines their reports and draft resolutions and, if appropriate, resolutions of a normative character are adopted.[43] Through these resolutions, the *Institut* seeks to highlight the characteristics of the prevailing law, *lex lata*, in order to promote respect and full observance. Furthermore, the *Institut* makes *de lege ferenda* determinations in order to contribute to the development of international law. However, in contrast with the method of the International Law Commission,[44] no consultation rounds with States or other bodies are held, although governments and international organisations are informed of the resolutions adopted by the *Institut*. The International Law Commission, when adopting a draft, submits it to the General Assembly with its recommendations. The General Assembly then decides what kind of action to take.

It is interesting and rewarding to note that the work of the *Institut* and the work by the International Law Commission over the last 70 years have informed, developed and reinforced each other on many occasions. When taking a look at the subject matters dealt with by the International Law Commission, many of them are, or have also been dealt with, by the *Institut*: in their entirety or partially, and

Koskenniemi, Sergei B. Krylov, Manfred Lachs, Sir Hersch Lauterpacht, Antonio de Luna, Ahmed Mahiou, Donald M. McRae, Václav Mikulka, Djamchid Momtaz, Shinya Murase, Zhengyu Ni, Georg Nolte, Alain Pellet, A. Rohan Perera, Christopher Walter Pinto, Pemmaraju Sreenivasa Rao, August Reinisch, Paul Reuter, Shabtai Rosenne, Emmanuel J. Roucounas, José María Ruda, Milan Sahovic, A.E.F. Sandström, Georges Scelle, Stephen M. Schwebel, Bernardo Sepúlveda, César Sepúlveda-Gutiérrez, José Sette Câmara, Bruno Simma, Sir Ian Sinclair, Nagendra Singh, Jean Spiropoulos, Sompong Sucharitkul, Dire D. Tladi, Peter Tomka, Christian Tomuschat, Grigory I. Tunkin, Endre Ustor, Sir Francis Vallat, Alfred Verdross, Stephen Verosta, Sir Humphrey Waldock, Xue Hanqin, Alexander Yankov, Mustafa Kamil Yasseen, Jesús María Yepes, Kisaburo Yokota, Jaroslav Zourek.

42 Chapter I, IDI rules.

43 Chapter III, Part Three, IDI rules.

44 Articles 16–26 of the ILC statute.

previously, concurrently or at a later stage. Reference can be made to such diverse topics as diplomatic immunities, diplomatic protection, State responsibility, extradition, the law of treaties, expulsion of aliens, the most-favoured nation clause, and arbitral procedure. In drawing a balance, I believe it is no exaggeration to state that the progressive development and codification of international law until today can to some extent be measured by the work of our two institutions.

VI Some Examples of Common Efforts at International Law-Making

Let me now proceed to providing some examples of common efforts in international law-making. An early example, starting late nineteenth century, relates to the subject-matter nationality including statelessness. The *Institut* has adopted several resolutions[45] and the International Law Commission considered it during the early 1950s,[46] leading to the adoption of the United Nations Convention on the Reduction of Statelessness in 1961, with currently 71 parties.[47] A second example is the non-navigational use of international watercourses on which the *Institut* adopted a resolution as early as 1911,[48] another one in 1961[49] and more specifically one on the pollution of watercourses in 1979.[50] The International Law Commission took up the topic in 1971 in its programme of work,[51] leading to the adoption of the Convention

45 1892 Geneva (admission et expulsion des étrangers), 1896 Venice (nationalité), 1928 Stockholm (nationalité), 1929 New York (droits de l'homme), 1932 Oslo (capacité des personnes (amendant la loi applicable à la capacité des apatrides mineurs, aliénés)), 1936 Brussels (Statut juridique des apatrides et des réfugiés), 1950 Bath (L'asile en droit international public (à l'exclusion de l'asile neutre)) <http://www.idi-iil.org/en/publications-par-categorie/resolutions/>.

46 See 'Analytical Guide to the Work of the International Law Commission: Nationality including statelessness' <http://legal.un.org/ilc/guide/6_1.shtml>.

47 Adopted 30 August 1961, entered into force 13 December 1975, 989 UNTS 175.

48 IDI, 'Texte des Résolutions adoptées en ce qui concerne la Règlementation internationale de l'usage des cours d'eau internationaux.' (Madrid 1911) 24 AnnIDI 365.

49 IDI, 'Utilisation des eaux internationales non maritimes (en dehors de la navigation)' (Salzburg 1961) 49-II AnnIDI 370.

50 1911 Madrid (Réglementation internationale de l'usage des cours d'eau internationaux en dehors de l'exercice du droit de navigation), 1961 Salzbourg (Utilisation des eaux internationales non maritimes (en dehors de la navigation)), 1979 Athens (La pollution des fleuves et des lacs et le droit international) <http://www.idi-iil.org/en/publications-par-categorie/resolutions/>.

51 See 'Analytical Guide to the Work of the International Law Commission, Law of the non-navigational uses of international watercourses' <http://legal.un.org/ilc/guide/8_3.shtml>.

on the Law of the Non-navigational Uses of International Watercourses in 1997, currently counting 36 parties.[52] A final early example relates to the regime of the territorial sea, more in particular the issue of the breadth of the territorial sea. In its first resolution on the territorial sea in 1894,[53] the *Institut* endorsed the "cannon-shot rule" coined by the Dutch lawyer Van Bijnkershoek (I come from the same West Frisian region), that is a territorial sea corresponding to the range of the coastal State's defence weapons on our dikes, so to say.[54] In view of the tendency in State practice to extend the territorial sea beyond the three nautical miles for purposes of protecting their coastal fishery interests, the *Institut* made an attempt to align theory and practice by proposing a six nautical miles limit. This discussion was still ongoing when, in 1928, the *Institut* adopted another resolution proposing a draft regulation concerning the territorial sea in times of peace, but even its two rapporteurs had a difference of opinion on whether it should be three or six nautical miles.[55] In the end, the three-nautical miles limit was adopted, as well as an article on the additional contiguous zone not exceeding nine nautical miles. As discussed, the 1930 Codification Conference of the League also proved to be deeply divided on this and failed to take a decision. In the 1950s, the topic of the breadth of the territorial sea was revisited, both in the International Law Commission and the *Institut*. However, both institutions left the actual breadth of the territorial sea open, only indicating that it could not extend beyond 12 nautical miles.[56] It was only in the context of the Third United Nations Conference on the Law of the Sea that the international community of States settled, in 1982, for a territorial sea of 12 nautical miles.[57]

---

52 Adopted 21 May 1997, entered into force 17 August 2014, UNTS registration no 52106.

53 IDI, 'Règles adoptées par l'Institut de droit international, à Paris, le 31 mars 1894, sur la définition et le régime de la mer territoriale' (Paris 1894 – 1895) 13 AnnIDI 328.

54 Cornelis Van Bijnkershoek, *De dominio maris* (Leiden, 1703) (and see also second edition of *Opera minora* in 1744); 1894 Paris (Règles sur la définition et le régime de la mer territoriale) <http://www.idi-iil.org/fr/publications-par-categorie/resolutions/>.

55 IDI, 'Règlement sur le régime des navires de mer et de leurs équipages dans les ports étrangers en temps de paix' (Stockholm 1928) 34 AnnIDI 736.

56 See e.g. Amsterdam (1957) 47-II AnnIDI 169; [1952] II ILC Ybk UN Doc, A/CN.4/53, 26; [1953] II ILC Ybk UN Doc, A/CN.4/61, 59–65; and [1956] II ILC Ybk UN Doc, A/CN.4/104, 256, article 3. At both places the Dutchman J.P.A. François played a leading role, respectively as Special Rapporteur for the International Law Commission and as President during the Amsterdam Session of the *Institut*.

57 United Nations Convention on the Law of the Sea, adopted 10 December 1982, entered into force 16 November 1994, 1833 UNTS 3, article 3.

Probably the most well-known and most successful topic taken up by the International Law Commission so far is the law of treaties. This was prioritized during its first session in 1949 and led to the adoption of the Vienna Convention on the Law of Treaties 20 years later,[58] with full participation of developing countries as also demonstrated by the recognition of the concept of *jus cogens*[59] and the clause on the fundamental change of circumstances.[60] Currently, the treaty has 116 parties.[61] Equally important, if not more important, is that most of its provisions are found to reflect, in the view of the International Court of Justice,[62] prevailing customary international law. In my view, this Convention is the real beauty, the crown jewel of the International Law Commission. Let me briefly mention that the *Institut* also discussed the issue of interpretation of treaties earlier, in 1956, on the basis of the work of a commission led by Sir Hersch Lauterpacht, who also served as the International Law Commission's Special Rapporteur on the law of treaties in the early 1950s.[63] Furthermore, the topic of termination of treaties has always faced some challenges and remains regrettably topical in these days of Brexit, clexit (climate exit) and the withdrawal by the United States of America from the so-called "Iran deal"[64] and the Intermediate-Range Nuclear Forces (INF) treaty.[65] Termination of treaties was addressed by the *Institut* in its resolution of 1967, in which it recognized the value of the work accomplished by the International Law Commission and addressed certain aspects of the general problem of the termination of treaties.[66]

A topic that was excluded from the scope of the Vienna Convention was the effect of armed conflicts on treaties.[67] Following the 1907 Hague Conference,

58 Adopted 23 May 1969, entered into force 17 January 1980, 1155 UNTS 331 (VCLT).

59 Article 53 of the VCLT.

60 Article 62 of the VCLT.

61 See for a recent contribution on treaties Georg Nolte, *Treaties and their Practice. Symptoms of Their Rise or Decline* (Brill/Pocket Books of The Hague Academy of International Law 2018).

62 See e.g. *Legal Consequences for States of the Continued Presence of South Africa in Namibia (South West Africa) notwithstanding Security Council Resolution 276 (1970)* (Advisory Opinion) [1971] ICJ Rep 47.

63 IDI, 'L'interprétation des traités' (Grenade 1956) 46 AnnIDI 358.

64 Joint Comprehensive Plan of Action (JCPOA), concluded 14 July 2015, adopted as part of UNSC Res 2231 (20 July 2015).

65 Treaty Between the United States of America and the Union of Soviet Socialist Republics on the Elimination if Their Intermediate-Range and Shorter-Range Missiles (INF Treaty), signed 8 December 1987, entered into force 1 June 1988, 1657 UNTS 2.

66 IDI, 'La terminaison des traité' (Nice 1967) 52-II AnnIDI 556.

67 ILC, 'Report of the International Law Commission on the work of its fifteenth session' [1963] II ILC Ybk 188, 189 at para 14.

the *Institut* adopted a resolution in 1912 on the effects of war on treaties.[68] The abolition theory, i.e. that war ended all relations between belligerents, was rejected in the resolution. As a rule, the outbreak of hostilities would have no effects on the existence of treaties, with the exception, *inter alia*, of treaties of a political nature and treaties of which the interpretation or application was the direct cause of the war. Similarly, multilateral treaties would in principle remain intact, but collective treaties on the law of war would apply only when all belligerents were contracting states (unless the treaty contained a formal clause to the contrary or the parties clearly intended for it to apply).[69]

Following the adoption of the Vienna Convention, which explicitly excluded in article 73 the effects of war on treaties from its scope, the *Institut* created a commission in 1973 to re-examine the matter. After extensive deliberations, it adopted in 1985 a resolution on the effects of armed conflicts on treaty regimes.[70] Subsequently, the International Law Commission put it on the agenda in 2004, pointing out that whereas the law remained, to a considerable degree, unsettled, the subject seemed now ready for codification and/or progressive development.[71] Inspired in part by the resolution adopted by the *Institut* and new developments in international law, including with respect to intra-State conflicts or non-international armed conflicts,[72] the International Law Commission drafted a set of substantive articles on the matter and adopted these in 2011.[73] A final and very recent example of our interactions relates to the work

68 IDI, 'Règlement concernant les effets de la guerre sur les traités' (Christiania 1912) 25 AnnIDI 648.

69 Unless a formal clause to the contrary or clear intention by parties. (Christiania 1912) 25 AnnIDI 611ff. It was acknowledged that the work of the *Institut* in 1912 had a relatively strong influence on the cases that were decided during the First World War and immediately thereafter, including by the courts of various countries. See Bengt Broms 'The effects of armed conflicts on treaties. Provisional Report and Proposed Draft Resolution' (Dijon 1981) 59-I AnnIDI 201, 213.

70 IDI, 'The effects of armed conflicts on treaties / Les effets des conflits armés sur les traités' (Helsinki 1985) 61-II AnnIDI 278.

71 ILC, 'Report of the International Law Commission on the work of its fifty-second session' [2000] II(2) ILC Ybk 1, 131 at para 729.

72 The International Law Commission uses a definition of "armed conflict" that is mainly based on the definition as set out in the *Tadic Case* [*Prosecutor v Dusko Tadic a/k/a "Dule"* (Decision on the Defence Motion of Interlocutory Appeal on Jurisdiction) ICTY-94-1 (15 July 1999)] which includes non-international armed conflicts (excluding the situation in which only two or more organized armed groups are involved), see ILC, 'Draft articles on the effects of armed conflicts on treaties, with commentaries' [2011] II(2) ILC Ybk 108, 110, commentary to draft article 2 para (4) at footnote 401.

73 ILC, 'Report of the International Law Commission on the work of its sixty- third session' [2011] II(2) ILC Ybk , Chapter VI. On 7 December 2017, the General Assembly decided that

of our Secretary-General Marcelo Kohen on the question of State succession in matters of State responsibility. Based upon his extensive report, the *Institut* adopted a resolution on this in 2015[74] and the topic has now been included by the International Law Commission in its programme of work in 2017,[75] to be discussed at the current session.[76]

VII The Future: Is Standard-Setting in International Law Completed or is There Still an International Law Agenda for the Future? What Roles for the Commission and the *Institut*?

This leads us to consider where we stand at the moment and what the future will bring for the development of international law and its codification. Could it be said that standard-setting in international law has been completed? Or is there still work to be done? If so, what are the respective roles of the Commission and the *Institut*? As mentioned in the beginning of my contribution, the *Institut* was created shortly after the Franco-German War out of a deeply felt desire to address the need for the progressive development of international law as a means to bring peace, or at least to render war an exception. It was for that mission and for the quality of its work in the initial decades that the *Institut* was granted the Nobel Peace Prize in 1904.

After every war, the importance of progressive development of international law and its codification has been reaffirmed, even though the effectiveness of international law to prevent or reduce the horrors of war has sometimes been severely questioned. Similar sentiments led to the establishment of the International Law Commission after the Second World War. If we look at the situation today, it is appropriate to recall the opening remarks at a press conference last week by the United Nations Secretary-General. Mr. Guterres referred to contemporary dangers and challenges including the threat of terrorism, the multiplication of armed conflicts, climate change, and dramatically increased inequalities, to which we can easily add the refugee crisis and the issue of migration and human security, a topic on which our *Institut* adopted

---

it would revert to the question of the effects of armed conflicts on treaties at an appropriate time. UNGA Res 72/121 (7 December 2017).

74 IDI, 'La succession d'Etats en matière de responsabilité internationale' (Tallinn 2015) 76 AnnIDI 703.

75 ILC, 'Report of the International Law Commission on the work at its sixty-ninth session' (2017) UN Doc A/72/10, para 263.

76 ILC, 'Provisional agenda for the seventieth session' (13 April 2018) UN Doc A/CN.4/709/Rev.1.

a substantive report and resolution in 2017.[77] The Secretary-General rightly stressed that "in this dangerous world, it is absolutely essential to preserve [...] the rule of law in international relations."[78]

I do not subscribe to those academic colleagues who portray international law merely as a "belief".[79] Rather, I view contemporary international law as the embodiment of shared global values such as peace, justice, humanity, freedom and sustainability. In our deeply divided world it is *our common language*. That is something to cherish. Moreover, international law also functions as a concrete regulatory framework for concrete action. And we need more of that function, as the recent Paris Agreement on the curbing of climate change demonstrates.[80]

It took a long period of gestation to arrive at the body of international law that we currently have. We know all too well that it is still fragile and in need of constant maintenance, if not reform, in order to remain relevant as the rule of law in global affairs. The International Law Commission has made a magnificent contribution to this, especially through the progressive development of international law and its consolidation through extensive and effective codification in the United Nations era.[81] Its task is certainly not yet completed, nor is ours. It is my pleasure and great privilege to wish our younger sister institution a great future, in the interest of all of us.

---

77 IDI, 'Mass Migrations' (9 September 2017) <www.idi-iil.org/app/uploads/2017/08/16-RES-FINAL-EN.pdf>.

78 Antonio Guterres, 'Opening remarks at joint press conference with European Commission President, Jean-Claude Juncker' (16 May 2018) <www.un.org/sg/en/content/sg/speeches/2018-05-16/remarks-press-conference-jean-claude-juncker>.

79 Cf. Jean D'Aspremont, *International Law as a Belief System* (CUP 2017).

80 Adopted 12 December 2015, entered into force 4 November 2016, UNTS registration no 54113.

81 See for an evaluation of the work of the Commission Arthur Watts, 'Codification and Progressive Development of International Law' in Rüdiger Wolfrum (ed), *The Max Planck Encyclopedia of Public International Law* (OUP 2012), vol II, 282–296; Pemmaraju Sreenivasa Rao, 'The International Law Commission' in Rüdiger Wolfrum (ed), ibid, vol V (2012), 875–888; Rosalyn Higgins et al., *Oppenheim's International Law. United Nations* (OUP 2017), vol II, 929–946.

SECTION 9

Commemorative Speeches Delivered in Geneva

Discurso de Eduardo Valencia-Ospina

Presidente de la Comisión de Derecho Internacional en su septuagésimo período de sesiones

(*Spanish original*)

Constituye un gran honor para mí, en nombre de la Comisión de Derecho Internacional, dar la bienvenida a todos Ustedes a esta sesión solemne – la segunda en conmemoración del septuagésimo aniversario de la Comisión, después de la realizada en Mayo de este año en la Sede de las Naciones Unidas en Nueva York.

Permítanme expresar el agradecimiento de la Comisión a nuestros invitados de honor por su presencia aquí en el día de hoy. Deseo reconocer en el podio: al Sr. Miguel de Serpa Soares, Asesor Jurídico de las Naciones Unidas, en representación del Secretario General; a la Sra. Corinne Cicéron Bühler, Directora General de Derecho Internacional del Departamento Federal de Asuntos Exteriores de Suiza, el Estado anfitrión de la Comisión; a la Sra. Kate Gilmore, Alta Comisionada Adjunta de las Naciones Unidas para los Derechos Humanos; y a Su Excelencia el Juez Abdulqawi Yusuf, Presidente de la Corte Internacional de Justicia, quien dictará la Conferencia magistral con la que concluirá esta solemne jornada.

Es también muy grato para la Comisión saludar entre la concurrencia a varios otros jueces de la Corte Internacional de Justicia, representantes de Estados Miembros y de agencias Especializadas y otros Organismos Internacionales y asesores jurídicos de Cancillerías, así como a eminentes académicos y profesionales del Derecho, incluyendo a antiguos miembros de la Comisión.

La conmemoración del septuagésimo aniversario de la Comisión de Derecho Internacional es una celebración del derecho internacional.

Al asumir la primera presidencia de la Comisión en Lake Success, Nueva York, el 12 de abril de 1949, el Sr. Manley Hudson, se refirió a la Historia como el motor de las actividades de la Comisión. De hecho, consideró que era imposible para un jurista "olvidar las lecciones de la historia" ("to forget the lessons of history").[1] La Comisión –continuó él- debería tomar en consideración los muchos logros graduales que la precedieron, pero reconocer al mismo

1 CDI, 'Actas resumidas y documentos de la primera sesión, incluido el reporte de la Comisión a la Asamblea General' [1949] Anuario de la CDI 1949, 10.

tiempo el perpetuo movimiento entre el presente y el futuro, para así evitar convertirse en una mera esclava del pasado.

Siendo el año el de 1949, sus palabras fueron una clara referencia a los desarrollos históricos más recientes. Naciente, como empezaba a serlo de entre los escombros dejados por el horror y aflicción de la Segunda Guerra Mundial, la comunidad internacional de naciones que, abatidas por dos grandes guerras que se sucedieran en un breve período, habían fracasado en el logro de su promesa de una paz duradera y estable, emprendió el proceso de reconstruir la promesa incumplida, a través del mantenimiento y avance del derecho internacional. Mirar al pasado era, por tanto, una forma de crear el futuro. El lema de nuestros eventos conmemorativos, "estableciendo un balance para el futuro", refleja ese deseo muy humano de introspección y prospección: aprender las lecciones del pasado para perfeccionar el futuro.

Dadas las circunstancias imperantes en el momento de su creación, la Comisión fue establecida precisamente para transitar con cuidado por este sendero entre el pasado y el futuro, iniciando estudios y formulando recomendaciones para promover el desarrollo progresivo del derecho internacional y su codificación, que es la misión que le asignara la Asamblea General con miras a la aplicación del Artículo 13, párrafo 1, de la Carta de las Naciones Unidas.

Personalmente he tenido el privilegio de observar y participar de cerca en ese andar de la Comisión desde varias aventajadas posiciones tanto internas como externas: formando parte de su Secretaría en los años 60 y 70; en mi condición de Secretario Adjunto y Secretario de la Corte Internacional de Justicia en los años 80 y 90; y, desde 2006, como miembro, luego Relator Especial, y ahora Presidente de la propia Comisión. En cada una de esas etapas he podido constatar a todo momento la continua relevancia en el transcurso del tiempo, de todos los aspectos del trabajo de la Comisión para nuestra tarea profesional de juristas internacionales. En este sentido, me refiero no sólo a los muchos tratados multilaterales que surgieron como resultado de las labores de la Comisión, sino también a otros diversos elementos que entran en juego en el proceso de desarrollo progresivo y codificación, a los que hacemos constante referencia en nuestras actividades cuotidianas. En efecto, es posible tomar en consideración la extensa práctica de los Estados recopilada por la Comisión y su Secretaría a lo largo de los años; las observaciones y comentarios expresados por los Estados oralmente o por escrito; la variedad y la pluralidad de los puntos de vista emitidos por los miembros de la Comisión durante los debates. Con frecuencia, repasamos los esfuerzos realizados en el pasado, en particular las opiniones de los miembros de la Comisión en las décadas a partir de los años cincuenta, a fin de afianzarnos en la búsqueda de las mejores soluciones para el futuro dentro del proceso de desarrollo progresivo del derecho internacional y su codificación.

Un tal proceso implica inherentemente períodos de una cierta extensión, a diferencia de lo que sucede cuando se trata de acordar un "derecho instantáneo". Y posee un significado que connota además una concepción unitaria del desarrollo progresivo del derecho internacional y su codificación. Como es bien sabido, el artículo 15 del Estatuto de la Comisión establece una distinción, "por comodidad", entre ambos conceptos. En la práctica, sin embargo, el trabajo de la Comisión sobre un determinado tema involucra al tiempo ciertos aspectos de desarrollo progresivo así como de codificación, y el equilibrio entre ambos varía dependiendo del tema de que se trate. Durante el Congreso organizado en el marco del Decenio de las Naciones Unidas para el Derecho Internacional en 1995, tuve la oportunidad de señalar que la codificación y el desarrollo progresivo, a pesar de estar formalmente diferenciados en el Estatuto, en realidad se han fusionado en un concepto más amplio de "codificación", que ya no se ve sólo como la mera transposición de "ley no escrita" a "ley escrita" (lo que podría denominarse codificación "clásica").[2] El futuro, entonces, resulta estar siempre plegado al pasado. A su vez, esta concepción más amplia de la codificación está estrechamente vinculada a la observación de que la forma final del trabajo de la Comisión, ya sea éste plasmado en artículos independientes destinados a traducirse en una convención, o directrices, conclusiones, principios o simplemente en un informe, sea tal vez de menor trascendencia para el futuro que el complejo proceso de desarrollo progresivo y codificación considerado en sí mismo.

Si bien tradicionalmente se consideró que el objetivo final de todos los esfuerzos de la Comisión sobre un determinado tema debería ser la elaboración de un instrumento internacional que consagrara en forma vinculante los resultados de su trabajo, la experiencia más reciente ha demostrado que esto no necesariamente es así en todos los casos. Algunos de los textos más autoritativos e invocados con mayor frecuencia que hayan surgido de la labor de la Comisión, redactados en forma de artículos, no se han convertido hasta el momento en tratados multilaterales. La travesía es pues tan importante como el destino; un ejercicio en perpetuo movimiento, el pasado informando el presente para hacer realidad un mañana mejor.

La anterior constatación fáctica no debe dar lugar a interpretaciones erróneas: el hecho de que se pueda dar una de las varias formas posibles a un proyecto definitivo de codificación, no significa que los tratados hayan llegado a convertirse en instrumentos obsoletos. La realización del anhelado "mañana

2 Naciones Unidas (ed), *International law as a language for international relations/Le droit international comme langage des relations internationales/El derecho internacional como lenguaje de las relaciones internacionales* (Kluwer Law International 1996) 523.

mejor" requiere con frecuencia la fuerza de la concertación internacional en la elaboración de tratados para expresar todo su potencial: puede ser necesario establecer instituciones, o que las leyes nacionales sean armonizadas gracias a normas comunes vinculantes. A este respecto, es altamente significativo que, recientemente, la Comisión haya recomendado explícitamente por consenso a la Asamblea General que el último proyecto definitivo a ella sometido sea convertido en una convención multilateral. Tal fue en 2016 el caso del relativo al tema sobre el que tuve el honor de ser Relator Especial: la "Protección de las personas en caso de desastre";[3] y se espera que sea el caso también el año próximo en relación con el proyecto definitivo a adoptar sobre los "Crímenes de lesa humanidad". Ambos proyectos tienen el potencial de conducir a tratados que demuestren ser históricamente trascendentales para la cimentación del ansiado futuro jurídico internacional.

La Historia, por supuesto, es creada por seres humanos, no por entidades abstractas. El papel autoritativo atribuido a la Comisión a lo largo del tiempo y la relevancia de sus resultados, incluso cuando éstos no se transforman en un tratado multilateral, reposa en última instancia en el reconocimiento generalmente extendido hacia las grandes mentes de juristas, gigantes intelectuales, de todo el orbe que han recorrido los pasillos del *Palais des Nations* en ejercicio de su noble oficio. Esta es la dimensión humana de la Comisión. Podemos referirnos a ellos como a las muchas voces que han articulado el trabajo de la Comisión con el transcurso del tiempo: a pesar de (o debido a) su pluralidad, diversidad y, a veces, divergencia, todos ellos han contribuido en alguna medida a crear la voz colegiada de la Comisión. Los métodos de trabajo de la Comisión están diseñados para que el producto final sea siempre plural y mayor que la suma de sus partes: es el destilado, la síntesis de las opiniones de muchas mentes jurídicas que trabajan por un objetivo común. La interacción de una balanceada representación regional, aunque no de género todavía, y de diferentes tradiciones y sistemas jurídicos en la composición de la Comisión es esencial a este respecto, como lo es también la independencia de los individuos que son miembros de la Comisión frente a los Gobiernos. En este esfuerzo colectivo -un punto que no debe olvidarse- también ha sido esencial, desde el principio, el destacado papel que ha sido reservado a la Secretaría de la Comisión, cuyos estudios preparatorios y asistencia jurídica sustantiva, que forman parte de los métodos de trabajo de la Comisión, son cruciales para su buen funcionamiento.

3 CDI, 'Informe de la Comisión de Derecho Internacional sobre el trabajo de la Comisión en su sexagésima octava sesión' (2016) Documento de Naciones Unidas No. A/71/10, 13.

Excepto en un par de ocasiones, la más reciente cuando sesionamos en la Sede de las Naciones Unidas en Nueva York por cinco semanas, Ginebra siempre ha sido el hogar de la Comisión. Su trabajo sustancial se ha desarrollado aquí. Los antiguos miembros, así como los miembros actuales, guardan cálidos recuerdos del *Palais* y de la ciudad y sus alrededores. La Comisión está profundamente reconocida al Gobierno del Estado anfitrión por el constante y generoso apoyo que le ha brindado a lo largo de su historia. Y la Comisión manifiesta también su agradecimiento a la Oficina de las Naciones Unidas en Ginebra, en especial su Biblioteca y Servicios de Conferencias, por su continua cooperación y eficaz atención, indispensables para el buen funcionamiento de las reuniones anuales de la Comisión.

Statement by Eduardo Valencia-Ospina

Chair of the International Law Commission at Its Seventieth Session

(*Translation from the Spanish Original*)

It is a great honour for me, on behalf of the International Law Commission, to welcome you all to this solemn meeting. This is the second meeting to be held in commemoration of the Commission's seventieth anniversary, the first having taken place at United Nations Headquarters in New York in May of this year.

I would like to express appreciation to all those who have graced us with their presence today. I wish to acknowledge, on the podium, Miguel de Serpa Soares, United Nations Legal Counsel, representing the Secretary-General; Corinne Cicerón Bühler, Director-General of International Law at the Federal Department of Foreign Affairs of Switzerland, the Commission's host nation; Kate Gilmore, United Nations Deputy High Commissioner for Human Rights; and H.E. Judge Abdulqawi Yusuf, President of the International Court of Justice, who will deliver the keynote address that will draw this solemn session to a close.

It is also a very great pleasure for the Commission to welcome among today's participants several other judges of the International Court of Justice, representatives of Member States and specialized agencies and other international organizations, as well as legal advisers to foreign offices, eminent academics and legal practitioners, including former members of the Commission.

The commemoration of the seventieth anniversary of the International Law Commission is a celebration of international law.

When he took up the position of first Chair of the Commission in Lake Success in New York on 12 April 1949, Manley Hudson referred to history as the driving force behind the Commission's work. Indeed, in his view, it was impossible for a jurist "to forget the lessons of history".[1] He went on to say that "the Commission must take into consideration the many gradual achievements of the past", while recognizing that history was in "perpetual motion", and that Commission members "must not be slaves of the past".

It being the year 1949, his words were a clear reference to the most recent historical developments. Barely emerging from the ravages and suffering

1 ILC, 'Summary Records and Documents of the First Session including the report of the Commission to the General Assembly' [1949] ILC Ybk 1949, 10.

© THE UNITED NATIONS, 2021 | DOI:10.1163/9789004434271_044

of the Second World War, the international community, beset by two world wars in close succession, had failed to fulfil its promise to secure a lasting and stable peace. It set about honouring that unfulfilled promise through the maintenance and advancement of international law. Examining the past was therefore a way of creating the future. The topic that we have chosen for our commemorative events, "Drawing a Balance for the Future", reflects the very human desire for introspection and exploration: learning the lessons of the past in order to create a better future.

Given the circumstances prevailing at the time of its establishment, the Commission was set up precisely to carefully tread this path between the past and the future, embarking on studies and formulating recommendations to promote the progressive development of international law and its codification, which is the mission assigned to it by the General Assembly pursuant to Article 13, paragraph 1, of the Charter of the United Nations.

I personally have had the privilege of observing and participating closely in the Commission's history from various advantageous positions, both internal and external: as part of its secretariat in the 1960s and 1970s; in my capacity as Deputy Registrar and then Registrar of the International Court of Justice in the 1980s and 1990s; and, since 2006, as a member, then as Special Rapporteur and now as Chair of the Commission itself. During each of these stages, I have seen for myself the continued relevance over time of all aspects of the Commission's work to our professional task as international lawyers. Here I am referring not just to the many multilateral treaties that have arisen as a result of the Commission's work but also to the various other elements that play a part in progressive development and codification, and to which we constantly make reference in our daily activities. Indeed, it is possible to take into consideration the extensive practice of States compiled by the Commission and its secretariat over the years; the observations and comments made by States, orally or in writing; and the variety and plurality of opinions expressed by members of the Commission during debates. We frequently refer back to past efforts, particularly the opinions expressed by members of the Commission from the 1950s onwards, in the search for better solutions for the future and as part of the process of the progressive development of international law and its codification.

Such a process inherently requires a certain amount of time, as opposed to "instantaneous law". It also connotes the concept of unity in the progressive development of international law and its codification. As you well know, article 15 of the Commission's statute drew a distinction, for the sake of convenience, between both concepts. In practice, however, the Commission's work on a given topic involves certain aspects both of progressive development and of codification, and the balance between the two varies depending on the topic in question. During the congress held as part of the United Nations Decade of International Law in 1995, I had the opportunity to say that codification and progressive development, despite being formally differentiated in the statute, have in fact been merged into a broader concept of codification, which is no longer simply viewed as the transposition of unwritten law into to written law (what might be called "classic codification").[2] The future, then, always yields to the past. In turn, this broader concept of codification is closely linked to the observation that the final form of the Commission's work, whether already embodied in stand-alone articles that will become part of a convention, or guidelines, conclusions, principles or simply a report, could perhaps be less important for the future than the complex process of codification and progressive development itself.

While the ultimate goal of all the Commission's efforts on a given topic is traditionally considered to be the development of an international instrument that enshrines, in binding form, the outcome of its work, recent experience has shown this not always to be the case. Some of the most authoritative and most frequently invoked texts that have emerged from the Commission's work, drafted as articles, have not yet become multilateral treaties. The journey is thus as important as the destination; an exercise in perpetual motion, the past informing the present to build a better tomorrow.

This statement of fact must not be interpreted incorrectly: the possibility of a final text for codification taking one of several forms does not mean that treaties have become obsolete instruments. Bringing about the long-desired "better tomorrow" often requires international consensus in treaty-making to express its full potential: it may be necessary to establish institutions, or for national laws to be harmonized through binding common rules. It is therefore highly significant that the Commission has explicitly recommended to the General Assembly, by consensus, that the most recent final draft text submitted to it be made into a multilateral treaty. This was the case, in 2016, in relation to the topic for which I had the honour to be Special Rapporteur: "Protection of persons in the event of disasters";[3] and it is hoped that the same will be true next year for the final text to be adopted on "Crimes against humanity". Both texts have the potential to become treaties of great historical importance that will help to secure the desired future of the international legal system.

---

2 United Nations (ed), *International law as a language for international relations/Le droit international comme langage des relations internationales/El derecho internacional como lenguaje de las relaciones internacionales* (Kluwer Law International 1996) 523.

3 ILC, 'Report of the International Law Commission on the work of its sixty-eighth session' (2016) UN Doc A/71/10, 13.

Of course, history is made by human beings, not by abstract entities. The authoritative role given to the Commission over time and the relevance of its outputs, even when they do not become multilateral treaties, ultimately derives from the generally recognized intellectual prowess of the jurists and great minds from all over the world who have walked the corridors of the Palais des Nations as they perform their noble duties. This is the human dimension of the Commission. We can refer to them as the many voices that have articulated the Commission's work over time: despite or because of their plurality, their diversity and, on occasions, their divergences, they have all, to some extent, helped the Commission to find its collegiate voice. The Commission's working methods are designed in such a way that the final outcome is always an expression of plurality and greater than the sum of its parts: it is the essence, the synthesis of the opinions of many legal minds working towards a common goal. The interplay between balanced regional representation – albeit not yet not balanced in terms of gender – and the different legal traditions and systems represented in the composition of the Commission's membership is essential in this regard, as is the independence of individual members of their respective governments. In this collective effort there is also something that we must not forget, something essential from the very outset, namely the prominent role played by the Commission's secretariat, whose preparatory studies and substantive legal assistance, which are part of the Commission's working methods, are crucial to its proper functioning.

Except on a handful of occasions, most recently when we met for five weeks at United Nations Headquarters in New York, Geneva has always been the home of the Commission. Its substantive work has been conducted here. The former members, and the current members, have warm memories of the Palais, the city and its surroundings. The Commission is deeply grateful to the Government of the host State for its constant and generous support over the years. The Commission likewise wishes to thank the United Nations Office at Geneva, in particular its library and conference services, for its continued cooperation and effective efforts, which are vital for the smooth running of the Commission's annual meetings.

Statement by Miguel de Serpa Soares

Under-Secretary-General for Legal Affairs and United Nations Legal Counsel

On behalf of the Secretary-General, I am delighted to be with you in Geneva for this commemorative meeting marking the seventieth session of the International Law Commission.

It is pleasing to see many legal advisers in the audience, as well as present and former members of the International Law Commission, academics, and representatives from regional bodies and other organizations. An occasion like this presents us with an opportunity to honour the International Law Commission and to exchange thoughts, insights and ideas on its past achievements and future challenges. I encourage all of us to actively participate in the discussions.

During the earlier commemoration in New York, on 21 May, I recalled that the Commission held its first session in Lake Success, New York, in 1949. On this occasion, it seems appropriate to add that the Commission's predecessor met here, at the Palais des Nations in Geneva, 25 years earlier. On 12 December 1924, in the room that we are meeting in today, the Council of the League of Nations established the "Committee for the Progressive Codification of International Law". The Committee consisted of 17 experts in international law and was tasked to identify questions that were "sufficiently ripe" for codification.

Similar to the Commission, the members of the Committee served in their personal capacity and, as a whole, represented the main forms of civilization and the principal legal systems of the world. It comprised many noted international lawyers of the day, such as José Gustavo Guerrero, from El Salvador, who later served as the last President of the Permanent Court of International Justice and the first President of the International Court of Justice; Simon Rundstein, the Polish expert on judicial and arbitral procedure; and a young professor from the United Kingdom, James Brierly, who was later elected as one of the first members of the International Law Commission in 1948. With him, the baton of excellence, study and reflection was passed on to the next generation of international lawyers.

With this commemorative meeting today, we not only pay tribute to the achievements of the International Law Commission in the past 70 years; we also honour the efforts of those who laboured towards the ideal of the progressive development and codification of international law prior to the Commission's establishment.

DOI:10.1163/9789004434271_045

Over the years, Geneva has remained at the heart of the codification effort. The successes of the International Law Commission over seven decades can be ascribed, in part, to the unrivalled facilities, library and surroundings of the Palais des Nations, as well as the generous hospitality of our Swiss hosts. At a distance, though not isolated, from the dynamics in New York, Geneva has proven highly conducive for serious study of and debate on complex questions of international law. It is only fitting that the Commission retains its seat here, where the first organized international efforts to codify and progressively develop international law started almost a century ago.

At the very first session of the Commission, in 1949, my erstwhile predecessor Ivan Kerno said the following: "International law is like a great and ancient edifice the doors of which are being opened so that it can ... serve as a shelter to mankind. Only under its protective roof can the Members of the United Nations find the international peace which the Organization has been established to ensure and maintain."[1] These words still hold true. The framers of the Charter of the United Nations affirmed the central role of international law in the architecture of peaceful relations between States, and more than seven decades later this role has not changed. The International Law Commission remains at the centre of the development and strengthening of the international legal order. As we reflect further on what our Commission can do, I can only affirm the continuing relevance of international law, and express the conviction that it will continue to provide a shelter to mankind in future years. Let me conclude by wishing us all a fruitful and inspiring two days.

1 ILC, 'Summary Record of the 1st meeting' (1949) UN Doc A/CN.4/SR.1, 9 at para 10.

Déclaration de Corinne Cicéron Bühler

Directrice de la Direction du Droit International Public et Conseillère Juridique du Département Fédéral des Affaires Étrangères Suisse

(*French original*)

C'est un honneur pour moi de participer aujourd'hui à la séance solennelle, en tant que représentante de l'Etat hôte des réunions de la Commission du droit international. J'ai le plaisir de vous adresser, au nom du Conseil fédéral, quelques mots pour marquer le soixante-dixième anniversaire de la Commission du droit international, qui est placé sous le thème ambitieux « Dresser le bilan pour l'avenir ».

Depuis la fin de la guerre froide, le monde est en constante mutation. Les rapports de force au niveau international se modifient dans un contexte marqué par la globalisation et la fragmentation. Les relations internationales ont gagné en importance mais sont aussi devenues plus complexes, notamment en lien avec le climat de volatilité qui prévaut. Le droit international aurait-il fait son temps ? Non, bien au contraire. C'est pourquoi il est capital de reconnaître et de souligner son rôle fondamental dans les relations entre États.

Le développement progressif et la codification du droit international sont ainsi essentiels au maintien d'un ordre international stable, juste et pacifique, particulièrement dans un monde confronté à des bouleversements. Le droit international constitue ainsi le garant de relations internationales basées non pas sur le droit de la force mais au contraire sur la force du droit.

En tant que petit Etat, fortement interconnecté, la Suisse a un intérêt marqué au maintien et au renforcement du droit international. Un tel renforcement constitue non seulement un élément fondamental de la Charte des Nations Unies mais est également essentiel pour la politique extérieure suisse. Ce constat valait il y a 70 ans déjà. Force est de constater qu'il conserve toute sa pertinence de nos jours.

Aucun pays, aucun acteur sur la scène mondiale n'est en mesure de trouver, seul, les réponses aux défis d'aujourd'hui. Il en va de même pour les questions juridiques, d'où l'importance des travaux de la Commission du droit international.

Si la Commission continue de s'engager pour les sujets de droit international général, tels que le droit des traités ou l'immunité des représentants des Etats, elle s'est déjà saisie de problèmes plus contemporains telles la protection de l'atmosphère, la protection de l'environnement en lien avec les conflits armés

 | DOI:10.1163/9789004434271_046

et la protection des personnes en cas de catastrophe. En effet, la Commission du droit international est appelée à se concentrer également sur le développement progressif de nouvelles règles visant à appréhender les enjeux du monde actuel. La pertinence et l'efficacité du droit international n'en seront ainsi que renforcés. Il est vrai que la Commission a été créée dans le but de promouvoir le développement progressif du droit international et non pas seulement sa codification.

La valeur des travaux de la Commission du droit international n'est plus à démontrer, les projets d'articles de la Commission du droit international jouissant d'une grande autorité dans la pratique et étant souvent interprétés comme des énoncés de droit par les tribunaux nationaux.

C'est donc un grand honneur pour la Suisse d'accueillir à Genève la Commission pour ses travaux et de pouvoir, par ce biais, contribuer à son importante activité. Je souhaite rappeler les propos tenus par mon collègue l'Ambassadeur Jürg Lauber le 21 mai à New York lors de la réunion solennelle : le choix de Genève comme siège des réunions de la Commission permet notamment de garantir la complète indépendance de son activité par rapport à la Sixième Commission, qui siège à New York, et dont le travail est aussi grandement apprécié par la Suisse. La diversité des cultures juridiques propres à ces deux organes constitue un atout pour le développement du droit international. Une présence à Genève assure des synergies avec les nombreuses organisations internationales, les plateformes et les acteurs internationaux qui se trouvent à Genève et exercent une influence sur le quotidien de chacun.

Par ailleurs, la Suisse estime très important que le droit international soit promu non seulement à New York mais également au siège européen des Nations Unies, à Genève. Cela me donne aussi l'occasion de rappeler le Séminaire du droit international qui se tient chaque année à Genève et qui permet à ses participants – fonctionnaires, professeurs et étudiants – de suivre les travaux de la Commission du droit international de très près. Une de mes tâches, en tant que Conseillère juridique du Département fédéral des affaires étrangères, est précisément de suivre le développement et la codification du droit international et je suis particulièrement heureuse que la Commission mène une importante partie de ses travaux en Suisse.

Au nom du gouvernement suisse, je souhaite vous assurer que la Suisse, Etat hôte de la Commission, va continuer à soutenir le travail de cette dernière et à faire le nécessaire pour que ses membres puissent travailler dans le cadre le plus propice au bon déroulement de ses travaux.

Comme indiqué, c'est un grand honneur pour moi d'être parmi vous aujourd'hui pour célébrer cet important anniversaire Je ne doute pas que les discussions que vous mènerez aujourd'hui sur le thème « Dresser le bilan pour l'avenir » seront fructueuses et me réjouis déjà de prendre connaissance des résultats de vos réflexions. Il me reste à vous souhaiter d'excellents travaux et vous remercier de votre attention.

Statement by Corinne Cicéron Bühler

Director of the Directorate for International Law and Legal Advisor of the Swiss Federal Department of Foreign Affairs

(Translation from the French original)

I am honoured to participate today in this solemn meeting, as a representative of the host State of the meetings of the International Law Commission. I have the pleasure to address to you a few words, on behalf of the Federal Council, to mark the seventieth anniversary of the International Law Commission, commemorated under the ambitious theme "Drawing a balance for the future".

Since the end of the Cold War, the world has been in a constant state of flux. The balance of power at the international level is shifting in a context marked by globalization and fragmentation. International relations have become more important, but also more complex, particularly against the backdrop of the prevailing volatile environment. Has international law had its day? No, quite the opposite. This is why it is crucial to recognize and emphasize its fundamental role in inter-State relations.

The progressive development and codification of international law are essential for the maintenance of a stable, just and peaceful international order, especially in a world faced with upheavals. International law constitutes the guarantee that international relations will be based not on the law of force but, on the contrary, on the force of law.

As a small, highly interconnected State, Switzerland is particularly interested in the maintenance and strengthening of international law. This strengthening is not only a fundamental tenet of the Charter of the United Nations, but is also essential for Swiss foreign policy. This observation was true 70 years ago, and it remains fully relevant today.

No single country or actor on the world stage is capable of finding the solutions to today's challenges alone. The same holds true for legal issues; hence the importance of the work of the International Law Commission.

While the Commission continues to address topics of general international law, such as the law of treaties and the immunity of State officials, it also has been dealing with more contemporary issues, such as the protection of the atmosphere, the protection of the environment in relation to armed conflict and the protection of persons in the event of disasters. Indeed, the International Law Commission is mandated to focus on the progressive development of new rules aimed at addressing the problems of today's world. This focus

 | DOI:10.1163/9789004434271_047

will increase the relevance and effectiveness of international law. After all, the Commission was established to encourage the progressive development of international law, not only its codification.

The value of the International Law Commission's work has been well established; its draft articles are considered authoritative legal texts and often are interpreted as statements of law by domestic courts.

It is therefore a great honour for Switzerland to host the Commission's meetings in Geneva, thereby contributing to its crucial work. I wish to recall the remarks made by my colleague, Ambassador Jürg Lauber, on 21 May at the solemn meeting in New York: the choice of Geneva as the seat of the Commission's meetings guarantees that it carries out its work with complete independence vis-à-vis the Sixth Committee, which is based in New York, and whose work Switzerland also highly appreciates. The diversity of legal cultures specific to these two bodies is an asset for the development of international law. A presence in Geneva ensures synergies with the many international organizations, platforms and international actors which are based in Geneva and which influence everyone's daily lives.

Furthermore, Switzerland considers it very important that international law is promoted not only from New York, but also from the European Headquarters of the United Nations, in Geneva. In this context, I wish to highlight the International Law Seminar, held annually in Geneva, which enables its participants – officials, faculty and students – to follow the work of the International Law Commission from up close. One of my duties, as the Legal Advisor of the Federal Department of Foreign Affairs, is specifically to monitor the development and codification of international law. I am therefore particularly pleased that the Commission carries out a substantial portion of its work in Switzerland.

On behalf of the Swiss Government, I wish to assure you that Switzerland, the host State of the Commission, will continue to support the Commission's work and to do whatever is necessary for its members to conduct their work successfully in the most conducive setting.

As I mentioned earlier, it is a great honour for me to be among you today to commemorate this important anniversary. I have no doubt that today's discussions on the theme "Drawing a balance for the future" will bear fruit, and I am already looking forward to hearing the outcomes of your deliberations. It remains for me to wish you all the best for the work ahead of you, and to thank you for your attention.

Statement by Kate Gilmore

United Nations Deputy High Commissioner for Human Rights

It is a great honour, on behalf of the High Commissioner for Human Rights, to welcome you to Geneva on the occasion of the 70th anniversary of the International Law Commission.

We come together today to celebrate the Commission, its achievements and its current work and further to examine the challenges it may confront in the future.

The Commission founded seven decades ago on the solemn purpose of progressive development and codification of international law is coincident in genesis with the Universal Declaration of Human Rights[1] – which thus also celebrates its 70th anniversary this year.

Conceived in Holocaust – a child of two world wars – threaded together from centuries old but unfulfilled longings across cultures and faiths, forged neither in privilege nor in prosperity, but amidst the wrack, rubble and ruin of reckless rancour, 70 years ago our foremothers and fathers gifted us an enduring encapsulation of what makes for a legitimate, humanizing relationship between power and relative powerlessness.

Born of that same era and that same courageous international spirt for the dignity of an inclusive human family, the Commission too manifests those longings – that truth might triumph over prejudice; that justice might serve fairness not fear; that access to justice be universal not a by-product of dumb luck of place of birth, colour of skin, gender or any other identity; that wound not only be healed but that those who cause such wound be made to give account and those who should have prevented that wound should give remedy.

Friends, among its many subsequent achievements, the Commission has played a leading role in developing and codifying international legal norms that today are at the centre of the work to defend the values that the Universal Declaration of Human Rights describes and that United Nations members states have pledged to uphold.

The Commission has made enormous contributions in developing the international law of State responsibility.[2] These achievements in the codification and promotion of the progress of international law also helped the work

1 Adopted 10 December 1948, UNGA Res 217 A (III).

2 See 'Draft articles on responsibility of States for internationally wrongful acts' [2001] II(2) ILC Ybk 26.

undertaken by the Commission to pave the way for the establishment of the International Criminal Court.[3]

For the work of our Office and fulfilment of the panoply of human rights mandates, the Commission has been essential. In all that the human rights system does – from treaty bodies and independent experts to our direct work with local communities – we call on the law that the Commission has expertly crafted, and we seek to extend the application of those standards as we work to address gaps in human rights protection, and help State and civil society actors to develop the capacity to provide that protection, as government officials, security forces, and civil society groups, including through trainings on, for example, how to question people without resort to torture and how to manage public demonstrations without resort to excessive force.

Our commissions of inquiry and fact-finding missions for investigation of grave violations of international human rights law and international humanitarian law confirm further the importance of the Commission's current work addressing proposals for a Convention on crimes against humanity – crimes so atrocious and inhumane that they threaten the peace and security of humankind itself. The prohibition of crimes against humanity is a clearly established and widely recognized norm of the international community. Yet in many contexts of conflict, crisis and State collapse, these crimes are a daily reality.

The International Law Commission's work on the draft convention on crimes against humanity therefore carries great import and holds deep promise.[4] The Convention will form a vital part of the legal framework our Office's work in assisting States to comply with their obligation to prevent gross human rights violations that may amount to crimes against humanity, particularly as the draft convention sets out in article 4 an obligation to cooperate with intergovernmental and other appropriate organizations.

We also note the draft convention's requirement in article 6 that States harmonize their domestic legal frameworks with international norms and standards regarding crimes against humanity. In view of the importance of international cooperation in preventing, investigating and prosecuting crimes against humanity, we also take note of the *aut dedere aut judiciare* obligation of States to extradite or prosecute alleged perpetrators in their jurisdictions contained in article 11. By promoting mutual legal assistance in article 14, the

---

3 See the draft statute for an International Criminal Court with commentaries in ILC, 'Report of the International Law Commission on the work of its forty-sixth session' [1994] II(2) ILC Ybk para 91.

4 See ILC, 'Report of the International Law Commission on the work of its sixty-ninth session' (2017) UN Doc A/72/10, paras 35–46.

draft convention will improve accountability and the efficiency of national and international responses to these crimes.

We further welcome the draft convention's inclusion of related obligations, such as the non-applicability of statutes of limitations for such crimes in article 6, and the universal application and non-derogability of these obligations even under exceptional circumstances, as set out in article 4. Every one of these developments would bolster the work of the Office of the High Commissioner for Human Rights.

Our Office also follows with particular interest the Commission's work on immunity of State officials from foreign criminal jurisdiction as well as on peremptory norms of general international law (*jus cogens*), in which the Commission examines, among others, the distinction between *jus cogens* and customary international law as well as the distinction between *jus cogens* and other possibly related concepts such as non-derogable rights found in international human rights treaties and *erga omnes* obligations.

We also take note of the Commission's work on subsequent agreements and subsequent practice in relation to the interpretation of treaties, and its conclusions 8 and 13 on interpretation of treaty terms as capable of evolving over time and on pronouncements of expert treaty bodies.

The cooperation between our Office, the United Nations Human Rights Mechanisms and the International Law Commission is simply essential and the value of its endeavours is felt by all who strive to hold high the banner of rights – so that it may cast far and wide a shade of shelter to those who rights are betrayed.

Excellencies, in a speech made in the final months of his short life, Martin Luther King Jr. said:

> ... it may be true that morality cannot be legislated, but behaviour can be regulated. It may be true that the law cannot change the heart, but it can restrain the heartless. It may be true that the law cannot make a man love me, but it can restrain him from lynching me ... while the law may not change hearts ..., it does change habits ... if it is vigorously enforced, and through changes in habits, pretty soon attitudinal changes will take place and then, even the heart may be changed.[5]

Today we celebrate the International Law Commission's determined invaluable contributions to changing hearts too.

5 Dr. Martin Luther King, Jr., 'Speech on Receipt of an Honorary Doctorate in Civil Law' (University of Newcastle upon Tyne, 13 November 1967).

Keynote Address by Abdulqawi A. Yusuf

President of the International Court of Justice

I am honoured to have been invited here to deliver the keynote address, and I am particularly happy that my first speech before you as President of the International Court of Justice should be on the occasion of the seventieth anniversary of the International Law Commission.

As a judge of the International Court, but also first and foremost as an international lawyer, the work of the International Law Commission has played, and continues to play, a crucial role in my daily work. Your dedication – and that of your predecessors – has allowed the international legal system to develop into what it is today. For that, on behalf of international lawyers everywhere, I thank you. Of course, in the first rank of these international lawyers are my colleagues at the International Court of Justice, many of whom have passed through the Commission and have asked me to convey to you their congratulations on this 70th anniversary as well as their best wishes for the future.

The theme of today's celebration is "Drawing a Balance for the Future", but I want to take a few minutes to look back into the past in order to understand the role that the International Law Commission has played over the past seven decades. This brings to mind an African proverb, which says: "If you want to know the end, look at the beginning."

The twentieth century was a time of particular upheaval for the international legal system. On the one hand, the century marked the evolution of the international law from a system that was applicable only among a small circle of European States to one that has a credible claim to be a universal legal system, one in which States from all corners of the globe participate. On the other hand, international law moved away from a Westphalian, State-centric system towards a legal order that recognizes and responds to the needs of a plurality of actors, including international organizations, individuals, and corporations. These are only two of the many challenges that the International Law Commission has had to deal with from its inception in 1947.

I The Evolution of the International Community

Resolution 174 (II) of the United Nations General Assembly entrusted to the Commission the task of "the promotion of the progressive development of international law and its codification".

The question that I want to address is the following: how did the International Law Commission fulfil its mandate in light of these challenges, and in particular in respect of the changes to the structure and composition of the international community that have occurred over the past 70 years? How did the Commission contribute to the adaptation of international legal rules to the profound societal changes on the international plane?

To respond to this question, we need to look back to the predecessor of the International Law Commission, the Committee of Experts for the Progressive Codification of International Law of the League of Nations, which was created in 1924. That Committee, although purportedly composed of "the main forms of civilization [...] of the world", manifested the deeply Eurocentric character of the international law of the early twentieth century, both in terms of its membership and its mission.

With regard to the composition of the Committee, although it included jurists from China and Japan, most of the Afro-Asian members of the League, such as Siam, Ethiopia, Liberia and Egypt, were not represented on the Committee. In relation to the mandate of the Committee, the codification of international law was, at that time, understood in a narrow sense of the term. The intention was the codification or systemization of the usages and practices of a self-styled club of "civilized States" that arrogated to itself the right to exclude or admit other nations into the scope of application of international legal rules.

The debate in the League of Nations on the Italian invasion of Ethiopia testifies to the continued prevalence of this 19th century conception of international law until the 1930s.

However, by the time the International Law Commission was established in 1947, the world was undergoing dramatic changes. The Atlantic Charter and the Charter of the United Nations, which were adopted in 1941 and 1945, respectively, laid the foundation for a new international law with universalist aspirations organized around the principle of equal rights and self-determination of peoples and on a universal protection of human rights. These emerging norms were enriched by the views and positions articulated by the newly-independent States, and in particular by two instruments through which they proclaimed those views.

The first was the Bandung resolution that was adopted by the Asian-African Conference in 1955, which declared that "colonialism in all its manifestations is an evil which should speedily be brought to an end". That resolution also demanded the admission to the United Nations of Cambodia, Ceylon, Japan, Jordan, Nepal, and Vietnam, laying the groundwork for the influential Non-Aligned Movement.

The second milestone was the adoption by the General Assembly of resolution 1514 (XV) of 14 December 1960, entitled the "Declaration of the Granting of Independence to Colonial Countries and Peoples". That resolution recalled "the necessity of bringing to a speedy and unconditional end colonialism in all its forms and manifestations" and proclaimed that "the subjection of peoples to alien subjugation, domination and exploitation constitutes a denial of fundamental human rights, is contrary to the Charter of the United Nations and is an impediment to the promotion of world peace and cooperation."

These declarations marked the beginning not only of a wide-spread process of decolonisation in Asia and Africa in the decades that followed and the resultant changes in the composition of the international community, but also the emergence of new perspectives of and attitudes to international law.

II The Response of the International Law Commission

As Wolfgang Friedmann stated in his famous book *The Changing Structure of International Law*:

> The main significance of this horizontal extension of the members of the family of nations does not, however, lie in the explosive increase of the numbers. It lies in the increasing dilution of the homogeneity of values and standards derived from the common Western European background of the original members.[1]

At the time of the creation of the Commission there were only 57 Member States of the United Nations; there are now 193. This change is not merely numerical; it represents a profound societal change involving the emergence of a diverse body of actors, each with their own culture, customs and legal traditions. These changes strengthened the mission of the International Law Commission and laid the foundations for its ability to contribute to the formation of a universal international legal order.

Similarly, it was not so much the increase in the membership of the International Law Commission, which was enlarged from 15 to 21 in 1956, then to 25 in 1961, and finally to its current 34 members in 1981, but its ability to account in its work for the diversity of perspectives of international law, which was born

1 Wolfgang Friedmann, *The Changing Structure of International Law* (Columbia University Press 1964) 5–6.

as a result of decolonization, that has smoothed the way for its achievements in the last 70 years. This was in turn rendered possible by the provision, in article 8 of the statute of the International Law Commission, that members of the Commission shall represent "the main forms of civilization and ... the principal legal systems of the world",[2] an article that reflects the wording of article 9 of the Statute of the International Court of Justice. That article reproduces the corresponding provision of the Statute of the Permanent Court of International Justice, which has become much more important today than the drafters of the Statute of the Permanent Court of International Justice could have ever imagined. The same may be said of article 8 of the Statute of the International Law Commission.

As I mentioned before, the rules of customary international law that existed at the time the Commission was created were derived from the practice of European States. But against the backdrop of decolonisation, the International Law Commission realized that codifying these rules, in the sense of their systemization, no longer reflected international reality. It therefore decided two things: first, that it was necessary to take into account the views and perspectives of the new States and their legal systems. Secondly, in order to do that, the Commission decided to consider as one the two limbs of its mandate, codification and progressive development. As you put it, Mr. Chair, the Commission merged the two limbs. One of the reasons why this was done was to avoid that the Commission's work be limited to a systemization of practices and rules, some of which were out of tune with the new realities of the international community.

The challenges faced by the Commission were described by the Dutch jurist, Bert Röling, who, in his 1960 book *International Law in an Expanded World*, concluded that:

> A new international law, consonant with the new sociological structure of the community of nations, and consonant with the new legal conceptions expressed in it, must be evolved. Such an evolution is [a] prerequisite for the existence of "one world" which should be both a welfare community and a community of peace.

Let me explain why I think this is so important. I would mention two reasons. The first is the need for diversity in the international legal sphere. It is not a

---

2 UNGA Res 174 (II) (21 November 1947), as amended by UNGA Res 485 (V) (12 December 1950), UNGA Res 984 (X) (3 December 1955), UNG Res 985 (X) (3 December 1955) and UNGA Res 36/39 (18 November 1981).

paradox to say that the universality of international law depends on diversity. For international law, universalization means borrowing and adapting concepts and principles from different legal traditions. The more international law can draw on multiple legal traditions, the more universal it will be considered.

The second reason is legitimacy. The legitimacy of international law depends, to a great extent, on its ability to reflect the perspectives of all components of the international community. As observed by Georges Abi-Saab:

> [I]f we really want international law to take hold and be taken seriously by all, it has to be, and be seen to be, both in its creation and in its interpretation and application, the product of this community as a whole, reflecting, by synthesis or symbiosis, the legal visions, needs and aspirations of all the components of this community.[3]

The work of the International Law Commission demonstrates a willingness to reflect the international community in all its multifaceted splendour. The International Law Commission demonstrated this early on not only through its work but also through the recognition of the importance of the individual contributions of rapporteurs from Afro-Asian countries, starting in the 1960s with Abdullah El-Erian, and followed by Mohammed Bedjaoui, Sompong Sucharitkul, and Doudou Thiam, to name but a few.

Although the work of these individuals was important, the work of the Commission as a whole demonstrates an openness to diverse perspectives, which have left an indelible mark on the contours of contemporary international law. Due to the constraints of time, let me mention just two examples of the concrete manner in which the Commission took into account the viewpoints of the newly-independent States in its early work on codification and progressive development already in the 1960s and 1970s, in an area which was profoundly marked by the practices and usages of the old club of the "concert européen", i.e. the law of treaties.

i *The Termination of Treaties*

I will start with the inclusion in the Commission's work on the law of treaties of provisions related to the termination of treaties. Newly independent States spoke out against the imposition of treaties thrust upon them by force or fear,

---

3 Georges Abi-Saab, 'The Portrait of the Jurist as an International Judge' in Connie Peck and Roy Lee (eds), *Increasing the Effectiveness of the International Court of Justice: Proceedings of the ICJ/UNITAR Colloquium to Celebrate the 50th Anniversary of the Court* (Martinus Nijhoff Publishers 1997) 166, 171.

as well as treaties of capitulation. During debates on the International Law Commission's 1966 draft articles on the law of treaties, delegates to the Sixth Committee of the General Assembly expressed the view that:

> [T]he draft articles on the law of treaties could not acknowledge unjust, unfair or unequal treaties, which in many cases were the consequence of the colonial system. Instruments imposed without the consent of the populations concerned, instruments which were the price of accession to independence, instruments taking advantage of the situation of the developing countries … could not be protected by the law of treaties, and should be eliminated from international relations.[4]

The work of the International Law Commission took into account these concerns by including, in particular, what would become article 52 of the Vienna Convention on the Law of Treaties, providing that "[a] treaty is void if its conclusion has been procured by the threat or use of force …".[5]

ii *Succession of States to Treaties*

A second example is the work of the Commission on the succession of States in respect of treaties. At the time of independence, a number of African States adhered to what later came to be known as the Nyerere doctrine of State succession. According to this doctrine, newly independent States would provisionally apply bilateral treaties on a reciprocal basis for a two-year period from the date of independence, to the extent that those treaties were compatible with the sovereign rights of the new States. This two-year period was considered as a time of reflection by a decolonized State on whether it decided to be bound by the treaty, to renegotiate it, or to abandon the treaty altogether.

During this period, the International Law Commission was also conducting its work on the "Succession of States and Governments", in relation to which the General Assembly urged the Commission to undertake its work "with appropriate reference to the views of States which have achieved independence since the Second World War", including – importantly – the principle of self-determination.[6]

This led the Commission to state that:

---

4 Felix Okoye, *International Law and the New African States* (Sweet and Maxwell 1972), 191.

5 Vienna Convention on the Law of Treaties, adopted in Vienna on 23 May 1969, entered into force 27 January 1980, 1155 UNTS 331.

6 UNGA Res 1902 (XVIII) (18 November 1963).

> The traditional principle that a new State begins its treaty relations with a clean slate, if properly understood and limited, was in the opinion of the Commission more consistent with the principle of self-determination.[7]

The Nyerere doctrine was thus fully reflected in the International Law Commission's draft articles, which served as the basis for the Vienna Convention on Succession of States in respect of Treaties.[8] In particular, article 16 of that Convention provides that:

> A newly independent State is not bound to maintain in force, or to become a party to, any treaty by reason only of the fact that at the date of the succession of States the treaty was in force in respect of the territory to which the succession of States relates.

iii *The Future of the International Law Commission's Work*

These two examples illustrate, in my view, how the International Law Commission has successfully taken into account views of diverse actors in order to develop progressively and codify an international law with universal aspirations. That is an exceptional achievement.

Let me briefly mention two other notable examples. First, the inclusion of the concept of peremptory norms (or *jus cogens*) in the International Law Commission's work on the law of treaties, and its subsequent inclusion as articles 53 and 64 of the Vienna Convention on the Law of Treaties, has had a lasting impact on the structure of international law. As eloquently put by Mustafa Yasseen, the Chair of the Drafting Committee of the Vienna Conference, *jus cogens* are "those higher norms which [are] essential to the life of the international community and [are] deeply rooted in the conscience of mankind".[9] Although initially controversial, the concept now commands widespread acceptance among States and other international actors. This is in large part thanks to the efforts of the Commission, and its on-going work on *jus cogens* attests to the enduring importance of the topic.

Second, the Commission's work on the succession of States in respect of matters other than treaties, is particularly notable insofar as it acknowledged

7 ILC, 'Report of the International Law Commission on the work of its twenty-fourth session' [1972] II ILC Ybk 227.

8 Vienna Convention on Succession of States in respect of Treaties, adopted in Vienna on 23 August 1978, entered into force 6 November 1996, 1946 UNTS 3.

9 United Nations Conference on the Law of Treaties, First Session, Vienna, 26 March-24 May 1968, Official Records, A/CONF.39/11, 295 and 296.

explicitly the principle of permanent sovereignty over natural resources, a principle which was strongly promoted and defended by the newly-independent States. This led to the inclusion of the principle in article 15, paragraph 4, of the Vienna Convention on Succession of States in respect of State Property, Archives and Debts.[10]

Through its work, the Commission has clearly shown the adaptability of legal rules to societal change. The scope and number of international legal rules recognized by all members of the international community has increased through the Commission's efforts, and it has succeeded to shift the principal source of law-making from custom to multilateral conventions and a codified set of rules in which, as the Court said in its advisory opinion on the *Genocide Convention*, "the contracting States ... have, one and all, a common interest ...".[11]

At the start of my address, I noted that two changes over the course of the twentieth century were particularly important for international law: first, the decolonization process and the resulting changes in the structure and composition of the international community; and, second, the movement away from a Westphalian, State-centric system of international law to one that recognizes a plurality of actors.

As I have mentioned above, the Commission has responded convincingly to the first of these changes. In relation to the second, however, as my colleague (and former member of the Commission), Giorgio Gaja, has noted,[12] there is still some work to be done. Let me mention just one example.

Whilst certain elements of the International Law Commission's work recognize the ability of individuals to hold rights under international law, such as article 33, paragraph 2, of the articles on State responsibility, the Commission has only acknowledged as recommended practice, under the articles on diplomatic protection, the important fact that reparations should accrue to an aggrieved individual in cases where their rights are breached.

The Court has not done much better. In the *Diallo Judgment on Compensation*, it simply recalled that "the sum awarded to Guinea in the exercise of diplomatic protection of Mr. Diallo is intended to provide reparation for the latter's injury".[13] In my view, both the International Law Commission and the

10 Vienna Convention on Succession of States in respect of State Property, Archives and Debts (adopted in Vienna on 8 April 1983, not entered into force yet), (1983) 22 ILM 306.

11 *Reservations to the Convention on the Prevention and Punishment of the Crime of Genocide* (Advisory Opinion) [1951] ICJ Rep 15, 23.

12 Giorgio Gaja, 'The Position of Individuals in International Law: An ILC Perspective' (2010) 21 EJIL 11, 12.

13 *Ahmadou Sadio Diallo (Republic of Guinea v Democratic Republic of the Congo)* (Compensation) [2012] ICJ Rep 324, 344.

Court should have asserted that reparations accrue to individuals in case of injury to their rights. To borrow the words of Giorgio Gaja, this would create a "comprehensive" and "coherent" approach to the place of individuals under international law.

But the future holds greater challenges for the Commission, and for the international legal system more generally. Recent developments show that the most fundamental rules and principles of international law are under threat. As the International Court of Justice stated in the *Corfu Channel* case, certain international obligations are based on "elementary considerations of humanity, even more exacting in peace than in war".[14] These norms are being questioned today by those that want to promote unilateralism and turn their back on a world order based on multilateralism. We also see the sanctity of treaties and *pacta sunt servanda* increasingly under tension, as international treaty commitments are repudiated virtually before the ink has dried on the paper on which they were written. There are attempts to render agreements among States the world over less durable and more fragile, and to equate a change of government or of political parties in power to the doctrine of *rebus sic stantibus*.

The International Law Commission must play a role in responding to these threats. In particular, the Commission must promote multilateralism and inclusiveness, and create awareness among governments of the need and the importance of these concepts to the rule of law at the international level. In sum, the Commission has to continue to show the way for a better observance of the rules of international law in the interest of humanity as a whole.

Throughout the 70 years of its existence, the International Law Commission has played a pivotal role in ensuring that international law responds to the needs of all the members of the society it serves. It is now needed more than ever. It must spread the word that the well-being and progress of all nations depends on multilateral co-operation based on the rule of law – and that peace and harmony among nations requires shared values and common standards and rules based on those values. That is a difficult challenge, but one that I have no doubt that the Commission will live up to.

14 *Corfu Channel case* (*United Kingdom v Albania*) (Merits) [1949] ICJ Rep 4, 22.

www.ingramcontent.com/pod-product-compliance
Ingram Content Group UK Ltd.
Pitfield, Milton Keynes, MK11 3LW, UK
UKHW022225051026
15624UKWH00002B/355

9 789004 434264